Year
of
the
HANGMAN

Year of the HANGMAN

GEORGE WASHINGTON'S CAMPAIGN
AGAINST THE IROQUOIS

Glenn F. Williams

WESTHOLME

Yardley

Published by Westholme Publishing, LLC
Eight Harvey Avenue
Yardley, Pennsylvania 19067
www.westholmepublishing.com

ISBN 13: 978-1-59416-041-7
ISBN 10: 1-59416-041-4

First Printing
0 9 8 7 6 5 4 3 2

Printed in the United States of America
on acid-free paper

To two of my mentors, role models, and heroes, my uncles
EDWARD VLADIMIR KAMINSKI, and JOSEPH KAMINSKI JR., COMMANDER, USNR (RET.)

Contents

Introduction

WE CALLED YOU "TOWN DESTROYER"

T HE "Year of the Hangman," 1777, represents the turning point of the American War for Independence. That was the year when the regulars and militia of the Continental Army's Northern Department defeated the British invasion from Canada, resulting in the surrender of Lieutenant General John Burgoyne at Saratoga. As the events on the Hudson were unfolding, farther south, around Philadelphia, the American Main Army demonstrated that it had come a long way since the humiliating defeats at New York and the retreat across New Jersey. Although unsuccessful in stopping General Sir William Howe's army at Brandywine, General George Washington's audacious but somewhat overambitious counterattack in the near-victory at Germantown demonstrated that the American soldier was far from being vanquished on that front. Together, the two campaigns contributed to the entry of France into the war, which ultimately proved decisive.

The year 1777 was also noteworthy in that it signaled the participation of Six Nations of Iroquois, and those Indian nations and tribes allied to or dependent on them, into the conflict. Since the first shots were fired at Lexington and Concord in 1775, the Commissioners of Indian Affairs appointed by the Continental Congress tried to enlist the active military participation of native peoples in the fight against the Crown. Failing that, the American commissioners attempted to keep the Indians neutral. The deputies of the British Indian Department also exerted great efforts to maintain the Indians in an alliance with the king. Although hesitant to abandon a policy of neutrality, most of the Six Nations decided that supporting the British in defeating the rebellion was in their national interest, and "took up the hatchet" in the Year of the Hangman.

With the Indians' taking sides in the conflict, the Revolutionary War entered into a new and brutal phase. British and Provincial regulars, including the famed corps known as Butler's Rangers, in conjunction with their Indian allies attacked lightly defended and highly productive agricultural settlements along the frontiers of New York and Pennsylvania. Before the end of 1777, back settlements from Fort Stanwix, New York, to the Ohio River had been touched by war. Stopping the raids with militia alone proved ineffective, and even the stationing of Continental troops in static defenses enjoyed only limited success. After more than two years of these attacks, Washington ordered a concerted effort against the Indian nations that had allied themselves with Great Britain, culminating in the Indian Expedition led by Major General John Sullivan in 1779.

A large detachment composed of some of the best units in the Continental Army under the command of some of its ablest general and field officers invaded the land of the Iroquois, destroying virtually all of their towns and laying waste to their cornfields. When Garganwahgah, or Cornplanter, a leading warrior of the Six Nations, met with the new President of the United States in 1790, the chief told him: "When your army entered the country of the Six Nations we called you Caunotaucarious, "Town Destroyer;" and to this day when that name is heard our women look behind them and turn pale, and our children cling close to the necks of their mothers."

This book is about the fighting during the American Revolution on what was then the western borders of New York, Pennsylvania, and Virginia (which now also encompasses areas in West Virginia, Ohio, and Kentucky), which came to be known in the U.S. Army as the Iroquois Campaigns of 1778 and 1779. The political atmosphere leading to the Revolutionary War and the state of Indian and Colonial relations along the backcountry settlements when the war began set the stage for the events that follow. Most of the narrative focuses on fighting between the forces of the British Crown and their Indian allies on one side, and the American Continentals, militia, and their Indian allies on the other.

The Iroquois Campaigns bear striking similarities with other operations conducted by the U.S. Army later in its history. Combatant polities used aspects of guerrilla, psychological and economic warfare. Some may find it ironic, and maybe a challenge to some popular perceptions, that in the summer of 1779 the American Western Army constituted a conventional force, conducting search-and-destroy operations deep in the forest, away from its logistical base, against an elusive indigenous enemy that was assisted by British special operations troops. Others will undoubtedly see the similarities between the Continental Army's operations in Tryon and Ulster counties, New York, in 1778 and more recent efforts to combat global terrorism. As always, the application or misapplication of the time-tested principles of war contributed to success or failure on the battlefield, and as always, commanders and troops were concerned about the need to balance combat power with adequate logistical support.

Finally, some believe that the U.S. Army's Iroquois Campaign in 1779 was a strategic failure. Those holding this view maintain that the expeditions led by Van Schaick, Sullivan and Clinton, and Brodhead did little more than destroy the Indians' towns and corn harvests, and had little or no impact on the outcome of the Revolutionary War. Others hold the opinion that instead of bringing those of the Six Nations that were allied to the Crown to peace terms or neutrality, these operations proved counterproductive by driving the Indians even more firmly into the British camp. These beliefs are some of the reasons why these major military operations have not garnered the popular attention they deserve. Upon investigation, these arguments fail to take into consideration the role of the struggle for the frontier in the overall course of the war, both before and after open hostilities erupted between Britain and America in 1775, as well as the important results of the Iroquois Campaigns, such as the expense they placed on an already overstrained British war machine that ultimately influenced the direction of the war and the precedent they set for future Indian and American relations. I believe that the Iroquois Campaigns accomplished their tactical and strategic objectives as laid out by George Washington, produced the desired calculated effect, and were a significant factor in the American victory in the War for Independence. It is my hope that this book will provide a better appreciation for the complex history of the early American frontier that spun into bitter war during the "Year of the Hangman."

Chapter 1

THE KING'S INDIAN ALLIES

THE Revolutionary War was not simply the story of Great Britain's American colonies breaking away from the mother country. Nor was it a confrontation between two well-identified antagonists, each of whom represented two distinct but internally cohesive groups. The Revolutionary War was a long, bitterly fought, and bloody struggle that was as much a civil war as a revolution, and which drew participants to each side from a variety of ethnic groups, religious beliefs, and ideological movements. Even though united in a common cause, the thirteen rebellious colonies engaged in disputes with their neighbors, some of which had been carried over from before the War for Independence. Virginia and Pennsylvania were at odds over which rightly controlled the area known as the "Forks of the Ohio," Pennsylvania and Connecticut contested dominion over the Wyoming Valley on the North Branch of the Susquehanna River, and New York faced challenges from settlers awarded land within its boundaries by New Hampshire, known as the "Hampshire Grants," which became Vermont. Nor was the Revolutionary War fought entirely by clearly defined forces of Americans versus British, as colonists of differing political beliefs called themselves Patriots or Loyalists. Likewise, many native peoples were drawn into the conflict on one side or the other, further complicating an understanding about that turbulent period.

The War for American Independence was also not a regional conflict on the Atlantic seaboard of North America. Following the colonies' signing of a political treaty and military alliance with the government of King Louis XVI of France in 1778, the conflict went from a colonial rebellion to a global war, with fighting at sea, and in Asia, Africa, and the West Indies. To offset the threats posed by the Franco-American alliance and in an attempt to regain the initiative after the previous year's campaigns failed to crush the rebellion, Britain turned its attention to the vulnerable frontiers of the united colonies, especially those of New York, Pennsylvania, and Virginia, where it decided to maintain a campaign of terror waged by its Provincial rangers, Tories, and allied Indians. The goal of this effort was to draw soldiers and supplies away from the main

1

body of the Continental army so that it could be defeated by the British army, either in a single decisive battle or destroyed piecemeal if it chose to disperse. As the war in the principal theaters along the coast settled into stalemate, which could only be good for the American cause, this bold strategy would test the resolve of independence-minded Patriots on the western frontiers, and raise the stakes of victory and defeat for not only the British and Continental governments, but also for the Indian nations along those borders.

Britain had reason to believe its unconventional tactics would succeed. Many, but not all, of the Indian nations were allied with the British. This was true for the Indian polity known as the Six Nations, or Iroquois Confederacy, arguably the most powerful and influential Native American entity of the period, which dominated the territory directly to the west of the northern colonies, from the shores of Lake Ontario, the northern branch of the Susquehanna, and the upper reaches of the Allegheny Rivers to the banks of the Saint Lawrence River and the Finger Lakes region. The majority of the confederacy—the Seneca, Onondaga, Mohawk, and Cayuga, nations which could bring more than 3,000 warriors to bear—backed England during the revolution largely because of their long alliance with the Crown and the belief that it was the best means of contending with white encroachment on their lands. These reasons did not sway members of the two other nations, the Oneida and Tuscarora, who although much smaller in number of warriors than their confederates, would choose an alliance with the Americans. Even so, the British could feel confident that they had more than adequate support from their Indian allies to carry out the campaign.

By taking different sides, members of the Six Nations did not believe they were breaking with tradition or violating previous agreements and covenants as much as they were pursuing policies in their own national interests. This can be explained by how the Six Nations viewed the British-American conflict. The Six Nation Iroquois did not consider themselves subjects of King George III of England, but they welcomed his protection from France and its Indian allies by virtue of their long history of friendship. The English and Iroquois had different concepts of property, dominion, and civilization, however, and these would remain a continuous source of conflict between the two cultures. While the British acknowledged the natural title and right of prior occupancy of native peoples, they also used a definition of domination shared by other European empires that considered the American Indians subjects by virtue of discovery, or by the taking of possession lands inhabited by heathen or uncivilized people. Each of the Iroquois nations, however, saw their policies during the American War for Independence as reflecting their adherence to treaties of friendship forged before the Revolution. When they spoke of English, or British, the Iroquois applied that description to whites born in North America as well as in Europe, who were now seen as fighting among themselves. During the wars against France and its Indian allies, the Six Nations fought alongside the British, but now that that the English were divided, honoring their covenant chain could therefore be interpreted by each in deciding which side, Patriot or Loyalist, they chose to befriend. Obtaining the alliance, or at the least neutrality, of the Six Nations became a major part of the political and military policy of both the British and Americans; the Iroquois were seen as critical to the success or failure of the rebellion given their proximity to the most populous colonies, their location between Canada and the other colonies, and the threat they represented to the multitude of small farming communities along the frontier whose food and supplies would be necessary to sustain the Continental Army. Understanding Iroquois culture became paramount for both sides in the northern theater of the American Revolution.

The very name by which both British and Americans knew them, Iroquois, came from their traditional enemies, the Algonquian peoples. From their earliest contact, the Algonquian solicited help from the newly arrived French explorers and settlers in combating their traditional foe. The name Iroquois is thought to be derived from a French rendering of the Algonquian words Ireohkwa, meaning "real adders," or Iriakhoiw, translated as "the rattlesnake people," with the addition of the French suffix "-ois." When speaking of themselves, however, the Iroquois used Haudenosaunee, which means "people of the longhouse."

As their name implies, the Haudenosaunee dwelled in longhouses. These distinctive dwellings were the sites of all activities that had bearing on the life of the tribes. The traditional longhouse was typically constructed on a frame fashioned from forked wooden poles anchored in the ground with crossed poles secured to these uprights to form an arched roof. The frame was then covered with sheets of bark, rough side facing out, and earth. Generally measuring twenty-five feet in width and from fifty to eighty feet in length, these buildings housed more than one, and as many as five or six, families plus their dogs, in a communal living arrangement. By the mid-1770s, an increasing number of Haudenosaunee dwelled in houses built of hewn logs or timber with glass windows resembling those of white settlers. Indian homes were also being furnished with European goods that were acquired through trade or plundered in war. The Iroquois soon prized the items they could not make themselves, such as firearms and scissors, or preferred items they acquired from Europeans, like steel knives and tomahawks, to those they had once made themselves from stone and other naturally occurring materials. European-made axes, fishhooks, needles, awls, brass and copper kettles, brass wire, and linens were soon commonplace in Indian towns.

The Haudenosaunee lived in established towns of numerous longhouses surrounded by fields cleared for vegetable gardens. The communities were located on or near lakes, rivers, or streams that provided not only a source of drinking water, but also a connection to the primary routes of trade and travel. At one time, Iroquois towns were usually located on defensible terrain and enclosed within palisades, or walls of sharpened logs placed upright in the ground, to enhance the natural defenses. European settlers often referred to the fortified villages as "castles." Later, "castle" was used to identify principal Iroquois towns. Every ten to twenty years, when their agricultural fields were exhausted, the entire community moved to establish another town.

In the division of labor, farming was primarily the work of women and girls. They tilled the soil using a variety of implements originally fashioned from wood and animal bone and antlers, planted the seed in the spring, weeded the fields throughout the summer, and harvested crops in the fall. The most important crops were the "three sisters" of corn, beans, and squash. They also grew pumpkins, cucumbers, potatoes, and watermelons in their fields. Some villages cultivated apple and peach trees, and after European contact raised and tended cattle, hogs, and horses. The female members of the tribes also gathered wild berries, fruits, nuts, sassafras roots, maple sugar, and other products from the forest. Hunting, fishing, and war were considered the men's domain. Iroquois men were skilled hunters who trapped and killed animals, primarily deer, bear, beaver, partridge, and wild turkey for both food and clothing. After European contact, trading in beaver pelts became the basis of the Indians' economy and source of goods.

Every male in the tribe between the ages of sixteen and sixty was a warrior, and Haudenosaunee boys began training for war at the early age of twelve or fourteen.[1] Practicing with war clubs, knives, tomahawks, bows and arrows, and firearms, they were usually ready for their first raids into enemy territory by their mid-teenage years. Fighting other tribes or intruding European settlers, young Iroquois could gain prestige and respect in their society by showing bravery and martial skill.

The Haudenosaunee pictured their collective society as an extended family figuratively living in an immense longhouse. The Mohawk were the easternmost, dwelling on the northern bank of the river that bears their name, and were therefore considered "keepers of the eastern door." The name Mohawk is also Algonquian, not Iroquoian, and translates as "eaters of men," because their enemies accused them of practicing ceremonial cannibalism. The Mohawk called themselves Kanienkahagen, or "people of the place of flint." The Seneca, located in the area from Seneca Lake to the upper Allegheny River, were the westernmost tribe, and were therefore "keepers of the western door." Their native name is Osininka, "people of the stone." The Onondaga, whose Iroquoian name Onondowagah, or Nundawaono, means "people of the great hill," or "people of the hills," occupied villages in the vicinity of Onondaga Lake and the Oswego River, south of Lake Ontario. As the central tribe in the Iroquois League, they were the keepers of the council fire and held the Six Nations' wampum belt record. The Oneida occupied the area between Oneida Lake

Stylized eighteenth-century drawing of an Iroquois warrior. Note that he is armed with both a musket and traditional war club, and wears snowshoes. (*New-York Historical Society*)

and the upper Mohawk River. Their tribal name was derived from the Iroquoian word Onayotekaona, or "people of the upright stone," referring to a large boulder within their homeland. The Tuscarora, or "hemp gatherers" (for their distinctive hemp-cloth shirts), remained close to their Oneida sponsors. (The Tuscarora originally inhabited northeastern North Carolina and southeastern Virginia but were driven out by their Shawnee enemy and English settlers, and at the invitation of the Oneida, were invited to settle among them. They were admitted to the Iroquois Confederacy in 1722 as the sixth nation.) The Cayuga, who controlled the smallest territory, inhabited an area largely covered in marshland between the Seneca to the west and Onondaga to the east, and were known as "people of the great swamp." Their native name is Guyohkohnyoh, or "people of the place where the boats were taken out."

According to oral tradition, the five original tribes had been brought together by the Huron prophet Deganawida, or Peacemaker, and the Mohawk warrior Hiawatha, or Hayonwatha, "he who parts the waters," in a form of civil government known as the Five Nations around the year 1570.[2] (Hiawatha was not the character of the same name in the Longfellow poem.) In an acceptance of the Great Law of Peace and Power, the primary tribes of Iroquois united in an attempt to make reason and the peaceful mind prevail among the Five Nations. They joined together for mutual defense, as well as to resolve perceived injustices and end blood feuds between clans and among the member tribes, in a great council that promoted inter-tribal tranquility. Governing by consensus of the chiefs assembled in the Great Council, the People of the Longhouse spoke with "one voice, one mind, one heart," rather than being divided by revenge, feuds, and war. The agreement united them under the sheltering branches of the Great Tree of Peace, a giant white pine that became their collective symbol. In its imagery, the tree is reaching skyward, spreading its branches over the snow-covered earth, and surrounded by the totems representing each clan. An eagle, watching warily in all directions for the approach of any invader, soars above the tree. To symbolize the nations' peaceful intent toward other members of the league, a war club and tomahawk (representing the traditional weapons of war) lie buried in the ground between the five roots representing each of the original confederation nations.

The Great Council was composed of fifty sachems, or civil chiefs, who were appointed by the clan mothers for life, unless removed. The matrons selected each sachem from among the royaneh, a title inherited by the sons of the clans' most influential families through their mothers' lineage. The closest English translation of royaneh is "lord." The clan mothers also selected war chiefs from among the royaneh. During the 1600s, the power of the military chiefs took on more importance in the Great Council. Using the advantages in strength and purpose provided by their confederacy, and the technical advantage afforded by acquiring firearms, the Haudenosaunee expanded their territories in every direction by conquest and migration in an effort to dominate the fur trade with Europeans: first the Dutch and later the English. Ruthless in war, they brutally destroyed their non-confederation Iroquoian cousins, like the once powerful Huron, and numerous other smaller Iroquoian-related tribes to their north, like the Neutral, Tobacco, and Erie, and the rival Susquehannock to the south. They made war almost constantly on the Algonquian tribes, including the Algonkin, Ottawa, Illinois, Miami, Potawatomi, Delaware (or Lenni Lenape), Mahican, and Wappinger. The Iroquois soon controlled an empire that stretched beyond their traditional homeland between the Adirondack Mountains and Niagara Falls, that at its height in 1680 included territory either occupied by them or by tribes that were conquered and made dependent on them, from the Ottawa River in the north to the Tennessee River in the south, and from the Kennebec River in the east to the Illinois River and Lake Michigan in the west.

In earlier times, Iroquois warriors went into battle armed with bows and arrows for inflicting casualties on the enemy from a distance, and war clubs, tomahawks, and knives for close combat. After European contact, these weapons gave way to muskets, metal-headed hatchets, and metal knives. During

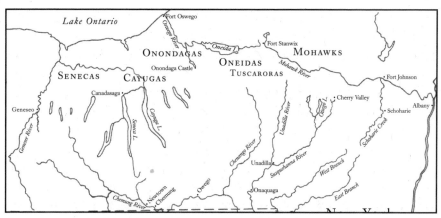

General geographical distribution of the tribes of the Six Nations.

the colonial wars and American Revolution, the Iroquois were an efficient military force, specializing in a form of guerrilla warfare of extreme ferocity. As described by James Smith, an Englishman captured during the French and Indian War and adopted by Canadian Mohawks, their conception of the art of war consisted of "ambushing and surprising our enemies, and in preventing them from ambushing and surprising us."[3] When under good command they could work in concert and execute their leaders' plans quickly. Their warriors were disciplined and punctual in obeying orders. Each warrior swiftly complied with orders to change formations, disperse, or concentrate by watching the movements of the warrior to his right, and in turn, relaying it to the man on his left. As the situation dictated, they could march several abreast in a compact group, or in scattered lines or files over a mile long, traveling considerable distances with a minimum of confusion. They could form circles and semi-circles to surround or outflank their enemies, and form large hollow squares facing out from behind trees if they found themselves surrounded.[4]

The Iroquois believed in fighting wars of annihilation rather than wars of attrition. The basic aim of a war party was at all times to attempt to "annoy [inflict casualties on] their enemy, and save their own men." The leaders of Iroquois war parties never sought to bring on an engagement unless they possessed a considerable advantage, or a prospect of certain victory with the loss of as few men as possible. Once engaged, if the tide of battle was against them, or if they were likely to lose many men in gaining a victory, they felt it their duty to retreat and wait for a better opportunity for defeating the enemy at a lesser cost. Smith commented that, "They commonly retreat if their men are falling fast." He cautioned that this was not a sign of cowardice, but in compliance with their rules of war. If surrounded, they would continue to fight as long as there was a man alive rather than surrender.[5]

In a military engagement, the Haudenosaunee, armed with muskets, practiced a form of fire and movement in which, "they proceed by divisions, so as to keep up a constant fire; while one division moves and fires the next is holding on and so on." This contemporary account went on to describe their method of fighting in the forest that gave them a particular advantage over a foe that could not adapt his tactics to their style of warfare: "In general except upon very important cases they carry on a kind of desaltory warfare which must be very distressing to an enemy; they go out in small parties, conceil themselves under the bushes and when they see an opportunity of gaining any advantage, they Sally forth and are guided according to circumstances."[6]

The most common Iroquois military operations were raids on enemy villages, or ambushes of enemy traveling through the country or just outside the protection of village palisades. Pitched battles between large groups were not uncommon, but after closing with the enemy, they resembled a series of individual combats. When victorious, women and children captured in battle or raids were usually adopted by the Haudenosaunee into the tribe. Enemy males who were not killed and scalped on the battlefield were made to run the gauntlet, where prisoners had to move between two lines of men, women, and children who struck them repeatedly with sticks and thorny branches from start to finish. Those who survived the ordeal could then face further torture and death, sometimes inflicted by the widows and orphans of fallen Iroquois warriors in revenge for their loss, or could be adopted into the tribe as replacements in consolation for men who met untimely death in battle or from disease. Such adoption decisions were made by the tribal matrons. In order to extend their influence and domination, the Haudenosaunee were also known to adopt whole tribes as allies or dependents to secure their borders.

The Mohawk were the first Haudenosaunee nation to establish peaceful relations with Europeans when they concluded the Two Row Wampum Treaty with Dutch settlers in the Hudson River valley in 1664. The wampum belt, depicting two parallel rows of colored shells on a background of white, symbolized the agreement of each party not to interfere with the other, as they existed in close proximity. When the British replaced the Dutch as the dominant European colonial power, they assumed the terms of the treaty, eventually replacing the wampum belt with the Silver Covenant Chain of Friendship. The British government used the covenant chain to extend the alliance to encompass the entire Iroquois Confederation, and through the Iroquois' political and military domination, to other tribes. Both the Iroquois and British government entered into agreements that were mutually beneficial. Through commercial trade arrangements, the Iroquois acquired iron tools, agricultural implements, and cookware, textiles, and firearms. In return, British mercantilism had access to a lucrative market for its products and a steady source of beaver pelts to supply the enormous demand for clothing, particularly hats, made from this fur. Both groups also benefited from their military alliance. With British arms and ammunition, the Six Nations crushed their enemies and controlled their dependencies, while providing the Crown an effective buffer between New France and the English colonies on the Atlantic coast. In an effort to strengthen the covenant in their struggle against the incursions of pro-French Indians in 1701, the Five Nations (the Tuscarora had yet to join the confederacy) signed a Deed of Trust for placing their hunting grounds under the king of England, their "Protector and Defender."

The long-lasting friendship of the Six Nations and Great Britain was largely due to the effort and skill of one man, William Johnson. Johnson was born in Ireland in 1715, and came to the colonies in 1737 to manage the New York estates of his uncle, Peter Warren, at Warren's Bush, a vast tract of land located south of Amsterdam, New York. Ambitious and energetic, Johnson invested in land, supplied military garrisons, and engaged in a profitable and honest business trading for furs with the Indians. From the very beginning of his dealings with the Indians in 1738, he earned a reputation among them as one of the few Europeans they could trust. Johnson developed a liking for the Indian people, especially the Mohawks, and the affection soon proved mutual. He was frequently among them. He visited their "castles," shared communal feasts, offered them generous gifts, attended their ceremonies and rituals, and took a seat to observe their councils. He learned native languages and spoke frequently with clan mothers and sachems, and immersed himself in the Indian culture. Johnson soon managed what was probably the largest trading operation in the New York frontier from his own Mohawk Valley estate, Mount Johnson. His business soon grew to include contracting with local farmers to supply the trading posts and Indian towns, and dealing imported English goods directly to the Indians. So astute was he in this commerce that the Iroquois named him Warraghiyagey, or "one who does much business."

Johnson married his first wife, Catherine Weissenberg, a former German indentured servant woman, at an early age. The marriage produced three children, Ann, John, and Mary. Although he lived with her until her death in 1759, William was reputed to have had affairs and fathered a number of children with several Indian women. After "Catty" had passed away, Caroline Peters, niece of the famous Mohawk Chief, King Hendrick, bore him several children. After her death five years later, he kept his home at his baronial manor, Johnson Hall, with a Mohawk woman named Koñwatsi-tsiaién-ni, or Mary "Molly" Brant.

Molly became his "prudent and faithful housekeeper," common-law wife, mother of eight children, and his companion for the remainder of his life.

Respected by the Iroquois, he displayed an unrivaled ability to get along with the native people. That ability led to his being granted the status of a "blood brother" by the Mohawks, and later being made a chief of the Iroquois. Johnson also proved to be a capable diplomat and soldier. He received appointments to the New York Council and as a colonel in the provincial militia by the royal governor, George Clinton. Johnson was instrumental in gaining the Mohawks' friendship for the British king in the many wars for empire among the European powers in North America. He was not as successful in bringing all the Six Nations to the king's assistance, but when the Mohawks were in the field, those Iroquois accompanying French forces usually declined to fight their brothers. During King George's War in the 1740s, he wore the clothes of an Indian war chief, painted his face, and joined them in the war dance. At the request of the confederacy's sachems, Clinton appointed Johnson as Indian Commissioner, and commissioned him as "Colonel of the Six Nations of Indians," in recognition of his ability to influence the Iroquois alliance with the Crown.[7]

Although Johnson's record qualified him as the ideal man to handle Indian affairs and regulate all colonial trade with them, colonies adjacent to New York preferred to handle relations with the Indians individually, or in conjunction with others. This was not only confusing for the Indians, but also made developing a coherent British policy for dealing with native peoples very difficult.

The lack of a unified Indian policy also affected diplomatic relations with the Indians. With another war against France threatening in the early 1750s, a military alliance with the Iroquois would help secure the western borders of the British colonies, and prove essential to defeating France and her native allies in backcountry fighting. As the native peoples became increasingly vocal over seizures of their land by settlers, the Lords of the Board of Trade and Plantations in London, who were responsible to the Crown for the management of the colonies and Indian affairs, called for a conference at Albany of colonial administrators and representatives of the Six Nations in June 1754 to rectify abuses and inconsistencies in Indian policy, and to gain the nations' alliance against the French.

As a result of this meeting, the Board of Trade and Plantations decided to appoint single agents to manage the Indian affairs of the northern and southern departments of the colonies. Johnson's nomination to become the first agent for the northern department was backed by the requests of the Six Nations. In April 1755, at the beginning of the French and Indian War, Johnson received a warrant of appointment as Superintendent of Indian Affairs, with authority to negotiate treaties with the Confederate Nations of Indians in the northern department on behalf of the British government, from Major General Edward Braddock, the commander in chief of the Crown's forces in North America. That same month a young American officer who had led an expedition of Virginia militia the previous spring against the French at Fort Duquesne, George Washington, was appointed volunteer aide-de-camp to General Braddock.

William Johnson, the British Crown's longtime Superintendent of Indian Affairs in the Northern Department was a skilled diplomat, military officer and businessman. His expertise in Indian matters and affection for the Six Nations were instrumental in establishing a British-Iroquois alliance before the Revolutionary War. (*New-York Historical Society*)

During peacetime what became known as the "Indian Department" was primarily concerned with maintaining diplomatic relations and regulating trade between the government of the British Empire and the Indian nations. In the north, the department operated commissaries for the exchange of Indian and European goods at British military posts and monitored the activities of fur trappers, traders and other whites doing business in Indian territory. The department employed agents, interpreters, clerks, storekeepers, and blacksmiths to perform its routine functions, as well as to be self-sustaining. Although not part of the British Army, the Indian Department included a military service function, and its officers held military ranks and wore red-coated uniforms. Its principal officers, called deputy superintendents, were charged with "conciliating the affections of the Indians and of steadily attaching them to the British government," by distributing "presents," and issuing arms, ammunition, and other equipment and supplies that they lacked, but which were essential in their military operations.[17] When poor harvests, the scarcity of game, or other circumstances caused the Indians to experience shortages of food and shelter, the department procured clothing and provisions from British military stores or other government sources for distribution.

"The Duty of a Deputy," William Johnson's nephew, Guy Johnson, wrote, "is to confer with the Indians, obtain Intelligence and transmit it to the Superintendent, and negotiate all Matters committed to him." The department's officers did not lead native warriors in combat, but its officers and rangers (enlisted men) did help to plan their operations, and frequently accompanied war parties. They also helped to coordinate the Indians' actions with other forces of the Crown, to ensure that they contributed to the overall military effort against an enemy. The department's rangers could usually speak one or more Indian languages and were well acquainted with the native methods of warfare. "The Rangers are very Necessary to accompany Indian Parties, serve as Expresses [messengers or couriers], and assist the Officers," Johnson explained.[8] Because of their knowledge of the Indians and Indian country, the department's officers and rangers frequently acted as translators, scouts, and spies, and provided liaison between the Indian war chiefs and British commanders. They were expected to restrain the Indians from exercising those practices of warfare permitted by their own traditions, but which eighteenth-century Europeans considered uncivilized, or characterized as savage. More often than not, so as to not alienate their allies, Indian Department personnel looked away while the warriors tortured and executed prisoners, took scalps, or mutilated bodies of the fallen enemy.

In June 1755, Major General Braddock with a force of about 1,500 regular British soldiers and colonials, including George Washington, marched to take the French stronghold of Fort Duquesne. On July 9, along a heavily wooded trail not far from the Monongahela River, several miles south of Fort Duquesne, Braddock's army was surprised and defeated by a smaller detachment of French troops and Canadian irregulars joined by a united Indian force of several hundreds. While Braddock and his officers attempted to direct the battle from horseback in the custom of the time, the French and Indians decimated his ranks and mortally wounded the general as they moved in and out of the forest surrounding the trail. With the general incapacitated, Washington assisted in command, despite being ill from poor water, and organized a successful retreat. The destruction of Braddock's expedition at the Battle of the Monongahela highlighted the usefulness of Indian allies in frontier warfare and the need to consider native counsel: Braddock failed to heed the warnings of the Indians accompanying his forces. Both of these lessons would not be lost on Washington in the future. For the young Virginian officer, the battle also marked his notice as a military leader.

Following Braddock's defeat, Johnson, in his military capacity as a colonel of provincial militia and of the Six Nations, led a combined force of Indian warriors and British soldiers that successfully blocked a French invasion at the Battle of Lake George on September 8. For this welcome victory after a series of British disasters in the early stages of the war, Johnson received a baronetcy from the king and a grant of land and a cash award of £5,000 from the British government. The following February, Sir William Johnson was appointed to the "Sole Management & Direction of the Affairs of the Six Nations & their Allies," answerable only to the government in London through the commander in chief of North America, not the colonial governors, with an annual salary of £600.[9] Johnson now had firm control of British policy with the Indians and the Indian Department in the north, whose organization and operations would bear his imprint until the end of the American Revolution.

Over the course of the French and Indian War, Johnson was promoted to major general of provincial militia in New York, and led

Battle of the Monongahela, July 9, 1755. This representation depicts General Edward Braddock receiving a mortal wound. The early battles of the French and Indian War were a crucial training ground for officers who later served on both sides in the Revolutionary War, including George Washington. (*Wisconsin State Historical Society*)

troops and allied Indian warriors to victory at the battles of Crown Point and Niagara. He continually sought a dominant position for the Six Nations, and by extension, for himself as well. The supremacy of the Six Nations over all other tribes throughout the northern frontier and Ohio country led the British government to consider other Indian groups as lesser, or dependent, and their lands as belonging to the Iroquois empire. Proving himself a gifted politician and government administrator, Johnson addressed colonial assemblies, imperial offices, and Indian councils on Indian matters from 1756 to 1774. He had no peer in negotiating Iroquois affairs with the Crown and interpreting royal policies to the Indians.

In 1763, the Treaty of Paris formally ended the French and Indian War, or the Great War for Empire as it is also known, an extension of the Seven Years War, with Great Britain winning supremacy among European nations in North America. The result benefited Johnson both financially and politically. After France's defeat, the Indian Department assumed responsibility for the "Northern Indians" of Canada, and Daniel Claus, husband of Johnson's older daughter Ann, became superintendent of the Seven Nations in the Province of Quebec, while George Croghan, an old friend of Johnson, was stationed at Fort

Pitt, at the forks of the Ohio, to serve as the deputy for the "Western Indians," the nations of the Ohio Valley and to the west.

Britain now found itself ruling a vast territory that ran the entire length of the North American seaboard. Incorporating Canada as a new colony and winning the loyalty of its French Canadian and Indian inhabitants was another challenge in which Johnson and the Indian Department could contribute. But in an effort to reduce expenses, against Johnson's advice, British authorities curtailed the French practice of giving presents to the Ohio and Great Lakes tribes. With the French no longer a threat in North America, the commander-in-chief, Major General Sir Jeffrey Amherst, believed that the friendship of the tribes could be maintained without such lavishness. The British viewed gift-giving as a bribe for loyalty, while Indians perceived the practice as a symbol of mutual respect, not subordination. Furthermore, the former French-allied and neutral tribes, like the Six Nations with the English, however, had become dependent on the Europeans for supplies, powder, shot, and trade goods. Some western tribes became resentful that their presents were reduced or curtailed, while those of the Six Nations had not, leading to animosity. Tensions with the western tribes worsened with increased encroachment by white trappers on their traditional hunting grounds. Indian nations that had refrained from actively supporting the French, or had come over to the British side trusting that the king would honor his promise to curb further settlement, felt betrayed. Rumors began circulating about an impending Indian uprising. In the spring of 1763, those fears were realized when the Ottawa chief Pontiac led his warriors in a series of attacks on British military posts and settlements (in what became erroneously described as a "rebellion") that was soon joined by the Shawnee, Delaware, Munsee (a Delaware subgroup), Miami, Wyandot, Mingo (an independent group of Haudenosaunee, mostly breakaway Seneca and Cayuga, who migrated down the Allegheny and eventually settled in the Ohio River valley in the early eighteenth century), and even some Seneca. The frontier was in turmoil, and the British could do little in response.

In an attempt to reduce this and other conflicts and impose the authority the colonial governments seemed unwilling to exercise, Parliament passed, and the king approved the Royal Proclamation of 1763. This proclamation, issued on October 7, among other provisions, forbade the granting of land "beyond the heads or sources of the rivers which fall into the Atlantic Ocean from the west or northwest." This in effect defined a boundary line separating the colonies from the lands to the west of the Appalachian mountain chain.[10] These lands were declared off-limits to colonial governments, being "reserved" to the Indians under the cognizance of the British Crown, which reasserted its sovereignty and control over the entire area.

Pontiac's War still raged in the western frontier, however, but by the autumn of 1764, the British took the offensive with two expeditions, led by Colonels John Bradstreet and Henry Bouquet, into the Ohio country and Great Lakes region. Sir William Johnson held numerous Indian councils where he successfully persuaded most of the Six Nations and Caughnawaga Mohawks to renew their alliance with Great Britain. As the tide of war turned against the western tribes, and their realization that the British-Iroquois alliance would not be broken, Pontiac's followers lost their fighting spirit, and before long most Indian leaders, but not Pontiac, sued for peace. In the autumn of 1764, several councils were held at Johnson Hall, Fort Niagara, and throughout the Ohio country that formally ended hostilities.

The Lords of the Board of Trade sought the advice of their superintendents of Indian affairs for establishing a more permanent arrangement. Johnson called a conference of the northern Indians at Fort Stanwix on the upper Mohawk River in 1768. In the negotiations, the Six Nations conceded the lands south and east of the Ohio River for European settlement. These lands were inhabited not by the Iroquois, but by tribes whom they considered their dependents by right of conquest or alliance, and therefore presumed domination to speak for, particularly the Delaware and Shawnee. In return for giving away territory along the Susquehanna, Delaware, and Allegheny Rivers that was not theirs, the Iroquois' own land was proclaimed secure from further European encroachment. The Treaty of Fort Stanwix furthermore proposed to make the Ohio River the permanent boundary between Indian territory and areas open to Europeans for hunting and settlement. Meanwhile, Johnson's counterpart in the south, Colonel John Stuart, had concluded a series of treaties, principally with the Cherokees and Creeks, that established a similar line to the west. Stuart's demarcation overlapped the boundary Johnson had negotiated at the confluence of the Great Kanawha and Ohio, thus forming a continuous boundary from north to south.[11] The Lords of the Board of Trade ordered the superintendents to ratify and confirm the "Stanwix Line," and to have it surveyed and marked in 1770.[12]

Almost as soon as the boundary between Indian lands and those open for settlement had been defined, it was violated by trappers, traders, and land speculators. In attempting to protect the Indian lands by enforcing the treaty, or at least regulating the establishment of new settlements, the British government alienated many frontier inhabitants and those wishing to migrate into Indian country. The pace of settlement along the frontier quickened, as veterans of the French and Indian War took possession of land granted them for their service to the king. The displaced Indians were not pleased. They felt betrayed by their Six Nations overlords, who gave away their lands without their consent. The

Benjamin West's portrait of Colonel Guy Johnson, depicted with Joseph Brant in the background. Guy Johnson was Sir William Johnson's successor as Superintendent of Indian Affairs in the Northern Department, and ranking officer of the Indian Department. Notice that he has modified his officer's uniform with articles of Iroquois garb. (National Gallery of Art)

Delaware were forced from their territory along the lower Allegheny River in Pennsylvania, and the Shawnee found that their hunting grounds in Kentucky were opened to settlement. Meeting in a congress of western Indian nations on the Scioto River in the autumn of 1771, the Shawnee, Delaware, Wyandot, Mingo, Miami, Ottawa, Illinois, and others agreed to join forces to oppose further white encroachment, regardless of any agreements made for them by the Six Nations. Under the leadership of the Shawnee chieftain Keigh-tugh-qua, or Cornstalk, the powerful alliance, resentful of the expansion of European settlement, prepared to defend the country beyond the Ohio.

The American Indians were not the only ones prepared to fight for land along the Ohio. In January 1774, the royal governor of Virginia, John Murray, Earl of Dunmore, in a boundary dispute between his colony and neighboring Pennsylvania (along the border of present-day West Virginia), forcibly took possession of the area around Pittsburgh. Fort Pitt was occupied, its name changed to Fort Dunmore, and the post became the judicial seat of the District of West Augusta, Virginia. The situation was further complicated when some Virginians killed several peaceful Indians, resulting in Shawnee and Mingo retaliatory raids against white settlements along the Ohio. To secure the frontier, the Virginia governor called out the militia to take part in a campaign that became known as Dunmore's War.

On July 11, 1774, while attempting to convince the Six Nations to remain neutral in the conflict, Sir William Johnson took ill and died. The Indians of the Six Nations were devastated at the news. Johnson, they believed, had been their sole benefactor in their relations with the British government. Through his efforts over the past thirty-five years, they were recognized as dominant among all Indian nations, and they wielded their influence over "subordinate" tribes to their own benefit accordingly. Johnson's sudden death brought an apprehension and uncertainty about future Iroquois-British relations. His son, John, inherited the baronet title. Although esteemed by the Indians who so admired his father, Sir John Johnson preferred the life of an English aristocrat. Educated in England, the young Johnson had been knighted in 1765, but he was not interested in managing the king's Indian affairs.

Sir William's nephew, son-in-law, and departmental secretary, Guy Johnson, assumed the role of Superintendent of Indian Affairs for the northern and western nations. Like his uncle, Guy was born in Ireland, and came to North America to find his fortune working for his influential relative. Through his uncle's patronage, Guy was not only granted a position in the Indian Department, but was commissioned a field officer in the militia and exerted considerable sway in provincial politics. He became Sir William's protégé, and at the time of his uncle's death was considered a likely candidate to succeed him. The choice met with the approval of the tribes.

Daniel Claus, Sir William's other son-in-law, retained the office of Deputy Superintendent of the Seven Nations of Canada. Claus had originally come to the Mohawk valley in the employ of the Pennsylvania government to learn Indian languages and customs under his future father-in-law's tutelage, but accepted a position to serve in the Indian Department instead of returning to Philadelphia. Through Sir William's help, Claus had obtained a commission as an officer in the 60th Royal American Regiment of Foot in the regular British army. After service with the regiment during the French and Indian War, Claus went on captain's half-pay while working with the Indian Department. Alexander McKee, who became Deputy Superintendent for the Western Indians in 1772, remained stationed at Pittsburgh.

As tensions between American Whigs—those who supported a break from England—and the English government worsened through the series of political crises between 1763 and 1775, Colonel Guy Johnson made several important appointments in the department to prepare for a possible war of rebellion. The men he promoted were already seasoned by years of experience in maintaining the friendship of the Iroquois for the Crown. They were trusted by the Six Nations' leadership, knew what motivated them, and understood their culture and ways of fighting. All of them would play crucial roles in the upcoming war and all were ardent Tories—resulting in a major blow to any future Whig efforts to gain Iroquois support. John Butler, a gifted interpreter who was fluent in several Iroquois dialects, became the Deputy Superintendent for the Six Nations with the rank of lieutenant colonel. Butler was also a long-time friend of Sir William, and had served as a captain in the Indian Department on five

campaigns during the French and Indian War, including as Sir William's second-in-command at the battles of Crown Point and Fort Niagara. When war
between the Patriots and Loyalists finally came, Butler developed a concept for
using a corps of rangers, such as had been organized by Major Robert Rogers
during the French and Indian War, which could cooperate with the allied-
Indian warriors to help achieve the Crown's operational objectives in the
absence of conventional British forces.

Joseph Brant, or Thayendanegea ("two sticks together," indicating strength)
in his native language, was named Guy Johnson's departmental secretary for
Indian affairs with the rank of captain in 1775. A member of a prominent
Mohawk family, Brant had been a translator for the department for some time.
As the brother of Molly Brant, and therefore Sir William's brother-in-law,
Brant also had close ties to the Johnson family. Sir William had acted as his
benefactor, and saw to his education at Moor's Indian Charity School in New
England (now Dartmouth College). Brant was a charismatic leader, and gained
a reputation as an influential orator at Mohawk councils. His martial skill and
bravery in combat during the French and Indian War had resulted in his elevation to the status of a leading warrior among his people. His service as a scout
for the Bradstreet Expedition during Pontiac's War had gained him familiarity
with the methods of European warfare and a most favorable reputation among
British officers. Brant was a true Loyalist and a dutiful adherent of the Church
of England. Later, when he visited England with Guy Johnson, he quickly
gained the admiration of London society and duly impressed the British leadership, so much so that his elevation to war chief among the Mohawk was promoted by his British benefactors.

Maintaining the frontier along the Stanwix Line and honoring their commitment to the Crown—to remain the king's Indian allies—was the only guarantee that many Iroquois believed would secure their borders in the face of an
impending rebellion. Already large areas of the Mohawk homeland had become
interspersed with European settlements. If the Whig faction emerged dominant
among frontier inhabitants in the coming struggle, it would likely result in more
encroachment. In the absence of a French threat from the northward in which
the Six Nations had presented a buffer for the British colonies in return for their
own security, the Indians now had to contend with the possibility of an
American threat from the east. But even before the expected war became hot,
an unexpected one along the western frontier provided the first glimpse of what
was to pass.

Chapter 2

DUNMORE'S WAR

A T the time of Sir William Johnson's death, the frontier was marked by the Fort Stanwix Treaty line, which separated the lands of the Six Nations and its dependents from those of the colonists. The line ran roughly south along the Oswego River through Oneida Lake, past the colonial settlements along the Mohawk River in Tryon County, New York, across the upper reaches of the Susquehanna, and down the upper Delaware River below the Catskill Mountains. It then moved west into northern Pennsylvania and ran adjacent to the colonial settlements along the Susquehanna River's main north and west branches; moving west, the line eventually picked up the Allegheny and Ohio rivers, which flowed south to define the western frontiers of Virginia and Pennsylvania.

This line made new lands, including a large area ceded by the Six Nations on behalf of their dependents just east of the Ohio River, available for settlement, and colonist families moved south and west to the frontier regions of Pennsylvania. But in addition to the influx of settlers and disputes with the dependent Indians who failed to acquiesce to the Six Nations' right to give away their land, the same area was the source of contention between the colonies of Pennsylvania and Virginia. The conflict grew out of a territorial dispute stemming from the 1750s, when Virginia considered the area where the Allegheny and Monongahela rivers combine to form the Ohio as part of its Augusta County, and therefore within the colony. The Penn family considered the same area as part of its Westmoreland County, and claimed it was within the boundary defined by the proprietary charter for Pennsylvania.

In January 1774, the royal governor of Virginia, John Murray, Earl of Dunmore, commissioned area resident and Pennsylvania native Doctor John Connolly as a captain commandant in the Virginia militia, and ordered him to seize the town of Pittsburgh. On January 27, 1774, after occupying the abandoned works at Fort Pitt and renaming the post Fort Dunmore, Connolly issued a proclamation on the governor's authority calling for the local inhabitants to embody as Virginia militia to enforce the laws of the province.[1] Arthur

St. Clair, the magistrate for Westmoreland County, Pennsylvania, was appalled by this action. He issued a warrant against Connolly in the name of Pennsylvania's proprietary governor, Thomas Penn, and committed the Virginia officer to jail at Hannah's Town (just north of present-day Greensburg), the seat of justice for Westmoreland County. Arrest followed counter-arrest, and governors Penn and Dunmore continued a lively correspondence justifying their respective claims.[2]

Dunmore maintained that his actions were justified based on his obligation to support and enforce Virginia's charter rights, and driven by a concern for the safety of the frontier. It may, more than likely, also have masked his involvement in a business enterprise to speculate on land in the frontier region of Vandalia, south and east of the Ohio River. Politically, Dunmore was also probably motivated by the prospects of garnering some much-needed popular support in a turbulent political climate. Virginia's veterans had been promised warrants of land in reward for their service in the French and Indian War, and in the months leading up to his takeover of Pittsburgh, surveyors had been swarming into the land along the Ohio River to mark the military grants. Connolly, a business agent and relative of Dunmore, and a nephew of former British Indian agent to the Ohio nations George Croghan, was a recipient of one of the land grants, and was acting on his own financial interests as well as out of loyalty to Virginia's royal governor.

To further justify his action and prevent open fighting between Virginia and Pennsylvania settlers, Dunmore used the pretense that it was necessary to defend the frontier from a perceived imminent Indian attack. He maintained that the Ohio Indians had failed to honor the terms to which they agreed at the end of Pontiac's War. Of the principal tribes in the area, only the Shawnee showed any inclination to fight, but that solely to counter the encroachment of white settlers beyond the Ohio. They demonstrated their resolve in early April 1774, when a band of Shawnee took captive members of a survey party scouting prospective land tracts in Kentucky. The Indians later released the surveyors with the admonition to tell others that all Virginians found on the north bank of the Ohio would be killed. Of the other principal tribes, the Delaware seemed the friendliest, and the Mingo, although pledged to honor the treaties then in force, were the least welcoming. Many frontier whites, however, did not usually bother to distinguish between Indians of different nations, much less determine which were friendly or potentially hostile. Some settlers, believed to be in league with Connolly, tried to provoke both warlike as well as otherwise peaceful Indians into a conflict. Following a few minor skirmishes, some Indians, including two relatives of the Mingo chief Logan, were murdered by frontier ruffians while visiting a trader named Joshua Baker on April 30. Within days, the Indians retaliated, attacking the settlements of even unoffending whites. As the alarm spread over the frontier, Dunmore had his war. He proposed a campaign to secure Virginia's western border by invading the the land reserved to the Indians north of the Ohio River.[3]

The turmoil on Virginia's frontier was not the only dispute which captured the attention of American colonists. Since the end of the French and Indian War in 1763, a number of political differences soon threatened to rupture the bond between Great Britain and its colonies. As a means of increasing revenues to pay the debts incurred because of that war, Parliament had passed a series of acts that levied both internal and external taxes on the colonists. External taxes were duties on imported commodities, which were added to the price of sale. People not wishing to pay the tax had only to refrain from purchasing the taxed merchandise. An "internal tax," however, was one in which the taxpayer had no choice since it was part of the price of a commodity traded within the colonies. In addition, internal taxes were authorized without any representation from the colonies and the tax monies went back to England. While Americans in general conceded Parliament's right to tax and regulate trade, they resented the imposition of taxes without their consent. As freemen and British citizens, the colonists had elected representative assemblies to enact laws for their own government. If Parliament wanted to tax the colonies, they insisted that the bills to levy them had to originate with the legislatures representing the citizens who had to pay. Any laws passed by Parliament for the internal collection of taxes were considered arbitrary and unconstitutional.

When the British government attempted to exert its supreme authority to regulate trade, levy both internal as well as external taxes, and legislate law in all cases, colonial resistance stiffened. The opposition usually took the form of non-importation agreements, which were formed by committees from within the provincial assemblies, and then carried out by those at local levels and Patriot organizations like the Sons of Liberty. By denying colonial markets to British manufacturers, the colonists repeatedly rendered the hated acts ineffective, hastening their repeal, and encouraged competition from American manufacturers as an unintended consequence. With the success of such resistance efforts, the idea that the colonies should be more autonomous within the empire slowly gained in popularity.

Reflecting the growing rift between colonies and mother country, in March 1773, Virginia's House of Burgesses, the elected lower legislative house, had proposed to the other provincial assemblies in the colonies that they form a standing Committee of Correspondence. The committee kept watch on the acts of Parliament and served as a network to share information. The committee system gave the emerging Patriot movement a way to show solidarity and plan collective action by all thirteen colonies in opposition to ministerial action affecting them all. Perceiving the action as subversive, Dunmore was compelled to act. Supporting his superiors in the Council of Ministers in London, and therefore raising the ire of his colony's Whigs in the process, the royal governor dissolved the House of Burgesses. But it was too late to stop the inevitable drift toward rebellion and war.

In May 1773, the administration of Prime Minister Frederick Lord North passed the Tea Act. Unlike previous regulations, it was less a tax bill than a government effort to financially revive the East India Company which, due in part to a European economic downturn and an American boycott of English goods, was nearing bankruptcy. Under the terms of the act, the company was allowed to ship tea directly to the North American colonies, avoiding the expense and taxes involved in having to first stop in England. The savings resulted in making the retail prices of tea in America lower than in Britain. Americans still had to pay an import duty, but even after that was added, the net reduction in cost still made tea less expensive than previously. Outwardly, it seemed to benefit all concerned. The East India Company got an exclusive market to save it from bankruptcy, the colonists gained access to less expensive tea, and the government collected the revenue. The law, however, stipulated that the tea could be sold only by specially commissioned agents. The Tea Act also created a monopoly in which the government managed the retail distribution of goods. If not opposed, this signaled a frightening development for American merchants and consumers, as well as introducing means of collecting another internal tax, and one which could be raised at the direction of the Privy Council. The Tea Act held ominous ramifications for the colonies.

American colonists turned again to their non-importation committees not only to organize a boycott, but also to refuse consignment of the tea in American ports. It was not long before ships laden with East India Company tea rode at anchor, unable to unload their cargo. Sons of Liberty and merchants joined in holding "tea parties," which in four port cities resulted in the confiscation or destruction of the cargo. In New York City, the Liberty Boys threw at least one shipment into the harbor. At Annapolis, Maryland, Patriots succeeded in inducing the owner of the ship *Peggy Stewart* to burn his own vessel rather than unload its cargo of tea. The most famous, and audacious, was the Boston Tea Party. Led by Samuel Adams, the Sons of Liberty, disguised as Indians, boarded three vessels in the evening of December 16, 1773. While a crowd of 8,000 looked on and cheered, the Patriots dumped 342 chests, containing 15,000 pounds of tea, into the harbor.

Tea Party in Boston Harbor. In the most famous of the protests against the Tea Act, crowds on the wharf cheer them on as Boston Sons of Liberty, disguised as Mohawks, dump tea into the harbor on December 16, 1773. (*Colonial Williamsburg*)

When the Virginia Assembly prepared to convene in the spring of 1774, both the members of the House of Burgesses and the royal governor, Lord Dunmore, hoped for a more cordial relationship. When the session opened, the governor sought an authorization and financing to prosecute his Indian war on the western frontier, which the House of Burgesses granted on May 12. During the months since he previously dissolved the body, however, the Boston Tea Party and other incidents of colonial resistance were viewed by the king and North government as a threat to the British constitution. They maintained that Parliament was the supreme authority to legislate in all cases in the British Empire. Instead of backing down, as it had when faced with colonial opposition before, the administration of Lord North introduced a series of four measures known as the Coercive Acts. One closed the port of Boston to all commerce until the revenue for the destroyed tea was paid. Another revoked the Massachusetts Charter, dissolved the Massachusetts General Court, or Assembly, and prohibited town meetings. A third permitted the trial of British officials charged with capital offenses in the colonies to be tried in Great Britain, away from potentially hostile judges and juries. The fourth, a new Quartering Act, authorized the stationing of British regulars in towns and housing them in quarters other than barracks, including private homes with or without the consent of the inhabitants. Another piece of legislation, the Quebec Act, enlarged the province of Quebec southward to the Ohio River. The Quebec Act caused much resentment, particularly in Virginia. It effectively questioned Virginia's claim to the same land and nullified the grants promised to veterans as a reward for service during the French and Indian War. Designed to remind the colonies in general of their subordinate status in the empire, and to punish Boston in particular for its rebellious behavior, the new laws collectively became known as the "Intolerable Acts" to many Americans.

On May 24, the Virginia Burgesses called for June 1, the date the Boston Port Act was to go into effect, as a "Day of Fasting, Humiliation and Prayer" in support of the Massachusetts Bay colony, and to protest Parliament's act closing the port of Boston. Confronting them on their stance, Dunmore voiced his displeasure and dissolved the House of Burgesses once more. In defiance, eighty-nine Burgesses adjourned to Raleigh Tavern in Williamsburg, where they proposed the convening of a congress of all the colonies and the formation of another non-importation association through the Committee of Correspondence. While Dunmore, and those Burgesses who were also officers in the militia of the affected counties, set about the task of assembling an army, twenty-five of the defiant Burgesses met again and called for a Provincial Congress, to be known as the Virginia Convention. The convention delegates, including Patrick Henry, Thomas Jefferson, and Francis Lightfoot Lee, met in Richmond in August, and resolved for Virginians to work alone as loyal subjects of the king against the "ill advised regulations" and "unconstitutional Acts" of Parliament, and in concert with the other colonies by electing delegates to the Continental Congress. Elsewhere, every colony except Pennsylvania had a provincial committee of correspondence through which to coordinate united action. At the local level, Committees of Correspondence were even formed in the frontier districts. On August 7, for example, Whigs in Tryon County, New York—the home to staunch Tories Guy Johnson and John Butler—elected a Committee of Correspondence to convey the "sentiments of this County" to the committees in the towns of New York and Albany, and the Provincial Assembly of New York.[4]

On September 5, 1774, fifty-six delegates representing every colony except Georgia met in Philadelphia at Carpenters' Hall as the First Continental Congress. After electing Peyton Randolph of Virginia as its president, the Congress adopted the Suffolk Resolves, which called for the implementation of some radical measures. Passed by a 6-5 vote over a more conservative alternative called the Plan of Union, the resolves demonstrated that the Whig faction, although not ready to press for autonomy, was gaining strength. As a result, the Congress resolved that the Coercive Acts were unconstitutional and need not be obeyed. It advised Massachusetts to form its own government and collect taxes, but to withhold the revenue from the royal government only until the Coercive Acts were repealed. It urged the people to arm themselves and form an independent militia in preparation for a possible conflict with royal authority. Most important, Congress recommended the application of harsh economic sanctions by a united action that would withhold American wealth from the British economy. That could be done by calling a boycott of British imports and an embargo on American exports on a greater scale than had been used against earlier unpopular laws. The Continental Association was thus formed to implement these trade conditions.

To give the boycott widespread and popular support, the Congress urged the formation of local committees to act as the agents of the Continental Association. Every colony, town, and county was encouraged to elect Committees of Observation and Inspection by all those qualified to vote for representatives in their respective provincial legislature. The committees enforced the boycott by punishing violators with public censure and social ostracism. Although they did not supplant local government institutions, the committees assumed "authority" for acting on issues of "continental" importance, and represented the first steps taken toward forming revolutionary shadow governments.

The First Continental Congress provided a means for all of the colonies to speak against Parliament with a united voice and coordinate their opposition activities for the first time. Although the conservative Tory delegates succeeded in softening the resolutions, Congress issued its "Declarations of Rights and Resolves," which denounced the Coercive Acts and the Quebec Act and called for their repeal. It also denounced the various revenue acts passed since the end of the French and Indian War, the use of vice-admiralty courts, and the stationing of British troops in colonial towns. The declarations reaffirmed allegiance to the Crown and acknowledged Parliament's right to levy external taxes, but denied Parliament's right to levy internal taxes as a means of raising revenue. In a reflection of popular sentiment, Congress laid the blame for making such action necessary on the administration of Lord North and his ministers, not on the king. After agreeing to meet again in May 1775, the First Continental Congress adjourned on October 26, 1774.

When Dunmore left Williamsburg in July to organize his military expedition, relations between the royal governor and Virginia's freeholders could not have been more strained. As the Virginia Convention met and selected its delegates for the First Continental Congress, Lord Dunmore had gathered an army of 2,700 militia men from the western counties. He organized the force with two divisions, or wings. The 1,300 men embodied from Frederick, Dunmore, Hampshire, and Berkley counties formed the Northern Division, or Right Wing, at Pittsburgh under his personal command. The Southern

Division, or Left Wing, was organized at Camp Union (present-day Lewisburg, West Virginia) from the Augusta, Botetourt, and Fincastle county militias, and commanded by the county lieutenant and member of the House of Burgesses from Botetourt County, Colonel Andrew Lewis.

As the First Continental Congress was meeting in Philadelphia, Virginia's royal governor was marshalling his forces for a war against the Indians. His original plan was for Colonel Lewis to move his division to the mouth of the Great Kanawha River at Point Pleasant, build a fort, to be named Fort Blair, and wait to be joined by the other wing. Instead, after Lewis' Right Wing was on the march in late September, the plan was revised for the two wings to cross the Ohio independently, and converge to attack the Indians in their Scioto River towns. By October 9, a Sunday, Dunmore's wing was already across the Ohio at the mouth of the Hockhocking River, and he sent orders for Lewis, still waiting for the rest of his army to arrive, to cross and join forces near Pickaway Plains.[5]

None of Colonel Lewis' scouts had reported seeing Indians in the Point Pleasant area, so the men encamped with relatively little security posted. They were unaware that Cornstalk had seized the opportunity to defeat the two wings of the Virginia army in detail, and had crossed the Ohio to their north with 800-1,000 warriors. During the night, they marched south and took positions about one mile north of the Virginians' camp, ready to attack before daybreak on Monday. The surprise was foiled early on October 10 when two Virginians out hunting deer encountered a party of Indians arrayed for battle. After an exchange of gunfire, one surviving hunter made it back to alert his comrades. They were quickly under arms. Colonel Lewis deployed two regiments for battle, and kept the rest of his available force in reserve while building a defensive breastwork. The deployed regiments formed a line of battle as the Indians attacked, and the battle was joined. The close-in backwoods fight lasted most of the day. Finding the Indians in greater strength than anticipated, the Virginians retreated, but rallied as Lewis reinforced the line by committing reserves to the fight. By around noon, the Virginians pressed their own attack. Cornstalk's warriors gave ground grudgingly until late in the afternoon, when they broke off the engagement and retreated. As the battle evolved into pockets of scattered gunfire, Cornstalk's Indians re-crossed the Ohio. The remainder of Lewis' wing arrived to reinforce the corps after the battle had ended.[6]

Up on Hockhocking River, Dunmore heard the musketry of Lewis' battle, and took the opportunity to steal a march on the Indians by advancing on their undefended towns. As the Virginians at Point Pleasant recovered from the

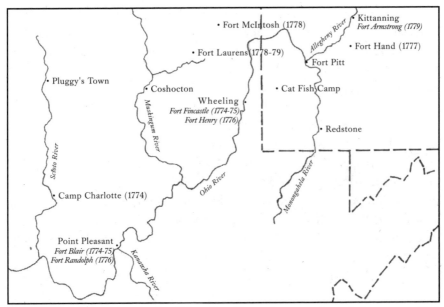

Early settlements and forts in the Ohio valley. The modern state boundaries are provided for reference.

hard-fought battle, buried their dead and tended to their wounded, the advance of Dunmore's wing had the desired effect. He was quickly between the Indian force and their towns. The day after the battle, Lewis sent Dunmore an express informing him that the Southern Division had defeated the Indian attack. After two more days, the chiefs of the fighting Indian nations sued for peace. The two sides agreed to discuss peace terms at Pickaway Plains on the Scioto River, where the Virginians established Camp Charlotte, named in honor of Dunmore's wife. Lewis' division crossed the Ohio on October 17 on its way to join Dunmore's. On the twenty-second, while still fifteen miles from Camp Charlotte, the men from Point Pleasant learned that the treaty had been signed.[7]

During the negotiations, Dunmore produced the Treaty of Camp Charlotte, in which he listed nine articles establishing "The Terms of Our Reconciliation" with the Indians. Quite draconian in its requirements, the treaty made the Indian nations agree to "give up, without reservation, all the prisoners ever taken by them in war with the white people, and to never again wage war against the frontier of Virginia." The Indians further agreed to "give up all negroes . . . pay for all property destroyed . . . [and] surrender all horses and other valuable effects taken from the white people in the last war." The Indians were forbidden "to hunt or visit the south side of the Ohio river, except for the purpose of trading with the white people," or to "molest boats . . . descending or ascending" the river, and "To agree to such regulations for trade . . . as should hereafter be dictated by the King's instruction." Finally, the Mingo and Shawnee were to "deliver up hostages as a guarantee" of their compliance with the treaty, "to be kept by the Whites until convinced of the sincerity" of the nations, until the supplemental treaty council convened at Fort Dunmore. In return, no white people were to be permitted to hunt on the northern side of the Ohio, and the governor guaranteed that this land was reserved to the Indians. Both sides agreed to meet the following spring at Pittsburgh to conclude a supplemental treaty that would ratify the agreements made at Camp Charlotte.[8] Always the more accommodating, the Shawnee voluntarily sent five of their chiefs to be held at the capital in Williamsburg. The more aggressive and supposed more treacherous Mingo were not as easily persuaded to accept the peace terms. Twelve of their warriors were taken prisoner and held hostage at Fort Dunmore until the treaty was ratified.[9]

As Dunmore's two divisions were marching back toward Pittsburgh and Point Pleasant from Camp Charlotte, the delegates of the First Continental Congress and the Continental Association were implementing those actions that had been agreed upon at Carpenters' Hall throughout the colonies. Whig sentiment was growing stronger in Virginia as in other colonies. The situation became ominous when Patriots convened the Second Virginia Convention at Richmond in April 1775, despite the royal governor's proclamation forbidding it. Dunmore directed his Tory subordinates throughout the colony to rally inhabitants to remain loyal to the Crown. He also specifically instructed John Connolly and Indian Department deputy Alexander McKee at Pittsburgh to cultivate the friendship of the Indians, and to impress upon the tribes that their best hope of stemming the flood of American settlers was to be in sympathy with their protector, the king. Connolly, now the major commandant and royal authority at Fort Dunmore, reported to the governor that he had secretly organized a group of Tories, whom he described as either officers of the militia or magistrates of the West Augusta district, in an association dedicated to restoring constitutional government.

Realizing war with Great Britain was drawing near, on April 20, 1775, the Second Virginia Convention had passed "An Ordinance for the Raising and Embodying a Sufficient Force for the Defense and Protection of the Colony." The measure was also taken up by the House of Burgesses when it assumed control of the government.[10] Local defenses were organized according to the established Virginia procedure. The Burgesses later ordered the militia in the area to organize and be ready in case of an Indian war on the border, anticipating the possibility that the British would incite the Indians to fight against the Americans.

When the news finally reached Virginia that tensions had escalated to open conflict, with British regulars and American militia exchanging gunfire at Lexington and Concord on April 19, Dunmore vainly tried to keep the situation in his colony under control by calling the Provincial Assembly. When the House of Burgesses opened its session in Williamsburg on June 1, 1775, Dunmore urged them to ratify the Treaty of Camp Charlotte. Five days later, he presented the legislators a document that included the peace he had negotiated with Cornstalk on behalf of the colony. Dunmore also wanted the Assembly to consider Prime Minister Lord North's conciliatory propositions for resolving the impasse between the colonies and Parliament, but the measure was not well received by the lower house. There were even mobs voicing their opposition to Parliament on the streets of Williamsburg. It was soon apparent that the House of Burgesses could no longer work with the royal governor, and he feared for his personal safety. On June 8, Lord Dunmore removed his seat of government to the safety of the British warship HMS *Fowey* standing off Yorktown, and the Burgesses seized governmental authority.

The measure for the supplemental Indian treaty remained on the table until June 20, when the House of Burgesses took the up matter, considered it, and passed "An Act for appointing Commissioners to ratify and confirm the late treaty of peace with the Ohio Indians." The upper legislative house, the Loyalist-dominated and appointed Council of State, however, did not concur with the lower house and its elected Patriot majority. By the final day of the session, June 24, the Burgesses learned that the Indians were growing increasingly dissatisfied over Virginia's failure to call the council, thus placing the treaty in jeopardy. The inhabitants of the frontier settlements began to fear that hostilities with the Indians would be renewed. The Burgesses therefore passed a resolution that appointed commissioners and appropriated £2,000 for the expenses necessary "to meet the chiefs or head men of the said Ohio Indians . . . to ratify and confirm the said treaty."[11]

Before fleeing his capital at Williamsburg, Dunmore sent orders to the commanding officers of the three frontier forts to disband the garrisons and abandon the posts. When Captain William Russell received his orders at Fort Blair in early June, he immediately prepared for departure, and marched his company home from Point Pleasant within the week.[12] Sometime during that summer, Indians crossed the Ohio River and burned the deserted post to the ground. Connolly also complied with his orders to disband the garrison and abandon Fort Dunmore on July 20, after which Patriot militia promptly seized control of the post, and changed its name back to Fort Pitt.

In July, unwilling to leave the frontier unguarded against raids or invasion, the Revolutionary government of Virginia authorized the establishment of a line of fortifications. The posts at Wheeling Creek (now the site of Wheeling, West Virginia; although the settlement was not named such until after the Revolution, the name Wheeling will be used to prevent confusion), Redstone (now Brownsville, Pennsylvania), and Pittsburgh were supplied with powder by the colony, and were to be manned by the local militia during times of emergency. Fort Fincastle, the post at Wheeling built during Dunmore's War and named in honor of the Royal Governor, was later renamed Fort Henry, in honor of the state of Virginia's first governor, Patrick Henry, after the new Virginia constitution became law.[13]

Four independent companies of "standing," or full-time, soldiers were then authorized to be raised by the state between August 1775 and September 1776 to provide garrisons at Pittsburgh, Point Pleasant, and Wheeling from among the militia in Botetourt, Augusta, Hampshire, and Frederick counties and the West Augusta District. Their complements each included one captain, three lieutenants, one ensign, four sergeants, two drummers, two fifers, and 100 privates. The company raised in Botetourt County, commanded by Captain Matthew Arbuckle, was ordered to Point Pleasant on the Ohio to establish a garrison and replace the ruined Fort Blair. The new post was named Fort Randolph, in honor of Virginia Patriot and president of the First Continental Congress Peyton Randolph, who had died suddenly in October while serving as a Virginia delegate to the Second Continental Congress in Philadelphia. The fort completed the line of defense and housed the garrisons serving under the orders of the commanding officer at Fort Pitt.

The dispute over the area near the Forks of the Ohio, claimed by both Virginia and Pennsylvania, still caused bitter feelings. Although the animosity increased after Dunmore's forcible seizure of Pittsburgh for Virginia, the two colonies agreed to settle their differences following the war with Britain. To help ease tensions, Virginia reorganized the old District of Augusta into three counties, and transferred the seat of government from Pittsburgh to Cat Fish Camp (present-day Washington, Pennsylvania).

In Tryon County and throughout the colony of New York, Patriots had agreed to unite with other Americans in support of Boston's suffering under closure of the port, and to "faithfully abide by and adhere" to the restrictions and regulations agreed by the First Continental Congress.[14] It was not long before local companies of independent militia were drilling in communities throughout the county. Patriot organizations like the Friends of Liberty, akin to the Sons of Liberty in other colonies, were holding political meetings and erecting Liberty Trees, upright trunks or poles that symbolized American opposition to the oppressive acts of Parliament, in almost every town. Despite the show of solidarity with the Rebels of Boston by many of their neighbors, the "friends of government" were not passive. Led by the Johnsons and Butlers, who had long dominated Tryon County and area politics with their wealth and influence, local Tories challenged the legitimacy and authority of the committee. Standing for "Order and Legal Government," Sir John Johnson threatened the captains of independent militia companies and members of the Continental Association with arrest and imprisonment whenever he saw them conducting treasonous activities. Sir John ordered the sheriff to disperse those attending meetings of the Friends of Liberty, and led posses of like-minded citizens to cut down their Liberty Poles. In March 1775, Sir John succeeded in getting the county government at Johnstown to pass a resolution affirming the loyalty of local residents to the king.

The Provincial Assembly of New York was still controlled by conservative Loyalists like Guy Johnson, one of the Tryon County representatives. The Assembly had voted not to consider the proceedings of the First Continental Congress by a vote of 11-10 in January 1775. When it met for the last time, on April 3, 1775, the legislative body again refused to endorse the Continental Association, voted not to approve the proceedings of the First Continental Congress, and voted against appointing delegates to the Second Continental Congress, which was scheduled to convene the following month. The hard line of the Loyalists incensed those of the Patriot faction. Throughout the colony, the Patriot organizations had coordinated their efforts during the non-importation efforts through New York City's Committee of Observation, which was commonly referred to as the Committee of Sixty by the spring of 1775. Angered at the action of the New York Assembly, the Committee of Sixty began to urge as early as March 1 that a Provincial Convention meet in April to elect delegates to represent the colony at the Second Continental Congress in May. Meeting on April 20, with representatives from all parts of the colony except Tryon, Gloucester, Cumberland, and some districts of Queens counties, the convention completed its business and adjourned on the twenty-second, just a day before the news of the confrontation at Lexington and Concord reached New York City. A wave of excitement swept the city. British regulars had fired on American militia, initiating a state of war. Militia companies broke into the armory and distributed some 600 muskets and ammunition to the most active members. Public stores and the Customs House were seized. Local government disintegrated, and Loyalists were openly threatened on the streets. The royal governor, William Tryon, moved his government to the safety of HMS *Duchess of Gordon*, a British man-of-war anchored in New York harbor. Although the upper legislative house of the province, the New York Council, continued to meet with the governor aboard the vessel, it no longer had any influence.

Throughout the colony of New York, the royal government structure ceased to function, while the apparatus that linked the local and provincial committees in support of the Continental Congress emerged from the shadows to seize control. On April 28, the Committee of Sixty called for the formation of more permanent governing bodies that were friendly to the Continental Congress for both the city and colony. The committee sent all the county and town committees an invitation by circular letter to hold elections of all freeholders and freemen in order to send representatives to meet in a Provincial Congress on May 22, 1775. On April 29, the committee declared a "general association," or willingness to execute the orders of the Continental Congress, in the name of the people of New York.[15]

When the Provincial Congress convened in May, it was composed of delegates from throughout the colony, representing both the Patriot and Loyalist factions, although the former were clearly in the majority. Some areas were still not represented, including Tryon County. As the result of its deliberations, the Provincial Congress, and its standing committee, agreed to support the Continental Congress in its direction of the war to protect the rights and liberties of America. The Provincial Congress, although still an extralegal entity, assumed responsibility for legislative functions, financial management, and the direction of government, including the internal police powers and military defense effort within the colony. By June 3, 1775, this once extralegal body had assumed the mantle of government throughout the entire colony of New York.[16]

That same day, the Provincial Congress invited Tryon County to send delegates for its representation, and specifically warned Guy Johnson not to interfere with or oppose the recommendations of either the Provincial or Continental Congresses. Before it adjourned for a recess on July 8, the Provincial Congress appointed a Committee of Safety to act as its executive agency during the interim. Representing each section of the colony, the Provincial Congress directed each town and county to do likewise at the local level to keep the military organization functioning and suppress the Loyalist faction. The Tryon County Committee of Safety identified Guy Johnson as a threat, due to his influence over both the local electorate and the Indians on behalf of the Crown, and sent a formal letter protesting his open Loyalist leanings. Knowing that other uncompromising Tories were being imprisoned and their property confiscated, Johnson realized it was time to leave. Johnson abandoned Guy Park, the home Sir William had built for him and his bride. Accompanied by Daniel Claus, John and Walter Butler, Joseph Brant and other Indian Department personnel, Loyalist members of his regiment of militia, and a party of faithful Mohawk warriors, nearly 250 men in all, he headed for Canada.

On the way, Johnson halted briefly at Fort Stanwix—its works now abandoned—to assemble a council attended by some 260 Oneidas and Onaquagas. A few days later after reaching Oswego on July 17 some 1,485 Indians from the various Iroquois nations and about one hundred Loyalists, including Indian Department members, met in council. Johnson was encouraged, and urged them to assist the king's troops in defending Canada from the Rebels, "annoy" the enemy in their own country, and send 120 of their warriors with him to Montreal to convince the other Indians, their "dependents," who were meeting there, to support the king.[17] The Six Nations, if united, could have fielded a force estimated at more than 2,400 warriors: 1,000 Seneca, 260 Onondaga, 200 Cayuga, 300 Oneida, 200 Tuscarora, and 300 from the two communities of Onaquaga.[18] These numbers could be substantially increased if the numbers of warriors from their dependent and allied tribes were added.

In the early months of the war, both sides attempted to enlist the aid of the American Indians. It was not lost on the British Commander in Chief for North America, General Sir Thomas Gage, that the ranks of the Rebel army besieging him at Boston included Indians from the Christianized community of Mahican Algonquin Indians at the Stockbridge Mission in Massachusetts. In June 1775, following the capture of Fort Ticonderoga and Crown Point by the Americans, which effectively cut his communications with Quebec by the Lake Champlain-Richelieu River route, Gage wrote to the Secretary of State for the Colonies, the Right Honorable William Legge, Lord Dartmouth. Gage said, "It will justify Carleton [British Royal Governor-General and Commander in Chief of Canada] to raise bodies of Canadians and Indians to attack them [the American rebels] in return; and we need not be tender of calling on the Savages, as the rebels have shown us the example, by bringing as many Indians down against us here as they could collect."[19] In response, on July 24, Lord Dartmouth wrote to British officials in North America that the "King, relying upon the attachment of his faithful allies, the Six Nations of Indians, might be under the necessity of calling them for their aid and assistance." He then directed Guy Johnson, who was still on his way to Montreal, to "lose no time in taking such steps as may induce them to take up the hatchet against his rebellious subjects in America." Johnson was also instructed to distribute "presents" to the various sachems, and that once enlisted into the king's service, the Indians were to be used however the commander in chief saw necessary.[20]

After he reached Montreal in July, Johnson called another council at which 1,700 representatives of both the Six Nations and Seven Nations were present. Each of the assembled tribes was given a war belt, and sang their war songs. At first, the Indian Nations professed a desire to remain neutral in what they saw as a quarrel between brothers. Major General Frederick Haldimand, Gage's second in command who would later report to the new Secretary of State for the Colonies, Lord George Germain, urged the gathered Indians to "assist the King now, and you will find it to your advantage."[21] Johnson urged them to rise up and attack the Rebels, but when they agreed, Governor-General Carleton rejected their offer to devastate the New England frontier based on humanitarian grounds. In a letter to Lord Dartmouth following the council, Carleton reported that the Indians had promised "great Things," although they could not be depended on for much in action. Still, he urged the necessity for maintaining their friendship, despite the expense.[22]

Johnson and Carleton had serious disagreements over the use of the British Indian allies. Johnson believed that the Indians could be of great use in helping to crush the rebellion by raiding and terrorizing the frontier settlements. Such employment, he reasoned, could cause the Rebels to divert military strength that would otherwise be employed against British forces, as well as intimidate inhabitants from supporting the rebellion. Carleton, in contrast, was reluctant to unleash the fury of the "savage" style of warfare on the frontier, where he thought the Indians would prey on Rebel and Loyalist, soldier and civilian, alike. Carleton did not oppose using Indian warriors in the conflict. He considered them as valuable allies when used in conjunction with or as auxiliaries to British and Provincial troops in the defense of Canada. As such, he first turned to the warriors of the Seven Nations of Canada, the former French allied Wyandot, Algonquin, Nipissing, Abenaki, and three tribes of "French" or "Catholic" Mohawks. Furthermore, Carleton despised Johnson's deputy for the Seven Nations, Lieutenant Colonel Daniel Claus. On his own authority, Carleton appointed Colonel John Campbell as the Superintendent for Canadian Indians in the Department of Quebec. Johnson believed that not only confused the state of British-Indian relations, but challenged his authority as superintendent of Indians in the northern department. The dispute grew more intense in September 1775 when Carleton refused Johnson permission to lead a body of rangers from his department and Indian warriors in independent offensive action against the Rebels. In desperation, Johnson applied for a leave of absence and sailed for England to personally discuss the matter with Lord George Germain. He wanted the Secretary of State for the Colonies to personally clarify his position as superintendent of Indian affairs and the role of the Indian Department. He was accompanied by Claus, his now displaced deputy for the Seven Nations, and Joseph Brant, the charismatic Mohawk and Indian Department officer. Once in England, Brant quickly became a favorite with members of the British government and English society, especially after he assured Lord Germain that, "the Six Nations will continue firm to their engagements with the King their father."[23]

Unlike Carleton, Governor Dunmore had no reservations about using the Indians offensively against Rebels on the frontier of Virginia from the very beginning of the conflict. When Major Commandant John Connolly returned to Williamsburg from Pittsburgh in late summer of 1775, he made his way to the British man-of-war at anchor off Norfolk aboard which Dunmore had taken refuge. For two weeks, Dunmore and his loyal subordinate developed a plan to hasten the collapse of the rebellion by taking control of the Ohio frontier. Connolly was to proceed to Fort Detroit and recruit a battalion from among the Loyalists living at the settlement. After being supplied with stores, possibly artillery and reinforcements from British forces in frontier posts, Connolly was to lead an expedition against Fort Pitt. Along the way, he hoped to persuade some of the independent militia companies to remain loyal to the Crown, and rally them and Tory militia to follow him. Connolly was also directed to obtain the cooperation of the Ohio Indians by distributing liberal amounts of supplies and presents, along with guarantees of restrictions on white settlement, on behalf of the British government. With the forces he assembled, Connolly planned to capture and destroy Forts Pitt and Fincastle, as well as any settlements that offered resistance, before penetrating into the more settled regions of Virginia as far as Alexandria. While Connolly was moving from the west, Dunmore planned to raise two regiments of Loyalist volunteers. One, composed of white Tories, was to be known as the Queen's Own Loyal Virginia Regiment. The other sought black recruits. Dunmore offered emancipation to the slaves of Rebel plantation owners who joined the Virginia Ethiopian Regiment. The royal governor planned to lead the two Loyalist regiments, along with British seamen and marines from Royal Navy vessels at his disposal in Chesapeake Bay, in a campaign to crush Rebel forces in the Virginia Tidewater. Dunmore and Connolly then planned to converge at Alexandria, thus severing Virginia and the southern colonies from the rest, and facilitate a quick end to the rebellion.[24]

During that summer, the Continental Congress issued a resolution creating its own agency for dealing with Indians, quite similar in purpose to the British Indian Department, as it was deemed in the colonies' best interest to "be very active and vigilant in exerting every prudent means to strengthen the [Indians'] friendly disposition" to the American cause. Recognizing that the "Indians depend on the Colonies for arms, ammunition, and clothing," which they could no longer do without, there was a mutual benefit to maintaining good relations. Congress appointed its own commissioners of Indian Affairs, and organized them into three departments, to urge the Indians to remain neutral. The three commissioners each in the northern and middle departments and the five in the southern were delegated the "power to treat with the Indians" in their respective departments, "in the name, and on behalf of the united colonies, in order to preserve peace and friendship . . . and to prevent their taking any part in the present commotions."[25] Among those individuals the northern department employed to maintain good relations with the Six Nations were Reverend Samuel Kirkland and James Dean. Kirkland, an energetic Presbyterian missionary and redoubtable Yankee from New England, had found a great following among the Oneidas, and preached not only Calvinistic religious doctrine but also sympathy for the Whig political cause. Dean, a long-time interpreter for missionaries since his youth, had grown up in the mixed Iroquois community of largely Oneida and Mohawk Indians of Onaquaga, and was said to be the most proficient white man in the Oneida language.

At the same time that most of the Seneca, Cayuga, Mohawk, and Onondaga were pledging their assistance to King George III, they were telling the Continental Indian commissioners a different story. They said they were not willing to take an active part in the war against Britain, and expressed their preference to remain neutral in the fight between the "Bostonians" and the Crown. Earlier in the year, Iroquois representatives had made two such affirmations, one to Ethan Allen, the colonel of the Green Mountain Boys who had captured Ticonderoga in May, and another in a declaration of neutrality by twelve Oneida sachems in June. In a council meeting with American commissioners at Albany at the end of August, Six Nations representatives, the Mohawk sachem Little Abraham among them, again relayed a pledge of Iroquois neutrality. They reaffirmed their nonaligned status by saying it was in "the determination of the Six Nations not to take any part, but . . . to sit still and see you fight it out." As they saw it, they explained, this was a family quarrel, and professed "as much affection for the King of England's subjects on the other side of the water, as we do for you, born upon this land."[26]

In Williamsburg, Virginia's newly appointed Indian commissioners prepared for their first meeting with the Indians. They sent one of their fellows, Captain James Wood, to notify the Indians that the long awaited peace conference to complete the treaty they had agreed to with Lord Dunmore would be held at Fort Pitt on September 12. Leaving immediately, Wood completed his mission and arrived in Pittsburgh on August 11. In the meantime, the freeholders and freemen of the District of West Augusta elected a Committee of Safety. The committee forwarded a petition to the Continental Congress at Philadelphia on behalf of the district, asking for a resolution on the unfinished work of the Camp Charlotte Treaty, not aware that Virginia's government had taken action. Congress responded that it had appointed its own Indian commissioners to represent the united colonies, and the commission's middle department had

Originally a French post, Fort Niagara was captured by Iroquois and British forces under the command of Sir William Johnson in 1759. Located at the mouth of the Niagara River, the fort controlled the portage to Lake Erie and presented a key British military presence and source of support to the Six Nations during the Revolutionary War. The main building, known as the "State House," is still standing substantially as Johnson captured it.

responsibility for dealing with the Indian nations that were party to the Camp Charlotte treaty.[27] Doctor Thomas Walker, who had already been selected as one of Virginia's commissioners, was appointed by the Continental Congress to serve as one of its commissioners as well. Congress also passed a resolution to appropriate $8,666.63 for the commission's expenses and presents for the Indian sachems. When the news reached Pittsburgh, while waiting for the chiefs (who were slow in assembling), the Continental and Virginia representatives organized a joint commission for the meeting and elected Doctor Walker to serve as chairman. The Indian chiefs began arriving on September 15, and the largest Indian congress ever assembled to that date in the Ohio country formally convened on October 19, 1775.

During the next thirty-four days, the commissioners and the assembled chiefs, representing those Indian Nations who fought in Dunmore's War, as well as members of the Six Nations seeing to the welfare of their "dependents," discussed, agreed to, confirmed, and ratified the terms of the Camp Charlotte treaty. When the council adjourned, every Indian nation from the Upper Allegheny and from the Ohio to Lake Erie entered into a pledge of friendship with both Virginia and the United Colonies.[28] It appeared to the American commissioners that they had succeeded in gaining an assurance that the Indian nations preferred neutrality to taking sides. As a result, the Ohio frontier was somewhat peaceful for the next two years.

While the American commissioners were holding council with the Indians at Fort Pitt, Dunmore's scheme to forcibly take Pittsburgh and the Ohio territory was put into motion. After traveling to Boston to gain the approval for the plan by His Majesty's Commander in Chief in North America, General Thomas Gage, John Connolly returned to Virginia with his commission as lieutenant colonel commandant of Provincial forces. On November 13, 1775, six days after Dunmore declared martial law and offered freedom to slaves willing to fight, Connolly began his overland trek toward Detroit. He was accompanied by two other Loyalists, Allen Cameron, formerly an Indian affair's agent in the southern department, and John Ferdinand Dalziel Smith, a physician who was appointed as the battalion surgeon. Because he was once a Maryland resident and familiar with the area through which they were traveling, Doctor Smith acted as their guide. The journey was uneventful until November 19, when the three Loyalist officers traveling in civilian attire reached an inn just beyond Hager's Town. For some reason, the trio had aroused the suspicions of some Whigs, who notified the colonel of the local minutemen. Before dawn the next morning, the conspirators were rudely aroused from their sleep and arrested by the Patriot soldiers. The minutemen escorted the Loyalists back to town for examination by the local Committee of Safety, and then to Frederick Town for further examination and a hearing by the county Committee of Inspection.

A copy of Connolly's plan, which had gone unnoticed when the trio was first apprehended, was discovered during a search of his belongings the next day. The documents showed that the Tory lieutenant colonel commandant was "clandestinely making his way to Detroit in order to give intelligence to and otherwise aid the garrison at that place." The discovery prompted the men of the committee to notify Continental authorities and request instructions on what to do with their prisoners. Congress directed the committee to convey the Loyalist trio to Philadelphia under guard. Before they departed Frederick Town on December 28, Doctor Smith managed to escape. The other two were escorted to Philadelphia and when they arrived, Connolly was jailed and confined for being a "spy and emissary from the British army." Smith was recaptured near Pittsburgh about two weeks later, on January 12, carrying three incriminating letters from Connolly. One was addressed to Connolly's wife, who was still in Pittsburgh. Another was addressed to Alexander McKee, the British Deputy Superintendent for the Western Indians of the Northern Indian Department. The third was intended for delivery to Captain Hugh Lord of the 18th "Royal Irish" Regiment, who was believed to be at Kuskuski, a Delaware town on the Beaver River, with instructions to forward Connolly's message to Captain Richard Beringer Lernoult of the 8th "King's" Regiment of Foot, then commandant of the fort at Detroit.[29]

It seemed unlikely that the Six Nations could remain neutral for long with the war swirling about them. If the ardor of the Crown's local commander in chief, Carleton, in encouraging offensive operations by the Indians was somewhat lukewarm as 1775 drew to a close, Colonel Guy Johnson could claim some accomplishment on behalf of his king in treating with the Indians. His department had reunited the Caughnawaga Mohawks, who had left the confederation under French influence and had been French allies in the last war, with their Six Nations Mohawk brethren, who had long been staunch allies of the British. Johnson could also take satisfaction that he had obtained a pledge before he left for England from the Seven Nations of Canada and some members of the Six Nations of Iroquois to help defend Canada against rebel invasion.[30] And that opportunity came while Johnson was away.

In September, the Americans launched an invasion of Canada in an effort to induce their northern neighbors to join the rebellion as the fourteenth colony. One wing under Brigadier General Richard Montgomery moved from Crown Point to take Montreal, while a second under Colonel Benedict Arnold left Boston to capture Quebec. Carleton decided not to defend Montreal and fell back to Quebec. As bitter winter weather approached, the Americans launched a two-pronged attack on the British strongpoint. Having failed to lure Carleton out of the protection of Quebec and into a decisive battle—a strategy that worked against Montcalm during the French and Indian War—Montgomery and Arnold were forced to assault the city directly on December 31, as many of their troops were due to complete their service at the first of the year, and the opportunity to engage Carleton would pass. The attacks utterly failed, and with Montgomery mortally wounded and Arnold injured, the Americans fell back.

Confederacy Mohawks and Cayugas helped to defeat the Americans and proved themselves valuable allies. There were no better fighters in the woods, and they inflicted more than their share of casualties when attacking the invading American units. Despite the accomplishment, Carleton remained reluctant to employ Indian warriors in offensive maneuvers against the frontier districts of the rebellious colonies. He realized their value as scouts and in screening the movements of his army from American patrols, and he used them in that capacity later on during his counter-invasion in the summer and autumn of 1776. Although they performed their screening and scouting missions well, Carleton noticed that his Indian allies could be difficult to control. Once they satisfied their desire for scalps or plunder, or simply tired of the campaign tactics employed by the British, it was not unusual for the warriors to start heading home.

Sir John Johnson, like his brother-in-law Guy Johnson and John Butler, was also a staunch supporter of the king. After hostilities erupted in open warfare, and Patriots seized control of provincial and local governments, Sir John Johnson raised and armed 300 men at his own expense to protect their fellow Tryon County Loyalists.[31] This provoked the local authorities to call for his arrest in January 1776 for recruiting Loyalist volunteers. After agreeing to disband his volunteers and giving his parole to desist from "inimical" activities, Sir John was allowed to remain at his Fort Johnson estate by Revolutionary authorities. When he learned that he would be freed from his parole only to be immediately taken as a prisoner of war and his estate confiscated, Sir John followed Guy Johnson in fleeing to Canada in May. Making his way to La Prairie, near Montreal, he met with the royal governor to offer his services.[32] Carleton appointed Johnson a lieutenant colonel commandant and issued him a "Beating Order" on June 19 to raise a battalion of Provincial troops. A beating order was the authority for an officer to raise a military unit by enlisting men to serve the king. The formal permission to raise a regiment, and the attached conditions, were embodied in a "letter of service" addressed to the prospective colonel in the regular British Army by the Secretary at War, or by the respective commander in chief of America or Canada for Provincial troops. (Although popular in the militia, the rank of colonel was largely honorific in British regular and provincial service. The rank commensurate with the command of a regiment was that of lieutenant colonel commandant.)[33]

Sir John Johnson found willing if not numerous recruits among other Tory refugees who had fled from Albany and Tryon counties to avoid persecution by Committees of Safety and the militia. They were eager to fight for the king and exact revenge on their former neighbors. These loyal "friends of Government" took pride in their unit that was officially designated the King's Royal Regiment of New York, or KRRNY, but were more popularly known as the Royal Yorkers.

"Provincials" were American Loyalist soldiers who volunteered to serve in units raised by officers who were commissioned by the authority of the commanders in chief in America and Canada. They were paid, armed, fed, and subject to the same discipline as British army regulars. Like all Provincials, the men of the Royal Yorkers were initially uniformed in green regimental coats with white buttons and different colored facings to distinguish one regiment from another. Because they were supplied with green uniforms, Provincials were sometimes called "Royal Greens," and took pride in the distinctive identity. When British quartermasters began issuing the standard red coats to Provincial units of infantry in 1778, some Provincials insisted on retaining their green regimentals. From 1778 until they disbanded in 1784, the KRRNY wore red coats faced with blue. In addition to the regimental coats, members of the Royal Yorkers were also issued white waistcoats and breeches, dark brown gaiters, hats, and other accouterments of the standard British design. Like their counterparts in the British regulars, the weapon issued to the KRRNY was the standard "Brown Bess" musket, although some Provincials received the older "Long Land" model. Between spring 1776 and summer 1777, Sir John Johnson's regiment had recruited 283 men.

Although the Connolly-Dunmore plan had been discovered and foiled, and American commissioners had successfully concluded treaties or gained Indian assurances of neutrality, the British were undeterred. They continued in their attempts to enlist Indian aid, at least for acting defensively, against the rebellious colonies. While Sir John Johnson was recruiting and training his regiment of Provincials, in April 1776, John Butler, acting as superintendent of Indian Affairs in the northern department in the absence of Guy Johnson, called a council. He sent messages to the northern and western Indians to meet with him and his fellow British

Sir John Johnson, Sir William's eldest son by his first wife. Sir John served in Pontiac's War and was knighted in 1765, and inherited his father's Baronetcy on the latter's death. He was commissioned a lieutenant colonel of Provincial forces and authorized to raise the King's Royal Regiment of New York, the "Royal Yorkers." In 1782 he replaced Guy Johnson as Superintendent of Indian Affairs.

Indian Department officers, Captains William Caldwell and John Johnston, and Lieutenants William and Peter Johnson (sons of Sir William Johnson by Caroline Peters and Molly Brant, respectively) at Fort Niagara.[34] Reportedly, the sachems told Butler "that the Six Nations with the Caughnawagas and the Seven Tribes in that vicinity had all united and resolved to maintain peace" with both sides, and "receive no Ax from either." Butler responded saying that while he was glad to hear that the Indian Nations were united, he was surprised at their intention to maintain peace with the Americans at the same time that they had already agreed to support the king. After distributing a liberal supply of presents and some persuasive negotiation, Butler was able to convince most of the Iroquois leaders to support the king against the "Bostonians." Before the council adjourned, Butler sent a party of about fifty Seneca and Cayuga warriors, and fifty of other tribes, to Montreal, to await the arrival of Guy Johnson on his return from England, and escort him back to Fort Niagara.[35]

The following month, the Continental Congress' northern department Indian commissioners called a council at Albany. The Oneida chiefs informed Major General Philip Schuyler, commander of the Continental Army's northern forces, what had transpired in the meeting with his British counterpart at Fort Niagara. With regret, they informed him that they "dread the consequences" of the tribes pledging their assistance to the king.[36] In another attempt to attract the support of the Six Nations, on May 25, 1776, the Continental Congress passed a resolution to "engage the Indians in the Service of the United Colonies." Congress directed its own commissioners at Albany to "use their utmost Endeavors to procure the Assistance of the Indians to act against the enemies of these Colonies." Recognizing the strategic value in having the Indians attack the British stronghold at Fort Niagara, Congress authorized its Indian commissioners to pay warriors a bounty of "£50 Pennsylvania Currency" for every soldier of the Fort Niagara garrison they took as prisoner and turned over to Continental military authorities or Indian commissioners.[37] Congress followed with another resolution on June 17 encouraging General George Washington to employ Indian allies as he saw best for military purposes. Washington was keenly aware of how important Indians could be, having witnessed their devastating effect during pitched battles in western Pennsylvania during the French and Indian War. In September 1775, he had written the Massachusetts General Court to introduce an Oneida chief who had visited his camp; Washington hoped that his new army would make a good impression on the chief, leaving open the door for possible cooperation during the war against England. Congress further authorized Washington to reward warriors who captured enemy prisoners in Indian country or along the frontier at the rate of "one hundred dollars for every commissioned officer, and thirty dollars for every private soldier."[38] Despite these incentives, the Iroquois continued to communicate their professions of neutrality to the American commissioners.

On July 6, 1776, three Continental western department Indian commissioners—Major William Trent, Major Bernard Ward, and Captain John Neville—convened their own conference at Fort Pitt. The Indian leaders attending included Kayashuta, a Seneca chief who had just returned from Butler's British conference at Fort Niagara, Captain Pipe, a chief of the Delaware, a Shawnee chief known as Shade, and several other influential Delaware and Shawnee leaders. Reflecting the tributary relationship of the Ohio nations to the Iroquois, Kayashuta carried a wampum belt to the Shawnees, Delawares, Mingoes, Wyandots, and other western Indians from the Six Nations. The belt's message told its intended recipients that the Iroquois Confederation were determined to take no part in the war between the British and Americans, and

urged the western tribes to do the same. Kayashuta then told the American officers that the Six Nations appointed him to "the care of this country" and the
Indians on the north bank of the Ohio River. He warned the Americans not to
launch the expedition against the British at Detroit that they heard was being
considered, for the Indians would "not suffer an army to march through our
country" without serious consequences for violating their neutrality. Knowing
that frontier inhabitants would be quick to fix the blame for any hostile actions
on Indians in general, Kayashuta pledged the Iroquois' assurance that any "mischief" that chanced to be committed by Indians was not done with the approval
of their chiefs. The Six Nations, he said, "have strictly forbidden any of their
young men or tributaries to molest any people on their own waters."

Speaking for the Americans, Neville assured the Indians that Continental
forces would not attempt to march through Indian country without first making them aware of the purpose and seeking their approval. Unless, of course, "we
hear of a British army coming," in which case, he said, the Americans would
make all possible effort to stop them, and not cede any such advantage to their
enemy. In response, Kayashuta assured them there was no danger of that, as the
Indians would stop either an American or British army from passing through
their country.[39]

Despite the Indians' continued professions of neutrality to the Americans,
the British were confident that they had gained their allegiance. All pretenses
were soon dispensed with in September 1776. After being called by John Butler,
an Indian Grand Council met at Niagara. As Lieutenant Colonel John
Caldwell, then in command of the 8th, or King's, Regiment of Foot and Fort
Niagara, looked on, Butler and officers of the Indian Department prevailed in
gaining a definitive declaration of alliance. All the chiefs of the Wyandot,
Chippewa (Ojibwa), Ottawa, Potawatomi, Mississauga, Seneca, Cayuga,
Onondaga, Mohawk, Delaware, Nanticoke, Sauk-Mesquakie, and Conoy were
present, but there was only one representing the Oneida and Tuscarora. The
assembled chiefs adopted and unanimously agreed to go to war in support of
the Crown, and made an appeal for the Oneida and Tuscarora "to quit the
Bostonians, and . . . fulfil their engagements to the King."[40] Although each
member nation of the Six Nations was free to pursue its own interests, they
refrained from fighting one another. If that occurred, it would be the first time
they would be divided by warfare in the history of their centuries-old confederacy. But the alliance might not have to be tested because Great Britain had
made a decisive move.

In late June, while American forces retreated from Canada in the face of
Carleton's offensive, a British fleet of ten ships-of-the-line, twenty frigates, and

a number of lesser class warships, commanded by Admiral Richard Howe choked New York harbor. Over the next few weeks, 300 transports unloaded a massive army of 32,000 British and German regulars at Staten Island. Commanded by General William Howe, the admiral's brother who had succeeded General Gage as commander in chief of His Majesty's forces in North America, it was the largest army Great Britain had ever deployed overseas. Soon after arrival, Howe put the finishing touches to his plan to capture the strategic city of New York, destroy Washington's largely ill-trained and mostly militia force of 28,000 Americans, and crush the rebellion once and for all.

Among those sailing with Howe were Colonel Guy Johnson and Joseph Brant, who now held a regular captain's commission. Having been in England for the past ten months, they were greeted upon their return by a messenger from the Mohawk Valley with information that the Rebel government had destroyed Johnson's house at Guy Park, removed both Sir John Johnson's and John Butler's wives to Albany under house arrest, and confiscated the Johnsons' estates. In a July 9 letter to Lord George Germain, Guy Johnson recorded his reaction to the news that greeted him, and complained, "Rebels had carried off my Negroes &c and demolished everything on my estate."[41] But there was the king's work to be done, and Johnson sent Brant to make his way through American lines to Indian country.

Accompanied by Captain Gilbert Tice of the Indian Department, Joseph Brant visited numerous Iroquois towns as he headed toward Fort Niagara. At every stop, Brant shared with the assembled sachems and warriors his eyewitness report of the military might of Great Britain, and how it would decisively defeat the American forces defending New York City. He also brought them a message from Guy Johnson urging the Six Nations to be prepared to cooperate with Howe's mighty army. Brant's accounts of his meeting with Lord Germain heightened their resolve. He told them how the Secretary of State for the Colonies had assured him on the Indians' behalf of the king's help and pledge in preserving their land against the threat of expansion by the colonists after the war was over. Brant told his audiences that he answered Germain by saying that if the government would "take care and have the grievances of the Six Nations on account of their lands, particularly those of the Mohocks and Oughquagas [Onaquagas] . . . and all those matters settled to our satisfaction whenever the troubles in America were ended," that his people would "continue to behave with attachment to the King."[42]

Brant was eager for the Six Nations to demonstrate their friendship toward the Crown. Brant believed his people were ready to take a more active role in the fighting against the king's rebellious subjects. After gathering a mixed force

Sketch of Howe's fleet at anchor at Staten Island. (New York Public Library)

of Indians and Loyalists, who armed and equipped themselves at their own expense, Brant began planning to lead them in raids on American backcountry settlements. When he arrived at Fort Niagara in December 1776, however, he found that with Guy Johnson still in New York at Howe's headquarters, Governor Carleton continued to insist that the Six Nations refrain from unleashing their full fury on the American frontier for fear of alienating those who might still declare their allegiance to the King. To ensure his directive was obeyed, Carleton ordered John Butler not to supply Brant's volunteers with ammunition, supplies, or money for any such campaign. Carleton was not out of bounds. When Howe replaced Gage, Canada became an independent command under Carleton. This treatment once again disheartened those Indians who were eager to get into battle. Brant and Sir John Johnson were both vocal in their criticism of the Indian Department and how it had been managed by Carleton and their friend Butler while Guy Johnson was absent. They questioned the expenditure of great sums of money that thus far had only kept the Indians friendly but inactive, while Rebel forces had easily seized Fort Stanwix in the summer of 1776. Renamed Fort Schuyler by the Americans, that important post was the gateway to the Mohawk Valley, and on the "eastern door" of Iroquois country.[43]

Having failed to dissuade George Washington from pursuing military action on behalf of the Continentals, Howe launched his offensive from his Staten Island base in late August 1776. Crossing over to Long Island, Howe's army defeated the Continentals and forced George Washington, and those troops who could, to retreat quickly to York Island (as Manhattan was then known) to avoid capture. Pressed by Howe, Washington's troops made a stand at Harlem Heights and then abandoned New York City to the British in October. At the same time,

Carleton's offensive encountered unexpected American resistance on Lake Champlain. Commanded by Brigadier General Benedict Arnold, a flotilla of barges off Valcour Island slowed his advance and, after reoccupying Crown Point, forced Carleton to halt his operations, as the onset of winter weather would hinder any continued forward movement. But Carleton may have had a change in heart about making more use of the Indian allies. Anticipating the next year's campaign season, Carleton directed his lieutenant governor at Detroit, Lieutenant Colonel Henry Hamilton, to send any intelligence about American intentions to attack that vital post. He also advised Hamilton to "keep the Savages in readiness to joyn me in the Spring, or march elsewhere as they may be most wanted."[44] The Crown now had large bodies of troops along the Canadian-American frontier and in New York City, a disposition that did not go unnoticed.

During the winter of 1776-1777, Major General John Burgoyne, who had been appointed second-in-command to Carleton in Canada earlier in 1776, took leave from his duties and returned home, frustrated with his own lack of authority and apparent lack of initiative of his superior. While in England, he formulated a campaign plan that he felt was certain to turn the tide, and presented it to Lord Germain in a paper entitled "Thoughts for Conducting the War from the Side of Canada." Burgoyne's plan called for him to personally lead an army of some 11,000 British, Provincial, and German regulars, along with American Loyalist and loyal Canadian militia and allied Indians, to advance south along the Lake Champlain-Hudson River route to Albany. There, they would meet and combine with the main British army under General Howe moving north along the Hudson from the city of New York. Once united, the two armies would effectively sever the rest of the colonies from New England—always seen as the instigators of the rebellion. Once New England was crushed, the full weight of Great Britain's military and naval power could then turn against the remaining American armies in detail. The plan was approved, and Burgoyne was elevated to the permanent rank of lieutenant general, thereby outranking his former superior, Carleton. If all went according to his calculations, Burgoyne's invasion could change the outcome of the war, and possibly end the rebellion with an American surrender in 1777.

Chapter 3

YEAR OF THE HANGMAN

T HE year 1777 would prove to be the most crucial of the war. After the American invasion of Canada in late 1775 came to a jarring halt at the gates of Quebec, British forces under the command of Governor-General Guy Carleton drove them out of Canada the following spring. In March 1776, British forces evacuated Boston, but what appeared to be a victory for the Americans was actually an attempt by Britain to turn the tide. In late summer, the commander in chief of North America, General William Howe, led a massive attack of fresh troops and those who had been stationed in Boston against American forces in New York City with hopes of ending the rebellion. Carleton anticipated combining forces with Howe by continuing his counter-invasion down Lake Champlain. After a series of American delaying actions prevented him from completing his plan before winter, Carleton resolved to make another attempt with the return of warmer weather the next year. In the meantime, Howe, whose forces captured New York City, pursued Washington's retreating army across New Jersey, until it too stopped to go into winter quarters. Howe expected to resume his advance on Philadelphia and destroy the American army in the spring. These plans were upset by Washington's bold counter-strokes at Trenton and Princeton. Despite these late reverses, the British were certain 1777 would prove decisive. Once Lieutenant General John Burgoyne developed his plan for ending the war, national and military leaders in Britain were confident this next campaign could crush the American rebellion. After victory, they would then hang the leading Rebels. Such a fate was fitting, for as many realized, the numerals denoting 1777 bore a resemblance to a row of gallows. With approval to execute Burgoyne's plan for "Conducting the War from the Side of Canada" and high hopes for success, the "Year of the Hangman" had arrived.

The violence of 1777 began on the Ohio frontier when bands of marauding Indians, now supplied and encouraged by the British, became increasingly troublesome. A Mohawk-Mingo chief named Tecanyaterighto, known to whites as Captain Pluggy, led his men in one raid that attacked McClelland's Station (now Georgetown), Kentucky, on Christmas Day 1776, and again on New Year's Day. By March, some 200 Shawnee warriors under the leadership of Chief Blackfish were actively harassing Harrodsburg, Boonesborough, and Logan's Station, the three major settlements in Kentucky, as Major George Rogers Clark organized the militia for their effective defense. At first, the raids were mostly scattered and relatively minor attacks. This did not prevent presumably friendly Indians visiting the frontier settlements from bringing news, or rumors, about the threatening activities of hostile tribes. Typically, Indians attacked unsuspecting men in the fields or hunters in the forests. A favorite tactic was to send part of their force to attack men working outside the protective stockades of the settlements, and wait for the militia to sally out to their rescue. The Indians "retreated" when the militia appeared, presenting the appearance that the small party of offending hostiles was running away from them. After the militia went beyond the safety afforded by the fort in pursuit, they learned that the retreating enemy was only the bait for the rest of the war party waiting in concealment to ambush the soldiers. The Indian war parties rarely attempted to storm and penetrate stockade walls, unless an opportunity to do so successfully presented itself. Instead, they remained in the area of the engagement long enough to destroy or burn crops, and kill, scatter, or drive off the livestock. After a day or two, the warriors would move on to attack another station. It soon became apparent to Clark that the Shawnees he faced were being influenced by the British lieutenant governor at Detroit, Lieutenant Colonel Henry Hamilton, and were being directly supported by the British outposts at Kaskaskia in the Illinois country and Vincennes on the Wabash River.

Blackfish's warriors struck repeatedly, using the same or similar tactics, at all three stations from March until August, keeping the inhabitants in a state of alarm and calling for help from the Virginia state government. After the settlers had endured months of almost constant Indian attacks, Colonel John Bowman arrived at the head of 100 Virginia militia in August, and Major William Bailey Smith came with fifty mounted militiamen and the promise of yet more, from along the North Carolina border. The Kentucky frontier settlers could at last enjoy some relief. Learning of the increased numbers of "Big Knives" who had already arrived or were on their way, the marauding Indians turned their attentions further up the Ohio to seek easier targets.

By March, the Virginia state government authorized a call for 300 militia for an expedition to attack the Mingo and Shawnee renegades at their Pluggy's Town settlement. Knowing the frontiersman's tendency to not bother distinguishing between friendly and hostile Indians when on campaign, the Continental Congress' Indian commissioner at Fort Pitt, Colonel George

Morgan, feared such an action would only endanger the treaties currently in effect, and jeopardize his own efforts to keep the Indians neutral, if not win them over as allies. He warned that any campaign into their territory could prompt the Indians to abandon neutrality in favor of direct involvement on the British side. He successfully petitioned Congress to have Virginia cancel the expedition.

Realizing the danger posed by these hostile bands, Congress authorized the stationing of some regular troops at Fort Pitt, and directed Brigadier General Edward Hand, a Pennsylvania Line officer, be sent to take command of Continental forces in the Western Department area, and exercise control over Pennsylvania and Virginia militia units when their services were required. Hand arrived at Fort Pitt, and assumed command of the department on June 1. Congress also directed that enough provisions for 2,000 men for six months and boats to transport 1,500 men be gathered and maintained at Fort Pitt to be available "should it become necessary, to chastise Indian irruptions, by going to their towns."[1] Not long after the Continental Army established the Western Department, most of the 12th and 13th Virginia Regiments marched east to join the 4th and 1st Virginia Brigades, respectively, with the Main Army.[2] The forces that remained available to Hand included a few companies detached from the 13th Virginia to garrison Forts Pitt and Randolph, and a few independent companies of Virginia state troops, supplemented with Virginia and Pennsylvania militia. Virginia Governor Patrick Henry pledged his cooperation in a letter to Hand, and despite Morgan's protests, the two agreed that taking the fight to the Indians was more favorable than waiting to be attacked.[3]

By June, however, Congress was convinced by Morgan's pleas, and resolved to suspend the establishment of the magazines they had voted on the previous January to provision a possible Indian expedition. The Congressional record noted "the friendly disposition of the Indians" made the execution of such an operation improbable.[4] But British attempts to incite the Indians to assist in the suppression of the Revolution from the direction of Detroit had not ended when Maryland minutemen upset the Tory Lieutenant Colonel John Connolly's mission in 1775.

In February 1777, Lord Germain sent Carleton a letter notifying him of Burgoyne's mission, and that it was expected "that Operations in other parts will be judged proper to be carried on at the same time where the Assistance of the Indians will also be highly necessary."[5] In March, Germain further directed Carleton to have Hamilton send Indian war parties accompanied by officers of the Indian Department on diversionary raids along the Pennsylvania and Virginia frontiers to support Burgoyne's main effort.[6] Germain wrote, the "King commands that you should direct Lieutenant Governor Hamilton at Detroit to assemble as many Indians in his district as he can, place a proper person at their head," meaning a British officer, to "conduct parties" in striking targets that would benefit the military effort elsewhere. Aware of Carleton's early reluctance to employ the Indians offensively, Germain was careful to make the familiar appeal to restrain the Indians from committing violence on the "well affected" Americans who remained loyal. As Carleton prepared to send the Indian Department deputies with the Six Nations and Canadian tribes instructions to abandon the policy of restraint in order to support Burgoyne's invasion of New York in early summer of 1777, he ordered his lieutenant governor at Fort Detroit to encourage the western Indians to attack the exposed American frontier in a coordinated effort.

In the grand scheme, the Indian attacks in the Ohio country were intended to provide a strategic diversion by "exciting an alarm on the frontiers of Virginia and Pennsylvania" that would compel the Rebels to weaken their main army and therefore facilitate Burgoyne's planned operations by the Lake Champlain and Hudson River route, and Howe's expected offensive drive from the east. Furthermore, under proper British control, the Indians could help deliver the Virginia and Pennsylvania backcountry from the "tyranny & oppression of rebel committees." Hamilton was authorized to invite Loyalists to join Provincial military units, where volunteers would receive the same pay and allowances as "His Majesty's other corps raised in America" and a bounty of 200 acres of land.[7] As an additional objective, an Indian offensive in the Ohio country provided the only hope of interdicting the flow of supplies the Americans were obtaining through sympathetic Spanish sources in New Orleans. From that city, the supplies traveled the long water route up the Mississippi and Ohio rivers to Fort Pitt, from where they were moved overland to the supply magazines supporting Washington's army. The seizure of Pittsburgh or any location that could interrupt that tenuous supply route would be beneficial to the British war effort.

In preparation for assuming their mission, Joseph Brant and his volunteers moved to Onaquaga, on the Susquehanna River. Originally populated by the Oneida, Onaquaga grew into a diverse community that included Tuscarora, Delaware, Mahican, and Shawnee, as well as white and mixed-race people, that was politically dominated by Mohawks. They were welcomed on their arrival to the settlement by some 700 inhabitants, and Brant announced that he and his men were on the side of the British Crown, and the town was under his protection. In May, Germain ordered Carleton to employ the Six Nations directly in the invasion of New York as part of Burgoyne's campaign.[8] The aggressive Brant wasted no time in launching his own offensive, and later that month he struck at the settlement of Unadilla, located on the Fort Stanwix Treaty line about thirty miles north of Onaquaga at the confluence of the Susquehanna and Unadilla rivers. Arriving with about seventy-five volunteers and warriors, he informed the inhabitants of the settlement that they had one of two choices to make. If they remained in their homes, he would insure their protection as long as they declared their allegiance to the king. As Loyalists, he expected them to "voluntarily" provide his men with the supplies they requested. Those who sided with the Rebels were given eight days to pack up as many belongings as they and their families could carry, and leave without being harmed. After the time expired, however, they would face the consequences of being considered enemies of the king. After the local Whigs left for the safety of Cherry Valley, Brant burned their abandoned homes, confiscated what he needed from the cattle and provisions they left behind, and moved

Edward Hand. The former British Army surgeon's mate and infantry officer left his Philadelphia medical practice to accept a commission in the Continental Army from Pennsylvania. He commanded the Continental Army's Western and Northern Departments and a brigade that functioned as the "Light Corps" in Sullivan's Expedition. (*Pennsylvania Archives*)

on up the Unadilla River in search of forage and other supplies. Thus populated by Loyalists, Unadilla became a British outpost and a refuge, or what a member of the Schenectady Committee of Safety described as, "a common Receptacle for all rascally Tories, and runaway Negroes."[9] The alarm spread throughout the Schoharie and Cherry Valley regions, as Brant repeated the tactic against other settlements. American militia commanders and Committees of Safety appealed to the government of New York for help in defending against the raids that were sure to continue, and Loyalists made their way to Unadilla and Onaquaga for their own protection and to offer their services to the Crown.

Word of the Indian attacks spread quickly, and it was not long before British forces facing Washington's army were aware of their effect from intelligence gathered from American sources and from messengers who slipped through the lines. From his office with General Howe's headquarters in New York City, the British Superintendent of Indian Affairs, Colonel Guy Johnson, proudly wrote to Lord Germain that the "Six Nations had called in and assembled all their people, in order to make a diversion on the frontiers." With some satisfaction, Johnson reported that, "agreeable to my messages," they made "several attacks along the back settlements from Fort Stanwix to the Ohio," which Johnson believed was interfering with the American effort to recruit volunteers for the Continentals or summon levies from the militia. As a measure of the success of the Indian operations, he noted that "the rebels have been obliged to detach General [Edward] Hand with some troops to protect the frontier," thus accomplishing their mission to serve as a diversion for Burgoyne's invasion down Lake Champlain.[10]

In yet another effort to keep the Iroquois neutral in the coming campaign season, Brigadier General Nicholas Herkimer of the Tryon County militia marched toward Unadilla with 380 troops for a conference with Brant. Herkimer and Brant had once been neighbors in the Mohawk Valley, and perhaps their former friendship could help soothe the Iroquois leader's hostility toward the New York Rebels. In cordial but fruitless meetings on June 27 and 28, Brant reaffirmed his loyalty to King George III. As the meeting ended, Brant advised Herkimer to return home, but not before having his 500 warriors and Tory volunteers emerge from their hidden positions yelling their war whoops and firing their guns into the air to let the Americans know they could have annihilated them if he so chose.

The long wait of the native warriors to take part in the fighting had at last come to an end. Lieutenant Colonel Henry Hamilton convened a council of the Ottawa, Chippewa, Potawatomi, Miami, Shawnee, and western Delaware nations on June 17 in Detroit. Painted and dressed like an Indian, in the tradition of Sir William Johnson, Hamilton sang the war song, feasted with them, and distributed vast quantities of food, ammunition, firearms, scalping knives, war paint, and other presents. In compliance with Germain's instructions to Carleton, Hamilton called on the assembled warriors to attack the Rebels, but not to kill women, children, or old men. With nearly 1,000 warriors expected to take the warpath at his urging, it was impossible for the British Indian Department officers and rangers, much less the Loyalist French-Canadian militia officers who were also accompanying them, to impose any kind of restraint. Because he paid generous bounties for American scalps and offered little or no reward for prisoners, Hamilton became known as "Hair Buyer."

While Hamilton prepared his warriors for battle, Burgoyne's main force of 7,300 men, somewhat less than his plan had envisioned, assembled at Cumberland Point at the western shore of Lake Champlain on June 20, 1777. Burgoyne's plan called for his main army to make its way down Lake Champlain and along the Hudson River, while a secondary effort was sent to

An American political cartoon of Lt. Col. Henry Hamilton, lieutenant governor of Canada, paying bounties to Indian warriors for American scalps, although the uniforms and facial hair appear to be more appropriate to the War of 1812. (*Library of Congress*)

recapture Fort Schuyler and march down the Mohawk River where it would join the main body on the Hudson. The 1,700-man brigade tasked for this assignment was under the command of temporary Brigadier General Barrimore (Barry) Matthew St. Leger. The brigade was a mixed force consisting of companies numbering about 100 men each from the 8th and 34th British Regiments of Foot, an eighty-seven man company of jaegers, or German light infantry armed with short-barreled hunting rifles from the Hesse-Hanau Regiment, 133 men of the light and field officer's battalion of the Royal Yorkers under Sir John Johnson's personal command, a company of Royal Artillerymen with a train of two 6-pounder and two 4-pounder field pieces and four small cohorn mortars, and 100 Loyalist Canadian militia. Departing Montreal on June 21, the command moved down the St. Lawrence River to Buck Island, at the mouth of the Saint Lawrence River on Lake Ontario. There, they met Colonel Daniel Claus, commissioned to act as superintendent of Indians on St. Leger's expedition, who arrived at the head of 150 Seven Nations Indians, to join the expedition.

For several months, Lieutenant Colonel John Butler had been actively seeking permission to raise a corps of rangers that could act independently or in conjunction with the allied warriors in direct action, instead of in the traditional missions assigned to the rangers of the Indian Department. During the spring of 1777, he had recruited a number of Loyalist volunteers to serve in the coming campaign, in hopes of showing his superiors the utility of such a corps to the British war effort. The opportunity to demonstrate his idea came on June 5, when Butler received a letter from Governor-General Carleton to collect as many rangers and Indians as possible and join St. Leger's column at the site of Fort Oswego, where he would also act as Claus' deputy superintendent of Indians for the expedition. When St. Leger's troops arrived at Oswego, Butler and about eighty rangers, the Seneca war chief Sayenqueraghta with some 200 Seneca warriors, and Joseph Brant with another 200 white Loyalist volunteers and Mohawk warriors were waiting for them.

Surprisingly, a number of other parties, totaling about 800 Iroquois warriors, had also gathered to meet with them in council at the rendezvous. To entice them into the king's service, the Indians were given presents of beads, trinkets, and cloth. Every warrior who "took up the hatchet" was given a brass kettle, a suit of clothes, a musket, ammunition, tomahawk, scalping knife, a piece of gold, and a promise of a bounty for every scalp they should bring to Claus. Although most of these additional Indians decided not to join, Claus convinced them to come and watch the triumph of the king's arms. In doing so, Claus increased the numbers of Indians the Americans would see and assume were hostile to their cause, and many of the Indian spectators, he hoped, would join the fight in order to be on the winning side following the British victory. After the customary presentation of gifts and feasting, the combined force marched on toward its objective. By August 3, the lead elements of St. Leger's brigade, made up of light infantry and some Indian scouts, emerged from the woods within sight of the American garrison, signaling that Fort Schuyler was under siege. Captain Gilbert Tice of the Indian Department advanced with a musician and flag to the outer works of the fort and delivered St. Leger's official demand for the garrison to surrender. The Americans replied with a defiant refusal.

As the British began their investment, a message arrived from Joseph Brant's sister, Molly. Having remained in the Mohawk Valley following the death of Sir William Johnson, she was in an ideal location to gather information of American forces and pass them on to the king's men. She sent word that the Tryon County militia had mustered at Fort Dayton in German Flats (present-day, Herkimer, New York), and that an 800-man brigade commanded by Brigadier General Nicholas Herkimer was preparing to march to the assistance of the garrison and lift the siege. They were joined by a band of about sixty Oneida warriors along the route. On August 5, word came that, judging by their speed, the American relief column would arrive within twelve miles of the fort that night. Following the standard practice of armies on the march, they could be expected to bivouac before dark, and push on to the relief of Fort Schuyler early the next morning.

St. Leger's brigade was not yet concentrated. Many of his troops were busy on fatigue details, moving the supplies or cutting the road for the artillery, supply, and baggage trains. Between the fort and the approaching brigade of militia and Oneidas, the British had only a thin cordon of about 250 troops maintaining the siege. St. Leger immediately ordered Sir John Johnson to delay the approaching Americans while he concentrated the rest of his brigade. Johnson gathered the light infantry and colonel's companies of his own Royal Yorkers, Butler's Indian Department rangers, and Brant's and Sayenqueraghta's warriors, a total of about 650 men. He then called the leaders together and went out to reconnoiter the area.

Although in nominal command, Sir John Johnson deferred to Brant's judgment in selecting the site on which to prepare an ambush. Some six miles from Fort Schuyler, Brant found a section along the King's Highway, an old military road the militia was following, that seemed ideal. The winding road dipped down steep wooded slopes into a ravine where two streams draining into the Mohawk River cut the swampy bottomland. After returning to camp, Johnson convened a council of war to discuss the possible deployment of their forces in the ambuscade. Suddenly, scouts arrived with the news that Herkimer's brigade was camped at Oriska, an Oneida town just a few miles from the site of their planned trap.

The Loyalists and Iroquois headed out in the dawn haze toward the rising sun in the east. On their arrival, the Tories and their Indian allies deployed and waited. Most of the warriors and rangers were positioned along the high ground on both sides of the ravine where they would fire into the long American column's flanks. Lieutenant Colonel Johnson positioned his Royal Yorkers near the center of the ambush where they could unleash deadly volley fire. Brant positioned eighty men he would lead to cut off the line of retreat and capture the baggage train. Once trapped, the plan called for the Rebel militia to be worn down and eventually wiped out.

The American brigade stretched over a half mile in length as the wagons and men lurched into motion. The heat of the blazing early-morning August sun was already beating down on the column. A detachment from the leading battalion moved a few hundred paces ahead to act as the advance guard. The rest of the 1st, Canajoharie, Battalion, under the command of Colonel Ebenezer Cox, moved at the head of the column of the main body. They were followed by the 2nd, Palatine, Battalion, commanded by Colonel Jacob Klock. The 4th, Kingsland-German Flats, Battalion was next in the order of march under

Colonel Peter Bellinger's command. The slow moving supply train of fifteen wagons trundled along between Bellinger's and the next unit. Ten of the wagons carried the brigade's baggage, rations, and supplies, and five were loaded with ammunition. Colonel Frederick Visscher's 3rd, Mohawk Valley, Battalion followed the wagons. A detachment from the battalion trailed the main body by a few hundred paces as the rear guard.

As the column entered the ravine, the day grew hotter, and the men and animals struggled with the difficult terrain. Waiting for the entire column to be within the ambuscade, Brant patiently held the signal to start the action that he would give with his British Army sergeant's whistle. Then, something went wrong. Before the trailing American battalion entered the ravine, the Americans' advance guard halted while crossing a stream to refill their canteens. Noticing the lax security, some impatient warriors and inexperienced war chiefs attacked the soldiers. After a deadly blast of musketry, the warriors rushed at the few surviving men of the advance guard with spears, tomahawks and war clubs. Realizing what had happened, the Indians and rangers opened fire in a rolling volley from their concealed positions. The ambush was sprung, although prematurely, on the halted column with devastating effect. The Americans immediately suffered heavy casualties, especially among their officers. The surviving American leaders desperately wheeled their men into position and returned fire. The eager Senecas who had massacred the advance guard went rushing up the road, against the advice of the older chiefs, and were met by a volley of musketry. The Royal Yorkers' light infantry, rangers, and more ably led Iroquois employed sounder tactics, rushing their adversaries as they attempted to reload their muskets. Slowly, the Tories and Indians began to encircle the three leading battalions, while the trailing American battalion still had yet to enter the ravine. Brant initiated his assault on the supply train. His warriors and Loyalist volunteers charged, captured the wagons, and cut them off from the trailing formation. Colonel Visscher's 3rd Battalion was alone and surrounded. A good number of the men panicked and ran. Many of those who did were chased down, killed, and scalped by Indians. Although cut off from the rest of the brigade, Visscher managed to rally the remnants of his battalion, which formed a perimeter, and fought on as best they could.

Surrounded, the brigade's main body fought to expand from its ragged defensive clusters into an organized perimeter, using some Indian tactics of their own. Herkimer, still mounted and among the men of the 1st Battalion, sent orders to the other battalion commanders to move their units forward to consolidate on the higher ground toward the western end of the ravine. Klock's 2nd and Bellinger's 4th Battalions and the Oneidas warriors doggedly fought their way toward the 1st and Herkimer. The militiamen then aggressively pushed out to the higher ground, away from the road. They paired off behind logs and trees, one man ready to fire while the other reloaded, to counter the enemy's rushes. After about an hour, the position of the main body of militia was still desperate, but it had stabilized. As he was riding along the lines and encouraging his troops, Herkimer received a mortal wound from musket fire. Still defiant, he continued to direct the fight and inspire his troops from an improvised sick bed.

A sudden heavy rain shower came on, and for about an hour both sides slackened their fire while trying to keep their powder dry. During the lull, the Indians exacted revenge for their heavy losses by massacring many of the militia who had surrendered, or who lay wounded within their lines. Although surrounded, the Americans' compressed positions had neutralized the British advantage of position to some extent. By noon the rain ended, and the fight resumed in all its violence.

The battle had become a wild mix of conventional and Indian fighting at their deadliest. Sir John Johnson attempted to break the final resistance of the Tryon County militia, and sent in his regiment's field officer's company. They advanced with dressed ranks and bayonets fixed. The militia met them with a volley of musketry, and then rushed out in a counter-attack. The battle in this quarter became a wild melee, as former neighbors from Tryon County faced each other in mortal hand-to-hand combat with bayonet, knife, and clubbed musket. Each wanted to avenge the wrongs the other had subjected them to in the tumultuous time leading up to and in the early days of the Revolution. When the sound of cannon was heard from the direction of the fort, the militia seemed to take new heart. They hoped that part of the garrison was sallying out to their aid as had been planned. By about two o'clock in the afternoon they heard sounds of an engagement from the direction of the British and Indian camps, and the survivors of Visscher's battalion finally managed to fight their way to the main body. Suddenly, it seemed that many Iroquois had lost heart for the fight. The firing began to taper off, and except for some scattered shots, by about three o'clock—five hours after it started—the battle was over.[11]

Herkimer's brigade had suffered heavily. Of approximately 800 soldiers and Oneida warriors who had entered the ravine, barely 150 remained unhurt. General Herkimer, mortally wounded, was among the many militia officers who were casualties. The Tories and Indians had stopped the American relief column before it could reach Fort Schuyler, but they had also been hurt, although not as badly. The British had suffered more than 200 dead, wounded, and missing. The battle had taken a disproportionate toll of Indian chiefs, particularly among those recently appointed at the Oswego council. Their inexperience had proved fatal. As a group, the Seneca suffered the most, losing five chiefs and sustaining sixty dead and wounded warriors. This had not been their kind of battle. As the Indians became discouraged, they started leaving the scene of action. Shortly after the Indians began withdrawing, the Indian Department rangers followed, having lost two of their officers in the battle. The battered remnants of the Royal Yorkers broke off the engagement. As they made their way to camp, their commander, Lieutenant Colonel Sir John Johnson, was visibly shaken.[12]

Once back within their lines, the Loyalists and Indians realized that the sounds of battle they had heard earlier were from a sortie by the Fort Schuyler garrison led by Lieutenant Colonel Marinus Willett. The Continentals had sallied out and engaged the force left to maintain the siege. While the warriors and Tories fought the Tryon County militia in the ravines of Oriskany, the Continentals succeeded in overrunning their encampment and plundered their supplies and possessions. Fort Schuyler now appeared too strong to be taken, and the British light artillery was ineffective against the fort's walls.[13] The Iroquois who had taken the British offer to come as spectators did not like what they saw and began to disperse. When St. Leger learned that Brigadier General Benedict Arnold was leading another American relief force, this time with regular Continental soldiers, he decided to raise the siege and retreat to Montreal. Butler and his Indian Department men retired toward Fort Oswego. The Battle of Oriskany was a turning point in the Revolutionary War on the frontier. Not only did the inability to capture the post contribute to the failure of Burgoyne's invasion and ultimate surrender at Saratoga, the battle marked a change in the participation of the Indian nations. As the Revolution was also a civil war between Patriot and Loyalist former neighbors, the pro-British Seneca and Mohawk had now faced the pro-American Oneida, their Iroquois brothers, in combat.

On his return from the battle, John Butler again approached Governor-General Carleton to reopen the discussion about his proposal to raise a full battalion of rangers, separate from the Indian Department, to serve with the Indians. Based on Butler's success in leading the department's rangers in cooperation with Iroquois warriors, and possibly with some animosity over the efforts of Colonels Guy Johnson and Daniel Claus to circumvent his authority with regard to Indian Department, Carleton consented. On September 15, Butler was appointed as the "Major Commandant of a Corps of Rangers to serve with the Indians." To enlist this body of troops, Carleton authorized and empowered Butler to, "by Beat of the Drum . . . raise on the frontiers of the

Province, so many of His Majesty's loyal subjects as will form one company of Rangers." The beating order went on to instruct that after the company was raised and "passed muster"—an inspection of their numbers to the prescribed strength, by the post commander at Fort Niagara, or another officer of the regular army—he was authorized to raise another until the corps consisted of eight companies. Each company, except the 1st, or Field Officer's, Company, was to have a captain, a lieutenant, three sergeants, three corporals, and fifty privates. (This is compared to a regiment of infantry on the regular establishment of ten companies—eight battalion companies and one each of light infantry and grenadiers. Battalion companies consisted of one captain, two lieutenants, one ensign, five sergeants, five corporals, two drummers, and 100 privates.) Two of the ranger companies were to be formed of "people speaking the Indian language and acquainted with their customs and manner of making war" to be paid four shillings per day. The remaining six companies were "to be composed of people well acquainted with the woods, in consideration of the fateague they are liable to undergo," and were to receive two shillings per day.[14] The officers were to be paid at the same rate as "Officers of like rank" in other Provincial regiments.[15] Although all rangers were required to clothe and arm themselves at their own expense, this was considered high pay compared to soldiers serving in British or Provincial line regiments.

The men were armed, equipped, and accoutered similarly to the light infantry companies in the conventional battalions. The ranger uniform consisted of dark green regimental coats for officers, and the shortened jacket as prescribed for light troops for the enlisted men, faced and lined with scarlet, a waistcoat of green cloth, and buckskin leggings reaching from ankles to waist. Their headgear were caps of black leather with a black cockade on the left, and brass plate in front inscribed with "GR" (for Georgius Rex, the royal cipher of King George III) and "Butler's Rangers." The men wore buff leather cross belts, held in place by a brass breastplate with the same inscription appearing on the cap plate. Although many men brought or purchased personal weapons, which were later exchanged, the standard arm of the rangers was the Brown Bess musket, in some combination of Short Land and Long Land variants. To ease the burden of providing their own arms and accouterments, however, each company was later allowed three "contingency men." This was actually an allowance equaling the pay of three private soldiers that the officers could use toward the purchase of arms and equipment for their companies. John Butler retained his position as Deputy Superintendent to the Six Nations with the Indian Department rank of lieutenant colonel, while at the same time holding the rank of major commandant of Provincial forces commanding the rangers.

As Butler began assembling his rangers and as Iroquois raiders struck down the Allegheny River from the Six Nations' country, war parties from among the Ohio nations were attacking farms and villages throughout the western frontier. Copies of proclamations that promised humane treatment to anyone affirming his allegiance to the king and taking refuge at a British post, and offering a bounty of 200 acres of land to all volunteers who would take up arms against the Rebels, signed and sealed by both Carleton and "Hair Buyer" Hamilton, were soon found along trails and near the settlements most vulnerable to attack.[16] Ominously, they were also found near the burned farmhouses and next to the scalped bodies of the "helpless people" who had "been cruelly massacred in each raid" after the Indians struck.[17]

The scattered nature of reported Indian attacks made the news no less alarming. At Fort Pitt, General Edward Hand began receiving news of raids and war parties moving throughout the area, and getting closer. In one, a soldier was reported killed and a boy taken captive at the trading post of Logstown, on the north bank of the Ohio just downstream from Pittsburgh. In another, a militia patrol surprised an Indian scouting party "skulking" near Wheeling. With the bad news spreading, some families prepared to return east. Others began constructing blockhouses, or moving closer to the garrisons, in a move that became known as "forting up." With Governor Patrick Henry's consent, Hand sought to call out more militia from the interior counties of Virginia. Rumors of Indian war parties were reported as far as the Clinch River and Greenbrier Valley settlements in the southwest Virginia frontier, and few towns were willing to send their militia where they would not be close to home.

The threat of attack and the distribution of the British proclamations fueled rumors that Fort Pitt was going to be attacked soon by a force of more than 10,000 British, Tories, Canadians, and Indians thought to be sweeping down on them. With indications increasing that the frontier was to be subject to an all-out Indian war, the Virginia militia county lieutenants in Monongahela, Ohio, and Youghiogheny counties, and those around Pittsburgh, called out their soldiers. Local militia companies posted small garrisons at Beech Bottom, Grave Creek, and Wheeling. In early August, General Hand sent a letter to Congress that was read to the assembled delegates, in which he outlined a plan to strike into the Indian country to destroy their settlements and force the hostile bands out of the region. But as fears of another Loyalist plot began to surface, Hand was distracted from planning his mission.

In the third week of August, the Supreme Executive Council of Pennsylvania issued letters directing the county lieutenants of Bedford, Northumberland, and Westmoreland counties to provide all possible assistance to General Hand. An informant told Colonel Thomas Gaddis of Westmoreland County, Pennsylvania, that local Tories had secretly "associated," or organized, and were planning to isolate Pittsburgh from any relief or reinforcement in advance of the anticipated British invasion. Gaddis warned Lieutenant Colonel Thomas Brown at Redstone Old Fort on the Monongahela River to increase the guard at the powder magazine, which supplied ammunition to all Virginia militia on that side of the mountains. Brown posted a guard of fifteen men on the magazine, while Gaddis led 100 men in rounding up or dispersing the Loyalists before their plot could be put into motion. Colonel Zackwell Morgan, the militia lieutenant of Virginia's Monongahela County, hurriedly mustered his men and concentrated 500 of them at Miner's Fort to halt what he styled the "unnatural unheard of frantic scene of mischief . . . in the very heart of our country." Writing to General Hand on August 29, he reported that after arresting and questioning several suspicious characters, many admitted to swearing allegiance to the king. Some of the detainees confessed knowledge of a plot calling on Loyalists to embody as militia and surrender Fort Pitt to the British without opposition. Morgan further warned Hand that many of the confessions implicated some of Pittsburgh's leading citizens, as well as both Continental and militia officers in the conspiracy.[18] In the wake of the apprehensions of their fellows, some known Loyalists fled into the Allegheny Mountains rather than risk interrogation and imprisonment.

Several of those named in the prisoners' statements were placed under arrest, and a commission was appointed by Congress to investigate the allegations. Even Congress' Indian Commissioner and the Continental Army's Deputy Commissary General for Purchases in the Western Department, Colonel George Morgan, was suspected of being among those "unfriendly to the cause."[19] Hand personally investigated and removed the charges against Morgan before the end of the year, and the commission restored his rank and privileges shortly thereafter. Others, such as Alexander McKee and Simon Girty, both of whom had pre-war ties to the British Indian Department, were considered especially suspect and were prudently placed under arrest. McKee was initially confined to the house at his farm, while Girty was put in the guardhouse at Fort Pitt. By late December, the commission of inquiry placed McKee on parole, and a magistrate acquitted Girty of his charges, although the action did little to remove the cloud of suspicion that had gathered around him.

Overall, the quick action by Gaddis, Brown, and Morgan in August had purged the neighborhood surrounding Pittsburgh of its Loyalist infrastructure and foiled their short-lived plot. The anticipated invasion from Detroit against Fort Pitt, however, had yet to materialize. General Hand now received credible intelligence that bands of pro-British Indians, primarily Shawnees, Mingoes, and Wyandots, were preparing to strike a more vulnerable and easily subdued target, somewhere in the belt of settlements along the south bank of the Ohio between Fort Pitt and Fort Randolph. When the British-Tory-Indian effort finally came, the target was Wheeling.[20]

The key to Wheeling's defense was Fort Henry, an imposing, if crude, structure, adequate to the purpose for which it was built. Located on a bluff overlooking the Ohio River to the west, and down a broad slope leading to Wheeling Creek one-quarter mile to the south, it occupied the highest elevation in the settlement. The white oak pickets were anchored in a deep ditch, and rose seventeen feet above the surrounding ground. The log curtain and the four corner bastions were pierced with loopholes that permitted the defenders to provide mutually supporting small arms fire while remaining under cover. The enclosed three-quarters of an acre held a number of cabins to shelter the neighborhood families during an emergency, a barracks intended for a small garrison, a military storehouse to house supplies for the local militia, a magazine for ammunition, a freshwater well, and a two-story house for the commandant. The roof of the house was configured to permit the mounting and operation of one light cannon, although none was installed. The ground surrounding the post was cleared and cultivated, which, depending on the season, denied attackers much in the way of a concealed approach, and offered the defenders an open field of fire for their small arms. Most of the houses and outbuildings of the Wheeling settlement, home to some thirty families, were located between the fort and the high wooded hills to the east.

The alarm reached Wheeling in late August, and recognizing their vulnerability as a likely target, the settlers who had not already fled to the safety of towns or with family farther east sought shelter in Fort Henry. The militia garrison numbered less than fifty men. Under the command of Ohio County's lieutenant, Colonel David Shepherd, and assisted by the commander of the local regiment, Colonel Silas Zane, they were determined to take all necessary measures possible to present an effective defense if attacked. Shepherd sent scouts, or patrols, out from Wheeling to provide warning of a possible enemy approach.[21] On the last day of August, the fifteen-man company led by Captain Joseph Ogle returned from patrol, but reported seeing no hostile Indians. Unknown to the militiamen, the Indians had left the trails and divided into small parties and scattered to avoid contact with the scout. The warriors approached the settlement through the woods from several routes before reconcentrating at Bogg's Island, about two miles below Wheeling Creek. They crossed the Ohio and approached the fort from the bottomland.[22]

Originally built during Dunmore's War and named Fort Fincastle, after one of Dunmore's other titles, Patriots changed the name to Fort Henry in 1776 to honor Virginia's first governor, Patrick Henry. The fort was located on the Ohio River near Wheeling Creek. The settlement that grew up around it was officially named Wheeling in the 1790s. (From *Early Settlement and Indian Wars of Western Virginia*)

The next day, September 1, a man named John Boyd and Loudin, the black servant of one of his neighbors, went out to catch and tend horses. Six Indians were waiting in ambush for any settlers to leave the protection of the fort. Seeing their unsuspecting targets approach, the warriors opened fire. Boyd fell dead of a gunshot wound. Loudin managed to return to the fort unhurt. Hearing the musketry, Captain Samuel Mason hastily assembled his fourteen-man company. On learning the supposed strength of the attackers from Boyd's companion, Mason believed they were facing only a scouting party that seized the opportunity to ambush the pair. The captain and his company sallied out, determined to drive off the Indians. The six warriors began to retreat, and Mason's men pursued them into the morning fog that clung to the bottomland of Wheeling Creek. Then, rising from their concealment, the rest of the Indian war party opened fire. The ambush took Mason's men completely by surprise. The militiamen found themselves outnumbered and nearly surrounded by painted warriors who rushed forward at them yelling their blood-curdling war whoops. The captain ordered his company to retreat, but it was too late. Most of his men were already dead or dying, and Indians went to work scalping the fallen militiamen. Only two survivors scrambled back toward the safety of the stockade, pursued by a host of angry warriors right behind.

As in the opening encounter, most of the action was hidden from the view of the rest of the garrison due to the dense fog, as well as by the smoke from the gunfire of the unfolding battle in the low ground. Hearing the sounds of the engagement growing more intense, and their comrades seeming to get the worse of it, Captain Ogle led his company out of the fort. Advancing down toward the creek intending to either reinforce or cover the retreat of Mason's company, Ogle's men found themselves directly in the path of the Indian onslaught. All but four were killed, including Ogle. In the brief time since the initial encounter, the militia force was reduced to twelve uninjured men and boys left to defend the fort and the eighty or so women and children sheltered there.[23]

The Indians closed in on the stockade, flaunting the scalps taken from the fallen militiamen. Half of the war party then took positions in the settlement, while the rest occupied the defile between the fort and riverbank, thus effectively surrounding the post and cutting it off from reinforcement or resupply. A red-coated Indian Department officer carrying the British colors and accompanied by a drummer beating the "Parlay" call then advanced to the fort. The officer read Lieutenant Governor Hamilton's proclamation, shouting the promise of the king's protection in return for surrender, or immediate massacre for continued resistance, to the fort's defenders. Colonel Shepherd refused the demand, and ended the parlay by firing a defiant shot into the air. The Indian attack then began in earnest.

The Indians rushed the east side of the fort in an attempt to force the gates open. When that failed, the warriors began an almost uninterrupted fusillade from three sides that lasted the remainder of the day, through the night and into the morning. Inside the fort, the defenders matched the attackers' efforts and energy. While the men and boys fired muskets from the loopholes, the women and girls, many of them now widows and orphans, made bullets, prepared cartridges, or reloaded and handed muskets back to the men. The defenders' ability to maintain their fire and keep their assailants at a respectable distance was possible only by having the arms and ammunition continually supplied to those manning the walls.[24]

On the afternoon of September 2, the second day of the siege, the Indians made several more attempts to breach the walls. While one Indian party laid down a base of supporting musket fire from the bottomland to the south in an effort to divert the defenders' attention, another party of attacking warriors rushed out from the cover and concealment afforded by the settlement's cabins in repeated attempts to enter the fort. Wielding a heavy timber as a battering ram, they tried to force their way in by breaking the gate open. After each of these attempts failed, the Indians withdrew a short distance, but maintained a constant fire on the defenders. Reflecting their frustration and being thwarted in their other efforts, several groups of warriors dashed up in desperate, but unsuccessful, attempts to set fire to the fort.[25] Toward evening, the Indian leaders called off further attempts for the day, and withdrew their warriors to prepare for a final assault that would decide the matter.

This respite providently coincided with the arrival of needed reinforcements. Fourteen men from Holiday's Fort, led by Colonel Andrew Swearengen, landed their canoes undetected during the lull, and made it safely into Fort Henry. Shortly thereafter, Major Samuel McCulloch led forty mounted men from Van Metre's Fort, on Short Creek, about ten miles north of Fort Henry. All made it past the stunned Indians to the fort and through the gate on the east wall in a successful dash except for McCulloch. The gate was closed while the major was still outside. McCulloch, who found himself surrounded by hostile Indians, dashed off again through the Indian lines, and headed back for the safety of Van Metre's Fort. After galloping up a hill, he reached the top thinking he had gained a lead over his pursuers. Before he could catch his breath in relief, he sighted another party of Indians returning from a raid on another settlement from the other direction. He was now caught between two groups of enemy, who were spreading out to surround him on three sides. McCulloch had but one chance to escape. There was a steep drop-off on one side of the hilltop, which the warriors had not elected to ascend, thinking it impassible to a rider on horseback. McCulloch reined his horse, and prodded the animal into a death-defying leap, and both crashed down through the brush and among the rocks. The stunned Indians gasped in amazement at the audacious move, as McCulloch escaped in a mad rush down the hill toward safety.[26]

Back at Fort Henry, the attacking Indians now faced a garrison reinforced by more than fifty fresh men. The defenses of the post showed no signs of weakening, or vulnerability to the repeated attempts to batter down the gate. Although they continued to fire a few desultory shots, the defending militiamen observed that the Indians started to gather or kill all the horned cattle, sheep, hogs, and horses in the settlement. Those they did not separate in order to drive homeward for their own use were slaughtered in the fields. The warriors then set fire to almost every house, outbuilding, and other structure in Wheeling. Having completed the destruction of the settlement, except for Fort Henry, the Indians withdrew, carrying their dead and wounded with them.[27] The settlers breathed a collective sigh of gratitude at their deliverance, bought at the price of twenty-six dead and five wounded.

General Hand was now more than ever determined to attack. Both the Virginia and Pennsylvania governments agreed to call out militia to take part in the campaign. Although there were some who protested that an offensive into Indian country to punish the tribes whose warriors had taken part in the summer raids might make the situation worse by inciting further reprisals by the Indians, the general feeling was that such action was warranted. Governor Patrick Henry, for one, responded that Indian depredations were far too serious to go unanswered, and more raids and attacks could be expected even if no action was taken. The impediment to the plan was that troops and supplies were simply not available. The settlements along the Ohio and all the way to Kentucky were not able or willing to strip men from their own defense for the general's expedition, while Washington's Main Army needed all the troops it could acquire to oppose Howe's offensive against Philadelphia. Washington had already detached some troops, and all available soldiers not with the Main Army were sent to Gates and the Northern Department to meet Burgoyne's offensive from Canada. Instead of leading an advance, Hand was forced to shorten his own lines by withdrawing the garrison from the outpost at Kittanning, upriver from Pittsburgh, to a smaller post, named Fort Hand.

Events on the northern frontier had unfolded dramatically. Lieutenant General John Burgoyne's army had advanced up Lake Champlain in June at a leisurely pace, confident of victory. In early July, Burgoyne forced the defending Continental troops, commanded by Major General Arthur St. Clair, to evacuate its principal defensive position at Fort Ticonderoga without firing a shot. The Americans executed a skillful, if embarrassing, withdrawal toward the Hudson River, giving up the fort that represented one of the Americans earliest victories. Colonel Seth Warner and his Continental Green Mountain Boys Regiment (not to be confused with Ethan Allen's Green Mountain Boys militia) conducted a highly effective delaying action against the advanced guard of the pursuing British at the Battle of Hubbardton. As Burgoyne pressed on through Skeenesboro, Fort Anne, and Fort Edward, heading for the Hudson River, American resistance, under the direction of Major General Philip Schuyler, began to stiffen. By the time Butler and Brant had defeated the Tryon County militia in the Battle of Oriskany, Burgoyne's advance had slowed, cutting a road through the forest for its artillery and baggage as it went. After breaking out of the woods, Burgoyne sent a mixed force of British, Provincials, and Brunswick troops and Indian warriors, a total of about 800 men under the command of Lieutenant Colonel Friedrich Baum, toward the town of Bennington in the Hampshire Grants (now in Vermont) to gather horses and forage. On the banks of the Walloomsac River in New York, Baum's force was attacked on August 16 by Colonel John Stark leading 1,500 men, mostly militia reinforced with the remnants of the Continentals who had fought at Hubbardton. The British force was overwhelmed and defeated, with about 200 killed and 600 being taken prisoner. Burgoyne's army had now been reduced to roughly 6,000 men, and he sent for reinforcements.

As Colonel Stark's troops destroyed Baum's forces, Major General Horatio Gates was appointed by Congress to replace General Schuyler, and Gates

Lieutenant General John Burgoyne meeting with the Indians at Cumberland Point on June 20, 1777. The British invasion of New York, and its supporting operations, represented the beginning of full participation by the Crown's Indian allies in the Revolutionary War.

assumed command of the Northern Department on August 19. Gates' first order of action was to establish a strong position at Bemis Heights, astride Burgoyne's intended route of march. Gates had about 7,000 troops under his command, and more were arriving every day. The British army began crossing to the west bank of the Hudson River on September 13. At the urging of Brigadier General Benedict Arnold, the Americans left the positions to engage the British at Freeman's Farm on September 19. The British suffered heavy casualties, but managed to stave off defeat in the daylong battle. On October 7, Burgoyne, whose force had since been reduced to about 5,000 men, attempted to locate and turn the American left flank. After the British reconnaissance was repulsed, the Americans, whose force had grown to about 9,000, counter-attacked. After they seized two key redoubts that made the British position untenable, Burgoyne was left with but one option. He ordered his forces to withdraw to the high ground near the village of Saratoga.

The same day Carleton signed the beating order enabling John Butler to form his ranger battalion, September 15, 1777, the governor-general ordered the new major commandant to march with every available ranger at his disposal and as large a body of Indians he could gather to reinforce Burgoyne's hard pressed army, which was now in serious trouble. As Butler secured warriors for this relief column, he learned that the Indians were disturbed by the news that the British command had decided to withdraw the troops it had posted to the garrison at Fort Oswego. The Indians protested, fearing that their allies seemed ready to abandon them. It was a bad time for such rumors to spread. The Senecas were still mourning their dead, and nursing their wounded warriors, as well as their wounded pride, from the bloody experience at Oriskany. Disappointed at their lack of success in the campaign, and the Crown apparently ready to renege on its assurances, created an opportunity of which the Continental Indian commissioners could possibly take advantage. The word was circulating among the Iroquois that General Schuyler had once more invited their chiefs to a council at German Flats to renew the chain of friendship with the Americans. Bad news was followed by worse, when it was learned that Burgoyne had been defeated and had surrendered his army.

Like Sir John Johnson, John Butler found enlisting sufficient numbers of men to serve in his corps was a slow process. When James Secord, a lieutenant in the new ranger battalion, led a detachment of thirty men to the Susquehanna to bring back cattle for the food supply of the garrison at Fort Oswego, and to recruit volunteers for the corps, they were surprised by Patriot forces. Most were captured, while the remainder were disbursed and returned to their homes. Such difficulties plagued the recruiting effort, that only one company of Butler's rangers was formed before the end of December, and by early February 1778, only two companies had been raised to the established strength and passed muster.[28] Competition among the Provincial units for the limited number of potential volunteers who had made it to Canada was so fierce that the royal governor eventually prohibited recruiting parties from entering Montreal. Recruiting agents turned to seeking potential recruits among the Loyalist refugees living in Indian towns, or traveled to the frontier settlements to convince the truly loyal, those "disaffected" by the Revolution, and those seeking revenge on their Patriot neighbors to accompany them back to Fort Niagara. Traveling in civilian clothes to areas they had frequented or lived in before going off to fight, they risked not only being discovered, but also treatment as spies or traitors if captured.

Such a fate befell Butler's son, Walter, now aged twenty-five, who had served as an ensign in the King's 8th Regiment of Foot at the siege of Fort Schuyler, and was to accept a captaincy in his father's new battalion. On a mission to recruit Loyalist volunteers in the Mohawk Valley, on August 13, he slipped through lines with fourteen soldiers and fourteen Indians from St. Leger's army and returned to his home at German Flats to encourage some of his former neighbors to serve the Crown. Butler was meeting with fellow Tories in the tavern of a Loyalist named Rudolph Shoemaker when the commander of the garrison at Fort Dayton learned of his presence. After surrounding Shoemaker's tavern, the American troops entered just as Butler was addressing a violent tirade against the Rebels to the gathered locals. Not wearing his uniform when arrested, he was charged with being a spy and tried by a court-martial. Walter Butler was convicted and sentenced to death. Given a reprieve, the death sentence commuted, the British officer was taken to Albany and imprisoned under heavy guard through the winter. The following spring, while Butler was suffering a serious illness, some influential Tory friends interceded on his behalf with the authorities. After giving his parole to remain under house arrest, he was allowed to recover at the home of a friend. With the help of some Loyalist rangers sent to his aid, he later managed to escape, and eventually made his way through Indian country back to Fort Niagara.[29]

Major John Butler's fears that the recent news that British forces were going to abandon Fort Oswego, coupled with the invitation for a council of the Six Nations with Indian agents from the American Congress, would drive the Six Nations into the American camp proved to be unfounded. With "Greatest Satisfaction," Butler reported that upon receiving a "Belt of Invitation" from Major General Philip Schuyler to attend the council at Johnstown he was planning, the Seneca chiefs sent it back to the Oneida, saying, "They had no ears to hear any Messages from them." The Seneca also added, "The blood of their people was still reeking," and blamed Schuyler for the blood spilling between the Oneida and Seneca. When the Iroquois sachems met in council at Onondaga in the fall, they resolved that the nations still loyal to the Great Binding Law that created their confederacy would "fall upon the Oneidas."[30] As Colonel Claus wrote to Secretary Knox, those of the Six Nations loyal to the Crown were ready to take revenge "upon the rebels for the loss of their chiefs at Fort Stanwix and for some of their peoples being put in irons and confined at Albany."[31] Because Oneidas had stood with the Americans and fought Senecas, Mohawk war parties planned to invade the land of their brethren and burn Oneida villages in retaliation.

The situation for the Americans on the western frontier was equally grave, as an incident occurred that negated much of the effort expended by state and Continental Indian commissioners in seeking favorable diplomatic relations with the Ohio Indian nations. In October 1777, the friendly and respected Shawnee sachem Cornstalk, along with a young chief named Red Hawk and one or two companions, arrived at Point Pleasant and visited Fort Randolph. Unhappily, they told Captain Matthew Arbuckle, commander of the garrison, that a council of their Shawnee Nation had agreed to accept the hatchet offered by the British, and that some warrior bands were already raiding settlements along the Ohio. The chiefs informed Arbuckle that they were obligated to follow the tribe's decision, however reluctantly, and regretted that in the next campaign, they would be fighting on opposite sides. Some traditional accounts even claim that the Indian chiefs offered to let Arbuckle kill them. Arbuckle did not wish to hurt the chief who had faithfully honored the pledges he had made in the treaties of Camp Charlotte and Fort Pitt, but was at a loss as to what to do. The captain decided to detain the Indian party as hostages, and sent an express to Hand asking for instructions.

When another group of Shawnee, including Cornstalk's son, Elinipsico, arrived looking for the chiefs, they too were detained. One day in early November, two members of the Botetourt County militia, who had been ordered to the post to reinforce the garrison in response to the threat of impending raids, crossed the Great Kanawha to hunt. The next morning, as they were returning to the fort, two Indians waiting in ambush shot and killed one of the militiamen, a man named Gilmore. His companion ran to the bank, and called across the river for help. A group of soldiers from the fort crossed over, and while searching for the hostile Indians, recovered Gilmore's scalped body. Shortly afterward, a group of Gilmore's enraged comrades, led by their officer, a militia captain named Hall, decided to kill the hostages in retaliation. Despite the efforts of Captains Arbuckle and Stuart to prevent it, the Indians were brutally murdered.[32] Upon learning of the killings, both Brigadier General Hand and Governor Patrick Henry were outraged, and a court-martial was convened. Although it was known that Captain Hall and his men had committed the crimes, witnesses refused to testify. The court-martial adjourned without a conviction.

Although attacks "by some savage tribes of Indians" had resulted in the massacre of a number of settlers, driven others from the homes, and generally exposed the frontiers of Virginia and Pennsylvania to the "barbarous ravages" of British troops and their Indian allies, Congress was optimistic that most Shawnee and Delaware Indians continued to be "well affected and disposed to preserve the league of peace and amity" with the United States. The majority of delegates continued to believe, or perhaps hope, that those two powerful tribes also felt threatened with attack from their "hostile neighbors." In response, Congress resolved on November 20 to send commissioners to repair the damage caused by the murder of Cornstalk and his companions, and to further cultivate the friendship of those two nations, engage their warriors in the service of the United States, and prevent American forces from committing any outrages against them. Congress also directed Hand to extend the war against the source of the preceding summer's Indian raids, the British garrison at Detroit, by mounting an offensive.

By drawing troops from the Virginia and Pennsylvania militia, calling for Indian auxiliaries, and with the Continentals at his command, Hand estimated he could possibly have a force of 2,000 men for the expedition.[33] But after the Stony Creek Glades settlement was attacked by Indians as the male inhabitants were attempting to gather the harvest, Hand was convinced that even a winter expedition against the villages of those bands known to be hostile was worth mounting if a larger operation against Detroit was beyond his department's capability.

With evidence that incursions were once again on the rise, Hand sent a letter to the Supreme Executive Council of Pennsylvania in late November detailing accounts of the recent Indian attacks and requesting their assistance. But again, troops and supplies were not forthcoming. The situation only increased Hand's frustration in attempting to command the Army's Western Department and safeguard the frontier. Hostile warriors were still reported roaming the rivers and woods, and local militia commanders were reluctant to send portions of their companies elsewhere for any purpose. Provisions and supplies for conducting a campaign were not adequate, nor were sufficient stocks to substantially improve the situation expected. The season was changing, and without adequate clothing and equipment, a winter campaign was out of the question. Plagued by the continuing quarrel between Virginia and Pennsylvania over the region near Pittsburgh, despite their professions of cooperation, and the inability to raise an adequate force for an offensive, Hand ceased making plans. He cancelled the expedition, and in a December 24 letter to the Board of War at Congress, Hand requested reassignment back to the Main Army in the east. The request would be granted in May.[34]

The British and their Indian allies saw the initial campaign against the western frontier a stunning success. When John Butler, tallied the accomplishments of the Indian Department, he reported to Governor-General Carleton that although the frontier had become fairly quiet: "The Indians of the Six Nations & those from the westward exerted themselves in laying waste the Country most exposed to them. From the Susquehanna to the Kiskismenitas Creek upon the Ohio [and Allegheny], and from thence down to the Kankawa [Kanawha] River is now nothing but an heap of ashes. Such of those miserable Rebels as have escaped have taken refuge in small forts. Affairs appear to be growing desperate about Fort Pitt. Some 200 wanting to pass to Detroit [were] told by Indians 'their country was always free & open to the King's good subjects, being only shut against rebels.'"[35] The Americans saw it differently. While the numerous raids and massacres of isolated settlements kept the frontier in a state of alarm, except for the raid on Wheeling, the feared invasion had yet to materialize.[36]

With a large force of Indians and Loyalists gathering at Fort Niagara to spend the winter of 1777-78, Major John Butler and Captain Joseph Brant shared their plan for a series of raids that would terrorize the frontiers of New York and Pennsylvania with Governor-General Carleton. They believed that by keeping the American inhabitants there in constant fear unless they declared friendship and support of the king, the raids would interfere with harvests that filled the American army's grain magazines and prevent the militia from being available to reinforce the Continentals. Furthermore, despite Burgoyne's loss, if the raids created enough havoc on the frontier, they could even drain the strength of the Continental Army enough to enable Howe's much larger and potent army, now in Philadelphia, to draw the Americans into the decisive battle that would doom the revolution. In early January, Butler held a council with the Six Nations to be sure of their continued support and cooperation, and to coordinate their participation. To maintain their allegiance, he distributed "large presents & in particular 300 of Burgoyns Silver medals to their young Warriors" if they would join in the fight against the Rebels.[37] To prepare for the spring campaign, Brant led his Loyalist volunteers and Iroquois warriors back to the bases they had established on the Susquehanna. There they would spend the rest of the winter as they had the previous year, offering protection in return for supplies and oaths of loyalty to the king, or taking what they wanted by force with a warning for professed Whigs to leave or face the consequences on their next visit.[38]

The Iroquois planned to postpone any violent attacks on New York settlements until spring. The war chiefs sent runners to inform the leaders of Indian villages and towns close to colonial settlements to relocate their populations behind the protective cordon provided by the war parties and Loyalist rangers operating principally from Onaquaga and Unadilla. This move, they believed, would protect the Indians from the retaliatory raids the Americans were sure to launch in response. While the Indian villages prepared to relocate, Butler further explained to his superiors the tactical "reasons for not alarming the rebels this winter on the Frontiers of the Province of New York." He said such a lull would better "deceive the Rebels & divert their attention in the spring," at which time the rangers and the Iroquois "intend to make a very formidable Irruption with their whole collected force into the frontiers of New York & glut that revenge they so impatiently wish for." To his satisfaction, the Cayuga and Seneca, whom he described as the "leading People of the Six Nations," were strongly behind the plan, and had given him their strongest assurances of fidelity to their alliance against the Rebels.[39]

To heighten their resolve in opposing the rebellion and assisting the British, the Six Nations had already received a report that the Americans were planning an invasion into the territory of the Seneca from the settlements along the Susquehanna. The Seneca had "unanimously resolved to defend themselves . . . as soon as the season of the year will permit."[40] With a number of war parties out in the direction of Fort Pitt and the western Pennsylvania settlements, Butler offered the Indians the assistance of his rangers until the return of their warriors. By early February 1778, Butler's rangers numbered about 125 men, two complete companies and part of a third, and they were eager for the campaign season to begin and their unit's baptism of fire.[41]

Word about the Indian council being held by the British did not take long to reach the Americans. While reporting on the improvements being made at Fort Schuyler that would enable the post to withstand a month-long siege, Colonel George I. Denniston sent the recently elected governor of New York, George Clinton (not to be confused with the former royal governor of the same name), intelligence on the Iroquois council gained from friendly Tuscaroras who had attended. He said the "infamous Butler" made the promise that Fort Schuyler would be taken in the spring. Denniston, however, was confident that another attack would fail as the one in the summer of 1777 had. He predicted, "Should he [Butler] come, I am in hopes he will go off (if he can) with greater Shame than he done before."[42]

If anything was certain, it was that the British were planning another offensive along the New York frontier, not the Americans. Only the details of which targets would be attacked were left to conjecture.

Chapter 4

THE APPROACHING STORM

As Major John Butler and Captain Joseph Brant finalized their plans, they had complete support of Crown officials who were aware of the psychological impact of the mere threat of Indian attacks had along the borders. Keeping the American inhabitants in these areas in constant fear, they believed, could undermine political, economic, and military support for the Continental Congress and Revolutionary state governments.

Ever since the American invasion of Canada in 1775-1776 had failed, a number of influential Continental leaders were still convinced that such a move could hasten a successful conclusion of the war. Politically, they believed that most Canadians, particularly the remaining French, would welcome an American invasion and be inclined to bring their province into the revolution as the fourteenth colony. Militarily, an invasion could conceivably cut Britain's long and tenuous Saint Lawrence River supply route on which their forces at Forts Niagara and Detroit, and by extension their Six Nations and western Indian allies, depended. In reality, such a venture would be difficult to execute. Major General Horatio Gates, who sought to replace General George Washington as commander in chief of the Continental Army, saw an opportunity to further his cause through his selection as the president of the Board of War at Congress. Gates had proved himself an able administrator and organizer when he served as the army's adjutant general and commander of the Northern Department. His military reputation was rising in the wake of the victory at Saratoga, but few in Congress realized that he lacked the qualities of a good field commander, and owed much of the credit for defeating the British invasion to the tactical competence and aggressiveness of subordinate commanders like Colonel Daniel Morgan and Brigadier General Benedict Arnold. In January, with Congressional confidence in Washington at an all-time low following the battlefield reverses that resulted in the British seizure of Philadelphia, Gates managed to convince Congress to bypass the commander in chief and resurrect the plan.

Following some deliberation, Congress cast ballots to select a commander for the second invasion of Canada. Although he was not among the original officers considered, Congress decided that the youthful French aristocrat, Major General Marie Joseph Paul Yves Roche Gilbert du Motier de Lafayette, was the logical choice. Despite his lack of experience as a division commander in combat, the delegates believed his presence at the head of American troops could rally the French Canadians to the American cause. Lafayette was hesitant, and sought his mentor's counsel. Although he did not endorse the planned invasion, Washington advised his twenty-year-old protégé to accept the appointment. Washington and Lafayette were not the only ranking officers with misgivings. Many of the army's most experienced officers, like generals Benjamin Lincoln and Nathanael Greene, were skeptical about the chances for success. Many members of Congress, like New York delegate and Indian affairs committee member James Duane, doubted the potential benefits of such a campaign as well as the lack of available resources to carry it out.

When he arrived in Albany to supervise preparations for his campaign, Lafayette and his staff found the units were severely under strength, and supplies and materials of every description were short. A growing chorus added their opinion that the assets committed to the venture could be used to better advantage elsewhere. George Clinton, a brigadier general of militia as well as the first elected governor of New York, wrote Lafayette in March 1778 to say that he believed the defense of the frontier was more important than a "Northern Expedition" at the time. Not only were the hostile nations of the Iroquois Confederacy still a threat, but there had been a noticeable increase in the activities of "a number of Persons employed recruiting for the Enemy's Service in the Neighbourhood of Albany." It was Clinton's opinion that these agents had "been but too successful."[1] Finally asked for his opinion by the Congress, Washington advised against the invasion, and much to the relief of those opposing it, the plan was cancelled.

In the meantime, the Continental Indian commissioners still maintained hope that they could bring representatives of the Six Nations to a council that would convince them to return to neutrality. On receiving the invitation from Major General Philip Schuyler and the Indian Commission, the Seneca, whose warriors outnumbered those of all the other Iroquois nations combined, were still defiant. Harboring a grudge about their losses at Oriskany, they expressed surprise that they were even asked to come while American "tomahawks were sticking in their heads, their wounds bleeding and their eyes streaming with tears for the loss of their friends."[2] Notwithstanding their hesitation, the council was scheduled for February, in hopes that the Seneca would reconsider, and all the nations would be represented. Schuyler and his fellow Continental commissioners waited for the council to meet at Johnstown with presents and promises of favor and protection as allies. But the Indians showed little interest in the council, and delayed their arrival until March 9. When they finally convened, few more than 700 attended, and they were mostly Oneida and Tuscarora, nations who were already friendly to the Americans. Only a handful of Onondagas, Mohawks, and Cayugas were present, and the commissioners were clearly disappointed in lack of attendance from the Seneca, the foremost nation they hoped to keep neutral. The American commissioners asked the sachems there to convene the whole of the Six Nations at Onondaga to discuss the matter of neutrality with the rest of the confederation.

One of Butler's spies at Johnstown reported that the Americans recommended "in the strongest terms" that Indians remain neutral. Schuyler told the gathered Indians that he was going to lead an army to take the British post at Fort Oswego, and hoped the Indians would not hinder his movement, lest they be considered enemies of the United States. According to the British informants, the pro-British Indians paid little attention to the threat, and their spies circulating among the American settlements reported that despite Schuyler's talk, there was no evidence that the Rebels were making any preparations or building boats for an expedition against Oswego. Before receiving orders to return to the Main Army at Valley Forge, Major General Lafayette also attended the Johnstown council. With the second invasion of Canada now aborted, Lafayette supervised the considerable improvement of frontier defenses. He had ordered the construction of forts at Cherry Valley and in the Oneida country, the arming and garrisoning of the three forts in the Schoharie settlements, and the improvement of other border fortifications. The Oneida had said they would send 300 warriors to General Washington's Main Army then fighting in Pennsylvania. When Lafayette reminded them of their promise, the Oneida expressed apprehension that the Seneca would send a war party to exact revenge for Oriskany while Oneida warriors were away helping the American army. The marquis responded by sending an engineer officer to their principal town, Oneida Castle, to speak with them and gain their pledge to send the warriors to Albany as soon as a "Small Piquet Fort is Completed ... to secure the families of those & the other Indians who stay behind" in case the Senecas attacked. Lafayette called on the militia to send 200 men to help their allies build the post, and the Oneida warriors were soon ready to depart.[3] When Lafayette commanded the American forces at Barren Hill in May, his division included a company of fifty Oneida warriors. The British were hearing talk on the frontier, however, of preparations for the expedition against Canada led by Lafayette, which they were not aware had been cancelled.[4]

Schuyler's threatened campaign against Fort Oswego caused the Seneca and other pro-British Indian nations to renew their requests to Lieutenant Colonel Mason Bolton, the commander of Fort Niagara, for maintaining, and even reinforcing, the post. They argued that its continued possession would give the king's troops access to Indian country, deny Rebel movement into the lands of the Six Nations, and keep the Americans from building ships on Lake Ontario that could threaten Fort Niagara and even Detroit. During the conference, only the Oneidas and Tuscaroras expressed agreement with the Americans, and solemnly predicted to their Iroquois brethren that war with the United States would end in the extinction of the nations who chose to remain hostile.

Iroquois representatives continued to announce to the American commissioners that they would remain neutral, while an Onondaga sachem explained that his nation's apparent support of the British was the action of a vocal minority of young and headstrong warriors. The conference accomplished nothing, except for an expression of allegiance to the United States by the Oneidas and Tuscaroras. At the close of the council, the commissioners warned the other Iroquois to refrain from military action on behalf of the British government, or they would suffer terribly. Schuyler wrote to Governor Clinton and the Continental Congress afterward, saying, "What Effect the firm Tone in which the Commissioners have spoke to the Indians will have on them is hard to say." Schuyler and his fellow commissioners were inclined to believe that when the Six Nations next held council, the Seneca, Onondaga, Cayuga and Mohawk would "commence Hostilities" and attack the frontier that spring. He further recommended that "it would be prudent to take the war into their country first."[5]

Even as Schuyler was warning of hostilities with the Iroquois, there were rumors of imminent attacks. The noticeable increase in Indian activity, particularly by Brant's men, caused many citizens to heed the Mohawk leader's warning. They abandoned their farms on the Tryon County frontier and moved to the protection offered by the settlements with forts and companies of militia or Continentals like Cobleskill, Schoharie, German Flats, and Cherry Valley. Militia commanders in the area found it increasingly difficult to respond to Clinton's earlier order to "raise a number of men in the counties of Albany, Tryon and Charlotte" for the garrison at Albany. One commander, Colonel John Williams, explained that the previous year's invasions and the more recent raids had created such a problem with available forage that he described the situation as "deplorable." To ensure the survival of the remaining cattle, many men who could have been drafted for active service were busy clearing away the snow to provide fodder for their animals. Although 200 men from Bennington were on the march in response to reports of "a number of savages" that had been "discovered at Oater Creek," Williams was concerned that any more drafts would only weaken the ability of the militia in his county to muster a credible force for local defense. Receiving orders to send troops to Albany or a frontier garrison led the militia colonel to implore, "[in] what manner are we to be guarded?"[6]

Benjamin Dickson (or Dixon) of the Albany Committee of Safety, like other civil and military leaders, also wrote to Governor Clinton in early April 1778 that he had received "Credible Intelligence" from the Cherry Valley committee that the community and the adjacent settlements were in imminent danger. Two presumably friendly Indians had appeared to warn the inhabitants that they should abandon their farms as the enemy was planning an attack at the end of the month. The informants said that Joseph Brant had assembled about 1,500 Indian warriors and Tories at Unadilla on the Susquehanna River, which was only about forty miles away, and was planning to strike the rich and populous Cherry Valley. The committee had also received reports that Brant's marauders were getting more violent. No longer content with demanding supplies and offering protection for allegiance to the king in return for not harming anyone, they began killing and taking the scalps of male inhabitants, taking women and children captive, and destroying isolated farms of those believed to be in sympathy with the Revolution.[7]

The Committee of Safety for the Peenpeck-Mamacotten Precinct notified the governor that an informant named Josiah Parks had come forward to provide information about the impending offensive. Parks said that in February, he had overheard a conversation between a Tuscarora Indian, who he knew only as Captain John, and some local Tories seeking to deliver "an Express of Letters" to a fellow Loyalist named Robert Lands. They had intended for Lands to take the letters to British headquarters in New York, but when they heard that he had already departed, his fellow Tories feared he had been captured by Patriot forces. Parks also learned, from a man named David Vaneveran, "That the Indians and Tories mean to strike on the Sisqueannah [Susquehanna] about Wyomah [Wyoming] and take that place first; with the Number of four thousand men, and then come through to the North River [the Hudson]." Before going to Unadilla with some fellow Loyalists, Francis Elswert, who was suspected of selling provisions to the Indians and believed to be secretly employed by the British Quartermaster Department, warned him "not to tell the Damn'd Rebels at Cashithtown [Coshocton] about the plot for fear they would move off" before the attack. Another informant, Joseph Gordens, added that Elswert and a man named Joseph Gooding vowed to return with the Indians and Tories to "take all the Wigs at Cashithtown," and leave the king's men unhurt.[8]

Understandably, the people of Peenpeck-Mamacotten and adjacent Goshen precincts were "filled with the Greatest Anxiety and fear of their Persons and

Families falling a Prey to their worse than Savage Neighbors" as the rumors circulated. Despite the apparent quiet that had settled along the frontier through the winter of 1777-1778, the inhabitants were fearful that "This Diabolical Plot" presented a danger to the frontier district inhabitants. Those in Orange County were especially fearful that the Delaware River town of Minisink was a prime and vulnerable target. Many New York settlers began to believe that the threat was even greater than Burgoyne's British invasion out of Canada the previous year.[9]

As tensions rose, the inhabitants of the towns on the northern frontier increasingly petitioned Governor Clinton for protection. They related that many who had fled for safety in 1777 were finally returning to their farms, months after the surrender of Burgoyne at Saratoga. With the onset of spring, they were "Engaged in Preparing to cultivate their farms, for the Subsistence of their families out of the Produce, and for the Support of the armies out of what they may Have to Spare." Their letters also

Joseph Brant, or Thayendanegea, the charismatic Mohawk leader and British Indian Department officer, viewed supporting the king as being in the best interest of the Six Nations. Note that in this 1776 portrait by George Romney, Brant is pictured wearing a British officer's gorget. (*National Gallery of Canada*)

expressed concern that if the Continental soldiers were withdrawn and sent elsewhere, the inhabitants would be exposed to "the Incursions of the Savages and more Savage abetters, the British troops and Tories from Canada," whose "depredations" were sure to ruin the crops, destroy their farms, and murder or take their families captive. The people of these frontier districts had every reason to fear the enemy, and were pleading for the necessity of guarding the frontiers, lest their farms be laid to waste, and "families be exposed to the Greatest distress."[10]

On April 3, the town of Manheim, New York, was attacked by Brant's Loyalist volunteers and Indian warriors, who carried off a dozen of the male inhabitants as captives. Four weeks later, they struck at Ephrata. Governor Clinton tried his best to respond with militia, and approached General Washington for the permanent stationing of Continental troops to garrison the important posts. At the very least, the governor asked the commander in chief to not withdraw those troops then stationed along the frontier until the alarms subsided. Whenever possible, Clinton sought to have the New York militia fill the void by keeping them active in defending the state, and sought relief from some tasks delegated by Continental officers that interfered with his troops' ability to respond to internal or frontier emergencies. Like many militia officers, Colonel John Cantine, the county lieutenant of Ulster County, received a May 1 letter from Clinton saying that the Tories and Indians at Onaquaga and Unadilla were reported gathering, and "for the Sake of Plunder may be tempted to commit Depredations on the Inhabitants." The governor directed his commanders to keep scouting parties out on the frontier, and hold the remainder of their regiments in readiness to "march on a Moment's Warning" to assist any community that was attacked.[11]

The state's militia was stretched to its limit. The brigade of Tryon County, for example, had not only taken heavy losses at Oriskany the year before, but was ordered out so often that Colonel Jacob Klock petitioned the governor to relieve his regiment from some of their many commitments. His men had already provided Lafayette a draft of eighty men for one month to help build the fort at Oneida Castle. When asked to raise two additional companies of sixty men each, Klock was not sure if his regiment, most of whom were farmers, could comply, as the call out at that time would interfere with the sowing of land. He reasoned that, since "there has not been as yet the least Appearance of any Danger from the Westward," instead of an additional commitment, the men called in the previous draft (but not already on duty at Fort Schuyler) could be used instead.[12] Overall, the harried militia commanders were doing their best to support the war effort and provide for their communities' own defense in the face of the increasing danger from the royal Provincial forces and the Six Nations.

With the forces of their American allies at the breaking point, the friendly Oneida were concerned about the menace presented by the raiding parties of their pro-British Iroquois brethren. After all, the Seneca had sworn vengeance on them following Oriskany. James Dean wrote to his fellow Continental Indian Commissioner Major General Philip Schuyler that the "Oneidas have been under great Apprehension of Danger," and were concerned that in the event of an emergency elsewhere, no troops would be available to march to their assistance. The Oneidas told Dean that they were not able to send any additional warriors to General Washington's Main Army, as their first duty was to stay and protect their women and children.[13]

Major General Horatio Gates, serving both as President of the Board of War at Congress and as the outgoing commander of the Continental Army's Northern Department, ordered Brigadier General John Stark, hero of the battle of Bennington in the summer of 1777, to Albany to assume command in his stead.[14] Gates specified that Stark's authority extended to the command of all Continental troops and militia posted to the northward and westward of Albany, with the exception of the garrison of Fort Schuyler. In the event of "any sudden irruption of the enemy" in the Mohawk or Hudson River valley areas, Stark was empowered to call for militia reinforcements from the Hampshire Grants, the counties of Hampshire and Berkshire in Massachusetts, and from the western and northern counties of the State of New York, "as will enable you to repel every hostile invasion."[15] Unfortunately, too few Continental troops were deployed in the area, and the militia was hard pressed to meet their military requirements and tend to their private or commercial obligations.

In many areas of Tryon County, and elsewhere in the colonies, not everyone was on the side of the Revolution. In some settlements, most if not all of the inhabitants were known to profess Loyalist sympathies. Even where the Whig faction was dominant, one could usually still find a "friend of the King" among his neighbors. Loyalists were at times subject to arrest or detention, and confiscation of property. One of the functions of the militia was to keep the Tories under control, and to prevent them from actively aiding British, Provincial, and Indian forces. When they were available, civil authorities asked for assistance from the Continentals. Such was the case for the new Northern Department. Three days after receiving instructions on his responsibilities from Gates, Stark ordered out "scouts," or patrols. One of them was led by Captain William Patrick, commander of a company in Colonel Ichabod Alden's 6th Massachusetts Regiment, one of the few Continental units at Stark's disposal. Patrick was ordered to the Cobleskill area to watch for the approach of invading Indian warriors and Tory rangers from the direction of the frontier. He was also to monitor the activities of area Loyalists who might be plotting to act against their Patriot neighbors or send information and supplies to invaders lurking in the woods beyond the settlement. If any of the local Tories were found under arms, or in any way aiding or assisting the enemy, Captain Patrick was ordered to arrest them and forward them on to General Stark in Albany. Patrick and his men were instructed to pay particular attention to the arrival of any known or suspected British officers in the area. The chances of such an occurrence were considered high, since "they [the British] have there so many friends" among the settlers. Patrick was to make every effort to detect and report on their presence, and capture them.[16]

On the British side of the lines, the winter of 1777-1778 had been a particularly hard one for the Seneca people. They were suffering from a lack of clothing and food, made all the more acute by the curtailment of trade with rebellious colonies, yet they were solidly loyal to the British. Lieutenant Colonel Mason

Bolton, in command at Fort Niagara, was impressed by the Seneca and other Iroquois allies, and wrote to Governor-General Carleton, "The savages . . . are determined to assist us." Based on reports he received from Butler and the Indian Department's officers, the nations were "calling in their people most exposed to possible Rebel attack" and "assembling their fighting men in each village" to oppose the American invasion of the Indian country that Schuyler had threatened to lead against Forts Oswego and Niagara. Bolton added, the "Savages may think it necessary to commence hostilities sooner" than wait for the American invasion. As his rangers prepared and trained at Fort Niagara, Major John Butler traveled to Canadesaga, also known as Seneca Castle, the principal town or "capital" of the Seneca nation (present-day Geneva). Located near the foot of Seneca Lake, this town of some fifty dwellings, some of them frame houses, was an ideal location to meet with tribal leaders. Butler had waited impatiently for the message that the Indians were ready, and was convinced that his presence with them would "accelerate their departure & direct their motions." While he was there, Butler consulted with Sayenqueraghta. Despite his advanced age of nearly seventy years, the Seneca still considered him their bravest warrior. An eloquent orator of the Turtle Clan, standing well over six feet in height, Old Smoke (or "Old King") as he was known to the whites, was an imposing presence at the council fire as well as on the battlefield. He was recognized as one of the two chief warriors of the Seneca nation, and the one whom the British reported "now has command over the Six Nations." The old chief told Butler that the Indians were still moving their people and friends living nearest the Rebels' settlements to places offering more safety, but the warriors were assembling and determined to strike the blow, as their council had decided the previous autumn.[17]

Satisfied that preparations were progressing, Butler returned to Fort Niagara and informed Governor-General Carleton on April 10 that he was nearly ready to march with the rangers in order to act with the Indians in launching the campaign. Butler was also having problems in maintaining the strength of his corps, which was evident by the returns that showed the number of officers and rangers dropped to 113.[18] Along the way back to the frontier, he hoped that his corps would be "considerably reinforced." He had sent a recruiting agent, John Depue, to bring in the rangers furloughed during the winter and after the Fort Stanwix siege was lifted, and to engage recruits on the North Branch of the Susquehanna. He also expected about 100 "Loyalists from the back settlements" who had been enlisted by the recruiting officer Captain Charles Smith. He assured Carleton that although Indians had not acted with "collective force," or bothered the settlements of the New York frontier over the winter, they had "not been idle." The Iroquois had frequently sent raiding parties to the Susquehanna, some of which were still out, where they destroyed several settlements and brought in a number of prisoners and about seventy scalps.[19]

As Butler's Rangers made ready to depart, their major asked Governor-General Carleton to arrange for an exchange of prisoners that would secure the return of his son, Walter. Yet unknown to those at Fort Niagara, Walter Butler managed to escape from his confinement at Albany on April 21, and was on his way to the safety of Indian country and ultimately to the British stronghold.[20] Until Walter actually joined the corps, Captain William Caldwell functioned as second-in-command and the senior company officer in the battalion.

When Major Butler finally led his command from Fort Niagara on May 2, he was joined by Captain John Johnston and a detachment of rangers from the Indian Department to superintend any warriors joining the force not already under the effective command of a competent chief. After about one week's march, during which twenty-six recruits were added to the corps of rangers' muster rolls, the command arrived at Canadesaga. To John Butler's great joy, his son Walter arrived there at about the same time Joseph Brant came in from the frontier. Brant and seventy Loyalist volunteers and warriors had been busy collecting food and cattle, taken forcibly from Whig settlers or voluntarily offered by those claiming to be Tories, and gathering the stores at Unadilla and Onaquaga for the upcoming operations. Brant had also encouraged those whites professing loyalty to go to Unadilla to enlist in Butler's Rangers. After a short meeting, Brant was on his way back toward the Susquehanna, reinforced with a detachment of about eighty rangers commanded by Lieutenant Barent Frey, to escort the remaining Mohawks living near white settlements in the Mohawk Valley back to the safety of Indian country.[21] Butler also sent Sergeant John Young and Ranger Richard McGinnis to Onaquaga and Unadilla to assist Brant and his Rangers in acquiring supplies and enlisting recruits.[22]

Major John Butler then met with Garganwahgah, or Cornplanter, the other chief warrior of the Seneca from the Wolf Clan. After meeting with Garganwahgah and Sayenqueraghta together, Butler wrote to Carleton that the two war chiefs expressed the "greatest desire to join me in an attack on the Frontiers of the rebellious Colonies." Sometime during the meetings, a war party of Senecas arrived from a raid toward the Ohio country, flushed with victory after an engagement with the enemy. The warriors related that they took two prisoners and thirteen scalps before the surviving Rebels retreated to the safety of a stockade fort, while the Indians sustained only one killed and four wounded. The chiefs told Butler that there were another 150 warriors still out along the back settlements of New Jersey and Pennsylvania, who were expected to return any day. Sayenqueraghta and Garganwahgah were preparing to lead another raid against American settlements on the West Branch of the Susquehanna. Such an operation would effectively screen Butler's movements from any enemy patrols, before the two joined forces for a major strike against the Americans. The major informed the chiefs and the assembled warriors that he would proceed with his corps to the Susquehanna and wait for them to rendezvous at Unadilla.[23]

Since Brant's raid of the previous year, the inhabitants of Unadilla who remained were known to British authorities and allies to be "friends to the Government." With its location on the Susquehanna and Unadilla Creek, the latter an avenue of approach to the Tryon County settlements, the town had become an outpost stronghold. It was a place for Loyalists to rally or seek refuge, as well as a base from which Provincial forces launched raids against Patriot communities. With two Loyalist-controlled grist mills and the provisions Brant's foraging expeditions had gathered, Major Butler expected to obtain sufficient supplies for his men on their arrival. From Unadilla, Butler could also choose the targets of his campaign. Cherry Valley, Schoharie, Minisink, and Wyoming Valley, with large populations known for their Whig sentiments, were all agriculturally productive and sources of supply for Continental Army magazines. All were within a few days' march—easy striking distance. Furthermore, between the volunteers Brant was securing, those enlisted by Captain Smith, or expected from his recruiting agent, John Depue, Butler was optimistic that he could add about 330 additional men, enough to complete the formation of the six companies needed to bring his battalion to full establishment strength.[24]

Major Butler decided that his son Walter was too ill and exhausted from the ordeal of his confinement and escape to go on the campaign, and sent him to Quebec with instructions to obtain some needed arms, clothing, supplies, and recruits for the battalion, and regain his strength before returning to assume command of his company. Walter proceeded on May 15, carrying a report from his father for Governor-General Carleton about the meeting with Sayenqueraghta and Garganwahgah, the situation as far as he knew it along the frontier, and his intention to rendezvous with the warriors of the Six Nations at Unadilla before raiding and pillaging settlements along the way down either the Delaware or Susquehanna Rivers, and possibly join "the Southern Army" of General Howe near Philadelphia.[25] Within two weeks, the rangers were on the march. Instead of marching toward Unadilla as originally planned, Butler changed direction, and headed for Tioga Point, not far from the Delaware town of Chemung, at the confluence of the Chemung and Susquehanna Rivers, from where it would be easier to join with the Indian warriors.

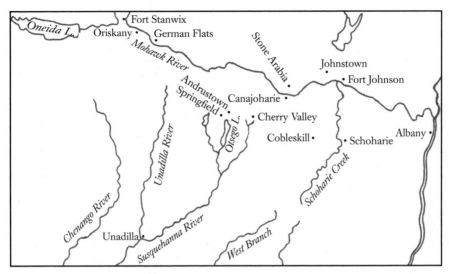

Settlements in the Mohawk River valley of New York.

While the British-allied Iroquois refrained from attacking the frontier of New York through the winter, they had not left the Pennsylvania back country undisturbed. Responding to increased hostile activity, the Pennsylvania government was also calling its militia to patrol and garrison forts in the threatened frontier regions. The state relied on its county lieutenants to fill detachments with volunteers or by drafting the necessary numbers of soldiers for periods of usually six months. In the spring of 1778, one such detachment of twenty "six-month's men" under the command of Lieutenant Moses Van Campen was directed by Colonel Samuel Hunter, the county lieutenant of Northumberland County, to build and garrison a fort on Fishing Creek, about three miles upstream from its mouth on the North Branch of the Susquehanna River, to safeguard the settlements in the area.[26]

The fort was nearly completed in May, when scouts reported a "large party of Indians making their way towards it." On hearing the alarm, many area residents left their homes and possessions behind and barely made it to the safety of the fort before the Indian raiders struck. The Indians burned and plundered all the houses and outbuildings in their path as they pursued the fleeing inhabitants to the fort. Although the attackers failed to get into the stockade, Van Campen said, "They kept a steady fire upon us all day." After nightfall, the Indians withdrew, "burning and destroying everything in their route" that had not been put to the torch earlier. Although his men had withstood the onslaught, the lieutenant continued, "What losses they [the Indians] sustained, we can not ascertain, as they carried off all the dead and wounded. From the marks of blood on the ground it must have been considerable."[27]

The well-established parts of Pennsylvania were also a focus of British strategy. One objective of General Sir William Howe's campaign of the previous summer and autumn was the capture of Philadelphia. He believed by taking the city that was considered the "capital" of the rebellious colonies, and possibly the members of the Continental Congress prisoner, he could sever the head of the rebellion. Despite being tactical losses, the skillful American withdrawal at Brandywine in September and the near victory at Germantown in October 1777 probably contributed to the French decision to support American independence that was sealed by the resounding victory at Saratoga that same month. Whatever General Howe may have gained, the heart and soul of the Revolution, the Continental Army, was as yet unvanquished. Even the capture of Philadelphia was a hollow triumph. Benjamin Franklin, when told of the event while representing the American cause in France, was unmoved, remarking with his characteristic wit and sagacity: "Howe has Philadelphia, or does Philadelphia have Howe?" Before Howe's army occupied the city, the Continental Congress adjourned, and reconvened in York Town, Pennsylvania, on September 30. As Butler and his Iroquois allies were discussing their next move at Canadesaga, the Continental Congress was back in session.

Many delegates still maintained the hope that a war against the Six Nations could be averted, despite the mounting evidence to the contrary. In a May 4, 1778, letter to Brigadier General Schuyler, Reverend Samuel Kirkland, once a Congregationalist missionary among the Six Nations, gave an optimistic outlook on Iroquois–American relations. Schuyler dutifully forwarded a copy of Kirkland's letter with his own report to Congress.[28] The information tempted the delegates with "a pleasing prospect of peace with the Six Nations," and prompted President of the Continental Congress, Henry Laurens of South Carolina, to believe that there was still a chance "to cultivate their present disposition into friendship by every proper means."[29] Before the end of the month, however, Schuyler's fellow Indian Commissioner, James Dean, dampened those hopes when he acquired news in conversations with various Iroquois that was "so various and contradictory," it was impossible to determine the Indians' real intentions. In contrast to Kirkland's optimistic missive, Dean learned that three different parties of Cayugas were out waging war on the frontiers of Virginia and Pennsylvania. Joseph Brant was leading a fourth war party, and gathering Tory volunteers and Indian warriors on the Susquehanna, in preparation for an attack on Cherry Valley. Other informants reported that a Seneca war party of 124 warriors had recently returned from an engagement in the Ohio country bearing thirteen scalps and two prisoners as trophies.[30] (Evidently this was the same party reported by John Butler to his British superiors from Canadesaga.)

Dean could only hope that the Onondagas were still divided in their senti-ments, and that at least the band of Senecas who were trying to arrange an exchange of prisoners being held at Albany wished to remain neutral, if not friendly to the United States. Unfortunately, Dean's overall assessment was that most Seneca felt "resolved to make no Terms" with the United States. The mat-ter of war or peace was still not determined, although Dean believed the border of Tryon County was not in imminent danger of attack as long as the prisoner exchange negotiations continued. Dean informed Schuyler the Onondagas had sent "runners," or messengers, to the Cayugas and Senecas to summon them to a meeting, but the council had not convened to discuss matters of alliance or neutrality with the United States. There being no "final Resolution" to declare on the subject, Dean told Schuyler that the council fire would be ritually extin-guished to signify a lack of agreement among the nations, and to expect the wampum belts extended to the Six Nations in invitation to a council by the Continental Indian Commissioners to be returned to him at Albany in the near future. There was also the news from his Indian informants of the council called by Britain's deputy Indian Superintendent Major John Butler at Canadesaga, which was attended by those Senecas and Cayugas not already on the war path on the side of the king.[31]

Schuyler dutifully made his gloomy reports to both Congress and Governor Clinton. To attempt to forestall disaster, Clinton directed Colonel Jacob Klock to take action. In a May 30 letter, Clinton's military aide-de-camp, Colonel Robert Benson, recognized that the governor was aware that a number of Tories had collected together near Unadilla, and were reportedly planning some hos-tile action against the inhabitants of the frontier districts. If this was true, the governor recommended that an expedition launched against them by a force of militia under the command of a "spirited & prudent officer" might make the region safer. Accordingly, Colonel Klock was authorized to order out a detach-ment for the purpose, if he thought his regiment was capable of the task.[32] But by the time the letter was delivered to Klock, Joseph Brant and his followers had already struck the first significant blow of the new campaign.

In the last week of May, Indians were seen in the vicinity of the town of Cobleskill. On May 24, Captain Christian Brown, commander of the local militia, took precaution, and spread the alarm for the men of his 4th Company to muster at his home just east of the main part of town. Fifteen men turned out. He then sent messengers to the garrison at the Middle Fort in Schoharie, and to his superior, Colonel Peter Vrooman, the commander of the 15th Regiment, Schoharie and Duanesburgh District, of the Albany County Militia Brigade, urgently seeking assistance to meet the emergency. Captain Patrick and a thirty-four-man company of Continentals were the first to respond.

Marching behind their drummer and fifer up to Brown's home the next day, the company joined the fifteen militia men who had already assembled. Over the next two days, more militia arrived until the American force had grown to about 100 men.

On Saturday, May 30, Captain Patrick led the mixed command through the cleared farmland up the valley from the settlement, searching for any sign of the enemy. At the same time, Captain Joseph Brant's approximately 350 warriors and Loyalists were moving down the valley, marching in the woods along the Cobus Kill creek toward the settlement in search of cattle, food, and other provisions. Gunfire broke the silence when three American scouts encountered two of Brant's. One of Brant's men fell dead, but the other returned to the main body and informed his chief. Brant decided to attack. Once its defenders had been dispersed or defeated, Brant resolved to destroy the town of Cobleskill.[33] The Mohawk-Tory leader hurried his men forward, and the advanced party soon emerged from the woods into the cleared fields on the farm farthest from the center of the settlement. It was the property of George Warren, a member of the local Committee of Safety. Had he been at home at the time, Warren's capture by Loyalist forces would have been quite a political coup.

When his scouts informed him what they had seen, Captain Patrick deployed his men and advanced in the direction the fleeing Indian had gone. When the leading elements of Parker's command reached the Warren farm, they found the house was already loosely surrounded by some twenty of Brant's men. Captain Patrick's troops immediately engaged, and after an exchange of musket fire, the Indians retreated into the adjacent woods. Although Captain Brown cautioned him about a possible ambush, Patrick's blood was up. The Continental officer ordered the soldiers to advance in open skirmishing order in pursuit of the retreating foe. As they were drawn deeper into the woods in a running battle, the enemy's strength steadily increased until the Americans found themselves in swampy ground, surrounded and outnumbered. As Brant's warriors and Tories swarmed about the American flanks, the firing became general, with both sides shooting from behind trees and other cover in deadly frontier fashion.

In a desperate attempt to break the enemy attack before it could completely encircle his command, Captain Patrick ordered a bayonet charge. But as soon as they left their covered positions, the captain and several of his men fell dead, and others were wounded. The counter attack came to a premature halt, accomplishing nothing. When the Indians rushed in to finish off those from Patrick's failed charge who had not retired or died, only Lieutenant Jonathan Maynard, the second-in-command of Parker's company of Continentals, was captured alive. Captain Brown took command of the survivors and prudently ordered a retreat. Three times the Americans halted to fire volleys as they fell back in good order until the ranks lost their cohesion in the woods.

Soon, the Americans were fighting from tree to tree. With Brant's warriors following them in close pursuit, the American withdrawal turned into a complete rout. As the retreating soldiers passed the Warren farmhouse again, three Continentals and two militiamen took position inside and continued the fight. Their action provided the cover necessary for the others to break contact. When the Indians stopped their pursuit to dislodge the men firing from the house, the retreating American survivors made their escape toward Middle Fort in the Schoharie settlement. The Indians then set the wooden building on fire. Three of the defenders burned to death inside, but two of the Continentals left the blazing structure to take their chances in the open. One was struck down soon after he emerged. The other was taken prisoner and later tortured to death.[34]

When they heard the sounds of battle the families back at Cobleskill were filled with dread, and when a few men ran back to warn the inhabitants to abandon their homes, their fears were realized. Many civilians fled into the forest to hide, some for several days, while others headed to the relative safety of the forts at Schoharie only a few miles away. Once Cobleskill's defenders were dispersed, Brant's band of raiders entered the village and plundered everything of use that they could find, before they set fire to about twenty dwellings and their associated barns and outbuildings. Judge William Dietz, the local justice of the peace and remaining civil authority, wrote to Brigadier General John Stark from Schoharie to inform him that "part of our Regiment of Militia with the Continental Troops have been attacked by Tories and Savages," whose numbers he estimated close to 500. Not being able to withstand the onslaught by this overwhelming force, he reported, the Americans gave way with considerable losses, including the dead Captain Patrick and Lieutenant Maynard. (Dietz knew that Maynard was missing and presumed dead, and was not aware that he had been captured.) At the time of writing, according to Dietz, although twelve of the Continentals were accounted for, the militia was still scattered. Unable to give an exact account of their losses, the judge was hopeful that more survivors would assemble. Dietz closed with a desperate plea for reinforcements and ammunition, especially grapeshot for their one small field piece, to help them withstand another attack that they expected to come in short order. In all, after the numbers could be confirmed, American casualties amounted to twenty-two killed, two wounded, and two captured. Some witnesses later said Brant's losses included about twenty-five killed and several wounded. An accurate count of enemy dead was difficult for the Americans to determine. In the usual Indian fashion common to all tribes, even when defeated, Brant's men carried away the wounded and dead after the battle. The bodies of their fallen comrades were said to have been hidden in the murky waters of the nearby swamp.[35]

Meanwhile, the area militia continued to respond. In all the surrounding towns, militia companies were mustering. Detachments were sent toward Cobleskill as soon as they were formed. Messengers were carrying expresses between commanders and their subordinates. Local civic leaders and militia officers sent requests for reinforcement by state troops to the governor's office in Poughkeepsie, or appealed to local Continental Army units for regulars. Lieutenant Colonel Christopher Yates of the 15th Albany County Militia Regiment sent a message to Colonel Abraham Wemple, commanding the 2nd, or Schenectady District, Regiment, to inform him of the situation. Yates arrived at Cobleskill at about three o'clock in the afternoon with a detachment of 150 men following the battle and "found the people in great disorder." Although the inhabitants escaped unhurt, all their buildings were destroyed. What food and cattle could not be moved by the refugees before leaving their homes was taken by the enemy when they withdrew. Yates learned from citizens that another, even larger, detachment of the enemy was on the move to join with those who had raided Cobleskill, and were believed to be intent on attacking Schoharie next. Yates closed his letter with a reiteration of Dietz's call for militia reinforcements and a resupply of ammunition.[36]

On Sunday, May 31, 1778, Brigadier General John Stark sent word to Major General Horatio Gates that although his resources were meager, he would send all the relief in his power to Schoharie. Stark confided, though, that it would "be a slender Reinforcement." Stark turned first to the Albany County Militia Brigade. Although their commander, Brigadier General Abraham Ten Broeck, was willing to muster his troops, he could not call them before church services were over "for fear of Frightening the Town into fits." Stark also set about seeking Continental reinforcements, even if it were only one regiment more, and specifically requested Gates to send any available field pieces. As he put it, although his department was weak in men, it was even weaker in artillery.[37]

On hearing the news of the attack on Cobleskill, Albany Mayor John Barclay and General Ten Broeck met to determine how their community could best respond. Together they wrote to Governor Clinton at Poughkeepsie about the situation in the hope he could provide some relief. The two men informed the governor that they feared further danger not only from Indians collecting together at Canadesaga under the direction of Major Butler, but also from the numerous Tories they had learned were going there to join him or to join Brant's band that had just destroyed Cobleskill. With a little desperation, they told the governor, "It is to be lamented that we still have too many Tories" in

Period illustration of an Indian attack on a frontier settlement. The scene depicts those horrors most associated with the war in the back country. Note the burning cabins while some settlers are killed and scalped, and other men, women and children are taken captive. (*Newberry Library*)

the area. A major concern about calling out the militia again was that so many of its members were also employed in vital public service occupations, such as carpenters, blacksmiths, and wagon drivers. Any large call-up was sure to affect the local economy, but the attack at Cobleskill prompted all the inhabitants of the Mohawk Valley to be in arms for their own protection. As Stark had said in his letter to Gates, Barclay and Ten Broeck added their voices urging the necessity of sending Continental troops to their relief, as well as the need for cannon, by writing "Not a single Field piece is left us, nor any artillery Men, nor any fixed ammunition [prepared cartridges of powder and ball]." The two added a concern about the presence of the large numbers of British and German prisoners in the area.

These prisoners were the men surrendered by Burgoyne's "Convention," or the agreement following the battles of Saratoga. For the most part, the soldiers were encamped or billeted in barracks, while the officers were quartered in the homes of local families, in communities in the Albany area. Gates had promised Burgoyne that he would refer to Congress the matter of allowing the troops to return home on the pledge they would no longer fight in North America. The delegates, as well as General Washington, hedged at the proposal. They correctly saw that such an agreement imposed no real loss on the British government if it was allowed to replace the "Convention Army" with soldiers from other posts and stations across the Empire. The presence of so many prisoners of war was a security risk that complicated the ability of Continental and militia forces to respond to the crisis at hand. Furthermore, it increased the possibility that the enemy would attempt to liberate and rearm these veterans, and return them to active service in the field. Barclay and Ten Broeck sought the governor's assistance in having the Convention Army moved to Poughkeepsie, eighty miles down the Hudson from Albany, or elsewhere as General Gates should direct.[38] Eventually, the Convention Army was marched to more secure camps in western Maryland and Virginia.

The urgency of the situation was best recognized by Colonel Jacob Klock, commander of the 2nd Regiment of the Tryon County Brigade of Militia and veteran of the Battle of Oriskany. In a letter sent from his headquarters at Canajoharie on Sunday, May 31, to General Ten Broeck in Albany, Klock reported that he had received three expresses from Cherry Valley within a half hour's time about enemy activity in that quarter. Fearing the worst, he mustered and marched about 500 men of Tryon County to within four miles of that location. He received word from fellow Oriskany veteran, Colonel Bellinger of the 4th Tryon County Regiment, that, based on what he learned from his Indian scouts, he expected the Flats to be attacked. To meet the threat, Bellinger asked Klock for a reinforcement of 300 men. Klock had already sent a scout of twenty-five men from his own battalion as soon as he heard the news of the attack on Cobleskill. The scout had been attacked and overwhelmed by a strong force of the enemy on May 31, possibly most of Brant's party, and all but three were killed. Of the three survivors, two returned unhurt, leading Klock to write, the "Enemy strikes in so many places, that we are not able to Stand them." He feared that any delay in reinforcement would cause the loss of all the settlements along the Mohawk River, and cost the lives of several hundred men, women, and children.[39]

Three days after the attack on Cobleskill, Colonel Abraham Wemple wrote to General Ten Broeck that he had learned a war party was heading toward Breakabeen. As a precaution, Wemple ordered a detachment of his 2nd Regiment to reinforce the upper Schoharie settlement, and was going to send additional forces as soon as some could be mustered. Looking to bring on an engagement with those who had ravaged Cobleskill, Wemple wrote, "If I am lucky Enough to meet them I hope to give them a Trimming." The events of the preceding days had nonetheless taken their toll on the energy and supplies of his men. He wrote Ten Broeck asking for a replenishment of his magazines, as he was "still waiting for ammunition" that had been previously requested, and was "in great want" of all classes of supplies and provisions, and even of sufficient quantities of paper on which to write his reports.[40] A "Return of Troops under the command of Coll. Wemple at Present at Schoharie 2d June 1778" submitted to the brigade commander shows that he had embodied parts of three regiments: Wemple's 2nd; Colonel Peter Vrooman's 15th, Schoharie and

Duanesburgh District, Regiments of the Albany County Brigade; Colonel John Harper's 5th, Frontier District, Battalion of Tryon County; and a company of rangers, for a total strength of almost 400 citizen-soldiers of all ranks.[41]

The militia on the New York frontier of 1778 would not have been unlike those found in other areas of the colonies. The Provincial Congress resolution called for the enrollment of able-bodied men between sixteen and sixty years of age, but the classes containing older men were usually called only for local emergencies.[42] Although some officers acquired uniforms at their own expense, most of the soldiers "turned out" in civilian attire, with a musket, bayonet, either a "cutting sword" or tomahawk, cartridge box, and knapsack. Unless called into "actual service," when these items might be issued from a state arsenal, it was likely that the soldier made do with items he acquired privately or improvised from what he had.[43] Ideally, each company consisted of one captain, two lieu-tenants, one ensign, four sergeants, four corporals, one clerk, one drummer, one fifer, and sixty-eight privates.[44] Regardless of the number of men enrolled in a town, village, or district, the local militia was organized as a company, but unless the emergency was local, ad hoc units were formed of volunteers or drafts. When companies were grouped into battalions or regiments, each was officered by a colonel, lieutenant colonel, two majors, an adjutant, and a quartermaster.[45]

News of the attack and the alarm quickly spread to Albany, where it was feared that Brant's raiders would strike next.[46] But after leaving Cobleskill in ruins, Brant and his men slipped away into the forest. A few days later, in early June, they captured several members of a gang working at repairing the wagon roads after the spring thaw, so important to the local economy of the Mohawk Valley, near Sacondaga. Hendrick Warmwood, whom they later released on account of his being crippled, lived to tell American officers that Brant's men, "about two hundred in number, all painted," were gathered about the late Sir William Johnson's fishing lodge at Summer House Point on the Sacondaga River. Using it as a base from which to operate, the Indians and Tories were building about twenty canoes, and had parties out to bring in captives and spread terror in the surrounding countryside. Before letting him go, Brant's men told Warmwood that what he saw "was not a third part of their number."[47] Not long after releasing the captive, Brant's men fell on the town of Sacondaga.[48]

At this stage of the campaign, Brant's primary objectives were to gather pro-visions, obtain recruits for Butler's Rangers, and avoid a major engagement if possible. Brant found a number of potential recruits among the "Disaffected," or those not supporting the Revolution, who went willingly to join him. Of the many male settlers taken captive in the raids, some accepted the offer of release in return for "volunteering" to take up arms for the British, while others felt compelled to swear their allegiance to King George III for fear of reprisal.

Most, when given the choice, seemed to prefer captivity to turning against their friends and neighbors. When Brant would ask the unrepentant Whig prisoners if they preferred to be held captive by the Indians, with the possibility of being adopted into Indian families, or as prisoners of war with the British at Fort Niagara, most chose the latter, knowing the Continental Army held three times as many prisoners as the British, and they therefore could expect to be exchanged. Two of these prisoners waiting to be marched to Fort Niagara managed to escape, and reported that Brant was boasting that he expected Butler and his Rangers to join forces with him when they arrived at Unadilla, after which he would return with an army of 1,000 men to "lay the whole County waste."[49]

One of the escaped prisoners, Robert Jones, told Judge Henry Wisner that in late May he was visiting in the strongly Loyalist Old England District and Butter Nut Creek area when Brant arrived with "Six Indians and 2 or 3 green Coat soldiers," most likely referring to Sergeant John Young and Ranger Richard McGinnis, and possibly the recruiting agent Captain Charles Smith. As he had done in numerous other settlements, Brant told the nine families living there that, if they were Loyalists, they should go to the safety of Onaquaga where they would be under his protection. If not, they could stay at their homes at their own risk. Regardless of their decision, he confiscated their cattle. Although Judge Wisner commented, "we have some reason to Suppose Jones to be a rascal," the members of the local Committee of Safety had "good Reason to believe in sundry Particulars" of his story.[50]

A week after the Cobleskill attack, June 6, Colonel Wemple wrote to Brigadier General Ten Broeck from Schoharie that at last, his regiment had completed the gloomy task of burying the dead from the battle. Fourteen American bodies were found in the fields, and five more were "burnt in the ruins" of the Warner house. The colonel continued his description of the carnage, and said the bodies had been "Butchered in the most Inhuman manner." Dead horses, cattle, sheep, and other livestock lay all over the fields. Ten houses and barns were destroyed. The people whose houses and effects were burned, he said, came away with only the clothing on their backs, and had lost everything to the hands of Brant's marauders. Most of the refugees were in need of food. As the militia supplies were the only source of possible relief, Wemple asked the permission of his superior to provision the unfortunate civilians with rations from the public stores.

The Indian and Tory raids of 1778 were already proving more troublesome and causing more damage than those of the previous year. The attack on Cobleskill renewed fears that Indian and Tory raiders were roaming the frontier areas of New York at will, causing much distress among the inhabitants. The situation prompted Governor George Clinton to call for militia to protect the frontier on June 2.[51] Brigadier General Ten Broeck responded that, due to the emergency, he had already ordered into "actual service" seven of the Albany County regiments. Under New York's Militia Law of 1778, being called into "actual service" meant the state government assumed the responsibility of paying, subsisting, and defraying other expenses associated with calling out the militia. Ten Broeck called no troops from his other regiments, preferring to hold them as a reserve. One of these was used to mount guard in the city of Albany. Three others were held ready for deployment to the northern frontier if necessary. Of those embodied after the governor's call, 100 men had been mustered to reinforce Wemple's force at Schoharie, and Ten Broeck sent a detachment of just over 200 to help protect Johnstown. As more men became available, Ten Broeck intended to use them to reinforce the Tryon County Regiments, but he admitted they "come on very Slow Indeed."[52]

As always, there was a question as to the numbers of enemy and the urgency of the alarm. Some officers believed the numbers being reported were greater than those actually present, thereby causing the crisis to be magnified and resulting in panic among the citizens. Ten Broeck explained, "However short the Enemy may be of the number Reported, they are Sufficient to Inspire Terror and Commit murder & Depredations in many of the defenseless Settlements." As proof, he cited the numbers of inhabitants who chose to flee their homes at the news that marauding Indians were approaching, and called for help. Although the rumors were unconfirmed, he and his officers had heard that the militia from Fishkill to Harpersfield had laid down their arms and that "all the Tories that were gone from Schohary were all with the Enemy," either Brant or Butler, and that town was going to be attacked on the following Saturday, June 6.

The general conceded the damage the Indian and Tory campaign was inflicting on the American cause, and feared the extent of the harm that would result. The situation, he believed, necessitated the quickest and most forceful effort on the part of the civil government, and both Continental and state military forces. Ten Broeck found the loss to the enemy in cattle alone was "Distressing to the Publick & the Ruin of Individuals in great numbers seems Inevitable." The Albany militia commander went on to tell Governor Clinton that although General Stark was doing his best to help, he could be of only limited assistance, for he was "a stranger" not familiar with the needs of the local inhabitants. Despite the lack of Continental troops at his disposal, Ten Broeck reported to Clinton that Stark was trying to do all in his power to assist in the security of the region, and had used his authority to request 100 men from Berkshire and Hampshire counties of Massachusetts.[53]

Colonel Wemple's regiment was completely mustered into service. The convoy of wagons carrying the promised resupply of ammunition and its ninety-man escort finally arrived, to his great relief. With his entire regiment under arms and stretched thin, Wemple informed Ten Broeck that he could not afford to draft only one-quarter of his regiment's enrolled strength into state service, as those in other districts had done according to the governor's order. Nor could he release three-fourths of those already on active duty, as that would leave his available force too weak to stop another attack. As it was, he had seventy men posted at lower Schoharie, the rest at upper part of the settlement, with patrols out scouting for any sign of renewed enemy activity. One of these scouts had ranged to the Susquehanna, where the colonel believed the enemy was assembling for yet another attack.[54]

After the state of alert continued into its second week, Colonel Klock reported an alarm that the Tories and Indians had exploited these tactics once more in Tryon County. After an express brought information that a party of Indians was sighted north of the river near the property of the fallen hero of Oriskany, Brigadier General Herkimer, he sounded the alarm. Before they could be engaged, however, the enemy broke into the settlement of Dillenburgh, near Stone Arabia, and destroyed it. Klock observed: "It is impossible for us to defend the County, for whenever we march from one place to defend another, the places we leave are attacked." Requesting assistance from Generals Ten Broeck and Stark to cope with the situation, he asked his general if it were not possible to be reinforced by calling upon the militia of other counties, especially those that were not immediately threatened, for the "assistance we owe each other."[55]

As the American recovery continued, some militia officers began suggesting the only solution to the menace presented by the Tories and Indians on the frontier was to take the fight to them in their own territory. Colonel Klock suggested as much to Governor Clinton when he wrote, "Unless a body of troops is marched directly to Unadilla in order to drive the enemy from thence and destroy the place, the Enemy will constantly make such Depredations upon the settlements."[56] Delegate James Duane in the Indian Affairs committee of Congress informed Governor Clinton that his sources agreed that "at least two parties of the Enemy" had entered the "Country for the sole purpose of ravaging and murthering the defenseless inhabitants." Consisting of "Indians under Brant's influence" and New York Tories, these forces, in Duane's assessment, presented a threat by the hope their actions were giving their Loyalist friends, as much as by the distress they caused those siding with the Revolution.[57]

The consequences of Congress having reassigned the Continental forces to other areas after Saratoga, and relying strictly on the militia for defense of the frontier, were now being realized. The warnings of Duane and other delegates in Congress of the necessity of leaving some troops in the Department were transmitted to General Gates without obtaining favorable consideration. Therefore, much as he may have wished to help, General Stark had no Continental soldiers at his command to send. According to Duane, the garrison at Fort Schuyler with respect to the present "Irruption, might as well be in the moon," as it was too distant to render any actual assistance. Likewise, Lieutenant Colonel Seth Warner's Additional Continental, or "Green Mountain Boys," Regiment was on the northern frontier to meet the potential threat of another invasion from that direction, and therefore too far from the people of Albany or Tryon counties.[58]

The governor, militia officers, and the commander of the Continental Army's Northern Department met and exchanged correspondence discussing the necessity of taking offensive action against the Tory base at Unadilla as a means of bringing some measure of security to the frontier. They realized the elusive enemy was capable of dividing into parties to strike at several places at the same time, then withdrawing before an effective response could be mounted. Simply calling out the militia in reaction to every alarm was exhausting the militia and harming the local economy by taking the men away from their farms, mills, and other businesses.

On June 11, Governor Clinton again contacted the ranking Continental officer in the area and his principal militia commanders in the most affected counties to continue the discussion of how best to protect the New York frontier settlements. As demonstrated at Cobleskill and Dillenburgh, reacting to enemy advances was not effective. Clinton observed, "no Force that can be collected will be able to afford full Protection to the Inhabitants unless the flying Party by whom they are distressed can be routed at the places where they usually rendezvous."[59] The governor told Brigadier General Stark that the "only effectual Means of giving Security to Inhabitants against future Ravages of the flying Party" was to attack their base. He then indicated that, according to their best intelligence, "Unadilla is the place on the Western Frontier at which the Tories and Savages who have lately committed Hostilities on the Inhabitants assemble & rendezvous." All agreed that attacking the enemy's base at Unadilla was the best course of action to take and made the most sense militarily. At the same time, Clinton wrote to Brigadier General Ten Broeck to advise that the expedition, if practicable, should be made with detachments drawn from the militia of Albany and Tryon Counties, and directed Colonel Klock for his regiments to "furnish their portion" of the necessary troops. To mount the operation, Clinton realized that he needed the support and participation of Continental troops as well as militia. Having learned that Alden's 6th

Massachusetts Regiment of Continentals was to remain in the area for the security of the western frontier, Clinton turned to Stark for having them join the expedition, and in obtaining additional detachments.[60]

The same day that Governor Clinton had notified his senior militia officers in the threatened counties and Brigadier General Stark of his decision to organize an attack against Unadilla, the Continental Congress passed a resolution that promised some relief to the frontier. Since the French had committed to an alliance with the United States, the Americans would benefit from money, matériel, naval power, and possibly ground troops to assist in fighting the British. The army had learned that the redcoats were planning to evacuate Philadelphia and concentrate in New York City. On June 11, 1778, in order to facilitate the success of the planned expedition against Detroit, Congress authorized a second expedition against the Six Nations from the Mohawk River to the Seneca country, "in order to chastise that insolent and revengeful nation, and to dispossess the enemy from Oswego." To execute the plan, Congress directed Major General Horatio Gates to "take the most expeditious measures" for planning the campaign, which was expected to "reduce to terms of peace, such of the Six Nations as are hostile" to the United States. Congress also directed its Commissioners of Indian Affairs at Albany, and elsewhere in the Northern Department, to co-operate with the general in executing their orders. Congress further instructed Gates, and the officer appointed to command the expedition against Detroit being prepared at Fort Pitt, to keep the Board of War informed, "in order that the two armies may, as far as practicable, act in concert."[61]

Despite the optimism in the American camp, the strategic situation was always changing. Although France entered on the side of the Americans and the enemy's evacuation of Philadelphia appeared to be imminent, the British were far from giving up the fight or reverting to a defensive war. Just a few miles inside of Indian country, Lieutenant Colonel Butler's "green coated soldiers" and the Indian allies were about to launch an offensive of their own from an unexpected quarter, with a level of intensity not yet seen on the frontier.

Chapter 5

BUTLER'S RANGERS

S OMETIME during the first week of June, as Joseph Brant and his Loyalist troops and warriors were gathering supplies, recruiting volunteers, and planning their next raid on a frontier settlement, a messenger from Major John Butler, then at Chemung, arrived at Onaquaga with an express. Butler wanted Brant to march immediately to the Chemung area for a council to discuss the progress and direction of the campaign. The Mohawk captain made the two-day trip down the Susquehanna from Onaquaga with a number of his follow-ers, as well as the recruits he had enlisted and much of the provisions he had gathered for Butler. For eight or nine days, the two leaders discussed their next moves. Brant advised the ranger commander that the Iroquois chiefs he had enlisted for the campaign refused to join any expedition against the American settlements along the New York frontier in the Mohawk and Schoharie areas unless Butler and his Seneca allies assisted by "cutting off" the Whig inhabi-tants of the Susquehanna to secure their flank, and protect the southern approaches to their country, first.

Butler agreed to attack the Wyoming Valley settlements as his first objective. Although also weighing the merits of a move south toward Philadelphia to join with Howe's army, Butler was still considering moving his rangers to the Tory stronghold at Unadilla. Using that outpost as a base of operations, Butler's Rangers could strike at targets down the Susquehanna or Delaware Rivers, or in the Mohawk or Hudson River Valley areas, depending on which could bet-ter support the overall effort to defeat the rebellion. The two leaders agreed that Brant would return to Onaquaga, from where he would lead an expedition against Lackawack on the Delaware River to collect provisions, and conduct other raids that would further confound and tie down the New York militia and any Continentals in the area. As soon as the council concluded in mid-June, Brant hurried back to his Onaquaga base.[1]

On the American side, Governor Clinton wrote to the Committee of Safety of Schenectady on June 18, 1778, as he had done with other towns concerned about the Indian and Tory menace on the frontier, that the forces of the state of

New York were doing the best they could to safeguard their lives and property. There was a continued need for militia to support Gates' proposed expedition against the Seneca, and Clinton suggested calling out one fourth of the men of each regiment in the area for that commitment. The governor told them that in the wake of the attack on Cobleskill, he had directed Brigadier General Ten Broeck to call out sufficient numbers of the Albany and Tryon County militia, continuously, for the defense in the Mohawk River area. Clinton also called out one fourth of the two regiments in Orange and part of the regiment in Ulster Counties to defend their own frontiers on the Delaware below the Catskills, instead of reinforcing Gates. Finally, the governor let the county lieutenants and militia brigadiers know that in return for having one quarter of their militia in "actual service," he had asked that Colonel Ichabod Alden's 6th Regiment of Massachusetts Continentals be ordered to remain in the area for defense of the frontier rather than join Gates' expedition. With the militia so heavily committed, Clinton petitioned Congress and General Washington to exempt the remaining militia of Albany, Tryon, and Ulster counties from additional duties so that they might also mount a credible defense for local emergencies.[2]

Militia commanders made the necessary preparations for the proposed expedition against Unadilla, and received their instructions for drafts to support Gates' expedition and other tasks ordered by Congress. With the prospect of yet more Indian and Tory attacks to come, many citizens were contemplating abandoning their homes and farms, and moving to areas that were not as threatened by the war. With harvest time approaching, that could have had serious consequences for the Patriot cause. Loyalist and Indian raids threatened to destroy the harvest before it was gathered, much less reach either the market or Army supply magazines, if there was no prospect for assistance from state or Continental forces. Colonel Klock requested that if the governor could not provide any reinforcement to help defend the frontier, that he at least provide a number of bateaux—flat bottomed, barge-like river craft—to evacuate the women and children to safety while the men remained in the valley.[3]

Meanwhile, the Tory Captain Charles Smith was actively recruiting volunteers for Butler's Rangers throughout the Albany and Schoharie areas. James Armitage, suspected by some of his neighbors of Loyalist sympathies, later told Brigadier General Ten Broeck of the militia that on Wednesday of the last week in June, two local men paid a visit to his home. When his wife told them he was not there, they told her to tell her husband that if "he Stayed home and remained Quiet, he would not be molested." On the following Friday, while Armitage and his neighbor Joshua Weeks were finishing breakfast, the two men returned, accompanied by a stranger who was dressed in a "Coloured Rifle

Shirt" and armed. The stranger was Captain Charles Smith who believed both men were sincere "friends of government." Smith sought "volunteers" from among the disaffected, but according to Armitage, "many were forced to be Tories by harassing of them." The "stranger" said he was in contact with a British Army major and superintendent of Indians who had collected 500 volunteers to fight the Rebels. Smith showed Armitage a letter from Major John Butler to General Sir William Howe, dated June 7, which read in part, "My Lord, these are to let you know that I am now in Readiness with 15,000 Indians and Government men, and hoping your Lordship will forward the army and fleet on the 15th of July I shall again begin my ruptures and hope to join you at Catskill." He then showed him another letter from Butler, addressed to Smith and the Loyalists he had collected, "desiring that they would come off Immediately" and join him. Smith then offered them four shillings in pay each per day of service. When they still appeared reluctant to join, Smith told them that if they did not, they could expect to "share the same fate as the Rebels as this was the last time of asking." To emphasize the threat of being treated as a Rebel, Smith also told them that he had commanded a "Party at Cobus Kill [Cobleskill]," where three friends of government had been killed owing to their not joining up when asked. Smith said he had also taken several reluctant Loyalists prisoner, and promised to take Weeks and Armitage too. Then, to emphasize the strength of the pro-British forces to further intimidate them, Smith said he had twenty-two Indians collected in lower Batavia, 500 Indians and government men "back of the Mountain," another "back of Cherry Valley," and a "Party back of Schoharie," ready to join the main body with Butler. Smith left, and vowed to return, but they never saw him again.[4]

As bloody as the attack on Cobleskill had been, just down the Susquehanna from Onaquaga, at Tioga Point, the largest raid yet carried out by Britain's Provincial Rangers and Indian allies was about to begin. With the recent recruits that had been enlisted during Brant's activities, engaged by Butler's agents, or who made their way to Unadilla to enlist, there were now some 210 green-coated soldiers in the corps of rangers, organized into three full companies and parts of three others.[5] Captain William Caldwell, Major Butler's second-in-command, saw to the building of canoes and bateaux, the stocking of supplies and provisions, and the training of new ranger recruits.

Sayenqueraghta arrived on June 20 with about 350 warriors, mostly Seneca, but with a good representation of Cayuga, Onondaga, and Munsee, or Wolf Clan Delaware, from a successful raid to the West Branch of Susquehanna. Queen Esther Montour, a Seneca clan mother who had once been married to a Munsee chief, gathered another 100 warriors from the various tribes and bands from the towns around Chemung and Tioga Point. Like her sister Queen Catherine, the fiery woman was well known to settlers along the Susquehanna from before the war. When the Iroquois and Wolf Clan Delaware living near Queen Esther's Town near Tioga Point considered going to war against the Americans, she not only urged them on, but accompanied the "Miscellaneous Indians" in a war party with Captain John Johnston of the Indian Department acting as their superintendent for the expedition. With a combined strength of more than 700 Provincial soldiers and Indian warriors, they began scouting down the Susquehanna to enlist more Loyalist volunteers, harass Whig settlers and plunder property, or intercept American scouting parties coming up the river. Britain was ready to hurl the first of its frontier thunderbolts at the Wyoming Valley.

Located on the North Branch of the Susquehanna River, the Wyoming Valley rests between the mouths of the Lackawanna River on the north, and the West Branch of the Susquehanna to the southwest. Today within the boundaries of Pennsylvania, on the eve of the Revolutionary War, it was claimed by that colony and Connecticut. The royal charters issued to both Connecticut and William Penn by England's King Charles II established overlapping rights to the land, and each believed they had rightfully purchased the land from the Indians.

The area had once been within the homeland of the Delaware (Lenni Lenape) Indian nation, in whose language "wyoming" translates to "large plains." Villages of the Nanticokes, Conoys, and Shawnee lined the river as it flowed for twenty miles "among the lofty, overshadowing trees, upon its margin, and the villages, hamlets, green woodlands, rich bottoms, and fruitful intervales."[6] Exerting their hegemony over their dependent Delaware in 1758, the Iroquois had sold the Wyoming Valley both to the Susquehanna Company of Connecticut and to an agent of the Pennsylvania province during the Indian Council called by Sir William Johnson at Albany the same year. Intertwined with the subordination issue was the Delaware alliance with the French, which displeased the pro-British Six Nations. Sir William Johnson called for an Indian council at Easton. The Delaware sachem Teedyuscung brought his nation into the war on the British side, and attempted to negotiate a reservation for his peoples' eastern branch in the disputed Wyoming Valley. The Grand Council of the Six Nations at Onondaga, however, sent its most powerful chiefs and persuasive orators to exert their hegemonic rule over the Delaware, as well as the other tributary tribes in the Susquehanna Valley, and precisely to silence the bid of the "Half King" Teedyuscung for autonomy.[7] Their plan succeeded. Teedyuscung acknowledged his subordination to the Iroquois sachems' authority, and British authorities recognized the Six Nations' dominion over the Delaware, Shawnee, and other "dependent" Indian nations in both the Susquehanna and Ohio River countries. The Iroquois then ceded large areas of their dependents' land on the Susquehanna and Allegheny Rivers, while the British agreed to recognize the lands west of the Ohio River as reserved to the western tribes. The agreements were formalized on October 25 and 26, 1758, with the conclusion of the Treaty of Easton. A small English settlement established there was destroyed in a raid by Delaware Indians during Pontiac's War in 1763. The way was opened again to white settlement in 1768 after the Treaty of Fort Stanwix placed the Wyoming Valley outside the "Stanwix Line," defining the border of Indian country.

Continually employed in the Indian Department's military service since 1755, John Butler also served as a judge in Tryon County before fleeing to Canada in 1775. After the war, he became a leading figure in the settlement of the Niagara region of Canada.

Seizing the opportunity thus presented, a number of Connecticut businessmen resurrected the Susquehanna Company, a joint-stock venture to develop the region for settlement of the fertile valley. The company made provisions for the establishment of five townships, each occupying five square miles along the banks of the North Branch of the Susquehanna River. When the first 240 "Yankee" settlers made the journey to their new homes in 1769, they found that the proprietary government of Pennsylvania had also begun selling the land in the area under a patent system to "Pennamite," or "Pennite," settlers. The error caused heated and sometimes violent disputes between the two colonies and their immigrants. Each rushed to beat the other in settling the Wyoming Valley, and the rivalry occasionally flared into an armed conflict between each group's militia in what became known as the "Yankee-Pennamite War." The dispute swayed back and forth when one side, then the other, gained a temporary advantage and evicted their antagonists from their new homes.[8]

By the summer of 1771, the Connecticut settlers were permanently established in their townships of Wilkes-Barre, Pittston, Kingston, Plymouth, and Nanticoke, which were organized and governed like those of New England, and in January 1774, the General Assembly of Connecticut formally annexed the

Wyoming area as the town of Westmoreland District to Litchfield County. Zebulon Butler and Nathan Dennison were appointed the first justices of the peace, and the community elected four deputies to represent its 2,000 transplanted Connecticut Yankees in the General Court at Hartford.[9] Despite this established order on the banks of the Susquehanna, neither the settlers from Pennsylvania nor that colony's proprietors accepted the situation graciously. Intermittent violence and legal wrangling continued until after the outbreak of the War for Independence, when the quarrel reached crisis proportions and threatened to disrupt the business of the Second Continental Congress. To prevent the Yankee-Pennite fray from causing irreparable damage to the fragile coalition of thirteen colonies in their common dispute with the Crown, on December 20, 1775, Congress "recommended, that that the contending parties immediately cease all hostilities, and avoid every appearance of force, until the dispute can be legally decided" after the war with Great Britain was concluded. The delegates further resolved that all property taken by the partisans of one side or the other be returned to the original owners, that neither interfere with the free passage of others through the disputed territory, and all persons seized or detained on either side be freed and charges dismissed. Congress further admonished that the parties to the "unhappy contest" should "continue to behave themselves peaceably on their respective possessions and improvements," or it would "take further order thereon."[10]

The Connecticut General Assembly, having convened in special session at Hartford on December 14, took up the matter when it received the Congressional resolution. Connecticut accepted the measures "pursuant to the advice of the Honourable Congress of the United Colonies" on peacefully settling the controversy. It also resolved that "in order to preserve the peace of [Westmoreland's] inhabitants, and harmony and friendship between the Colonies," it would curtail further settlement of the area.[11] The Connecticut legislation was immediately sent to Philadelphia, where it was read, agreed to, and accepted by the Continental Congress. Yankee and Pennite factions settled into an uneasy truce, and the two colonial governments agreed to suspend their grievances until after the hostilities with Great Britain were over.[12]

Most of the Wyoming Valley's inhabitants, the New Englanders in particular, were ardent patriots. The principal township was named in honor of two prominent Whigs who championed the rights of American colonists in the British Parliament, John Wilkes and Isaac Barré. The local militia was formed according to the New England model where the universal obligation of free males to have arms and participate in "trained bands" at the village-level was practiced as members of "Watch" or "Alarm" companies. The "Watch" companies were composed of men whose age and physical abilities enabled them to participate in general military service as the local need or the requirements of the province dictated. The "Alarm" companies included older and less physically capable men who could still defend their homes and communities in an emergency, as well as those otherwise exempted from regular militia service. The militia drilled on a regular, if not frequent, basis under the leadership of elected company officers and non-commissioned officers. Governor Johnathan Trumbull, the only royal colonial governor who remained in office as a state governor, reported in 1774 that each Connecticut town had its trained band and attended drill four times a year, as well as participating once or twice a year in regimental exercises.[13]

Shortly after the outbreak of the war, the Second Continental Congress passed its resolution recommending that all free males between the ages of sixteen and sixty, unless otherwise exempted, should be enrolled in the militia of the several colonies. The Connecticut government followed with its own militia law, which formed the adult male population of each town into companies, each with one captain, two lieutenants, one ensign, four sergeants, four corporals, one clerk, with a drummer and a fifer, and from thirty two to sixty-eight privates.[14] Under the provincial Connecticut Assembly, the militia belonging to all the companies or trained bands from the town of Westmoreland, or the Wyoming Valley townships and districts, and those from the "Up River" settlements, constituted the 24th Regiment of Foot of Connecticut Militia. Following the outbreak of war, the 24th Regiment had to be "established" by the new Revolutionary government, and conform to the militia organization prescribed by the resolution enacted by Congress. The Assembly appointed Colonel Zebulon Butler, Lieutenant Colonel Nathan Dennison, and Major William Judd as the field officers, who were then commissioned by Governor Trumbull.[15] In October 1775, the Committee of Inspection approved the establishment of nine companies, and the appointments of one captain, one lieutenant, and one ensign as the line officers in each. The companies were organized with an allocation of men to each district or township: 1st Company was formed in the lower half of Wilkes-Barre; 2nd Company in Kingston; 3rd Company in Plymouth; 4th Company in Pittston; 5th Company in Hanover; 6th Company in the upper-half of Wilkes-Barre; 7th Company in the lower part of the North District, which included Exeter and Providence; 8th Company in the Lackaway District; 9th Company in the upper part of the North District, or Tunkhannock, Mehoopany, and Meshoppen; and, 10th Company in Huntington and Salem.[16]

When the Continental Congress passed an act requiring each colony to form companies of minutemen equaling one fourth of its militia strength for the defense of their own and neighboring colonies, the Connecticut Assembly convened in December 1775 to enact the complying legislation. As Congress directed, the Connecticut law ordered the towns and militia regiments to enlist volunteers for companies "to stand in readiness as minutemen for the defence of Connecticut and the rest of the United Colonies." The minuteman companies were to be composed of able-bodied volunteers who would muster every two weeks for a half day of drill. Due to the remoteness of Wyoming Valley and the relatively small and spread-out nature of the population, the Assembly declared that the Act did "not extend to include or affect the 24th Regiment of Militia."[17] This was not a reflection of an unwillingness of the Wyoming Valley inhabitants to share the burden of fighting the war. The settlements proved fertile ground for Continental Army recruiting parties and furnished a high percentage of its military age young men to the cause. Despite the limited population, estimated at about 3,000 in 1777, about 275 men from Westmoreland, including thirteen officers, served with the Continental Army, mostly in units of the Connecticut Line.

Given the isolated and exposed nature of Wyoming Valley, far from the state's population centers and militia reinforcements and close to Indian territory and the potential dangers that presented, the officials of the Town of Westmoreland petitioned their delegates in Congress "concerning their apprehension of trouble from the Indians" for the raising of some companies of Continental soldiers. The application was referred to the delegates of both Connecticut and Pennsylvania before being introduced on the floor of Congress. On August 23, 1776, Congress authorized the raising of two companies of Continental soldiers to serve in defense of the frontier at Wyoming.[18] One company was commanded by Captain Samuel Ransom and recruited from the communities on the west bank of the Susquehanna. The other was recruited on the east side of the river, and was formed under the command of Captain Robert Durkee. Sufficient numbers of recruits were enlisted to achieve the established strength in both companies within sixteen days, and were mustered into service at Wilkes-Barre. Those who lived near enough were quartered and took meals at their homes, while the rest were billeted with residents of the town. Colonel Zebulon Butler, as commander of the 24th Regiment of Militia, saw to their training and other requirements, and fulfilled the duties of commissary and paymaster for the two companies.[19] By winter of that year, the news from the battlefield was not good. To make up the losses sustained in the disastrous campaign for New York City and the subsequent retreat across New

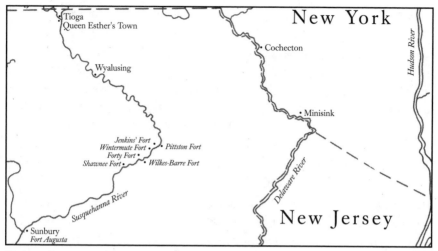

Early settlements and forts in the Susquehanna Valley.

Jersey, the Wyoming Independent Companies were ordered to join the Main Army of General George Washington on December 12, "with all possible expedition."[20] The security of the Wyoming Valley was once again the responsibility of the militia.

In the meantime, Colonel Butler relinquished his command of the 24th Regiment of Connecticut Militia to accept an appointment as a lieutenant colonel in the Continental Line on active service. In his place, Lieutenant Colonel Nathan Dennison rose to the rank of colonel and was appointed to command the regiment. Captain Lazarus Stewart was appointed to fill Dennison's lieutenant colonelcy, and Lieutenant George Dorrance became the major of the regiment in the place of William Judd.[21]

As in all communities in English North America, not everyone who lived in the Wyoming Valley was sympathetic to the Patriot cause. Some Yankees and Pennites remained loyal on principle, while some of the latter allied themselves with the British to even scores with the Connecticut interlopers. Likewise, some recent immigrants from the Hudson and Mohawk valleys, especially of German or Dutch backgrounds, had left their former homes due to persecution when Whig Committees of Safety had wrested civil government from royal authorities in New York. One group of Tories settled in their own community at the head of the valley around the property owned by the Wintermute[22] family, and erected a strongly fortified home they called "Wintermute's Fort," about eight miles upriver from Wilkes-Barre on the west bank, in Kingston Township.[23]

At first their Loyalist sympathies, then later their outward belligerence to the Patriot cause, resulted in the Tory minority attracting intense scrutiny by the local Committees of Vigilance and Safety. The most ardent Tories kept British officers at Fort Niagara informed of the contributions the valley was making to the American war effort, and when discovered, some were arrested and sent to prisons in Connecticut and their property was confiscated as punishment for aiding and abetting the enemy. Others, after being detained, were released when there was insufficient evidence to prosecute them. Once released, it was not unusual for unrepentant Loyalists of military age to find their way to Fort Niagara or Canada and enlist in Provincial units, such as Butler's Rangers and Sir John Johnson's "Royal Yorkers," to fight for the Crown. Others who remained at home became active in raising Indian hostility against the Patriot cause, or pledged that they would enlist if Loyalist forces would conduct them and their families to safety at Fort Niagara.

In the summer of 1777, when the British turned their Indian allies loose against American frontier settlements, the residents of the Wyoming Valley realized that their defenses had to be improved. Some work on the defenses had begun the previous summer when the authorities of Westmoreland ordered the construction of one fort in each township. With the renewed threat, it had become necessary for the inhabitants to erect the forts proposed by the town's proprietors as early as 1772, or improve the ones that already existed, as a defense against a common enemy. The cost or procurement of material and labor were borne solely by the local inhabitants without the assistance of the state government or the Continental Congress. The local citizens worked on the several forts by repairing the damage they had sustained from misuse and neglect, and made them ready should the need arrive. In addition to the forts ordered for the town's common defense, each township had a number of fortified homes or personal blockhouses, some of which were surrounded by palisades, located on property where the owner, his neighbors, and their families could find shelter in an emergency.

The two principal defenses were Wilkes-Barre Fort and Forty Fort. Wilkes-Barre Fort was built in the township of the same name on the east bank of the Susquehanna. Sited near the riverbank and adjacent to the town square, the fort had one gate, which opened toward the river. Its walls, constructed of a double row of logs set in a trench, rose sixteen feet above the ground and were surrounded by a ditch. The stockade walls were pierced by loopholes to allow the garrison to fire on an attacker without being exposed, and were strengthened by blockhouses on each corner. The fort enclosed about one half acre of ground, on which stood the structures of the Westmoreland courthouse and jail, as well as fort's barracks built into the walls. A spring, either within the walls or close at hand, supplied the garrison with fresh water. The fort boasted one 4-pounder cannon, but without a supply of shot, it was only good for use as an alarm signal.[24] Two private forts, originally built as strongholds for Connecticut and Pennsylvania immigrants, Durkee's and Ogden's Forts, respectively, remained as legacies of the Yankee–Pennamite Wars.

Artist's rendering of Wilkes-Barre Fort, the town defense which was destroyed in the Tory-Iroquois invasion of July 1778. A more sturdy installation was built on its ruins and named Fort Wyoming later that year.

Forty Fort, on the west bank of the Susquehanna, was the defense for Kingston Township. Constructed as an improvement of one of the original blockhouses in the settlement, it was named in honor of the first forty Yankee settlers, but was sometimes also referred to as "Kingston Fort." Situated close to the river, the fort had double log palisade walls similar to that of the Wilkes-Barre fort, and was strengthened and enlarged until it had a sentry box at every corner. It enclosed an acre of ground with a parade field, and cabins to house its defenders and their families in the event of attack. The fort had two gates, one on the north wall, and the other on the south. The latter led to a spring near the river via a "covered way," or sunken road protected by a timbered roof. Wintermute's Fort was located just upriver from Forty Fort, near the edge of Abraham's Plain, where the slope led down to the flats along the river.[25]

About two miles upstream from Wintermute's Fort, the Jenkins and Harding families built Jenkins' Fort, at the stockaded home of Judge John Jenkins, Sr., in Exeter Township.[26] Completed quickly, Jenkins' Fort provided the town's authorities with a check on the suspected Loyalist activities of the Wintermutes and their Tory friends. Jenkins' Fort was located near the river by the landing for the ferry crossing to another township, directly across the Susquehanna. On the east bank, the township of Pittston was defended by Pittston Fort, which consisted of three blockhouses surrounded by a stockade.[27] Since the township had originally been named Lackawanna, some area residents called the stockade "Lackawanna Fort," while others occasionally referred to it as "Brown's Fort," in honor of James Brown, who had built the first of the three blockhouses.

Down the river from Wilkes-Barre lay the townships of Plymouth and Hanover. Plymouth was located on the west bank along the road leading to

Shawnee Flats. For its defense, the township had a stockade named Shawnee Fort, sited on slightly higher ground than the surrounding area. The rise was popularly known as Garrison Hill.[28] Across the river on the east bank was Hanover Township. Built not far from the river, the Stewart blockhouse also occupied a slight rise in the ground. Constructed of logs with loopholes in the walls, it had an "overshot," or second story that projected over the first to enhance its defenders' fire against attackers below.[29]

It was not uncommon for those Tories who had joined the king's forces to return on occasion to visit their friends and family, or on military missions to enlist recruits of obtain supplies. In September following the Battle of Oriskany, a number of Tories whose homes were on the Susquehanna had returned on furlough for the winter, or shorter visits from Fort Niagara or their British units. On hearing the rumors of their presence, Colonel Dennison sent a detachment to search their homes. In a September 20 message to his superior, Brigadier General Oliver Wolcott of the 6th Brigade of Militia at Litchfield, Dennison reported that "A number of Tories left their possessions in this settlement and to Join the enemy at Niagary some time last spring." In response, he "Sent a party of men to make Prisoners of such as might be found." Although these Tories "took to the mountains for shelter," he reported that, "our people took two of them Prisoner and killed one," while sustaining the loss of one wounded militiaman. Dennison surmised that the surviving Tories had either gone to seek refuge in Indian settlements or were, more likely, "Lurking about" their families' homes. The prisoners were arrested and put in the Westmoreland jail while Colonel Dennison awaited Wolcott's decision on where to send them for long-term confinement. The colonel learned from questioning the prisoners that 160 Indians had returned to their own country from the battles at Fort Stanwix, instead of approaching Westmoreland. With some optimism, he hoped that some of the furloughed Tories would turn themselves in to the American authorities.[30]

With evidence of increased activity by Tory military units and the active involvement of hostile Indians on the side of the Crown, the American militia in the Wyoming Valley increased the frequency of their patrols. James Secord was one of the local inhabitants who had gone to Niagara to join the Indian Department. He was later commissioned a lieutenant in Butler's Rangers, but following the end of the siege at Fort Schuyler, he led eighteen rangers to plunder, seize provisions, and confiscate cattle on the Susquehanna and drive them to Fort Niagara. He and his entire party were surprised and captured by the militia after a local child had noticed they were hiding in a great swamp known locally as the "Shades of Death." Not long after the news of the victory at

Saratoga reached Wyoming in October, Lieutenant Asa Stevens of the local militia led a scout, or reconnaissance patrol, of nine men up the river from Wilkes-Barre. After being out for several days, they captured five suspected Tories. Another scout, led by Ensign John Jenkins, Jr., was not so lucky. They were ambushed near Wyalusing, and Jenkins was captured by Tories and Indians, and sent to Fort Niagara. Early in November, Lieutenant Colonel George Dorrance led a scout of 111 men, accompanied by a supply train of five packhorses, up the Susquehanna to Wysox, Sheshquin, and Towanda to capture Tories known to be gathered in those settlements. The militiamen returned from the successful raid with twenty-eight prisoners.

In December 1777, Colonel Dennison mustered a detachment of 126 officers and men from the 24th Militia Regiment after being informed of a band of Tories to the west of Westmoreland going to Tioga to purportedly enlist the aid of Indians there to kill the inhabitants and destroy the town. In a grueling eighty-mile march upriver, the militiamen took the Tories prisoner and pacified the Indians, at least for the time being, or so they believed. On returning to the Wyoming Valley, the Tories, some of whom were members of Butler's Rangers, were confined to Westmoreland jail while waiting to be turned over to the Continental Army. Seeing these green-coated soldiers up close, however, brought home to those living in Wyoming just how near they were to the fighting—and the vulnerability of their communities. By 1778, the Wyoming Valley settlements stretched along the Susquehanna for about twenty-five miles. The area's rich farms produced immense quantities of various grains, roots and other vegetables, fruits, hemp, flax, and livestock that made the area prosperous and a great source of food and supplies for the commissary and quartermaster needs of the American forces.

At the turn of the year, detachments of Butler's Rangers and Indian war parties began raiding Patriot settlements. In February 1778, they struck at Friedenshutten, an abandoned Delaware Indian village and Moravian religious mission near Wyalusing. At the time it was occupied by Amos York and some other settlers. The rangers and warriors stole food, plundered the inhabitants' possessions, burned their homes, drove off their cattle, and took prisoners, sending them into captivity at Fort Niagara or to Indian towns. In response, Colonel Dennison led 150 men to escort the survivors and the remaining families back to the relative safety of Wyoming.

The people of Westmoreland appealed to both the Continental Congress and the State of Connecticut for help. First Governor Trumbull approached General Washington for help from the Army. The citizens of Wyoming also sent messages to the commander in chief requesting that he send Continental troops to help defend their settlement. Other state governments, like New York, were sending similar pleas. Washington could not afford to weaken the hard-pressed Main Army by dispersing companies and regiments to every local emergency. In December 1777, General Sir William Howe led 6,000 men of the main British Army out of their Philadelphia defenses seeking to bring on a decisive engagement. Washington's White Marsh defenses proved too strong on that occasion, and Howe withdrew back to Philadelphia, but the American commander in chief expected his adversary to make another attempt. Washington's intelligence network was reporting that the British army was also planning to evacuate Philadelphia and march overland to New York. If that came to pass, he could attack and possibly damage them along the way. In either event, he could ill afford to detach Continentals to other missions.

Colonel Dennison reported to the state's General Assembly that Westmoreland was a "frontier town adjoining the wilderness and a country of savages which have been hired by our merciless enemies to murder the peace-able inhabitants of these United States," and expressed the need for more than militia for its defense. He explained that he had been sending detachments from the 24th Regiment on scouting parties, and when there was danger of being attacked by the Indians and Tories, he had called part of the regiment to "keep proper guards." In response, the Assembly voted to pay officers and men "in the same manner as is allowed to others of the militia of this State on like occasions."[31] When the requests reached the Continental Congress, it respond-ed on March 16 by resolving, "That one full company of foot [infantry] be raised in the town of Westmoreland," for the defense of the town and neighbor-ing settlements. Although the officers and men were to receive the same pay and rations as those in Continental service, they had to supply their own arms, accouterments, and clothing. Serving terms of enlistment for one year, they were not entitled to bounties paid by Congress to "regular" Continentals, who served terms of three years or for the duration of the war. In recognition of their local defense mission, Congress placed the company under the command of the colonel of the militia at Westmoreland, who was "empowered to superintend [and] . . . give orders relative to the station or stations it shall take for the defence of the country."[32]

By the end of May, State Representative Anderson Dana presented and read another petition requesting relief, reporting Indians had killed and taken twen-ty-five people captive on the Susquehanna and upper part of Westmoreland. The inhabitants, he said, "believe that the Indians Intend to make Warr." He further argued that unless there was a company to defend the town, the militia must be relied upon "to go a scouting & garding" to defend it. That, in turn, would result in "Neglect raising provisions for the support of the inhabitants." He therefore asked for the State to pay bounties to supplement the pay authorized by Congress as an inducement to potential volunteers.[33] On June 10, the Assembly agreed.[34] Lieutenant Asahel Buck, a subaltern in Captain Durkee's company, was sent to York Town, Pennsylvania, carrying letters from the Connecticut Assembly and Colonel Dennison in Hartford, regarding the issue of the bounty for the new Wyoming company.

The same day, news reached the Connecticut Assembly that Indians under the command of British captain and Mohawk leading warrior Joseph Brant had attacked settlers near the head of the East Branch of the Susquehanna. Representatives Dana and Dennison thought it prudent to return home. They arrived in Wyoming Valley ten days later to find the population in a state of high anxiety over reports that the green-coat soldiers from Fort Niagara and paint-

A German illustration published in 1784 of two Pennsylvania soldiers in the Continental Line at the beginning of the War for Independence: a riflemen on the left, and the member of an infantry musket company on the right. By mid-1778, except for corps like Posey's, most of the Continental Army's rifle units were disbanded.

ed Indian warriors were about to strike. Scouts reported that the enemy was at Tioga Point, preparing for the feared invasion of the Wyoming Valley. Settlers from the North District moved their families and belongings to Wilkes-Barre. Others, who had been away, returned to the upriver settlements to find their homes destroyed and families gone. Many of the missing families were taken to Tioga Point as captives, where Butler's Rangers and Sayenqueraghta's warriors gathered and built boats and canoes, and completed their preparations for the attack on the Wyoming Valley.

Chapter 6

THE BATTLE OF WYOMING

L IEUTENANT Colonel Zebulon Butler had arrived at his home in Wilkes-Barre on furlough from the Continental Army's 3rd Connecticut Regiment of Foot in early June. After being welcomed by his children and wife, Lydia, he learned that the town was in a state of alarm and pending emergency. After a brief stay, he decided to ride to York Town, Pennsylvania, where the Continental Congress was meeting. Going straight to the Board of War, he made an impassioned appeal for a detachment of Continental troops to help defend the Wyoming Valley settlements. If none were available, he proposed that the two Wyoming Independent Companies, then stationed at Lancaster guarding enemy prisoners, could be detached to return home. Then, Lieutenant Asahel Buck arrived with the letters from Hartford, and the Board of War also received a report from Brigadier General Oliver Wolcott about the situation in the Wyoming Valley.

The board was swayed. Colonel Timothy Pickering wrote General Washington with the recommendation to detach the two Wyoming Independent Companies for home defense on June 19. Pickering reasoned that their "absence from the army will be of small consequence, though probably their service against the Indians will be of considerable importance." He also recommended that Lieutenant Colonel Zebulon Butler be "permitted to remain in that quarter to direct the operations of the force which shall be collected there." Enlistments for the new company lagged, and only forty-six of the sixty-one men had been enlisted under the command of Captain Dethic Hewitt. So, the general was informed that the board was prepared to report to Congress on the advantage of offering financial encouragement for filling Hewitt's company, and recommending the consolidation of the two Wyoming independent companies into one.[1]

Recognizing the "apprehensions of the Public of an Indian war in the Western Department," Washington revealed that he was "induced on the 15th of the month to detach Durkee's and Ransom's companies for that command."[2] The commander in chief agreed with having Butler "remaining where he is and taking the direction of the Troops to be employed in that Quarter, if it is agreeable to Congress."[3] After receiving the recommendations of the Board of War and Washington's endorsement, Congress realized that the lack of incentives paid to the volunteers and the requirement for the men to arm and equip themselves at their own expense were inhibiting recruitment. On June 23, Congress finally voted to pay bounties for those men enlisted for service in the new Westmoreland Company, and to pay the non-commissioned officers and soldiers an additional stipend for providing their own arms and accouterments as soon as the unit passed muster at the required strength.[4] The June 23 resolution also agreed with the Board of War recommendation to detach Durkee's and Ransom's companies from the Main Army for service on the frontier. Noting that the companies had been reduced in strength "by various causes" to a combined strength of eighty-six noncommissioned officers and privates, Congress also resolved that the two independent companies be consolidated into one. Lieutenant Simon Spalding was appointed captain of the new unit, and Lieutenants Timothy and Phinehas Pierce were appointed subalterns.[5]

As the reorganized company prepared to depart from its post at Lancaster, Pennsylvania, Captain Ransom and Lieutenant James Wells, Sr., now supernumerary officers, were retired from the service. They departed for the Wyoming Valley ahead of twenty-five men who left without official leave. As soon as they arrived home, they offered their services as volunteers to Dennison. The remnants of the two units were then formed into a single company and, accompanied by Captain Durkee, were finally detached on June 26. They began the long forced march, about 120 miles, back to their homes, from Lancaster, through Berks County to Reading, then to Bethlehem and Nazareth, and on into Northampton County, through Wind Gap, and then over the "Lower road" from the Delaware River toward Wilkes-Barre.

Lieutenant Colonel Zebulon Butler reported to Colonel Dennison as soon as he arrived back in Wilkes-Barre. After meeting with other militia officers and civil authorities, Dennison and Butler made the best possible preparations against the impending attack. Scouts were sent up the river as far as Wyalusing every day, and a few went further, but none chanced going all the way to Tioga Point. All work in the valley, even routine farming chores, was done by armed men, some of whom were detailed to stand sentry as others labored. The cannon at Wilkes-Barre had powder, but still no shot, and remained an alarm gun to warn inhabitants and call militia to their various rendezvous. The entire 24th Regiment, as well as the Alarm List companies, were ordered to be ready at a moment's warning.[6]

Ensign John Jenkins, Jr., who had been captured the previous October, escaped from his captors while being moved from Fort Niagara to Canadesaga. He arrived home on June 2, exhausted and hungry, and reported that a large number of Tories from the upper Susquehanna had wintered in Fort Niagara. They were particularly abusive to him and other prisoners from Wyoming. They often repeated threats to return to their deserted homes with British troops and Indians to drive settlers off and take possession of the Whigs' property for themselves.

On June 5, the defenders learned that a band of Indians accompanied by six rangers had struck at Tunkhannock. After attacking, they captured the remaining settlers, and plundered the homes of those who had left to seek refuge in Wilkes-Barre. The flow of bad news spurred the inhabitants working to strengthen forts to intensify their efforts. Soon, those living in the outlying areas of Exeter were moving to the shelter of Jenkins' or Wintermute's forts, and families from the upper reaches of Pittston were moving to Pittston Fort.

Militiamen William Crooks and Asa Budd of Kingston went on a scout beyond Tunkhannock on June 12. After reconnoitering the area near the abandoned home of John Secord, a known Tory who had gone to Niagara to join Butler's Rangers, Crooks remained at the house while Budd went further up the river alone to hunt for game. That night, after Budd observed what he thought to be a scouting party of Indians fording the river, he paddled back to Secord's to tell Crooks. When Crooks went back into the house to retrieve some ammunition he had left inside, he was seen, shot, and killed by a group of Indians. When the warriors left to rejoin the rest of their war party, Budd made his escape. Crooks was the first casualty in the battle of the Wyoming Valley.

Five days later, a six-man scout from Jenkins' Fort went upriver in two canoes to determine the strength of the enemy and the direction it was moving. The men in the leading canoe beached on the west bank, about six miles below Tunkhannock. While ascending the bank, they encountered a band of Indian warriors and armed Tories running straight at them. They made a hasty retreat under fire while pursued back to their canoe, and sounded the alarm. As they attempted to hurriedly paddle to the shelter of the lee side of an island in order to escape, two of the men in canoe were wounded, one of them mortally.

Mysteriously, two Indians who had once lived in Wyoming and knew some of the inhabitants came for a visit accompanied by their wives. Not surprisingly, they were suspected of being spies for the British. One of the townspeople heard that an Indian, while under the influence of liquor, boasted to his host that warriors were preparing to attack the settlement soon. The two Indian men were arrested and confined in the town jail, and their wives were sent away under a flag of truce.

On Saturday, June 27, Butler's Rangers, the Iroquois warriors of Sayenqueraghta and the group of "miscellaneous Indians," about 700 in all, left Tioga Point, heading downriver by canoe. After several hours of paddling, they slipped past Standing Stone, and beached their craft near Wyalusing to spend the night. Early on Sunday morning, the raiders were back in their canoes heading downstream. After passing the Three Islands and opposite the mouth of Tunkhannock Creek, the rangers and warriors came ashore to camp for the night. On Monday, they reached the mouth of Bowman's Creek, about thirty miles upstream from Wilkes-Barre, and landed. The invaders broke camp early on Tuesday, June 30, and Major Butler and Sayenqueraghta led the main force to continue their approach march by land, following the creek before turning to the south-southwest behind the high mountain, which they kept between their column and the river. Butler detached a party of Indians accompanied by five rangers to march south along the right bank of the Susquehanna to scout the approaches to the settlement, with orders to rejoin him on Mount Lookout, behind the settlement of Kingston. After marching about twelve miles, Butler and the main force arrived on Mount Lookout, "an eminence which overlooks the greatest part of the settlement," and encamped. The position allowed Butler and his officers a vantage point from which to observe the townships of Kingston and Exeter, and the activities at Jenkins' and Wintermute's forts. Butler promptly "sent out parties to discover the situation, and strength of the Enemy."[7]

That same day, earlier in morning, twelve men and boys departed Jenkins' Fort in lower Exeter for the mouth of Sutton's Creek, about five miles to the north to tend their crops and other work. The group included three members the Harding family, Benjamin, Stukely, and Steven, Jr., and friends Ebenezer Reynolds, John Gardner, and a youth named Rodgers. They were accompanied by the Hadsall family, James, his sons James, Jr., and John, son-in-law Daniel Carr, and friends Daniel Wallen and Quocko, a black servant of a William Martin. While they were on their way out to the creek, Captain Dethic Hewitt was returning from a scout he had led up the river a few days before. The captain's patrol brought news that a large body of the enemy had been seen and was already in the area, but it was too late to warn the Hardings and Hadsalls.

When they arrived at Sutton's Creek, one of the Hardings stood guard while the rest went to work in the family cornfield on the flats on the river just above the creek. Four of the Hadsalls went to work in their family's cornfield, on an island out in the river just above the mouth of the creek, while the others went to the family's tannery on the west bank. Late in the afternoon, Michael Showers and Frederick Anker, refugees from upriver who were staying with the

Wintermutes, arrived and offered to stand guard while the sentry helped his companions finish the fieldwork before sun set. Agreeing, the sentinel quit his post to work in the field. Stephen Harding noticed that Anker and Showers were not at their post as he went to retrieve the horses for the return trip to Jenkins' Fort. Meanwhile, the other Hardings quit work and went down a ravine toward the river and a nearby saltlick. As Stephen was returning on the path through the ravine, he saw Anker and Showers with a group of Tory Rangers and Indians waiting in ambush for his companions coming from the river. Before Stephen could issue a warning, the enemy opened fire. Benjamin and Stukely Harding were wounded, but managed to return fire. The Tories and Indians then rushed the party, who fought desperately for survival in a furious melee. The unarmed John Gardner was taken prisoner, but young Rodgers managed to escape. Stephen Harding watched in horror as the Indians toma-hawked and scalped his brothers before he, too, escaped into the woods.

Another group of Indians and Tories surprised the men working at the Hadsall tan-yard. After taking James Hadsall, Sr., Daniel Carr, and Quocko Martin prisoner, the Indians set the building on fire, and waited for the four men working out on the island to return. As the farmers beached their canoes, the enemy began shooting. James, Jr., fell dead. Ebenezer Reynolds, although wounded, managed to escape with the aid of the uninjured Daniel Wallen. The youngest Hadsall, John, who was securing his canoe when the attack started, was not seen by the enemy and managed to elude capture by hiding in a thick-et of willows before finding his way home. The prisoners were taken to the British camp on Mount Lookout, where Major Butler reported that his patrols "brought in eight Prisoners, and scalps."[8] Ranger Richard McGinnis, who was in the party that raided the tannery (which he described as a mill), reported that "the Savages" had captured "two white men and a Negro, whom they afterward murdered in their own camp."[9]

John Hadsall made it back to Jenkins' Fort that night and reported on the ambush and the death of his brother. The three surviving members of the Harding party evaded capture and made it to Jenkins' Fort by early next morn-ing to tell of their ordeal. The alarm gun sounded at Fort Wilkes-Barre, and the call for the militia to assemble went through the valley. Some 400 men gathered in their companies at the various muster fields. Colonel Dennison, establishing his headquarters at Forty Fort in Kingston, sent for Lieutenant Colonel Zebulon Butler, at his home in Wilkes-Barre, to join him and the rest of the regiment's officers for a conference. As soon as he received the summons, Butler crossed the Susquehanna and reported to the militia colonel. Dennison offered to overlook the differences in their respective ranks and defer to Zebulon

Butler's more extensive military experience and status as a Continental. He then proposed that Butler assume actual command of all forces involved in the defense of the Wyoming Valley. The proposal was quickly endorsed by all of the assembled officers, and Butler accepted the responsibility without hesitation.

With the news of the previous day fully absorbed, it was time to act. With a view toward meeting the enemy outside the more heavily populated townships, the 24th Regiment mustered its available companies. After posting sufficient Alarm List company members to provide garrisons for the forts to protect the civilians, the regiment marched from Forty Fort. Although they expected to meet the enemy on the west bank as they headed toward Sutton's Creek, the troops encountered no Provincial soldiers or Indian warriors along the way.

After halting at Sutton's Creek, Lieutenant Roasel Franklin led a detachment from the 5th, or Hanover Township, Company forward to the scene of enemy's attack on the men tanning hides and tending their fields the previous day. They soon found the mutilated corpses of the two Hardings. They also discovered two Indian warriors waiting in ambush, presumably to attack anyone coming for the bodies. But seeing them first, Franklin's men were the first to fire. One warrior fell dead. The other was wounded, and when he tried to escape, he was pursued and killed by Franklin and one of his men. Tradition holds the two were sons of the Indian matron called Queen Esther. The bodies of the two Harding men were recovered, and carried back to Jenkins' Fort as the 24th Regiment made the return march. The men arrived at Forty Fort in the early evening after having marched more than twenty miles.

Throughout the day on July 1, while most of the regiment was marching to or back from Sutton's Creek, the valley's families were brought into the Forty Fort stockade or one of the other places of refuge, and some members of the militia were assigned to garrison each. Lieutenant Elisha Scovell of the 7th, or Exeter, Company was assigned to Wintermute's Fort, despite the fact that a number of the inhabitants were believed to be Loyalists. When most of the 24th Regiment was away, two members of the Wintermute family left their fort and climbed Mount Lookout, one mile to the northwest of their property, to contact the British commander. Major John Butler later reported that "Two loyalists who came into my camp informed me that the Rebels could muster about 800 men, who were all assembled in their Forts."[10] Intelligence of the enemy was not all the two Loyalists brought to camp. Ranger McGinnis related that "kind Providence was indeed very, very favorable," as "two men, Wintermots by name, hearing of our approach and distress for provision, came to our relief with 14 head of fat cattle." The animals were immediately butchered and divided among the Tories and Indians. McGinnis also said the Wintermutes "had a fort at Wioming of their own name" which they were prepared to deliver to the king's forces.[11]

That evening, guided by the two Loyalists through a gap on the northeast side of the mountain and into the valley, Major John Butler's men marched undetected by the Americans to within one half mile of Wintermute's Fort. Major Butler then sent a "flag party," an officer carrying a flag of truce accompanied by a drummer, to formally demand the fort's surrender. Advancing with the two Wintermutes, Lieutenant John Turney and Drummer John Phillips of the Rangers approached and called on Lieutenant Scovell to capitulate, after which they would take possession of the fort.[12] The Patriots of the garrison prepared to resist, but the Wintermutes told them that Major Butler and his rangers were welcome there.

Turney offered the garrison Major Butler's terms sparing their lives in return for surrendering. The Wintermutes and their Loyalist friends among the garrison prevailed on the militia officer's instinct to fight. Scovell executed the Articles of Capitulation for Wintermute's Fort, dated July 1, 1778. In return for surrendering all stores, arms, and ammunition, and the garrison's defenders pledging to not bear arms against the king again during the present war, Major Butler promised that all men, women, and children in the fort would not be hurt by the rangers or Indians. Butler then entered the fort with a number of his men. After establishing his headquarters, he began sending out scouts to gain information on American defenses, and parties to collect cattle and provisions at upper end of valley. All non-Loyalists were detained under guard and held prisoner until July 5, when they were released after giving their parole to abide by the articles of capitulation.[13]

The next morning, Butler sent Captain William Caldwell with another flag party, and a detachment of rangers made up of former Wyoming Valley residents, to demand the surrender of Jenkins' Fort. Approaching with a flag and drummer beating the "Parlay," Caldwell offered the same terms as granted the garrison at Wintermute's. With their numbers already reduced from June 30 skirmish at Sutton's Creek, Captain Stephen Harding of the 7th, or Exeter, Company and Squire John Jenkins agreed to capitulate. The "Articles of Capitulation between Major John Butler, on behalf of His Majesty King George III and John Jenkins" were signed. Like their comrades at Wintermute's Fort, the garrison of Jenkins' Fort and their families were placed under guard.

From his headquarters at Forty Fort, four miles away, Colonel Dennison sent out scouts of his own to determine strength and disposition of the enemy. Captain Dethic Hewitt led one such patrol. The scout encountered and skirmished with the enemy. They returned to the fort after suffering one wounded, one captured, and another, named Fitch, shot and left for dead near a gorge in the mountain known as Shoemaker's Hollow. Another scout sent out later in the day recovered Fitch's scalped body and brought it back to the fort.

While Captain Caldwell's flag party was at Jenkins' Fort, Lieutenant Turney's appeared at Forty Fort to present Colonel Dennison with Major Butler's demand for surrender. The defenders refused, vowing to "stand it out to the last and defend it to the last

The main defense for Kingston Township, Forty Fort was named in honor of the first forty Connecticut settlers in the Wyoming Valley. In July 1778, it was the place for the local militia to rally, and site where Colonel Dennison signed the capitulation document.

extremity."[14] Dennison had already sent urgent messages to Captain John Franklin at Huntington and Captain Asaph Whittlesey at Plymouth (Shawnee) to bring their companies to Forty Fort in Kingston, and send their women and children to safety in Salem. Lieutenant Colonel George Dorrance followed these with messages informing them of the capture of Wintermute's and Jenkins' Forts, and urged them to hurry with their two companies. Dorrance sent another urgent message to Captain John Clingman at Fort Jenkins near Fishing Creek requesting assistance. Although quite a distance away, the militia there could muster ninety men. They were, however, Pennsylvanians, and were not in Continental service. Considering the bitter Yankee–Pennite rivalry, the people of the Wyoming Valley did not place much hope in obtaining reinforcements from these neighbors. In the face of the emergency, however, Colonel Dennison at Forty Fort and Lieutenant Colonel Zebulon Butler at Fort Wilkes-Barre were summoning all men they could.

By July 1778, the 24th Regiment of Foot of Connecticut Militia had ten regular companies and two Alarm List companies. The 8th, or Lackaway District, Company, however, was not expected to arrive in time, and there was a possibility that their community, too, was going to be attacked by a strong Indian war party. The 7th, Exeter, Company was already in combat. Two of its officers had surrendered two of the township's forts, and they had suffered a number of killed, wounded, and captured in the skirmishes of June 30. The available remnants of the company were either in Forty Fort under the command of Ensign John Jenkins, Jr., or at Pittston Fort. The 4th, Pittston, Company was garrisoning the fort in their township under the command of Captain Jeremiah Blanchard. The 1st, Lower Wilkes-Barre, Company, under command of

Captain James Bidlack; the 5th, Hanover, Company under Captain William McKerachan; and the 6th, Upper-Wilkes-Barre, Company commanded by Captain Rezin Geer, were all mustered at Fort Wilkes-Barre, where Lieutenant Colonel Butler was in charge. In addition to Captain Dethic Hewitt's Westmoreland Company of volunteers in Continental service, Forty Fort was manned by the 2nd, Kingston, Company under the command of Captain Aholiab Buck. Some members of the 3rd, Plymouth, Company had already mustered at the Shawnee Fort stockade on Garrison Hill under the command of Captain Asaph Whittlesey, and along with part of Captain John Franklin's 10th, Huntington–Salem, Company were on their way to Forty Fort with as many men as they could spare after leaving sufficient garrisons to guard their families. The 1st and 2nd Alarm List companies of Captains James Bidlack and (Doctor) William Hooker Smith, respectively, were distributed among the forts or stockades nearest their homes.

On the morning of Friday, July 3, Major John Butler sent a flag of truce carried by David Ingersoll, one of the prisoners at Wintermute's, escorted by a ranger and an Indian warrior, with a message demanding the unconditional surrender of Forty Fort and all remaining forts in the valley not yet surrendered, along with all public stores, and all Continental officers and soldiers. In return, the Provincial Ranger commander offered "good terms" if they submitted without further bloodshed. If the offer was refused, however, Butler threatened to use all the force at his command to subdue them. Colonel Dennison refused, but asked for time to consult with those officers who were not present. Dennison believed that the Provincial rangers and Indians would advance to attack Forty Fort as soon as his message of refusal was relayed to the Tory commander, but he needed all available time to weigh the options or gather sufficient forces to meet the inevitable assault.

During the time allowed for consideration, Dennison sent a messenger to Lieutenant Colonel Zebulon Butler informing him of what was happening, the British demand for surrender, and requested that he immediately come over to Forty Fort for a conference. Dennison also sent orders for the Hanover, Pittston and two Wilkes-Barre companies, and all Alarm List company soldiers not yet detailed to a garrison, to march to Forty Fort. All the companies were ready to move by noon, except Captain Blanchard's Pittston men. Manning Pittston Fort, just across the river from the now enemy-occupied Jenkins' Fort, Blanchard thought it more prudent to remain there instead of leaving the women and children defenseless. His company also had no way of crossing the river at that point, since the enemy seized all the boats at Jenkins' Ferry. The only way to Forty Fort was by a march down the east bank to the ferry at Wilkes-Barre.

When Lieutenant Colonel Zebulon Butler arrived, the assembled officers held a council of war. Colonel Dennison moved, Lieutenant Colonel Dorrance seconded, and all officers agreed, that Zebulon Butler should take command again, as he did on July 1 for the expedition to Sutton's Creek. Butler accepted, and the conference of officers and unanimously decided not to surrender, but "hold the fort at all hazards." While they were meeting, Lieutenant Timothy Pierce of Captain Spalding's Wyoming Independent Company arrived to tell them that the unit was en route, and would probably arrive two days later. Lieutenant Colonel Butler then sent the 24th Regiment's adjutant, Isaac Baldwin, to the Board of War at Philadelphia—Congress having just returned to the city after the British evacuated it in June—carrying a message informing them of the situation at Wyoming. To gain additional time, if not for Spalding's Continentals, then for Franklin's 10th company from Huntington and Salem and maybe Clingman's from Pennsylvania to arrive, Lieutenant Colonel Zebulon Butler prepared a message to Major John Butler requesting a conference to discuss the terms of the surrender proposal.[15] The message was sent with an officer carrying a flag of truce, but he was twice fired on by Indians before going very far, and returned.

Scouts were sent to determine British strength and intentions. Those sent earlier, some of whom were still out, had learned little. Finally, returning scouts reported that the enemy was burning all the farms above Kingston and collecting the cattle. It appeared that the rangers and Indians would not risk attacking the fort. Instead, they feared the enemy would burn and plunder the upriver settlements, cross the river to Lackawanna, burn Pittston and massacre its defenders, and take their families captive back to Indian territory. The Council of War reconvened to discuss the possible actions open to the defenders.

Based on what had been observed, many did not believe the combined force of Indians and Tories outnumbered the American forces assembled at Forty Fort. Colonel Dennison and Lieutenant Colonels Butler and Dorrance, leading one group of officers, preferred to wait for the reinforcements that were surely on the way, and remain on defense at Forty Fort. A second group disagreed and wanted to attack the enemy immediately. They believed it was the only way to drive the invaders off before they inflicted much more damage to their homes and crops. This faction also argued that the fort was ill-provisioned to withstand a long siege if the reinforcements did not arrive, and that many soldiers would leave to see to the protection of their families rather than wait for the enemy to attack them in the fortified post. The arguments not only split the officers, but spread to the men in the ranks as well. The proponents of attacking the enemy argued that the longer they delayed, the more crops would be destroyed, making it harder for the community to survive the following winter. The discussions became more heated, until those advocating immediate action accused the officers and men who preferred to wait for reinforcements of cowardice. The rift in the 5th Company from Hanover resulted in a near mutiny, and the members who advocated attack deposed their moderate captain, William McKerachan, and elected the outspoken leader of their faction, Lazarus Stewart, in his place. Rather than risk further loss of cohesion, or even disintegration of the embodied militia at this critical moment, Dennison, Butler, and Dorrance conceded to the demand of their subordinates pressing for an immediate attack.

By noon, the assembled force included Captain Hewitt's standing company, and the 1st, 2nd, 3rd, 5th, and 6th Companies of the 24th Regiment of Foot of Connecticut Militia. There were even some members of the two Alarm companies, remnants of the 7th, a few men from the 9th, and the lead elements of the 10th Company, led by Lieutenant Stoddard Bowen, who arrived after marching some twenty-one miles. The late-arriving militiamen were distributed among the five companies present. The lately retired Continental officers Captain Samuel Ransom, Lieutenants James Wells, Sr., and Peren Ross, and Ensigns Matthias Hollenbeck, Rufus Bennett, and John Pierce arrived to volunteer their services. They were followed by twenty-five enlisted men from Captain Spalding's company, who left Lancaster before the company was formally detached from the Main Army. Spalding's men joined the ranks of Captain Hewitt's company. Aside from those left to garrison the fort under the command of Ensign John Jenkins, Jr., there were approximately 375 men organized into a six-company battalion for impending battle. Some companies now included soldiers who had never trained with those they now stood beside, and despite the late addition of a few men to their ranks, they were unaware that the enemy they were soon to face outnumbered them by almost two to one. Yet, they felt ready and confident. At about two o'clock in the hot afternoon of July 3, the battalion marched out in column behind the two mounted figures of Colonel Dennison and Lieutenant Colonel Zebulon Butler, the color bearer, and the combined fifes and drums playing "St. Patrick's Day in the Morning." As they moved to the northeast, the column passed Colonel Dennison's home, and halted for a rest on Abraham's Creek. Despite the short distance of the march, the July heat was sapping the energy of the troops with every step. During the halt, Lieutenant Colonel Butler advanced another officer with a flag of truce to request a parlay with Major John Butler, while fresh scouts went forward.

Back at Wintermute's Fort, Major Butler's scouts informed him that the Americans were on the march in their direction and preparing to attack. Butler said, "This pleased the Indians highly, who observed they should be upon an equal footing with them in the woods." The Tory commander sent messengers recalling his troops and the dispersed parties of Indians to concentrate at his headquarters. He sent a runner to Captain Caldwell with orders to set Jenkins' Fort on fire, and bring his company back to Wintermute's Fort. He then ordered Wintermute's Fort to be abandoned and burned in order to deceive the Americans into thinking that they were retreating.[16]

Captain Robert Durkee, his black servant Gershom Prince, and Lieutenant Phineas Pierce of Spalding's Company arrived at Forty Fort on lathered horses, having ridden ahead of the company from Wind Gap the previous day. Finding that the battalion was on its way to fight, the three rode on to join them and offer what assistance they could, despite their exhaustion. They managed to catch up with the column as it was halted at Abraham's Creek, just before the scouts and the flag party, having been fired on again, returned. Shortly before 3:00 PM, Lieutenant Colonel Butler ordered the men to cross Abraham's Creek, reform into column, and resume the march toward Wintermute's Fort. So far, the Americans had marched about two miles without engaging or even observing any enemy. Halting again within one mile of Wintermute's Fort, Lieutenant Colonel Butler sent Captains Ransom and Durkee and Lieutenants Wells and Ross to select and mark off the ground on which the regiment would align its ranks. Once accomplished, Butler ordered the column forward and to deploy to the left into a line of battle, two ranks deep. The right of the line ended where the ground sloped down from Abraham's Plain ten or twelve feet to the flat bottomland that bounded the river. From there, the line stretched northwestward across the plain for 300-400 yards.

Hewitt's Continentals, now reinforced with the advanced elements of Spalding's company, took the right of the line. With Bidlack's Lower Wilkes-Barre Company formed to their left, and Geer's Upper Wilkes-Barre Company to the left of Bidlack's, these three companies constituted the right wing under the direct command of Lieutenant Colonel Butler. Whittlesey's Plymouth Company, brought closer to establishment strength with Bowen's Huntington and Salem men, was the last unit on the extreme left. To their right were posted Stewart's Hanover men, followed by Buck's Kingston Company to the right of Stewart's. These three companies formed the left wing under the command of Colonel Dennison. The currently serving and recent Continental officer volunteers were positioned as field aides. Captain Durkee and Ensign Hollenback took their posts on the right wing, and Captain Ransom on the left. Major Garrett assisted Butler as his second in command on the right wing, while Lieutenant Colonel Dorrance was second in command to Dennison on the left.

With the battalion so disposed, Lieutenant Colonel Butler called for volunteers to scout ahead for the location of the enemy. Abraham Pike and an unknown companion stepped forward. The two went ahead, undetected, and found the enemy gathered about Wintermute's Fort in strength. On their way back to report to Lieutenant Colonel Butler, they had a running encounter with two of Major Butler's Indian scouts, who fired on them, before they reached the American line. Pike and his friend told the American commander that with Wintermute's Fort being set afire and the Indians and rangers gathered about, it appeared that the enemy was about to evacuate the valley. This news heartened the American militia. Meanwhile, the two Indians that Pike and his friend had encountered had proceeded back to Wintermute's Fort to inform the British commander of the Americans' activity. Every movement the Americans had made since leaving Forty Fort had been watched by Major Butler's scouts, and his scattered detachments were now concentrated. By three o'clock, except for some scouts and pickets he had posted elsewhere, Major Butler's entire force was assembled, and the Americans appeared to have taken the bait in believing the rangers and Indians were preparing to withdraw. It was now time to set the trap.

Wintermute's Fort lay directly ahead of the American right wing, near the edge of the steep slope leading to the flats. To the north and west of Wintermute's Fort lay a field of six or seven acres, with its far boundary marked by a log fence. Major Butler formed his rangers behind the fence, "in a fine open wood, and for our greater safety lay flat upon the ground, waiting their approach."[17] Butler took off his regimental coat and military hat, covered his head with a black handkerchief, and took his post behind the log fence to command the left wing, where he positioned most of his battalion of rangers. To the left of the field and log fence, as the Americans faced it, was a large, heavily wooded swamp, or "morass," bordered by dense thickets. The Indians, with the Indian Department's and a few of Butler's Rangers, were posted in the swamp, on the right of the British line. Ranger McGinnis said, "We immediately treed ourselves and secured every spot that was any way advantageous to our designs."[18] Organized in six bands, the warriors and rangers were ordered to lie on the ground and hold their fire until Sayenqueraghta gave the signal to commence shooting. In the vicinity of the burning fort, and scattered behind trees and elsewhere on the open field, Butler deployed Indian warriors and rangers dressed and painted like them to act as skirmishers. He then sent the American prisoners under guard to the rear with the women and other noncombatants. As it drew close to four o'clock, Major Butler learned that the Americans, now less than a mile away, had deployed into line of battle.

After his scouts returned and made their report, Lieutenant Colonel Zebulon Butler decided to advance. Before giving the command, he addressed the forces, saying: "Men, yonder is the enemy. The fate of the Harding's tells us what we have to expect if defeated. We come out to fight, not only for liberty, but for life itself; and what is dearer, to preserve our homes from conflagration, our women and children from the tomahawk. Stand firm at the first shock, and the Indians will give way. Every man to his duty!"[19]

After Lieutenant Colonel Butler ordered them to advance, the line stepped off. As they moved forward toward Wintermute's Fort and the enemy, Hewitt's Company on the right guided along the edge of the slope. When the line was about 150 yards from Wintermute's, Butler ordered a halt. Believing the enemy was close by, the veteran Continental field officer gave some final instructions to his subordinate company officers. It was nearly five o'clock, and the bright July sun promised another two and a half hours of daylight. Seeing all was ready, Lieutenant Colonel Butler ordered the line to resume the advance. Emerging into open ground that was partly cleared and cultivated and partly covered by scrub oak and yellow pine, the advancing line became visible to the waiting enemy. Maintaining their deliberate cadence, the members of the 24th Regiment of Foot came steadily on and passed the burning ruins of Wintermute's Fort. Suddenly, enemy skirmishers, singly at first then in pairs, began to leave their concealed places to fire their muskets at the militiamen, before disappearing into the thickets, swamp, or beyond the log fence at the edge of Wintermute's field. As they advanced, with Butler in command on the right and Denison on the left, the American line crossed the level plain.[20]

Major Butler's fire and withdrawal tactics convinced the advancing Americans that they were facing the rear guard of a retreating enemy. Most of the skirmishers headed for the log fence at the far end of Wintermute's field, now only 200 yards away, and into the woods beyond. The Americans then saw the prone figures of Butler's Rangers, just visible in the gaps between the stringers of the log fence. Lieutenant Colonel Butler then committed his battalion by initiating the "the evolution" for "firings on the advance" by giving the preparatory command, "Take care to fire by battalion!" He then gave the orders for the companies to "Make ready! Present! Fire!" The muskets erupted in a sheet of flame and smoke. Each captain then had his company prime, re-load, and shoulder firelocks, before Butler ordered them to advance. After pacing off about another thirty yards, they halted, fired another volley and reloaded. As soon as their muskets were shouldered, Lieutenant Colonel Butler ordered, "To the front, March!" The companies advanced another thirty yards or so until Butler ordered them to again halt, "Make ready! Present! Fire!"[21]

After firing the third volley, the enemy still had not answered with return fire. Ranger McGinnis said some Americans came on shouting "Come out, ye villainous Tories! Come out, if ye dare, and show your heads, if ye durst, to the brave Continental Sons of Liberty!" as they advanced.[22] When they had closed to within 100 yards of the fence, the Americans halted and prepared to fire a fourth volley. With their attention focused to the front, the Patriots were unaware of the warriors lying silent and concealed in the dense thickets of the swamp off to their left flank. Sayenqueraghta then gave a shrill war whoop, the signal to attack, which was then repeated by each of the six Indian bands as they opened fire in succession. When the rangers took up the war whoop, they rose to their feet and fired a deliberate and deadly volley that tore gaps in the American ranks. The battle was joined, and heavy firing became general along both lines.

The rangers, now all on their feet, fell back on order to reform and reload. Lieutenant Colonel Zebulon Butler called out, "See the enemy retreat! Stand fast and the day is ours!"[23] His men answered with a cheer. The right wing of the American line, guiding on Hewitt's company, advanced another thirty yards closer to the log fence. Although the companies to their left had yet to advance that far, all were at least maintaining their positions and keeping up a good rate of fire. To the Americans, it appeared as if the enemy line to their front was beginning to falter, and if they could only hold fast on their own left, they might prove victorious. Lieutenant Colonel Butler, satisfied with the progress his right wing was making, reined his horse and rode toward the left to see how that wing was faring. Appearances were deceiving.

With the American right wing moving ahead of the left, the Tory rangers responded with defiant yells and epithets of their own and their resistance began to stiffen. At the same time, casualties mounted on the vulnerable and exposed American left flank, and Major John Butler observed, "Our fire was close and well-directed."[24] It appeared the king's forces had gained an upper hand. More Americans fell dead or dying, Major Garrett and other key leaders among them. The American officers had underestimated the enemy's numbers in deciding to attack, and were now paying the price in killed and wounded. Colonel Dennison ordered Captains Whittlesey and Stewart to have their Plymouth and Hanover Companies, respectively, "flank off" and refuse the left flank by falling back to re-form at a right angle to Captain Buck's Kingston Company. This move was intended to reduce the Americans' vulnerability by presenting the attacking foe with a cohesive front. But just when a well-timed volley might have broken the Indian attack on the flank, and the enemy's own left flank was in danger of giving way to the American right wing, something went terribly wrong. Although those officers and soldiers who had understood the order tried to execute, others did not. When the command for certain platoons to fall back was issued to begin the evolution for the companies to flank off, some soldiers misunderstood it as an order to retreat, and began to retire.

Just then, Indian warriors charged from out of the swamp yelling their wild, blood-chilling war whoops, and the American left wing was thrown into confusion. Ranger McGinnis said the Tories and Indians on the right of the British line soon had the Americans "entirely surrounded."[25] Seeing the attack on the American left gaining momentum, the rangers arrayed behind the log fence rallied and assaulted the American front. McGinnis continued, "The white men [Tory rangers] . . . on the left drove and defeated the enemy on every quarter."[26] Rushing in with spear, war club, and tomahawk, the warriors swarmed among the confused militiamen of the American left wing. Amid the deadly hand-to-hand combat, Colonel Dennison and the surviving officers tried to reestablish order, reform their lines, and have the men stand their ground. The Indians, however, with a superiority in numbers, pressed their advantage.

Lieutenant Colonel Butler made his way through the smoke and noise of the musketry that had obscured his view from the right, but halfway down the line he realized that the gap between the two wings was dangerously wide. Butler found himself between the two halves of the American line, one of which was quickly losing its cohesion. He saw that the enemy now advanced with renewed vigor, and the Americans on the left flank were retreating despite the best efforts of their officers (many of whom were killed and wounded in the attempt) to rally them. The error was fatal and unrepairable. The remnant of the left wing gave way and fell back on the right wing. Panic and confusion spread along the line, and some men began to flee. Lieutenant Colonel Dorrance and Captain Ransom were wounded and taken prisoner. Dorrance was executed later in the day by his captors. Captain Durkee fell wounded and was helped from the field. Captain Bidlack was wounded and taken as a captive to the British rear.

Seeing that the Indians had gotten behind them, one of Hewitt's subalterns shouted, "The day is lost!" Pointing to a group of warriors who had gotten behind them to the rear, he asked his captain, "Shall we retreat?" Hewitt replied, "I'll be damned if I do!" He then called, "Drummer, strike it up!" Hewitt died fighting. With all the American company commanders dead or wounded, the surviving Americans, including the leaders Colonels Butler and Dennison, fled the field. The British commander, Major John Butler, later wrote, "the affair was soon over, not lasting above half an hour, from the time they gave us the first fire till their flight."[27]

With the battle ended, the massacre started. Knowing the "cruel treatment" they could expect from "wrathful Indians and offended countrymen," the Patriots tried to escape.[28] Some of those Americans on the right wing ran down the slope and across the flats to the bank of the Susquehanna in their effort to get away. From there, they plunged into the river and swam or waded to Monocanock Island, which was about one and a half miles from the scene of battle. The island and its vegetation provided temporary safety from enemy musket balls, as the fleeing Americans ran to the far shore, reentered the water and swam across the main channel of the Susquehanna to the eastern bank. The fortunate few who made it, then headed for Wilkes-Barre Fort. But soon, this temporary refuge was lost as Tories and Indians crossed over in pursuit. Hector Saint-John Crèvecoeur, the French immigrant who wrote as the "American Farmer," said that only thirty-three made it to the opposite bank, while the rest were overtaken and tomahawked or pierced by lances while in the water.[29] Some Americans gave themselves up to the enemy, trusting their lives would be spared. A widely circulated story after the battle told how a number of those who had made it safely to Monocanock Island were lured back to the west bank with the promise of safe quarter if they surrendered. One group of sixteen returned to shore to give themselves up as prisoners. They were marched back up the slope from the bottom lands, and ordered to sit in a ring around a large boulder, which measured six feet in length and three feet in width showing about eighteen inches above ground, facing inward toward each other. While a warrior stood behind each of the men to hold him down and prevent his escape, another went around the ring of men with a war club, or "death maul," and smashed each of their skulls. Although not verified, tradition holds that Queen Esther Montour, her heart burning with vengeance over the death of her sons at Sutton's Creek two days before, was the executioner. The scalped and mutilated bodies were later found around the stone that was thereafter called Bloody Rock, or Queen Esther's Rock.

The wounded Captain Durkee was helped as far as the river bank with the aid of Lieutenant Asa Gore and Ensign Matthias Hollenback. With Indians pursuing them, Durkee recognized that their faithfulness in aiding him was only jeopardizing the lives of all three. The veteran captain ordered the two subalterns to leave him in order to save themselves. Gore and Hollenbeck reluctantly obeyed, and after running a short distance, they heard the distinct sound of a tomahawk being driven into the captain's skull.

Most of the beaten Americans ran back in the direction from which they had come, toward the safety offered by Forty Fort. As the Americans fled, pursuing Tories and Indians followed, or rushed ahead and tried to cut off their

This familiar rendering of the Wyoming Massacre is accurate in that it depicts Butler's Rangers and Indian warriors killing and scalping militiamen who are wounded or no longer armed, as well as those who continued to fight. (*Library of Congress*)

retreat. Many Yankees were taken prisoner and herded back toward Wintermute's Fort, where all but a few were forced to run the gauntlet before being tortured and executed. The Indians were not inclined to give quarter, and most of the American militiamen were hunted down, killed, and scalped, even as they attempted to surrender. Survivors later claimed that few Americans actually fell in the engagement, and that most were killed during the pursuit that followed, or after surrendering. Crèvecoeur wrote that the Indians scalped the dead, and tied the prisoners to small trees and burned them.[31] Even Major Butler remarked, "In this action were taken 227 Scalps and only five prisoners." He justified the savagery by saying, "The Indians were so exasperated with their loss last year near Fort Stanwix [in the battle of Oriskany], that it was with the greatest difficulty I could save the lives of those few."[32] The major's statement neglected to explain the murderous behavior of his own men. After the battle, stories abounded about Loyalist volunteers and Tory rangers exacting the same wanton brutality on their defeated former neighbors and even relatives. The massacre of the Wyoming Valley militia illustrated the savagery of frontier fighting and civil war at their bloody worst.

After the American line broke, the men and their surviving officers saw no honor or purpose in remaining on the field to be slaughtered. Militiamen attempted to gather as best they could into squads, and frequently halted to fire a few individual shots or an occasional ragged volley at their pursuers, or to lend support to others trying to escape, in a running but fighting retreat. Colonel Dennison, still mounted on his horse, made it to Forty Fort at the head of an exhausted handful of men. Likewise, Lieutenant Colonel Butler, also still mounted, was among the last to leave the field. He rode into Forty Fort accompanied by four or five others, just as Captain Franklin arrived with some men from his Huntington–Salem Company. The rest of Franklin's company was still waiting at Fort Shawnee in Plymouth for the balance of the company to muster, before catching up to him at Kingston. When they paused to take stock of the situation, Dennison and Butler found that only fifteen to twenty survivors had thus far made it back to join the small garrison left at Forty Fort. After a brief discussion, Butler crossed the river back to Wilkes-Barre to see to the situation there.

At both forts, as the sun set, sentinels were posted, and the garrisons prepared to meet the next enemy onslaught. Throughout the night, a few frightened battle survivors straggled to Forty Fort, or to the forts at Wilkes-Barre and Plymouth, while others went to their homes to gather their families and fled the valley. Frightened civilians, who had remained in their homes during the day, gathered what provisions they could carry and sought refuge in the forts. Conditions were getting crowded. At Forty Fort, the garrison left behind during the battle, Captain Franklin's advanced party, and the stragglers from the battle numbered about fifty, while the noncombatants brought the total occupants in the small post to several hundred. Other civilians loaded possessions into boats on the river, or into wagons and on the backs of horses and oxen, and prepared to flee for safer quarters. The men at Pittston Fort later reported that they could hear the sounds of the Indians, cheered on by the Tories, torturing the wounded prisoners. By the light cast from still-burning Jenkins' Fort, they claimed to have watched helplessly from the east bank of the Susquehanna as Captain Bidlack and other unfortunate captives were stripped, tied to stakes in the ground, and tormented by Indians performing a "Scalp Dance," before being burned alive. Others later reported that prisoners, including the wounded Captain Ransom, were tortured and executed near Wintermute's Fort.

The long day was finally at an end. The American Patriots had been soundly defeated, and there was little hope that they could hold off a British attack or withstand a siege for long. Captain Spalding's Wyoming Independent Company was still more than a day's march away. Many of the women and children in the fort were now widows and orphans. Throughout the night, the enemy kept up an annoying fusillade that wore on the nerves of the garrison and occupants of Forty Fort. Surely, if the Provincial Rangers, Loyalist volunteers,

Another rendering of the Wyoming Massacre. Note the circle of prisoners being executed in the background, while women and children flee their homes as the militia line crumbles in the foreground. Although Joseph Brant, shown here holding a tomahawk and musket, was not present, popular accounts claimed he was. (*Library of Congress*)

and their Indian allies did not try to storm the remaining forts that night, they would renew the attack in the morning. With the glow of burning buildings visible upriver, there was a sense of dread about the morrow.

In the Wyoming Valley, any observance of the second anniversary of the Independence of the United States of America on July 4, 1778, had to be tempered with the realization of disaster. July 3 had been a costly day for American Patriots. Ranger McGinnis recorded that of the Rebel force that attacked him and his comrades at Wintermute's field that he estimated at 450 men, only about forty-five survived and were captured. According to his account, British casualties included only two Tories wounded, one of them mortally, and one Indian killed.[33] In his report of the operation, Major John Butler wrote that between 300 and 400 Americans had been engaged, and boasted that his Rangers and Indian allies took 227 scalps and only five prisoners. The Tory major listed his own losses as one Indian and two rangers killed, and eight Indians wounded.[34] Some surviving militiamen, however, reported to have witnessed the warriors and Tories, in the manner typical of the Indian way of fighting, carrying as many as eighty bodies of their fallen comrades into the swamp to be hidden from the Americans. Regardless of how one counts the corpses, it was an overwhelming Indian and Tory victory.

Chapter 7

THE WHOLE COUNTRY MAY MEET THE SAME FATE

E ARLY in the morning on July 4, Major John Butler sent a detachment of rangers, accompanied by some Indians, across to the east bank of the Susquehanna River to demand the surrender of the American militia in Pittston. With no hope of relief or reinforcement, Captain Blanchard could see no alternative but to submit. He signed the articles of capitulation for the "three forts at Lacuwanack," or Pittston Fort, Rosecrans Blockhouse, and another blockhouse he called Brown's Fort. The terms required the commander of each to surrender his post, and deliver up all arms, ammunition, and stores they contained. In return, Major Butler promised to preserve the lives of all the men, women, and children in the township, provided they all gathered in the forts where Provincial officers could see to their safety. To identify which inhabitants were now under the king's protection, Indian warriors marked the captured settlers' faces with black paint, and instructed them to carry white flags if they had to travel outside the limits of the town. In this manner the Americans were told that other Tories or Indians would know that they had surrendered, and so they would not be harmed. As soon as the settlers complied, the Indians and rangers began demolishing the blockhouses and stockade fences and pillaging the homes of valuables and other belongings.

At about eight o'clock in the morning, Major Butler sent a flag party to deliver a message to Colonel Dennison requesting to meet him at the smoldering ruins of Wintermute's Fort, where they would discuss the terms of surrender. Having no options available, Colonel Dennison, accompanied by Obadiah Gore, Sr., and Dr. Lemuel Gustin, immediately assented. The two opposing commanders opened the negotiations with a discussion of the situation. Butler later reported that Dennison revealed the American losses as "one colonel, two majors, seven captains, thirteen lieutenants, eleven ensigns, and 268 privates."[1] Dennison and the legation from Wyoming then listened as Butler dictated his terms. He told them he would accept their surrender, immediately parole the militia, and promised not harm the civilians on the condition that all Continental officers and soldiers in the valley, particularly Lieutenant Colonel

Zebulon Butler, were delivered up as prisoners of war. Dennison was also to surrender any stores of ammunition or supplies belonging to the "Rebel government." Not wishing to condemn the Continentals to confinement at Niagara at best, or immediate torture and summary execution at worst, Dennison requested some time to discuss the terms with his other officers before giving an answer. Major Butler agreed on the promise that the parties met again at one o'clock that afternoon.

As soon as he and his companions returned to Forty Fort, Dennison hurried to Wilkes-Barre Fort to discuss the matter with Zebulon Butler. The two officers agreed that the only option was the surrender of the settlements on the British terms. They also agreed that before Dennison and Major John Butler reconvened the discussions, Zebulon Butler and the surviving men in Continental service, being those from Hewitt's company and the members of Spalding's who had arrived ahead of their comrades, should leave before the actual capitulation. In that way, Dennison would neither violate the conditions of surrender nor relinquish the Continentals to their fate. Lieutenant Colonel Butler assembled the fifteen to twenty remaining Continentals and ordered them to depart immediately for Shamokin. He told them that he would join them there after he took his wife and infant son to Fort Allen at Gnadenhutten on the Lehigh River. As the men prepared to leave, many of those who also had families in the valley saw to their evacuation. Butler then threw a feather mattress and a few possessions over his horse's back, and started over Wilkes-Barre Mountain. By nightfall, he and his family were twenty miles away. It is likely that Captain John Franklin received the message to leave as well. He and the small advanced detachment of his company were too little, too late, to contribute to the battle. By returning to the Salem and Huntington district, they could turn the thirty men of their company back toward home, and spare them from being included in the capitulation.

Meanwhile, the bulk of Captain Spalding's company, still twenty-seven miles away, met Ensign Matthias Hollenback. The officer, riding with some companions, had left Wyoming the previous day, July 3, carrying messages about the situation and pleas for help from Colonel Dennison. After hearing the news of the battle, they pushed on in a forced march to within twelve miles of Wilkes-Barre before halting for the night at Bear Swamp. Spalding sent scouts to the crest of Wilkes-Barre Mountain, who returned to report that they could see smoke rising from burning buildings in the upper valley. As the Wyoming Independent Company drew closer to Wilkes-Barre, they encountered increasing numbers of fleeing inhabitants who provided more details about the disaster. After considering the sightings of his scouts and what was learned from the refugees, Spalding decided that his men could serve no useful purpose by continuing on to the ruined valley that was under the control of a superior enemy force. He ordered his company to countermarch thirty miles back toward Shupps, where they took the road for Fort Penn.

With the Continentals no longer available to be delivered into captivity as demanded, Colonel Dennison returned to Forty Fort with Gore and Dr. Gustin. They were joined by the Reverend Jacob Johnson and Judge Zerah Beach, who accompanied them back to Wintermute's for the second meeting with Major Butler. When the surrender talks resumed, Dennison informed Butler that all the Continentals had fled the valley, and he accepted the remaining terms. The two parties agreed to meet again to formally sign a written capitulation document at four o'clock that afternoon in Forty Fort. In the meantime, as a precaution, Major Butler told Dennison to destroy any stores of liquor, for he would not be able to control his Indian allies from massacring everyone in sight if they discovered it and succumbed to its influence.[2] When Dennison and the rest of his surrender legation returned to Forty Fort, he immediately ordered the seven barrels of whiskey to be rolled to the river, the heads knocked in, and the contents dumped into the water. Next, Dennison ordered his officers to have the defenders ground their arms—lay their weapons down—on the fort's parade, no matter how painful it was to them, and open the gates to await the victorious enemy's arrival.

At four o'clock, Butler's forces were seen approaching in two parallel columns. The rangers, marching in a column of four files as one division behind Major Butler, followed by the "irregular" division of Loyalist volunteers, were on the left. The Indians, also in four files, followed behind Queen Esther and Sayenqueraghta on the right. Colonel Dennison went out to meet them, and according to the military convention of the day, escorted the victorious enemy officers into the post they were about to surrender. As they marched into the stockade, the rangers and Indians halted on either side of the grounded American weapons. When a few rangers began picking them up, Butler ordered his men to lay the weapons back down on the ground. He then turned to the Indians, and told his allies the arms were the gift of Colonel Dennison to them, hoping this would "console" them for the loss of any warriors in the previous day's battle. The warriors immediately began to inspect and take the arms into possession.

Finally, it was time to settle the disagreeable business at hand. Colonel Dennison, Dr. Gustin, and Judge Beach adjourned to a cabin, followed by Major Butler, Captain Caldwell of the rangers, Captain Johnston of the Indian Department, Sayenqueraghta, Garganwahgah, and a Delaware chief. As Judge

Beach wrote, the British commander dictated the "Capitulation made & completed between Major Butler on behalf of His Majesty King George 3rd and Colo. Nathan Deniston of the United States of America." The documents were reviewed, agreed upon, and signed. The terms required any Continental stores be surrendered, and "the inhabitants of the Settlement to lay down their Arms, and their Garrisons be demolished." The surrender encompassed all those at posts in the valley that had not already executed separate capitulations. The defeated Americans were allowed to occupy their farms peacefully and their lives "preserved entire and unhurt," and Major Butler further promised to "use his utmost influence" with the Indians to safeguard their private property. In return, "the properties taken from the People called Tories up the River" were be restored to their owners, and the Patriots were to allow them to remain in "possession of their Farms, and unmolested in a Free Trade."[3] All prisoners, except for any Continental soldiers, were to be immediately exchanged. The two Indians jailed for being spies the previous month were freed in return for one Samuel Finch, an American taken prisoner on July 2.

With the formal surrender executed, the militiamen were to be immediately paroled on condition they did not take arms again "in the present contest."[4] Tradition holds that as the American prisoners marched out to sign their paroles, Butler recognized one as a British deserter from Fort Niagara named Malcolm Boyd, who had since become a sergeant in the American militia. Despite Boyd's protests that he should be treated as a prisoner of war, Butler had him marched out of the stockade to a nearby tree where he was summarily executed by a volley of musketry.[5]

The terms were the best the Americans could have expected under the circumstances. Except for preventing the wholesale massacre of the inhabitants, however, the terms were almost immediately violated. The Provincial soldiers, Loyalist volunteers, and most of the Indians then withdrew to the area of the Wintermute property, except for about thirty warriors remaining in Forty Fort. Despite his pledge to safeguard the homes and possessions of the valley's inhabitants, as Butler's column marched along, every house along their route was ransacked and set on fire. Major Butler and the chiefs were powerless, if not also unwilling, to bring them back under control. Butler then promised Dennison he would honor any claim for damage to full value, knowing that any such accounting would be difficult, if not impossible.

The next day, Sunday, July 5, although they honored the pledge not to further harm women and children, Provincial rangers as well as the Indians began violating Major Butler's other assurances in earnest. After one detachment crossed the river, they found the town of Wilkes-Barre and its fort abandoned.

They proceeded to plunder and burn almost every house and destroy all the crops. Back on the west bank, roving bands of five to ten Indians or Loyalist "irregular" volunteers and detachments of rangers plundered and burned the forts, houses, barns, mills, outbuildings, and destroyed bridges and other improvements in the valley. While the barracks remained undamaged for housing the valley's refugees, the stockade walls at Forty Fort were demolished. The raiders laid waste to grain and other crops in the fields of every farm, and set fire to all that would burn. Parties of rangers were sent to the homes of the Whig inhabitants for "a total confiscation of all their property, such as oxen, cows, horses, hogs, sheep and every other thing of that kind." When the recently paroled Wyoming militiamen asked that their property be respected, as they had understood Major Butler's terms had promised, the rangers curtly told them to be content "that your lives are still spared and that you have not shared the same fate with your seditious brethren."[6]

Yankee families fled the Wyoming Valley in droves. Taking what belongings they could put in a wagon or oxcart or onto horseback, or load into boats or rafts at the river's banks or ferry landings, the fugitives headed across the mountains by the "Lower Road" for Fort Penn in Lower Smithfield Township and Easton, the "Upper Road" through Solomon's Gap and eventually toward New York and Connecticut, or downriver toward Sunbury, Catawissa, and other destinations in Northampton County, Pennsylvania. There were stories of families, once they were away from the settlements, being stopped, and their baggage plundered by Indians. The less fortunate saw their men killed and scalped, and women and children being taken captive. As the refugees fled, the panic spread, and the inhabitants of settlements along the river below Wyoming began to abandon their homes in what became known as the "Great Runaway."

On July 6, an express arrived from Fort Niagara with a message for Major Butler. After reading its contents, Butler called his officers and the Indian chiefs to a conference where he instructed them to complete the destruction of the settlement and to prepare for their withdrawal in two days. Those Americans still being held prisoner at the ruins of Forty, Wintermute's, Jenkins', and Pittston Forts were finally given permission to leave.

Butler ordered his drummers to beat the "General" to call his troops together early on the morning of July 8, and the rangers were soon assembled in marching order. The column moved off, the rangers marching behind their regimental standard, followed by the Loyalist volunteers who had joined them along the way, and the inhabitants of Wyoming Valley that rallied to the invaders. Some were going to Niagara to enlist in the Butler's Rangers and other Provincial forces and take up arms for their king, while others were relocating to where they could live under the protection of the Crown and let others do the fighting. The Seneca warriors came next, followed by the "miscellaneous Indians," then the women, and finally the captured horses and cattle, and those detailed as drovers. The column also included those prisoners who were not exchanged as specified in the articles of capitulation. Among these unfortunates were John Gardner and Daniel Carr who were captured at Sutton's Creek on June 30. There was also a Samuel Carey, a prisoner who, instead of being tortured and executed, had been quickly "adopted" by an Indian family following his capture on July 3 to take the place of a son who was killed in battle.

Major Butler halted his column for the night as it drew opposite Scovell's Island and the mouth of the Lackawanna River. As his men prepared to encamp and cook their evening meal, Butler sat down to complete a detailed report of the expedition. In the message, Butler proudly proclaimed the success of "this incursion" by reporting that his forces had "taken and destroyed eight pallisaded Forts, and burned about 1000 Dwelling Houses, all their Mills &c., . . . [as well as] killed and drove off about 1000 head of horned Cattle, and sheep and swine in great numbers." Butler went on to say, "But what gives us the sincerest satisfaction is, that I can ... assure you that in the destruction of this settlement not a single person has been hurt of the Inhabitants, but such as were in arms, to those indeed the Indians gave no Quarter." Certainly, the description "but such as were under arms" did not apply to those who were attacked at Sutton's Creek, or with the battle lost, those who surrendered on July 3. Nor did it include the male members of families who were stopped while attempting to flee the ravages of the Tories and Indians. Butler was not hesitant to express his pride for the members of his command. He told Lieutenant Colonel Mason Bolton, "I have also the pleasure to inform you that the Officers and Rangers behaved during this short action highly to my satisfaction, and have always supported themselves through hunger, and fatague with great chearfullness."[7] If Ranger McGinnis' account is any indication, the members of the Indian Department and Butler's Rangers also felt they had acquitted themselves well in the action. He wrote, "Every man behaved with uncommon bravery. They vied for each other for glory to se[e] who should do most in supporting the injured cause of our excellent constitution."[8]

Butler concluded his report by revealing his plan to raid the settlements at Schoharie or Minisink on his next foray, "both of which abound in Corn, and Cattle the destruction of which cannot fail of greatly distressing the Rebels." He also noted concern that the expresses he had sent to Generals Howe and Clinton had not returned. Increasing the chances that at least one copy would get through, he had sent ten copies with ten messengers by ten different routes, and was "in hopes that some of them will be able to make their way to them and return."[9] The news that the main British army in North America had evacuated Philadelphia and was heading for New York City, and that its rear guard had been engaged by a much-improved and more confident Continental Army at Monmouth Courthouse on June 28, had yet been received. Butler enclosed copies of the articles of capitulation for the surrenders of the Patriot forces in Wyoming Valley, and gave Lieutenant John Hare the report with instructions to ride ahead on one of the captured horses, and deliver it to Lieutenant Colonel Bolton at Fort Niagara.

The next morning, July 9, Hare began his ride to Fort Niagara, while the rangers and Indians prepared to continue their march back toward Tioga. Butler sought to further damage the American war effort and sent detachments of rangers and Indian war parties to "harass the adjacent country, and prevent them [American farmers] from getting in their harvest." Because the British and Indians were experiencing supply problems, Butler's forces were traveling light and therefore plundered farms and settlements, seizing what provisions they needed along the way, while creating havoc in the backcountry. To deceive the Americans as to which direction they were heading or where they would strike next, Butler "sent a party of men to the Delaware [River] to destroy a small settlement there, and to bring off prisoners."[10]

When the rangers and Indians arrived back at Tioga, Major Butler was struck by a violent attack of fever and ague accompanied by "rheumatism in the head." As soon as he was well enough to travel, he left for Fort Niagara, and placed Captain Caldwell in temporary command. Butler instructed Caldwell to proceed on to Onaquaga, where he was to inform the friendly Indians there that the rangers would help them defend their villages along the border of their country. He also instructed the captain to send out ranger patrols, as well as officers and rangers with Indian war parties, to scout and harass the Americans as much as possible. He encouraged Caldwell to conduct offensive operations within the capability of the force at his disposal, and "to burn and destroy everything you possibly can" to prevent the Americans from harvesting grain, and divert the attention and dissipate the strength of the Continental Army so as to assist the main British army under General Henry Clinton's command.[11]

Even before Butler's Rangers and their Indian allies evacuated the Wyoming Valley, stories were pouring in from express riders going from town to town, and from one military headquarters to another, and by word of mouth. The citizens of Goshen, New York, heard "the most disagreeable news of Wyoming on the River Sisquehanah being in possession of our most Inveterate Enemy" on July 5. As their town lay on the road to the Susquehanna, they were concerned that

"Butler and Brandt" had invaded the area with a large body of troops. (Brant, of course, was not at Wyoming Valley, although many rumors placed him there.) Having defeated the Wyoming Valley's militia in battle and "reduced them to the necessity of surrendering themselves and the whole Settlement Prisoners of War," the people of Goshen feared that their town was the next target.[12] Rumors and reports abounded that Joseph Brant was in the area with a force of Loyalists and Indians to execute the same kind of destruction that had been unleashed at Wyoming. The region was so alarmed that there were reports that people from Cochecton and Minisink were preparing to flee for safer regions unless action was taken to better secure the frontier. These pleas were echoed by the Minisink Committee of Safety, who informed New York Governor George Clinton that in their neighborhood there was the "greatest confusion," which prompted them to call out two regiments of the county's militia until the emergency abated.

Governor George Clinton replied to the local committees, and reminded them he had previously ordered out one fourth of two companies as a "Guard for the frontier" and to gain intelligence on the enemy in response to a similar alarm in June. He expressed that those troops would have been more useful closer to home. Clinton ordered Lieutenant Colonel Jacob Newkirk to strengthen the guards in Ulster and Orange counties by calling out detachments from other frontier companies. But Clinton hesitated to strengthen the border posts to the point of weakening the defenses along the rivers. Unless they could determine where Butler or Brant and their men would strike next, such action could make supplying the frontier posts more difficult without affording the settlements any added security.[13]

To add to the chaos, the rumors about Brant and his men being in the Minisink area were true. Brant led a force of 250 Indians and Tories toward the Delaware River settlements. They marched without being detected along the Mongaup River to within striking distance of the lucrative targets, and halted. Brant had originally planned to divide his force into small parties, and assigned each to certain parts of the settlement where they would strike, according to the report of an American militia captain named Cuddeback, and "execute their villainy at the same time." But when they reached the mouth of the river, Brant learned from scouts and area Loyalists that a large body of militia had been called out and gathered at Minisink, presenting an obstacle he wished not to challenge. Instead of proceeding any further down the Delaware, the Mohawk-Tory leader changed his plan and turned his wrath on the smaller, less-defended Lackawack settlements. They struck on July 8, the same day that Butler and his rangers and Indian allies left Wyoming. According to Captain Cuddeback, who led five militiamen on a scout, Brant's raiders murdered a number of inhabitants of Lackawack, took others prisoner, confiscated sheep, hogs, and other cattle.[14]

Receiving word that militia from the north had mustered in preparation for the long-anticipated attack against Unadilla, Brant decided to return to safeguard his bases. He immediately sent a number of his Loyalist volunteers and a band of warriors under the leadership of a Mohawk chief known as Captain Jacobs hurrying off to help defend the Unadilla Tory stronghold. Brant planned to follow with the rest of his command as soon as he was sure Onaquaga was secure.

Unknown to the British, Congress had directed George Washington to detach two veteran regiments of Continentals from the Main Army, Lieutenant Colonel Commandant John Gibson's 13th Virginia, and the 8th Pennsylvania commanded by Colonel Daniel Brodhead, for service on the Ohio. These regiments were to report to Brigadier General Lachlan McIntosh, who had replaced General Edward Hand as commander of the Western Department, and prepare to support a proposed expedition against Detroit. The 13th Virginia had been detached at the end of May and was making its way to Fort Pitt. The 8th Pennsylvania Regiment was detached, and, preceded by an advance party that would prepare the regiment's quarters at Fort Pitt, the main body left Valley Forge to join the Western Department at the end of June.[15] When they were between Lancaster and Carlisle, Colonel Brodhead received news of the attack on Wyoming and orders to march up the Susquehanna to drive the enemy away and encourage the settlers to return to their farms and homes. Leaving the regimental baggage under guard at Carlisle, the rest of the 340-man regiment marched in light order on July 12 toward Sunbury, where a garrison of 100 men held Fort Augusta. From there, Colonel Brodhead sent company-sized patrols up both branches of the Susquehanna, concentrating on the West Branch, searching for signs of the approaching enemy.

Although a few small parties of Indians ranged through the area to harass the remaining settlers and delay any troops on the way to the endangered settlements, the 8th Pennsylvania's commander found that it was too late to assist the inhabitants any further. Brodhead's regiment swept the area for any remaining Indians, guarded the roads, and posted detachments at the principal settlements to encourage the farmers to return and prepare their fields for harvest. Strong detachments ranged as far as Penn's Valley and were posted at Potter's Fort, the property of Brigadier General James Potter, commander of the Pennsylvania militia. In a report dated July 24, Brodhead wrote that "Great numbers of the inhabitants returned upon my approach, and are now collected in large bodies, reaping their harvests."[16]

At the end of July, Colonel Thomas Hartley, commander of an Additional Continental Regiment, was ordered to move his troops to Fort Augusta at Sunbury, downstream on the Susquehanna from Wyoming, to replace Colonel Brodhead's troops as they departed for duty on the Ohio. Hartley's force was to be joined at Sunbury by more than 1,000 Pennsylvania militiamen, but when he arrived on August 1, few of the promised troops had assembled. He established a supply magazine in that town by converting and fortifying the residence of William Maclay with a stockade. Then to augment his reduced-strength regiment, Hartley called on Pennsylvania Brigadier General Philip de Haas for the assistance of the local militia. Once relieved, Colonel Brodhead and the 8th Pennsylvania returned down the Susquehanna to Carlisle, and arrived on August 6 to recover their baggage. After a week's rest, they resumed the march to Fort Pitt.[17]

As Brodhead's regiment was nearing Carlisle, on August 4, Lieutenant Colonel Zebulon Butler was ordered to lead the 112 Continentals he had gathered at Fort Allen, Spalding's company, and the remnants of Hewitt's company, back to the ruins of Wilkes-Barre Fort. After they arrived, the troops started building a new post they named "Fort Wyoming" in memory of those who fell defending the valley in July. Over the next several weeks, a number of the refugee settlers returned to begin fixing or replacing their ruined homes. The local militia began to reconstitute, and Butler's force started to grow. Indian warriors were still in the area, and continued to kill and take a number of Wyoming Valley inhabitants captive in small-scale raids and ambushes for some time.

Colonel Hartley soon established a line of posts between Fishing Creek and Great Island. Other detachments garrisoned Fort Jenkins at Brier Creek on the North Branch, Rossley's Mills at the forks of the Chillisquaque, and at Fort Muncy on the West Branch. The presence of the soldiers reassured the local populace. It was estimated that about 80 percent of the inhabitants had fled their homes in the Great Runaway, but as the soldiers became more evident, many refugees started to return. As the garrisons improved their installations and began patrolling, Hartley and de Haas inspected and evaluated the effectiveness of the defenses. Hartley was charged with protecting a frontier stretching more than 150 miles from the West Branch of the Susquehanna to the Allegheny Rivers with barely more than 200 men. This was an impossible defensive task, and he realized that an offensive move offered the best chances for providing some security along the frontier. If nothing else, an offensive action could divert the enemy's attention from the vulnerable settlements, and possibly cause the Indians to curtail raiding in order to guard their own villages.[18]

The first hand stories brought by the Wyoming Valley refugees, undoubtedly embellished with every retelling, soon appeared in print, and were circulated in newspapers and on broadsides throughout the country. The *New York Gazette* carried one such account with the dateline of Poughkeepsie, July 20, 1778, and it was reprinted verbatim by the *Pennsylvania Packet* on July 30, the *Boston Gazette* on August 3, and others in the following weeks. The account related that Major John Butler, incorrectly identified as a cousin of Lieutenant Colonel Zebulon Butler, attacked the Wyoming settlement with a "whole body of the enemy, consisting it is supposed of near 1600 . . . about 300 of whom were thought to be Indians, under their own Chiefs, the rest Tories painted like them." It went on to describe the skirmish at Sutton's Creek on June 30, the capture of Jenkins' Fort the next day, and the ambush and destruction of the militia on July 3. It accurately related that Lieutenant Colonel Zebulon Butler escaped from the battlefield on that day, but portrayed the surviving militia, under Colonel Dennison's command, as holding "Fort Kingston" while Indians and Tories invested the post and maintained "a continuous fire" until capitulating on Sunday, July 5. It was reliable in the reports of the burning and looting of houses, barns, and other buildings, the ruining of crops, and driving away or the killing of cattle, but the account diverged from the truth by reporting the Indians had wantonly massacred women and children. The story was made even more sensational when it reported that seventy Continental soldiers were "inhumanly butchered" after surrendering "Wilkesborough." If that were not grisly enough, the article went on to say after "shutting up the rest [of the Continentals] with the women and children, in the houses, they [the Indians and Tories] set fire to them, and they perished together in the flames."[19]

With the inaccurate report of battle details and exaggerated tales of destruction which followed, the incident became known as the "Wyoming Massacre." The accounts of the merciless slaughter of Americans who had either been captured or were in the act of surrendering could rightly be termed a "massacre." The destruction and plundering of homes, slaughter or driving away of cattle, and laying waste to farms and food supplies were enough to justify retribution on the "savage" enemy. The wanton killing of civilian men "not under arms," and the murder of women and children on a large scale, however, did not actually happen. But the stories in the biased Whig press were believed, which helped to heighten the panic caused by the incursions of Brant and Butler, and were effectively used to urge that action be taken by the Continental Army.

Although they lost the tactical engagement, the Americans won the propaganda battle. Already, the public outcry that something be done was heard and answered. Delegate Roger Sherman wrote to Governor Trumbull that

"Congress sent two Regiments of Continental troops with some Militia to repel the enemy."[20] Judge John Cleves Symmes of Minisink wrote the commander in chief an account of the "massacre." General Washington responded on July 10 to say, "I am extremely sorry to hear of the melancholy stroke that has fallen upon the Wioming settlement." In an effort to show that the army was contemplating some kind of response, although it was beset by many such requests, the general explained that he "Lately ordered a considerable detachment from the Main Army to Fort Pitt, to quell Indian disturbances in that quarter, and due to losses at Monmouth can not spare more, but in the case of the greatest emergency." Washington's opinion was that the greatest danger in the area had passed now that the enemy had "struck the meditated Blow they will retire and not attempt to penetrate the Country" any further. He advised the governors, Committees of Safety, and militia commanders to remain active in order to gain intelligence of the enemy numbers, situation, and intentions. If the enemy forces persisted in their attacks, however, he reminded them that "all possible opposition should be given by the Militia" first, before seeking the assistance of the army.[21]

For now, however, there were more immediate concerns. Although the New York forces had been authorized to attack Unadilla the month before, and the Indian commissioners had been consulted, no commander for the expedition had been appointed. Brigadier General Abraham Ten Broeck wrote to Governor George Clinton on July 11 that if Lieutenant Colonel Marinus Willett of the 3rd New York Regiment of the Continental Army did not accept the offer of the command, he would appoint a militia officer to the position. To complicate matters, the thirty-day terms of the militia already called out had only twelve days remaining, and Ten Broeck feared that his officers would not be able to muster sufficient replacements in time to carry out the offensive. Already, there were complaints by the militia about being called out in a critical phase of the growing season.[22]

In the capital at Poughkeepsie, Governor Clinton was receiving reports from his militia commanders and Continental officers operating in New York that more trouble was expected. For example, a letter addressed to inhabitants of Kingston, allegedly by "Order of the Anandago [Onondaga] Indians" as a warning, contained accounts of the "Hostile Designs of the Indians and Tories" on the western frontiers. Colonel Peter Gansevoort, the commander of the 3rd New York Regiment of Continentals and Fort Schuyler, reported that his intelligence indicated that "a number of Regular Troops from Canada & Indians were assembled at Oswegatchie" and were preparing to attack his post. He believed that the increasing number of Indian attacks against the frontier settlements were planned so as to cut off supplies and keep the militia from reinforcing the fort.[23] Gansevoort sent Lieutenant Thomas McClellan in command of a detachment from Fort Schuyler to raid Fort Oswego and disrupt the enemy's preparations. McClellan's detachment returned after destroying the buildings at the unoccupied British post on July 10, 1778. If the enemy intended to use Fort Oswego as a base of operations in a new campaign, they would first have to rebuild it. Despite this success, Gansevoort's regiment saw little action, except for occasional attacks or ambushes of soldiers on fatigue details and other work parties outside the Fort Schuyler stockade.[24] The tactical situation had changed since the siege of 1777 and the failure of Burgoyne's invasion, so that Indian war parties and Tory raiding patrols from Six Nations' territory bypassed Fort Schuyler on their way to attack the Whig settlements in the Mohawk Valley.[25]

Clinton reminded the militia commanders of the need to remain vigilant, and with so many drafted soldiers serving temporarily with Washington's army in the strategic Hudson Highlands, he did not wish to call out more militia unless it was absolutely necessary. With harvest time approaching, the governor advised the regimental commanders to use their discretion in dealing with invaders. Trying to make the most of those already on duty, Clinton recommended regimental commanders in Ulster County, whenever possible, send strong detachments from the two regiments covering Minisink and Peenpack to gather and share intelligence, being always ready to cooperate, while the third increased the guards posted on the frontier by ordering out "the greater part of the Militia." If the situation dictated, Clinton urged local commanders to take actions they deemed appropriate without waiting for official authorization.[26]

Late on the morning of Saturday, July 18, 1778, Tryon County once again "experienced the Cruelty of a restless Enemy."[27] Without warning, Captain Joseph Brant and his forces descended on the prosperous farming settlement of Springfield, on the shore of Otsego Lake.[28] Houses, barns, wagons, plows, and even haycocks in the meadows were burned. After his men had killed eight male inhabitants, Brant, in an act of mercy that contributed to his reputation for being a "noble" enemy, put all the women and children in the one building that he did not set on fire. Although such acts were typical and earned him a great deal of respect from his foes, Brant did not hesitate to make widows and orphans of the same innocents by killing their men and adolescent boys, regardless of whether they were armed or offered resistance. Brant's men also rounded up as many as 200 horses and horned cattle, loaded them with as much plunder as they could carry, and drove them for their own use at Onaquaga and Unadilla, along with fourteen male inhabitants that were taken prisoner and marched into captivity when they withdrew.[29]

An exhausted rider delivered a frantic express to Colonel Jacob Klock with a call for help from Springfield. Klock immediately called the militia out to meet the enemy as an urgent message for help arrived from Colonel Bellinger requesting assistance, saying the enemy was burning houses in the neighborhood of German Flats as well. Klock ordered five companies to muster, and marched with the rest of his battalion toward Andrustown (near present-day Jordanville, New York) after sending word to Colonel Bellinger to move his battalion there in an effort to have the converging forces intercept the enemy. While Klock's battalion was still on the march toward Andrustown, however, he learned that the foe had already departed. As he still believed a "strong party of the Enemy was left to do mischief" in the area, he had his men "scour the woods" to flush them out of hiding. It was the same old story. As soon the militia from German Flats was on the march, some of Brant's men entered the German Flats settlements, killing one and capturing two men and inflicting relatively minor damage there.[30]

Meanwhile, the militia in the Cherry Valley vicinity mustered. As soon as he heard the musketry from nearby Springfield, Lieutenant Colonel Jacob Ford sounded the alarm for the militia of the district to gather near the meetinghouse. As the men began to assemble, he sent reconnoitering parties, and heard additional firing from the direction of Springfield. When his scouts returned, they reported that the town was in flames and the number of dead was unknown. Instead of risking a defeat in an ambush by hastily marching to the aid of the neighboring settlement, Ford kept the eighty men who had assembled ready to defend Cherry Valley, should the enemy attack there next. To prevent being surprised, he prudently kept patrols out constantly looking for signs of the enemy's approach. One of Ford's scouting parties returned late in the day and reported that the entire settlement of Springfield had been reduced to ashes.[31] The harried Ford then, like the officers in other close-by communities, sent an urgent call for reinforcements to Colonel Klock, with the news that Springfield and Andrustown were "Entirely destroyed by Indians and Tories, the houses Set on fire, several men killed and Scalped, [but] the Fate of the women is not known."[32]

Hoping that the additional militia and a company of Tryon County rangers said to be on the way would arrive by morning, Ford posted his men in a line of defensive "picquets" around the settlement's meetinghouse, where the women and children were sheltered, along with the few household effects they were able to carry from their homes. As he waited for the reinforcements, he lamented that, in its present posture, his small force was, at best, only "bait" for the enemy. Later, in his report to General Ten Broeck, he acknowledged that the post was vital for defending that part of the Mohawk Valley, but recommended a garrison of 500 Continentals to hold it properly.[33] The next day, Ford felt a little bolder. Having received some reinforcement and knowing Klock's and Bellinger's detachments were surely close at hand, he sent a scout to gain intelligence on the strength and intentions of the enemy, and possibly bring on a battle.[34]

But with Brant's departure the danger temporarily subsided. The militia commanders and Governor Clinton were now in agreement that the militia alone could not defend the Tryon County settlements. General Ten Broeck cited his apprehension at calling the militia out at this time, and urged the governor to seek the stationing of Continental troops in the area.[35] "If supporting troops do not come soon," Ten Broeck wrote, "I dread the consequences—it is now harvest and it is with the most difficulty I get the militia to turn out," no matter how dire the circumstances.[36] Colonel Klock reminded the governor and general that the Continental troops that had once been stationed in Tryon County were reassigned to the Hudson Highlands after Burgoyne's defeat. The militia sent out earlier under the command of Colonel Peter R. Livingston on a thirty-day tour of duty was on its march home as its term was expiring, so the inhabitants of the area were "Entirely Destitute of any Assistance." He repeated the plea heard so often through the difficult spring and summer of 1778 that the frontier was "too Extensive to be Guarded by the Militia alone," and if "no Continental Troops or a Standing Force can be Continued," he feared that "the whole Country may meet the same fate."[37]

Two days after the attacks on Springfield and Andrustown, the Oneidas at Oriska sent Indian Commissioner Brigadier General Philip Schuyler a message and wampum belt with news that the enemy had destroyed Springfield and Henderson's Purchase (Andrustown), and expected German Flats would be next, followed by Canajoharie and other villages in the vicinity. The report was particularly disturbing since the "finest Grain Country in the State is on the point of being ruined" because there were no Continental troops available. Schuyler recommended that if any were sent, they should immediately be used to save part of the settlements and fine crops of wheat by assuming security of the area from the militia so the embattled farmers could tend their fields.[38]

When Clinton passed along the "disagreeable account of Springfield and Andreastown [Andrustown] on the Western Frontier of Tryon County being destroyed by the enemy" to Washington, he added his apprehension that the enemy would lay waste to fertile country, which the militia could not prevent, despite their "utmost Exertions."[39]

Washington finally relented in his stance that regulars not be dispatched in response to Indian and Tory raids. On the same day that Captain Joseph Brant

Although sometimes described as the Wyoming Massacre, this period illustration is more accurate as a portrayal of the aftermath of the attack on Cherry Valley in November 1778. (*New York Public Library*)

and his Loyalist volunteers and Indians descended on Springfield, July 18, 1778, the General ordered a sizable detachment of troops from the Main Army to New York under the command of Lieutenant Colonel William Butler, "an enterprising good Officer, and well acquainted with the savage mode of warfare."[40] The detachment included Butler's own 4th Pennsylvania, a hard-fighting veteran regiment with an excellent combat record, and the Rifle Corps commanded by Captain Commandant Thomas Posey. Posey's unit represented the "remains" of the famous corps of riflemen that was commanded by Colonel Daniel Morgan and had distinguished itself in the Saratoga campaign of 1777. Originally a provisional battalion composed of men selected from among the best marksmen and Indian fighters in the Continental Army, all but the companies of Captains James Parr, mostly Pennsylvanians, and Gabriel Long, mostly Virginians, were disbanded and the men transferred back to their original units following the Battle of Monmouth. General Washington explained that the long-requested Continentals were sent to help guard frontiers from the relentless attacks by Indians and Loyalists. Washington expected Stark to employ them to "cooperate with the Militia and to check the Indians if possible."[41] Washington ordered Lieutenant Colonel Butler's Regiment to post at Wawarsink, instead of at Minisink on the Delaware as had originally been planned, to put them closer to the endangered border. This too was changed, and the regiment was ordered to only halt briefly in Wawarsink, and then march to the frontier of New York to await further orders.[42] As few of the promised Hampshire or Berkshire militia had arrived at Albany to augment the local brigade, Clinton asked Washington to have Butler's regiment "hasten the march," and proceed north to Schoharie without halting, as intelligence reports indicated the next enemy attack was likely aimed there.[43]

Governor Clinton wasted no time in informing his militia commanders in the frontier districts that a regiment of Continentals was joining them on the frontier. Clinton reminded his commanders that the presence of the regulars did not relieve the militia from its responsibility of guarding their communities or the frontier posts. He emphasized the need to comply with orders for calling out and keeping a "Respectable Force of the Militia" constantly on the frontier to assume their fair share of duty for the safety of the inhabitants. He reminded the militia commanders that with the border stretching from "Virginia Northward," the Continentals could not guard it even if they were not contending with the main British army.

It now seemed that at long last, American forces in New York would be able to take the fight to the enemy in their own bases of Unadilla and Onaquaga, and clear out the nests of Loyalists that aided and abetted the enemy from the safety of the frontier counties. The upcoming campaign had to succeed, and Clinton urged all commanders to "exert ourselves with double Vigour" to "exterminate those perfidious Villains who so wantonly disturb the Peace of our Frontiers." He called for a meeting of officers of the militia of Ulster and Orange counties to make the necessary defensive arrangements, and asked General Ten Broeck to do likewise in his brigade in Albany County. As with the regiments covering Minisink and Peenpack, to coordinate their efforts, he ordered the commanders of militia "guards" detachments on the frontier and south of Schoharie to communicate, share intelligence on movements of the enemy, and cooperate with Ten Broeck for the common defense of the frontier.[44]

Meanwhile, to the north, the desperation of the frontier inhabitants of New York was reflected in the appeal the militia officers and Committee of Safety members of German Flats made to Governor Clinton on July 22. Colonel Peter Bellinger explained, "If we can not get assistance, we can expect to Starve, as we are oblig'd to keep all in a body, to Protect ourselves our Wives & Families, not knowing how soon we may be attacked. By which means we have not time to get in our harvest." The previous year's harvest had been bad, owing in large measure to the emergency created by Burgoyne's invasion, and much of what had been salvaged had spoiled. Most people in German Flats feared that the harvest for 1778 would prove a great deal worse, with no one being able to bring in the precious crops.[45]

The reports that the enemy was active near Schoharie continued. A scout of Tryon County rangers led by Captain John Harper reported on July 24 that enemy strength at Unadilla was estimated at 3,000 men. Another patrol sighted a party of four Indians reconnoitering within fourteen miles of Schoharie, and reported that the enemy scouts spent the night at the residence of a known Tory named Christopher Service (or Servos), who was described as "a great enemy of the Country." Colonel Peter Vrooman, commander of the militia at Schoharie, appealed to Brigadier General Abraham Ten Broeck for reinforcements, and whatever assistance in men, field pieces, and ammunition could be obtained from the Continental authority, Brigadier General Stark.[46]

As the month drew to a close, General Ten Broeck learned that Indians and Tories were still active around Schoharie and Cobleskill in undetermined strength. When the inhabitants of the latter settlement left the shelter of Schoharie to return to their destroyed homes and gather their wheat, they found evidence that the enemy was still present. While the farmers were in their fields, a number of them heard shooting and sounds like hogs being slaughtered by Indians, they believed. Alarmed, they all returned to Schoharie by midnight. A militia officer quickly formed a scout and sent them to investigate, but the patrol returned to report that any remaining cattle were either killed or driven off by the enemy. Lieutenant Dietz Rainschers led another scout in the direction of Harpersfield. As the patrol returned toward Schoharie, they were fired on and pursued by a larger force of Indians. The scouts scattered in order to make their escape, and returned to Schoharie to sound the alarm. Major Baker requested reinforcements from Ten Broeck, because he felt an attack was imminent, and his command had "not men enough to stand and relieve Schohary" if attacked by a strong enemy force.[47]

As was the practice of field officers commanding detachments on active service and the end of their tours, Colonel Livingston submitted his report to the governor and brigade commander on the defenses in the western part of the state in late July. He explained that Continental troops needed to be posted without delay at Schoharie, Cherry Valley, German Flats, Stone Arabia, and Johnstown. Otherwise, those areas would be deserted and "the Granary of our Country be exposed to the Depredations of a merciless Banditti of Savages." He observed the wheat, pea, oat, and corn crops nearing harvest around those communities were "most extraordinary fine." He reported that while the posting of the 240 men of Colonel Alden's 6th Massachusetts Regiment near Cherry Valley was good, like numbers were required at all the posts mentioned, so that in an emergency they could cooperate. Ominously, scouts continued to report increased enemy activity in the area, and Continental and militia officers expected that a new series of attacks on one, if not more, of the posts was imminent. Livingston suggested, "There wants much a man of Spirit and prudence for a Brigadier General," referring to Stark, "as there seemed to be a lack of leadership among the militia."[48]

Not counting the men on furlough, detached duty, in the hospital, or on sick leave, when Lieutenant Colonel William Butler and his troops marched into Albany and reported to Brigadier General Stark at the end of July, the "Detachment of Rifle Men" reported its strength as 135 officers and men, and the 4th Pennsylvania as 190 of all ranks.[49] Butler then informed Stark of his command's supply requirements. His new superior had little to offer, which prompted Butler to complain, "The Rifle men have hardly a Shoe." When Butler showed him his instructions and suggested they plan an attack against Unadilla, Stark said "it was impossible to carry on Offensive Operations against the Enemy at present." He went on to explain that while Alden had just over 200 men at Cherry Valley, "it would be like pulling a Cat by the Tail to get out the Militia at this time." Butler felt that Stark's "Sentiments seem to differ widely" from Governor Clinton's.[50]

There were also professional jealousies at work. Butler expected to command the expedition against Unadilla, although Alden outranked him. When Stark ordered Butler to join with Alden's regiment at Cherry Valley, Butler complained to Washington that such a move "deprives me of the Honor your Excellency intended me in Command of the whole." To force a decision in his favor, the newly arrived commander of the 4th Pennsylvania Regiment asked Washington, "If your excellency thinks me worthy of the Command and impowers me to carry on Offensive measures against the Enemy I will do it at the Risque of my Honor & every thing I hold sacred. If I cannot be I will do my duty in the Command of my Detachment."[51]

Although not committing the Continentals to an attack on Unadilla right away, Stark believed Butler's troops could dampen the ardor of the Tryon County Loyalists and hearten the spirits of local Whigs. The aggressive Continental Line officer was anxious to get started on an operation, though, and sent off an advanced guard of fifty riflemen as soon as their weapons had been cleaned and repaired. The main body of Butler's force marched for Schoharie on the first day of August, and took one brass field piece and an "Iron 3 or 4 Pounder" with them, although there was no shot for the latter. Brigadier General Stark requested half of the Albany city militia and half of the company drawn from the area between the city and Patroon's Mills to march to Schoharie, knowing that the militia already posted there and at Cherry Valley had but two weeks of duty remaining before their terms expired. Ten Broeck planned a meeting with his regimental commanders to discuss what detachments from his brigade were to turn out for orders to "cooperate with Lieut. Col. Butler & be under his Direction to carry on Offensive Operations against the Enemy, & Cover the Frontier Inhabitants." The militia general informed Stark that he had 100 Albany County militia men already posted at Schoharie, had ordered out 200 more, and that Tryon County expected to turn out another 300, ready to support.[52]

When Lieutenant Colonel Butler arrived at Schoharie, he found that there were three forts erected by inhabitants for their protection on Lafayette's recommendation. Named the Upper, Middle, and Lower Forts, all were within four miles of each other. Butler established his headquarters at the Middle Fort, officially named Fort Defiance, the one he thought most likely to be attacked. He then sent a subaltern out in command of a small scouting party to reconnoiter the country and "make discoveries about the Enemy." After proceeding about twenty-five miles, they encountered one Christopher Service (or Servos), the "Noted Villain who had Constantly supply'd the Enemy with Necessaries," at his home. When Service resisted arrest and refused to surrender, the subaltern's patrol opened fire. Service fell dead, and the four other individuals found at his home were taken prisoner.

Before the scouts returned with their prisoners and information about Service, Brigadier General Stark sent Butler intelligence that the Loyalist recruiting officer Charles Smith had raised a number of Tories and was marching to join Brant for an attack on Schoharie. Butler sent a detachment commanded by Captain Long of the Rifle Corps to intercept them. After moving up the Schoharie River to about fifteen miles beyond the Upper Fort, Captain Long's men discovered a band of Tories, dressed and painted like Indians, moving on the far bank. Undetected by the Loyalists, Long deployed his men for a hasty ambush. As the leading "Indian" came into his sights, the captain fired. The man fell dead with a single rifle shot as the rest of the Americans opened fire. The remaining Tories, one of whom was believed to have been wounded, fled the trap. The Continentals advanced, but while fording the creek their charge was slowed enough to permit most of the enemy to escape. One American was wounded in the engagement, and one Tory surrendered when the Americans reached the far bank. When the Continentals searched the body, they learned that the dead man was Captain Charles Smith, and he was carrying incriminating letters addressed to Walter Butler and Joseph Brant. The contents of the documents in his possession disclosed the enemy plan to rendezvous at Service's house that Sunday where they would divide into two divisions to attack Cherry Valley and Schoharie.

Realizing the significance of the information he had discovered, Long returned to Fort Defiance with his prisoner, Smith's scalp, and the captured documents. Acting on this information, Lieutenant Colonel Butler sent Major Thomas Church of the 4th Pennsylvania in command of a detached battalion, 120 men strong, to a "Canoe Place" about five miles beyond Service's house. After arrival, they waited in ambush to prevent enemy agents from landing their provisions and supplies. When no enemy appeared, they drove off the cattle intended for the enemy's use and made their way back to Schoharie. Some of those who fled when Long sprang his ambush had evidently warned the approaching enemy that the Americans were aware of their intentions.[53]

Despite this early success, Lieutenant Colonel Butler was disappointed that he could not be more active against the enemy. He estimated that the enemy had 1,500 men at Unadilla, about eighty or ninety miles from Schoharie. While he desperately wanted to attack them in their own territory, he placed "Little dependence on militia" for assistance in the enterprise. Consequently, he and his Continentals mostly remained on the defensive, and erected additional defenses and mounted the two pieces of artillery to the fort to strengthen the position against enemy attack.[54] But the mere presence of the Continentals was having an effect. With both Christopher Service and Charles Smith dead, the Loyalists' place of rendezvous compromised, their source of supplies cut off, and their volunteers scattered, enemy activity in the Schoharie area was less noticeable. In a letter to New York Governor George Clinton, Butler reported, "Everything is very quiet." The officer also told the governor that although many in the area had not fully supported the Patriot cause in the past, "numbers of the disaffected People begin to have a proper sense of their Error and are Hourly coming in Begging Protection and are desirous of taking the Oath of Fidelity to the States."[55]

For the remainder of August, Lieutenant Colonel Butler sent his Continentals out on three scouts of 150 men each to the headwaters of the Susquehanna and Delaware Rivers in an effort to bring on an engagement. The Continentals encountered no enemy troops or Indian warriors, but arrested a few militant local Tories whom they turned over to the militia. Butler remained convinced of the necessity to attack the enemy's own bases at Unadilla and Onaquaga, and proposed a plan for such an offensive to Brigadier General Stark. Although the general agreed on the necessity, he continued to be pessimistic that the plan could be executed with the forces at hand. Undeterred, Butler busied himself with gathering intelligence.

One of Butler's best sources of information was John McKenzie, a soldier in Captain Parr's company. McKenzie made his way alone in a two-day journey to

Unadilla, where he encountered some former acquaintances from Pennsylvania who had joined the enemy. The spy convinced them that he was now a fellow friend of the king, and was permitted to move freely about the settlement from August 19 to 24. Through observation and in conversation with his new "friends," McKenzie estimated there were between 400 and 500 Loyalist fighters at Unadilla, and from 500 to 600 Indian warriors at Onaquaga under Brant's command, and another 1,100 Provincial rangers and Indian warriors at Chemung under Captain Walter Butler's command. On his return to friendly lines, he informed Lieutenant Colonel Butler that from the information he gathered, these enemy forces intended to attack the frontiers in order to terrorize the Patriot families living there. They also needed to acquire provisions and other necessities since the enemy was experiencing supply problems, and even bread was scarce. Furthermore, McKenzie learned that if the British troops under Sir Henry Clinton made an "excursion" out of New York, the Tories and Indians would support them by diverting strength or reinforcements from Washington's army to the frontier.[56]

Another four-man scout was sent to reconnoiter Unadilla in early September. They returned after capturing three prisoners, who confirmed enemy strength at 300 in Unadilla and 400 in Onaquaga. The prisoners, however, were uncertain about the numbers of their comrades at Chemung. After consultation, Brigadier General Stark agreed that a quick striking raid by 150 men could destroy Unadilla without weakening defenses elsewhere. As they would enable the expedition to move more quickly, Butler sought to impress some packhorses to carry the baggage and supplies for the expedition.[57] When the commander in chief was informed of Butler's intention by Brigadier General Stark, General Washington wrote back, "If Colo. Butler undertakes the Unadilla expedition, I hope he may have success."[58]

Chapter 8

ON DANGEROUS SERVICE

O N September 7, 1778, a patrol was sent from Cherry Valley to reconnoiter the vicinity of Unadilla. They returned with three prisoners two days later, and reported what they had learned to Lieutenant Colonel Barent Staats, who passed the information on to Brigadier General Abraham Ten Broeck in Albany. One of the prisoners, an inhabitant of Unadilla, reported that Captain Joseph Brant had issued orders for a meeting of 2,000 men to draw ammunition on September 8 for an expedition, but did not know where they were going to strike. The other two, who were suspected of deserting their Albany militia units, told the captain commanding the scout that they had been in Unadilla for only nine days. They confirmed the Unadilla man's story, but estimated the number of men available to Brant as between 400 and 600, although they actually saw only 100, and believed the rest were at Onaquaga.[1]

In fact, while Colonel William Butler was in Schoharie preparing to organize a strike against Unadilla, Brant planned a surprise raid on the prosperous grain and cattle growing settlement of German Flats. In addition to his own force of Loyalist volunteers and pro-British Indian warriors, Brant was reinforced by a detachment of 200 men from Butler's Rangers under the command of Captain William Caldwell, and a war party of thirty, mostly Mohawk, warriors who had recently arrived from Fort Niagara with Captain Gilbert Tice of the Indian Department. This increased Brant's numbers to some 300 Loyalists and Provincial Rangers, and about 150 Indians. In mid-September, they moved out, traveling through the woods toward German Flats.

The settlement stretched along both sides of the Mohawk River, and was defended by the 4th Regiment of Tryon County militia, under the command of Colonel Peter Bellinger, and a detachment of volunteer rangers in state service. German Flats had four fortified posts, including Fort Dayton on the north bank and Fort Herkimer on the south bank, where the inhabitants could seek shelter in an emergency. After receiving reports that Brant was preparing to advance on German Flats, Colonel Bellinger sent scouts out in the direction of Unadilla, a known staging area for raids on the frontier.[2]

Along the way to German Flats, Brant's advance guards surprised and captured five Oneida warriors. Despite Captain Caldwell's protests, Brant elected not to take them along, and placed them under guard of three of his men after the pro-American Indians gave their word not to escape. On September 16, near the head of Unadilla Creek, Brant's men clashed with a scout of nine New York rangers, which had been sent out by Colonel Bellinger. The enemy quickly overwhelmed and drove the party into the river, killing two and scattering the rest. One of the survivors was John A. Helmer. After he escaped to a nearby hiding place, he counted about 200 enemy, which he believed was only half of the total number. Then, without stopping, he ran the nine miles to German Flats to warn the settlement's garrison and people that their community was in danger. After Helmer arrived at Fort Dayton and delivered his report, Colonel Bellinger sent an urgent request for help to Colonel Jacob Klock and sounded the alarm calling the men of his own battalion to arms. The local inhabitants gathered a few possessions and moved their families to the shelter of the forts. When he received the call for help, Klock immediately sent orders for his regiment to muster and concentrate. He intended to send one detachment to the aid of German Flats, while another joined with Alden's Continentals and the militia at Cherry Valley in striking Brant as he moved along Unadilla Creek.

Meanwhile, after being slowed by a steady rain, Brant and his men came upon German Flats in the night, but delayed their attack until morning. Shortly before dawn on September 17, Brant divided his force into two divisions, each further broken down into smaller bands, and marched down both sides of the Mohawk River at once. They plundered whatever property the inhabitants left behind, and burned everything in their path they could not carry away. The raiders then attacked Forts Dayton and Herkimer, but were surprised at the resistance and driven off by the musketry of the defenders. When the raiders on the south side attempted to burn a barn just outside the stockade to aid in their taking Fort Herkimer, a detachment from the garrison sallied out and drove them back to a respectable distance.

By noon, although the forts remained unconquered, Brant was satisfied with the destruction he had inflicted on his former neighbors. In all, his men destroyed sixty-three homes, as many barns and uncounted outbuildings, three grist mills, and one sawmill. Large quantities of recently harvested grain and fodder, much of it intended for the Continental Army, were destroyed. Brant's forces carried off 235 horses, 269 head of cattle, and 269 sheep. Of the cattle, 100 head had been destined for the food supply of the garrison at Fort Schuyler. Those that Brant's men could not drive back to Onaquaga and Unadilla were slaughtered in the fields. As they withdrew, the raiders left only the forts, a barn, the church, and the homes of the minister and two known Tories standing, one of whom was Rudolph Shoemaker, Walter Butler's host at the time of his capture in 1777. Owing to Helmer's timely warning, only three Americans had been killed and one wounded in the raid. In all, 719 people, including 387 children, survived, although they had no homes or food with the change of season approaching. Colonel Bellinger's appeal to Governor Clinton had been prophetic. Not satisfied with inflicting such little pain on his enemies, Captain Caldwell lamented that the attackers "would have in all probability killed most of the Inhabitants of German Flats had they not been apprized of our coming by one of the Scouts getting in and warning of our approach, and perhaps got to their Forts."[3]

Colonel Jacob Klock mustered 300 men of the Tryon County militia and marched to Cherry Valley, and ordered the rest to German Flats. On receiving the news of the enemy attack, Colonel Alden sent part of his Continental regiment in an attempt to intercept the enemy as they retired toward Unadilla. When Klock's men approached to within four miles of Cherry Valley, an express overtook them to deliver a message that the enemy was marching toward Canajoharie. The colonel ordered a countermarch back toward the Mohawk River. When another express informed him that scouts found no truth in the earlier information, Klock ordered another countermarch. By that time, many of the militiamen had become weary and discouraged, and left for home. With their numbers reduced, those who stayed on duty followed Klock back toward Cherry Valley. When they finally arrived, Alden told Klock that he and his men were too late to serve any useful purpose. Although the Continentals went out in an attempt to intercept the withdrawing enemy and bring on an engagement, they discovered the enemy was too far gone to overtake. Other elements of the Tryon County militia arrived at German Flats, but Colonel Bellinger and the other regimental commanders chose not to pursue. After Colonel Klock marched the footsore members of the Palatine battalion home, he issued orders to dismiss the militia, and sent a letter informing Governor Clinton that German Flats was "laid to waste for ten miles along the Mohawk River."[4]

When Brant's men returned to where they left their prisoners under guard, they discovered that the five Oneidas had escaped. While Brant and Caldwell were burning German Flats, a war party of Oneidas and Tuscaroras had raided Unadilla and Butternuts in the Old English District, and took nine prisoners, including some of Butler's Rangers. Among the captured rangers was Richard McGinnis, who had participated in the attack on Wyoming the previous July. The friendly Indians also liberated a number of American captives being held at Unadilla. They took no scalps, and left the women and children unmolested.

The Oneida then marched their prisoners to Fort Schuyler where they were delivered to American forces.[5] When he was informed of the assistance provided by their Indian allies, General Washington wrote to General Stark and Governor Clinton that he was glad to hear the Oneida allies had attacked Joseph Brant's rear support area while the latter were conducting their raid on German Flats.[6]

In the analysis that followed, there was increasing dissatisfaction with the leadership Brigadier General Stark was exercising with the Continentals in aiding the militia in the defense of the settlements. Brigadier General Ten Broeck was so irritated that he told Governor Clinton, "I cannot account for Genl. Stark's conduct. It does not appear to me that he pays the least Attention to the safety of the Frontiers."[7] General Washington was left no choice but to replace the "hero of Bennington" with an officer who would show more aggressiveness in supporting the Continental and militia forces trying to check the ravishes of the Tories and Indians on the frontier areas of the Northern Department. In October, he ordered Brigadier General Edward Hand to take command of the army's Northern Department headquartered at Albany. With a more aggressive and energetic commander in the area, Washington sought other possibilities for defending the frontier and countering the Indian and Tory depredations. For example, he considered forming one expedition under the immediate command of Brigadier General Clinton, and a second one, under Brigadier General Hand or Lieutenant Colonel Butler, "composed of troops already to the Northward."[8]

Americans along the entire frontier were growing increasingly impatient for some offensive action in response to the Tory and Indian attacks. None sounded the call for action with more urgency than those who had been affected most by the destruction of Wyoming and the Great Runaway. The area remained far from secure. In late August several Indians and Tories were reported about Wyoming. Some of the intruders attacked and killed the members of a family fifteen miles below Wilkes-Barre, and two men were found dead and scalped near Nanticoke Falls.[9] Colonel Thomas Hartley, commander of the Additional Continental Regiment based in Sunbury, sent a detachment from his regiment under the command of Captain Lewis Bush to reinforce Fort Wyoming. Hartley was contemplating an offensive against Tories and Indians in the Susquehanna area, and wanted to assess the strength of the Wyoming garrison. On September 1, Lieutenant Colonel Zebulon Butler reported that he commanded a force of 193 men at Wilkes-Barre to defend those rebuilding the settlement.[10]

Colonel Hartley soon developed a plan of attack, writing to Butler on September 10: "I am informed many of your people have the highest inclination to go against some of the Indian towns, [that] they may revenge the murders of fathers, brothers, and friends, besides serving their country." He then revealed that his objective was the Indian town of Chemung, where reports indicated "a great part of the plunder taken from our unhappy brethren at Wyoming, and a body of Indians and Tories, are collected."[11]

So to not telegraph their move to enemy scouts or sympathizers who may have been in the area, Hartley decided to concentrate his forces from several posts, before the enemy was aware of his intent. Therefore, in his instructions to Lieutenant Colonel Butler, he wrote, "It is absolutely necessary that the troops at Wyoming, those on the West Branch, and in this department, should effect a junction before they proceed" to the objective. The expedition was to approach the target by the Lycoming path to the mouth of Towanda Creek. They would then attack and, if possible, destroy Chemung before sweeping down the Susquehanna River to root out Tories and Indians on the way back to Wyoming. If the plan succeeded, Hartley believed it would give some relief to the frontiers and intimidate the enemy.[12]

Hartley impressed on Butler the need to maintain secrecy, and urged him to inform no one of the plans, except Colonel Dennison and Captains Bush and Kenney. In developing his order of battle, he instructed Butler to remain at his post in Wyoming with Captain James Kenney of the Additional Regiment serving as his second in command at the garrison. In addition to the normal complement of officers, sergeants and corporals, Hartley instructed Butler to keep ten men of the Additional Regiment's detachment, twenty from Captain Spalding's company, and fifty of the militia in the garrison. In the event the enemy attacked, the other troops remaining in the region, at Nescopeck, would be available to reinforce Butler if needed. Captain Bush's detachment and Captain Spalding's company, minus those staying in garrison, and Captain John Franklin's detachment of as many militia as would volunteer, were to march from Fort Wyoming on September 14 for the rendezvous at Fort Muncy, bringing their unit baggage loaded on packhorses. Each soldier was to draw and cook four days' provisions for the march, and would draw rations and supplies from Colonel Hartley's quartermaster after reaching the rendezvous.[13]

Lieutenant Colonel Butler published his preparatory orders for the troops going on the expedition on September 13. Still maintaining secrecy, he revealed only "That a Detachment of 130 men of Continental Troops march from this post tomorrow under the command of Captain Bush, on an Expedition in readiness to march at 8 o'clock in the morning." Those scheduled to march, with their rations cooked and baggage packed, were ordered to be "paraded" that afternoon so that their officers could inspect them to ensure they were "complete with arms and ammunition." At eight o'clock on the morning of September 14, Captain Bush led the detachment out of Wilkes-Barre on the march to Fort Muncy on the West Branch of the Susquehanna. They proceeded with sixty men of Hartley's regiment, fifty-eight of Spalding's Westmoreland Independent Company, and Captain John Franklin's twelve-man "company" of Westmoreland militia. Despite their small numbers, the men from Wyoming should not be overlooked. Many survivors of the July battle gave their parole not to take up arms again in return for immediate exchange, although Tory rangers and their Indian allies had violated the terms their commander had dictated as soon as the ink was dry. Like the men of Spalding's company, the militia soldiers were familiar with the area and were crucial to the success of the operation, whatever their numbers. They crossed the Susquehanna River, then took the road leading north-northwest to a point a mile west of Toby Creek, where it turned southwest to cross North Mountain.[14]

The troops began to concentrate at Fort Muncy on September 18. To provide an advanced guard with increased mobility, the colonel mounted seventeen infantrymen from his regiment on horses to act as "dragoons," with Captain Henry Carberry as their commander. When Colonel Hartley asked his subordinate commanders for the strength reports, or "returns," he was disappointed to learn he had only about 200 "rank and file" present for duty. He later commented, "With volunteers and others, we reckoned on 400 rank and file for the expedition, beside seventeen horse, which I mounted from my own regiment."[15] Undeterred, Hartley started out at four o'clock in the morning on September 21, with every available Continental soldier that could be spared from the fort or other duties. The colonel resolved that since the enemy did not expect him to attack, his move would at least provide a diversion that would enable the farmers of the area to save their grain harvest without enemy interference.

The column crossed Loyalsock Creek at the ford, and moved up the road to its junction with the Sheshequin Trail. The weather was miserable, and the troops were soaked by rain as they crossed difficult terrain. The fatigue party cut through the woods, widening the Indian path to permit the easier passage of troops and horses as the route crossed "prodigious swamps, mountains, defiles, and rocks." The Sheshequin path, by which Hartley intended to penetrate to Tioga, followed up Bouser's Run and then crossed over the hills to ascend Lycoming Creek.[16] To describe the march as "difficult" was an understatement. The troops "waded or swam the river Lycoming upwards of twenty times" on their way toward their objective. As they moved through woods and groves, the colonel reported that the expedition found the "haunts and lurking places of the savage murderers who had desolated our frontiers" and the "huts where they had dressed and dried the scalps of the helpless women and children who had fell into their hands." Despite the heavy rains and rough terrain, Hartley's men made steady progress.[17]

On September 26, the American advanced guard of seventeen mounted troops, moving about one mile ahead of the main column, stumbled on a like number of Indian warriors on their way to raid an American settlement somewhere on the Susquehanna. In the brief meeting engagement, the troops fired first. One Indian, presumably a chief, fell dead, and was scalped. As the light infantry moved up to their support, the rest of the warriors escaped without becoming decisively engaged. A few miles further the Continentals discovered an abandoned camp where at least seventy warriors had recently bedded down while preparing for a raid. On learning of the approach of Hartley's force from the party that had been engaged earlier in the day, the warriors fled to spread the alarm. The element of surprise had been lost.

With no time to lose, Hartley ordered his force to advance rapidly toward Sheshequin, home of the enemy allied Delaware Chief Eghobund. When the Americans reached the place, the advanced guard came upon and liberated fifteen prisoners, some of whom had been taken by the enemy during the raids on Springfield, Andrustown, and German Flats. One of them told Hartley that an American deserter, allegedly from Spalding's company, had arrived from Wyoming to warn the enemy. Another prisoner told Hartley that there were 300 enemy, "mostly Tories dressed in green," under the command of Captain Walter Butler, who had left the area a few hours before their arrival, heading for Chemung, twelve miles away, to prepare its defenses. Hartley then ordered Captain Carberry and his mounted men to "close on Butler." They continued scouting three miles up the Chemung River without making contact before they returned to rejoin the main body at Sheshequin. Hartley, fearing that that his mission was thus compromised, and not wishing his command cut off far from any assistance, ordered his force to move "with the greatest dispatch towards Tioga" after setting the abandoned structures of Sheshequin on fire. The column forded the Chemung River near the point where it emptied into the Susquehanna. The Continentals took an Indian prisoner, who told them that "Young Butler" was preparing to give Hartley battle in the defiles and rough terrain as he advanced toward Chemung. The exhausted troops could go no further that day, so Colonel Hartley halted his men and bivouacked for the night in the evacuated Indian village of Tioga.[18]

When he initially set out, Colonel Hartley had set Chemung, the gateway to the British base at Fort Niagara, as the objective of his limited expedition. Hartley noted that "Niagara and Chemung are the asylums of those Tories who can not get to New York." With the enemy now alerted, had he 500 troops, 160 light infantry, and one or two pieces of artillery, Hartley was confident that he could probably have destroyed Chemung. The situation had changed, but there was still an opportunity to strike a blow before the end of the campaign season. Tioga was considered a "watch town" that, with Queen Esther's Town directly across the Chemung, guarded the "southern door" to the Iroquois longhouse and the approach to the British base at Fort Niagara. The area had also been used as the staging area for British and Indian raids against American settlements on the frontiers of New York, Pennsylvania, and New Jersey. If nothing else, Hartley's force could at least inflict some damage there.

With American troops literally on their doorstep, concerned British officials and Iroquois chiefs were calling in their available troops and warriors. The enemy was

An American rifleman drawn by Jean-Baptiste-Antoine de Verger in 1781. He wears the "hunting frock" or "rifle shirt" normally associated with soldiers in rifle units, instead of "regimentals" as worn in the musket regiments. Note that he carries a tomahawk in lieu of a bayonet, as a musket-armed soldier would have.

visibly disturbed at the audacity of the move. According to Captain Walter Butler, they believed that Hartley had advanced with a force estimated at 1,400 regulars and militia, allegedly "piloted" by Colonel Dennison and others who were in violation of their paroles, on an "invasion" of Iroquois land. Captain John Johnston of the Indian Department was collecting Seneca warriors to assist Captain Butler when runners reported three parties of Americans from Wyoming were "coming to demolish Six Nations country." Butler reported that the Americans ascended the Susquehanna, desolating Loyalist farms and Indian villages as they went. He quickly assembled a force that included Captain Caldwell and the rangers who had raided German Flats, some redcoats of the 8th Regiment of Foot from Fort Niagara, and about 400 Seneca warriors, giving him a total of about 600 men.[19]

To inflict any substantial harm on his foe and preserve his force, Hartley knew he had to move before the enemy concentrated against him. After discussing the situation with his subordinate officers, Colonel Hartley explained, "It was soon resolved we should proceed no further, but if possible make our way good to Wyoming." Hartley's men spent the day destroying Tioga and Queen Esther's Town, home of the Indian matron, which was done in retaliation for her alleged murder of American prisoners at Wyoming, along with some smaller settlements on Tioga Point, and captured a number of canoes and "some plunder."[20]

On the morning of September 28, having accomplished all he could hope to with his limited resources in light of the new situation, Hartley ordered his men across to the east bank of the Susquehanna, and to march south toward Wyoming. They arrived at Wyalusing at about eleven o'clock that night, with the "men much worn down, our whiskey and flour gone." The American troops remained in the area for twenty-four hours to kill and cook beef, but that delay gave the enemy, now reacting to the American incursion, a chance to close the distance between them. Hartley's expedition moved out at about noon with 120 "rank and file" in the column. The advanced guard, under the command of Captain Benjamin Stoddard from his regiment, led the way. (Stoddard would eventually serve as the first Secretary of the Navy in the John Adams administration.) The main body, formed into three divisions: the remainder of Hartley's regiment; Captain Spalding's Independent Company; and Captain James Murray's company of Northumberland County Rangers. The rear guard of thirty men, commanded by Captain Isaac Sweeney, trailed the three divisions. Seventy men, whom Hartley described as suffering "from real or pretended lameness," were loaded into the canoes or on the backs of now unburdened packhorses. Besides not slowing down the progress of the march, these lame or lazy at least served to strengthen the detail guarding the stores and baggage.

The American column had not gone three miles beyond Wyalusing when the advanced guard was taken under fire. They returned fire and deployed, but before Hartley could form his three divisions into line of battle, the enemy retired. Reforming their marching order, the column proceeded another mile before the advanced guard was attacked again, this time by a larger enemy force. After some sharp skirmishing with the advanced guard, the enemy again retired before Hartley could deploy. Later that afternoon, the Americans arrived at the plantation belonging to John Depue, the Tory recruiting agent for Butler's Rangers who was so active before the attack on Wyoming, at the mouth of Tuscarora Creek.

Captain Walter Butler had sent a company of thirty rangers and a war party of Indians with Captain Benjamin Pawling to Wyalusing to hold the Rebels as he prepared to bring his main force to bear. At about two o'clock in the afternoon, the American rear guard came under heavy attack. Captain Sweeney's company formed to repel the assault, but began to give way under the pressure, as Indians skirmishers worked their way around to advance on the American left flank. From the intensity of their attack, Colonel Hartley estimated the enemy strength was about 200 men. He and his officers conferred, and all agreed that the attacks were not just small parties sent to harass the column in its movement, but they were convinced that such a large body of enemy was attempting to bring on a general engagement.

The officers believed that due to their strength and position, the enemy must have felt overconfident and prone to act with undue "impetuosity," which could be turned to the Americans' advantage. Hartley ordered Spalding's company to reinforce Sweeney's on the rear guard, while he led the rest of his command, undetected, to the high ground on the Indians' flank. Hartley then sent Captain Benjamin Stoddard's Continentals around the enemy to attack them in the rear. "At the critical moment," Captain Hawkins Boone, who was serving on detached service from the 6th Pennsylvania, and Captain John Brady and Lieutenant Robert King, formerly of the 12th Pennsylvania now serving as officers of militia, led a "few brave fellows" landing from the canoes to join the fight. Hartley reported, "The War Whoop was given by our people" and "we advanced on the Enemy on all sides, with great shouting & Noise, the Indians after a brave resistance of some minutes . . . fled with the utmost Haste . . . & left ten dead on the ground."[21] After the firing ceased, the Americans retained the field, counting four of their own dead and ten wounded.

Hartley was disappointed that the enemy had escaped, but thought his officers and men had performed well. Captains Stoddard and Spalding were particularly commended for their performance, as was Captain Carberry with the mounted detachment that "was very active, and rendered important services till the horses were fatigued." Hartley praised the conduct of the men in his regiment, and attributed much of their success to their "buck and ball" ammunition—a single cartridge consisting of one musket shot and three buckshot, therefore producing a discharge of four projectiles on firing—and not marksmanship, in turning the tide. "The men of my Regt," he wrote, "were . . . no great marksmen, and were awkward at wood Fighting." But, he continued, "the Bullet and three swan shot in each Piece made up, in some measure, for the want of skill."[22]

After their attacks were defeated with considerable losses, the Indians did not pursue any further.[23] Butler described Hartley's fighting withdraw as a "retreat" with "every sign of haste."[24] The march back to Wyoming proved uneventful, and the remaining interference the Americans encountered was driven off with little effort.

Having engaged in considerable fighting, the American force suffered minimal casualties. In two weeks, "Hartley's Expedition" covered about 300 miles of difficult terrain, defeated the enemy when encountered, and destroyed the Indian towns between Wyoming and Tioga. It liberated fifteen prisoners and captives, and recovered about fifty head of cattle taken in raids by the enemy. The men also captured twenty-eight canoes, "besides many other articles" of value.

In the custom of the day, according to the Articles of War, when the American expedition arrived at Wilkes-Barre on October 1, Colonel Hartley issued an order that all the items taken as plunder, except for military stores, be turned in or showed to a board of officers for a proper accounting to be sold. The funds were then divided up according to rank. After leaving a detachment to bolster the garrison at Wyoming, the remainder of Hartley's command marched back to Sunbury, arriving on October 5. Hartley posted a number of the companies of his regiment in the several forts that defended the area, while he waited for the promised reinforcement he was sure must be on the way to bolster his little command.[25]

Although successful, it was still an operation that had not achieved its limited objective due to the lack of resources. As Hartley told the delegates to the Continental Congress and the members of the Pennsylvania Supreme Executive Council in his reports, "Considering our numbers we pushed our good Fortune as far as we dare." Although far from the main fields of effort, Hartley reminded the politicians of the importance of the defense of the frontier areas, by telling them, "We are here on a Dangerous service, which gives us few opportunity's of gaining Laurels; we have a Vigilant & Dangerous Enemy, but it gives us pleasure to think we serve our Country & protect the helpless and innocent."[26] He praised his men's performance: in spite of hardships, "they surmounted them with great resolution and fortitude." He closed with a warning that his "little regiment with two classes of Lancaster and Berks County (Pennsylvania) militia, will be scarcely sufficient to preserve the posts from Nescopeck falls to Muncy, and from thence to the head of Penn's valley."[27] The first important offensive against the Tories and Indians brought some security to the northern frontier of Pennsylvania, although the danger was by no means eradicated.[28] Despite the limited success, the expedition gave great satisfaction to Continental and state authorities, and the Supreme Executive Council unanimously passed a vote of thanks to Hartley for his "brave and prudent conduct in covering the northwestern frontiers of this State, and repelling the savages and other enemies."[29]

Although smarting from their defeat at the hands of Colonel Hartley, the Tories and their Indian allies still sought every opportunity to molest the settlers and attack the soldiers. Those Indians who were allied with Britain did not relax in their efforts to inflict pain and suffering on the frontier by securing captives and scalps. On October 7, the day before Colonel Hartley wrote his report, two sergeants of his regiment posted at Fort Muncy were ambushed a short distance from the stockade enclosure. One was immediately killed, and his scalped body was later found by comrades. The other was presumed taken prisoner when his corpse was not recovered. One week later, William Jameson, a private in the militia, left the garrison on horseback to visit the ruined homes of his father and brother in nearby Hanover to ascertain their condition. He was shot by Indians near the bridge across Buttonwood Creek, a short distance downstream from Wilkes-Barre. After he fell wounded from his horse, he tried to escape by running into the woods, but was overtaken and tomahawked and scalped. Mortally wounded, he died two days later.[30]

On October 21, at Wyoming, Lieutenant Colonel Zebulon Butler ordered out a detail to gather and bury the dead still laying on the field where they fell on July 3. Early the next morning, Lieutenant John Jenkins, Jr., now a Continental officer in Spalding's company, led a guard of one subaltern, two sergeants, two corporals, and twenty-five privates, followed by a detail of soldiers. They left Camp Westmoreland with two carts full of spades, mattocks, and wooden pitchforks to bury the remains. The soldiers were joined by a number of local inhabitants. They crossed the Susquehanna to the west bank and headed north toward Wintermute's Fort. Halfway between Forty Fort's ruins and Abraham's Plain, they began to gather the dried and shriveled remains of friends and family members with pitchforks. None of the bodies was recognizable by their features. The carts were filled up in a short time, and they halted by an open field near the road, where a detail of soldiers dug a hole and buried the first of the recovered remains. Throughout the day, the soldiers and civilian volunteers brought in more, and laid them in the common grave.[31] At the end of the day, the detail left its grim task to return to Camp Westmoreland.

The respite from enemy activity proved to be brief. On November 9, Colonel Hartley reported to the Pennsylvania Supreme Executive Council and the Board of War at Congress that a force of Tories and Indians was again operating in the area, having destroyed the settlement of Nanticoke. He asked for reinforcements, but did not wait on their arrival. By November 14, he was at Fort Jenkins, near Nescopeck, looking to bring on an engagement.[32] In the meantime, the remnants of Colonel John Patton's "Additional" regiment had been dispatched by General George Washington to reinforce Hartley's regiment at the Susquehanna frontier on October 24.[33] On December 16, Congress directed that Hartley's and Patton's "Additional" regiments, along with four independent companies, be consolidated into one, and designated the 11th Pennsylvania Regiment of Continental Line, and reaffirmed the decision on January 13, 1779.[34] When Hartley resigned his commission in February, Lieutenant Colonel Commandant Adam Hubely assumed command of the new regiment.

While Colonel Hartley was returning from his strike against Tioga, Lieutenant Colonel William Butler assessed the strength of his post at Schoharie. With little prospect for being reinforced by additional militia, and not counting those on detached service, furlough, or sick leave, he had 521 men of all ranks.[35] The detachments of militia on active service commanded by Lieutenant Rainschers, distributed to Upper, Lower, and Middle Forts, numbered 189. Lieutenant Dietz reported fourteen rangers in his company in New York state service. Major Posey had 122 men with the Rifle Corps. Butler's own 4th Pennsylvania Regiment of Continentals stood with 196.[36] Lest these numbers be reduced by the inability of the militia to meet their quotas of drafts and the approach on unfavorable weather, Butler decided to act.

On the first of October, Butler sent Lieutenant William Stevens of the Rifle Corps commanding a detachment of twelve men plus a subaltern and sixteen militia to the frontier. Their mission was to guard the roads and passes leading toward the enemy settlements to prevent Tory sympathizers from carrying intelligence to them, and to intercept enemy scouts attempting to reconnoiter and observe the preparations going on at the forts.[37] The next day, 267 troops marched out of Schoharie heading toward the Susquehanna. Leaving a sufficient force to guard the settlement, Butler led 161 men of his own musket battalion, the 4th Pennsylvania, under the command of Major Thomas Church, seventy-seven riflemen of Posey's Corps, and twenty-one New York rangers, plus a detachment of seven militiamen and one officer to act as guides and packhorse drivers.[38] The soldiers each carried six days' rations on their backs, with another five days' provisions loaded on the packhorses. On the first day's march, they covered twelve miles to Maticus without incident. On October 3, the men marched fifteen miles to the head of the Delaware in "Rainy, Disagreeable W'r [weather] and very bad roads."[39] By ten o'clock the next morning, the weather cleared, and over the next two days, the force marched down the Delaware, then crossed the mountains to reach the Susquehanna.

After beginning his march in early morning on October 6, Butler closed to within eight miles of Unadilla before halting at dusk. Lieutenants William Stevens and Reuben Long of the Rifle Corps went forward leading two small scouting patrols to capture some inhabitants who lived within four miles of the Loyalist town and base. After a short rest, the main body moved under the cover of darkness to concealed positions from which they would attack Unadilla the next morning. The scouts met them one mile from the town with a prisoner, who disclosed that the enemy had left the town a few days before, heading toward Onaquaga, another thirty miles down the Susquehanna. In the morning, Butler sent Stevens into the settlement with a small patrol to capture a Tory named Glasford to serve as their guide to Onaquaga. The lieutenant returned with his prisoner, and shortly after breakfast, Butler's troops were again on the move. When the troops arrived near the mouth of the Unadilla River the advanced party discovered tracks of a man they assumed to be an enemy scout left behind to observe and keep Brant informed of the Americans' approach. Butler sent three riflemen to track the enemy scout down, but they returned at sundown without success, after having pursued the man for eight miles.[40]

A heavy rain began early in the morning of October 8, making the soldiers miserable and slowing their progress. By eight o'clock, the weather cleared sufficiently for the troops to clean their weapons and continue the march. When they arrived to within three or four miles of Onaquaga, the column met Lieutenant Stevens and his scouts, who had just reconnoitered the enemy town from an adjacent mountain. After Butler listened to Stevens' report, he developed his plan of attack. In order to reach Onaquaga, the Americans had to cross water up to their armpits, as the Susquehanna was about 250 yards wide at that point. Clearly at a disadvantage if the enemy should ambush his men as they forded the river, Butler planned to cross at night and attack.[41]

The riflemen led the way, followed by the companies of musketry, then the baggage train, advancing up and over a mile long mountain, thick with woods and logs. At eleven o'clock they crossed the river, the two rifle companies in front posted to attack the flanks, while the musket companies charged the center with bayonets fixed meeting no opposition. It appeared that the enemy evacuated the town that day "in the greatest Confusion," leaving "at least 2000 Bush'ls of Corn, a Number of Horses, Cattle, Poultry, their Dogs, household furniture, &c., &c." behind as they fled. Butler described Onaquaga as "the finest Indian town I ever saw." Built along both sides of the river, it consisted of forty "good houses" made of hewn logs, with "good Floors" and shingle roofs, stone chimneys and other improvements like those found in those built by European settlers.

Satisfied with the ease at which his troops had seized the town, but always wary that the enemy lurked about, ready to attack, Butler took no chances. He ordered a number of fires made, to make it appear to enemy observers that he had more men than he actually did. Those soldiers not on sentry were ordered to "lay on their arms," or to sleep with them ready nearby instead of stacking them. At daybreak on the ninth, Butler ordered the trumpeter of the Rifle Corps to sound his "Bugle Horn" as the signal for all to get under arms.[42]

Major Thomas Church crossed to the other side of the river and burned the buildings in that part of the town, which also had ten "good Houses" and a large Quantity of Corn." The detachment also "brought off some Cattle" on their return to the main body. While the troops made preparations for marching away, some of the packhorse drivers went out to round up a few animals that had wandered off in the night. Contrary to Butler's orders, the men were unarmed. After going about a half mile beyond the main body of troops, they were fired on by the enemy. One man fell, with wounds in the side and head, but was still alive. As soon as he heard the gunfire, Lieutenant Colonel Butler put his entire force in motion. The column marched with the remaining pack-horses and baggage in the rear, so that any of Brant's "Spies & Scouts" who saw them would be deceived that the Americans were continuing their expedition farther down the Susquehanna. After marching about two miles, Butler halted. Expecting an attack from Brant's forces, Butler had his men assume concealed positions in the woods to receive it, while Captain James Parr of the Rifle Corps continued on with a thirty-man detachment to feign continued pursuit. Parr was ordered to march three miles farther to burn an Indian "Castle," or fortified town. The detachment executed their mission, and returned driving some captured livestock with them.[43]

Once Parr's detachment linked back up, Butler's force "march'd off from the left, in fine order" with the men of the "musketry" of the 4th Pennsylvania leading, at about three o'clock in the afternoon. The whole town of Onaquaga, except one house, was set on fire as they withdrew. The one house that was spared belonged to a "friend Indian" who then made his way to the protection of the Oneidas. Expecting to be attacked while recrossing the river and marching through two miles of "a very dangerous defile," Butler ordered Captain Edward Scull and his Grenadier Company of the 4th Pennsylvania to lead. With bayonets fixed they were prepared to force a crossing of the ford if any opposition was encountered. The crossing was made without incident, and conducted in "good order." Along the way, they burned another small village and some corn. Slowed by the poor roads and the burden of carrying the severely wounded man, the column halted at about eleven o'clock that night near the town of Callacrunty, after a grueling march of thirteen miles.[44]

The brief rest was interrupted at one o'clock the next morning, October 10, by another hard rain. With the water levels in the creeks rising fast, after marching about ten miles, they came to stream that was so high that the packhorses had to swim, and the troops could only cross by felling trees to span them. When they reached the Susquehanna, if the provisions had not been nearly exhausted, the American commander would have waited for the water to recede. Instead, Butler had the drivers assemble the packhorses. The soldiers waded part of the way, then were ferried, two at a time, across the deepest part of the river by the swimming horses, until they could continue wading. It took about twenty trips to get the entire unit across, with the loss of only some ammunition, provisions, baggage, and seven muskets, but not one soldier. Continuing on the south bank of the Susquehanna, the troops marched across the mountains to avoid crossing the swollen river again. On reaching Unadilla, they burned the saw and gristmills, and all the houses in the settlement, except for that of the reluctant guide, the Tory named Glasford. The next morning, October 11, as most of the troops dressed and cleaned arms, a detail was sent back to the river to prepare a raft to transport men to the opposite bank to burn the rest of Unadilla. Lieutenant Long and one private then crossed on the raft and burned all the houses and corn. Once back with the main body, the force marched another twelve miles against swollen streams, their provisions exhausted.[45]

On October 12, after a twenty-five-mile march, they arrived on the banks of the Delaware. Again, the water was too high to ford. In attempting to avoid crossing the river, the guides led the whole force into the woods for six miles, only to lose their way in the dark. After spending the night on the mountain, on the thirteenth they continued crossing the mountain until arriving at the first settlement between Unadilla and the frontier, the home of a family named Cawley. At about this time the packhorse driver died of the wounds he sustained at Onaquaga. From there, the troops quickened the pace to reach the Sawyer farm after a sixteen-mile march. On October 16, with a ration consisting of one ear of parched corn per man, the troops arrived back at Fort Defiance to a thirteen-round cannon salute and a "feu de joy" fired in their honor.[46] Butler was pleased with their performance. They had marched more than 300 miles, destroyed both Unadilla and Onaquaga, burned all their structures (except those mentioned) and 4,000 bushels of corn, and drove away all the enemy's livestock. He was "well convinced that it has sufficiently secured these Frontiers from any further disturbances from the Savages at least this Winter."[47]

Unaware that Butler's expedition was in progress, Governor Clinton continued to correspond with General Washington seeking additional aid for New York's embattled borders and urging him to allocate Continental troops to launch an expedition against the enemy bases.[48] In response, General Washington wrote that he would "immediately order one Regiment to be held ready for frontier service," and more if they could be spared.[49] This was good news for the governor, and he submitted a plan using Rochester, in Ulster County, as a rendezvous for Continental and militia troops approaching from several different areas of the state to concentrate, at which to gather supplies, and to use as a base from which to attack Onaquaga.[50] But Governor Clinton began receiving messages of alarm from the militia in Orange County to the south.[51] The enemy was sighted in the Minisink area, attacking in the middle of the grain harvest season. The militia turned out as best they could, and those on active service manning the frontier guard posts responded to the attacks; otherwise there was little organized opposition. Local commanders sent the governor requests for reinforcements of state troops or militia from other counties, and for more ammunition. One company commander pleaded for resupply as the recent actions had reduced his men to only three cartridges apiece with which to meet the next attack, which they expected at almost any time.[52]

Sure enough, at eleven o'clock on the morning of October 13, Brant's men struck the post at Peenpack. The guard fought them all day, until forced to retreat at about eleven o'clock that night. Colonel Newkirk believed that all the guards along the Delaware River frontier would be attacked, and called for his militia to turn out. Colonel Abraham Hasbrouk called his regiment, and marched seven companies to reinforce Colonel John Cantine's Ulster County militia, while leaving the other four companies to await further orders. Joseph Brant's men may have remained in the area to terrorize the inhabitants longer than originally planned, unaware that William Butler's small force of Continentals was at the same time repaying them in kind. But by October 16, Brant was gone. Hasbrouk dismissed his men, except for a sufficient guard who remained on duty until Colonel Cantine and the guards returned.[53]

Chapter 9

THE CHERRY VALLEY MASSACRE

WHEN the Mohawk war chief and Indian Department officer Joseph Brant and his men returned from the foray into Orange County, they were shocked by the sights that awaited them. Like numerous farms, settlements, and towns they had destroyed since initiating their campaign in the "Year of the Hangman," their own mills, barns, and homes, including Brant's, were now in ashes. Their corn was destroyed and cattle driven away. Their families, like those of their enemies at Cobleskill, Andrustown, Springfield, and German Flats, were now homeless refugees. The first concern was moving them to places of shelter for the winter, either in the interior Indian towns or at Fort Niagara. Over near Chemung, the Indians who had allied themselves with the Crown and their comrades in the Provincial forces must have been experiencing similar feelings. Their settlements proved no more secure than those they had attacked on the West Branch of the Susquehanna. The inhabitants of the towns where they prepared, gathered supplies, and built the canoes and boats that carried them to destroy the homes and farms in the Wyoming Valley were now without homes as well. For once in the war on the Susquehanna, Delaware, and Mohawk River frontiers, the Tories and their Indian allies were on the receiving end, and they did not like it.

They were determined to strike back. Lieutenant Colonel Sir John Johnson, commanding the King's Royal Regiment of New York, asked the Indians to join with his Provincial troops, which he planned to lead against the rebels, and hoped to give them an "eternal thrashing."[1] There were reports from the American commander at Fort Edward that 400-500 enemy were seen on Lake Champlain below Crown Point, and Colonel Lewis Van Woert heard from subordinates that "Lake George was full of Boats with Regulars, Tories & Indians" in the first week of November. On calling out three regiments of militia to reinforce the troops posted there, however, it appeared the intelligence was false, and the men were dismissed. But on November 10, an enemy raid reportedly struck in the Skenesborough vicinity of Charlotte County. Lieutenant Colonel Alexander Webster of the militia there sent expresses carrying urgent appeals for help and reinforcements. He described the destruction saying "the enemy are burning on both sides of the Lake all the houses & taking all the men prisoner, Striping all the women & Children the way they go, killing all the Cattle."[2] The raiders, about 350 British and Provincial soldiers and 100 Indian warriors, was commanded by Major Christopher Carleton. Johnson's force, however, did little "thrashing" during 1778.

Any true measure of revenge for the destruction on their bases by the expeditions of American Colonels Hartley and William Butler was left to the Tory Captain Walter Butler, temporarily in command of his father's corps of Provincial rangers, Captain Joseph Brant and his warriors and Loyalist volunteers, and any force the Six Nations could get into the field. With their forward bases destroyed, Butler and Brant were sure that the Americans felt more secure on the frontier, at least until spring. True, it would be difficult to mount a substantial attack before the winter weather made such an operation out of the question, but Butler and Brant saw it as their best opportunity. The two officers of the Crown called for a council with their Seneca allies at Tioga to discuss the object of their next raid. While the Americans were guessing where they would strike, Captains Butler and Brant informed the council of their decision to attack the settlement of Cherry Valley in Tryon County before retiring to winter quarters, and asked for their reinforcement.

Through the course of the discussion and planning, Butler and Brant became engaged in serious differences and disagreements. The tenor grew angrier when the young Butler made it clear that despite the differences in the levels of experience, he considered Brant his subordinate. Brant's men felt their captain had been insulted and ill treated, and many refused to serve under Butler's command and headed for home until spring. Brant even considered staying behind, but in the end his desire for revenge was stronger than his disdain for Butler. Ninety of his Loyalist volunteers and thirty Mohawks chose to stay and follow their captain on the raid.

This was Captain Walter Butler's first large independent command. As they prepared to move up the Susquehanna from Tioga, the Provincial captain considered his order of battle. He had three companies of Butler's Rangers, totaling about 150 men, reinforced by a company of fifty redcoats from the British 8th King's Regiment of Foot from Fort Niagara, which he formed into a battalion under the command of Captain John McDonnell of the rangers for this operation. Brant commanded the 120 men of his own force. The Indian chiefs brought 310 Indian warriors, primarily Iroquois. The mostly Seneca war party also included some Cayuga, Onondaga, and a few Tuscarora, plus some allied Delaware, all following their own war chiefs. Although called together under the command of Sayenqueraghta, the leading warrior of the Six Nations, the

actual raiding party was probably led by
Garganwahgah, known to whites as
Cornplanter, and accompanied by Captain
John Johnston of the British Indian
Department.[3] Despite the absence of many
of Brant's men, and with the element of surprise working in their favor, Butler was sure
the force of 620 men under his command
was sufficient to the task, and they began
their journey to Cherry Valley.

The Americans began receiving ominous
intelligence that the enemy was again
preparing to strike. The Oneidas passed
along to the Continental Indian
Commissioner word of the "Hostile
Intentions of the Senecas & other Tribes of
Savages" to respond to the American attacks
in their territory. Although additional
Continental troops were soon expected in

Garganwahgah, or Cornplanter. Note
that the Seneca war chief and second
in command of all Six Nations' forces
during the Revolutionary War wears a
British officer's gorget. (*Library of
Congress*).

the area, Governor Clinton thought it advisable to call out a "greater portion" of
the militia and felt that the Minisink area appeared particularly vulnerable.[4] In
Tryon County, Lieutenant Colonel William Butler detached the Rifle Corps to
Schoharie's Upper Fort to bolster the militia garrison, and he and Colonel
Ichabod Alden each agreed to come to the other's assistance if attacked. Before
the end of October, the governor requested that Colonel Phillip Van Cortlandt
move his Continental regiment to the Rochester area. This precaution was
prompted after Major Cornelius Wynkoop of the militia learned that Ulster and
Orange County inhabitants were alarmed by reports that Brant's command
expected to join with Seneca reinforcements in an attack on Coshecton.[5]

On Monday morning, November 9, Brigadier General Hand set out to visit
his subordinates at Schoharie and Cherry Valley. The new commander of the
Northern Department wanted to see in person if the quartering of troops in
those frontier garrisons was the most expedient use of them through the winter. After arriving at Fort Alden, he inspected the post's magazines and the
return, or inventory report, of what ordnance stores of ammunition were on
hand. If the recent intelligence was accurate, Hand did not want his units to
face the threat with inadequate resources.

Although Colonel Alden doubted there was any great danger of enemy
attack until spring, the inhabitants of Cherry Valley were concerned about
their present safety. They had heard that the enemy was intent on striking their

settlement, and many living outside the town wanted to bring their families and some belongings into the shelter of the stockade. Alden maintained that the worry about an attack was only the result of rumor. But the reports were more than just rumors. At dawn six days before, eight to ten Indians and Tories attacked a farmer named Peter Hansen near Johnstown, not too far from Cherry Valley. Although they let his wife and children leave unharmed, they took Hansen and his servant prisoner, and burned his house and barn.

While he was at the settlement, the leading citizens and militia officers presented Hand a letter addressing their concerns. The people told the general that they were aware that there were still men in the towns along the frontier who were corresponding with the enemy. These Loyalists were not only furnishing information, but actively assisting the Indians and Tories by giving them provisions, often by plundering and robbing their Patriot neighbors of cattle, then secretly hiding them for the enemy's use during their operations. Some of these "Notorious Villains," they said, "have been apprehended at ye Butternuts and Elsewhere" since Colonel Alden's 6th Massachusetts Regiment arrived. According to them, Alden acted "with great activity and prudence in Subduing these Rebbels to the States." Quite often, instead of being held to prevent them from doing further harm, the "Villains" were "set at liberty" on passes, free to return to Cherry Valley and assist the forces of Butler and Brant. "It can [be] proven" that these Loyalists, the citizens told the general, "have aided Brant in his way of burning & Slaughter," and some were known to have friends, relatives, and other associates who were involved with the destruction at Cobleskill, Springfield, Andrustown, and German Flats. To prevent their community from being next on that list, they requested the army to provide a "sufficient number of Troops," along with those under Colonel Alden who already know "the Roads and Haunts of our Enemies," so Cherry Valley's people may be "screaned from Slaughter & Devastation and this Quarter from Ruin & Distress."[6]

Meanwhile, an express arrived from Fort Schuyler warning Colonel Alden to be on his guard. The hastily written message was signed by Major Robert Cochrane of Colonel Gansevoort's 3rd New York Regiment. Cochrane had received information from two friendly Oneida Indians that the council called by the enemy leaders at Tioga decided to attack Cherry Valley.[7] Brigadier General Hand had the regiment turned out for his review. After complimenting them on their inspection, General Hand took his leave, promising to send them a large quantity of provisions and ammunition. Because of the warning of the impending attack, Colonel Alden sent out scout parties to detect any indication of the enemy's approach. Before he headed back to his headquarters in Albany, General Hand met with Colonel Jacob Klock to ask for a 200-man detachment of Tryon County militia to reinforce the garrison at Cherry Valley.

One scout of eight men led by Sergeant Adam Hunter made its way down the Susquehanna and halted. As his men built a campfire and prepared to bed down for the night, Hunter failed to post sentries. The sergeant and his men woke up in the morning of November 10 surrounded by Tory rangers and Indians. Ironically, Hunter had been one of the guards posted on the Albany home where Walter Butler was held under house arrest before breaking his parole and making his escape. The sergeant and his fellow prisoners were questioned by their captors, and revealed many details that would assist the enemy in preparing their attack. The British forces believed they faced 300 Continentals and 150 militia soldiers who would defend a wooden picket stockade and a detached blockhouse that had been built by the town's inhabitants shortly after the attack on Cobleskill the previous spring. They also learned that there were a few defended homes in the area, both with blockhouses or houses enclosed within stockade fences. More important, Sergeant Hunter and his men revealed that all the garrison's officers were quartered at the home of a local family, about 400 yards from Fort Alden's gate.

The Indians and Tories resumed their march, trudging through a blinding snowstorm over ground covered in wet snow and mud. When they arrived within six miles of Cherry Valley, the enemy moved into the concealment provided by a pine wood. After calling his principal officers and Indian chiefs to a council of war, Butler proposed his plan of attack. Initially, they would proceed toward Cherry Valley at moonrise. One party of Seneca would rush the house where the American colonel and his officers were quartered, while the rangers and the rest of the warriors stormed the stockade and forced their way inside the gates before the defenders could sound an alarm. When the time for their departure arrived, however, the snow had turned to rain, and the Indians refused to initiate the battle until after daybreak. Without tents, the Tories and Indians spent a cold, miserable night sheltered only by the pine branches of the woods. To prevent revealing their presence to the Americans, and thus losing the element of surprise, even campfires to keep the men warm were not permitted.[8]

The next morning, November 11, Butler altered the plan before the column began its march toward Fort Alden. He decided to have Captain McDonnell and two subalterns lead fifty rangers accompanying one party of Indians to overwhelm a picket guard, then surround the house of Judge Robert Wells to keep Colonel Alden and the American officers from reaching the fort. Butler and the main body of rangers would then support the main attack on the fort by the rest of the Indian warriors. All went according to plan at first. With the Senecas in front, the forces of the Crown approached their objectives without being detected by American patrols or challenged by pickets. Butler then ordered the column to halt. While the rangers and redcoats were told to check their muskets, change flints, and replace wet cartridges, two Indian scouts went ahead to reconnoiter the last mile to the objective.[9]

Shortly after starting out, the scouts encountered two men cutting wood and opened fire. One woodcutter fell dead, but the other, although wounded, escaped. The Seneca chiefs, on hearing the firing, ordered their men onward, leaving the rangers and redcoats behind to hurriedly complete their preparations. The wounded woodcutter ran back toward the stockade, passing the Wells house as he went, spreading alarm that the settlement was under attack. When they heard the shouting, Major Daniel Whiting and a few officers barely had time to leave and flee to the stockade. The Seneca warriors came rushing onward, quickly overwhelmed the picket guard manned by two subalterns and twelve soldiers posted on the Wells farm, and charged the house. The warriors were soon joined by some of the Tory rangers. Before setting it on fire, the warriors and rangers cruelly murdered Judge Robert Wells and seven members of his family. Others pursued the American officers and surviving pickets toward the fort. They killed Colonel Alden and captured his second in command, Lieutenant Colonel William Stacy, along with a lieutenant, an ensign, the surgeon's mate, and a few privates before they could make it to the stockade. The regimental colors were saved from being taken as trophies only because they burned in the flames that consumed the Wells house.[10]

The element of surprise was lost, but within ten minutes of the first shots, rangers, redcoats, Tory volunteers, and Indian warriors surrounded the fort. Once in position at a distance of seventy yards, they opened fire with a hot fusillade that the Americans "as briskly returned both by their Musquetry and Cannon," according to Butler.[11] Frustrated in their attempt to take the fort by storm, Butler and the rangers explored a means of forcing their way into the stockade by reconnoitering the approaches from all sides. In the process, they captured and destroyed a detached blockhouse the Americans had not manned, or abandoned early in the attack.[12]

With the defenders isolated in the fort, the warriors rampaged all over the Cherry Valley settlement, killing "a number of inhabitants including women and children," and carried off many others as prisoners. Brant, who knew most of these people, attempted to stop the killing of civilians, but the Seneca warriors paid him no attention. Many civilians who had professed their Loyalty remained in the homes, believing Brant's pledge that they would not be harmed when his forces raided their settlements. On this occasion, that pledge did not help them. All Brant could do was "capture" as many people as possible and claim them as prisoners of his Mohawk and Onaquaga Indians in order to spare their lives and scalps.[13] Throughout the settlement, women and children shrieked in terror as Captain Butler's marauding allies plundered and burned homes, barns, and other buildings, and killed or drove off cattle and horses. Those settlers who could do so escaped into the woods to hide until it was safe to return.

As his Indian allies, accompanied by Indian Department personnel, committed their depredations, Butler positioned his rangers and redcoats on a rise overlooking the gate of the fort to block any attempt by the soldiers to sally out of the garrison and interfere with the orgy of destruction. The Tories maintained the position, despite an incessant rain, until late in the evening, when they retired to a position about a mile away from the fort to collect their prisoners and captives, divide the plunder, and bed down for the night. Most of the houses, barns, and Continental stores found in the settlement were put to the torch as the raiders withdrew.[14] Away from the action, the captive civilians and military prisoners were herded into the center of a circle of large campfires for the night. Many were only half-clothed, and all were exposed to the cold and wet weather.

The next morning, November 12, Captain Butler sent Captain McDonnell leading sixty rangers, accompanied by Brant and fifty of his Mohawks, back to complete the destruction of the town. Satisfied with the damage they had caused, the Seneca headed for home. Butler sent the rest of Brant's Indians and Loyalists, along with those rangers who were suffering from illnesses and exhaustion, to guard their prisoners and to gather and drive the captured cattle and horses on the march back to their hastily rebuilt base at Unadilla. All of the military prisoners and thirty-four civilian captives were marched along with the column. The remaining forty-five civilian prisoners waited under guard near the settlement as the battle resumed.

To support Captain McDonnell's detachment as it went about its task of destruction, Butler again positioned the redcoats and the remainder of the rangers to guard against any attempt by Americans to sally out and catch them off guard. The American garrison was under constant observation so that Butler could respond to any move they might make. Butler fumed that the Americans had refused to take the bait presented by McDonnell's detachment and come out to counter attack. They had apparently learned their lesson from the accounts of the Wyoming massacre in July. Disappointed at not being able to draw them into his ambush, Butler later reported, "The Garrison all the while coop'd within their Breast-Works remained Spectators of our Depredations which they made no Attempts to interrupt." Knowing that his force was inadequate to storm the fort to complete the destruction of the settlement, Butler "thought proper to retire and leave it, the only remaining Building amidst the Ruins of the Place."[15] Captain McDonnell's detachment finished its work and "returned after intirely desolating the Settlement and adding a large drove of

Horses & Cattle to those already taken."[16] Butler then ordered his command to begin its march toward Unadilla.

Major Whiting noted that "there was no sign of them [the enemy]" the next day, November 13, and sent a scout of a sergeant and eight men to reconnoiter toward Butternuts to determine where the raiders had gone. They found that the Indians had burned more houses, and killed and captured more American inhabitants there as they retired. Whiting then dispatched an express to Brigadier General Hand informing him of the attack, the destruction of the settlement, and the losses they had suffered, both civilian and military. He informed the general of the garrison's status in the aftermath of the attack. Whiting explained that food was in short supply, and if the militia had not had a barrel of powder and a box of cartridges to give them, the garrison would have exhausted their ammunition quickly. At the time, the major reported the death of his regiment's colonel and the civilian and military casualties as best he knew them. Within a few weeks, these were revised until the full cost of the raid was known.[17]

In all, the Continental Army suffered thirty casualties. Eleven, including the regimental colonel, were killed. One soldier was wounded. Four officers, including the lieutenant colonel, one sergeant, and thirteen rank and file, or a total of eighteen soldiers, had been captured or reported missing. The wounded soldier suffered an injured leg requiring amputation, but the surgeon no longer had any instruments. Civilian casualties had also been high. Thirty-three, mostly women and children, were murdered by Indians and Tories, and two were wounded. Seventy-nine inhabitants, again mostly women and children, had been taken captive. Forty-five of them, many believed to be Loyalist in their sympathies, were released and sent back to Cherry Valley after the last of Indians and Tories withdrew. Thirty-two houses, thirty-two barns, two mills, and one smith shop were burned, and all the livestock and food supplies were seized, leaving about 182 survivors to face the winter without food, clothing, or shelter. Whiting urgently requested reinforcements, food for the soldiers and civilians, ammunition, and a surgical kit to be sent to Cherry Valley without delay.[18]

Colonel Jacob Klock had already sent Brigadier General Hand word that Cherry Valley had been attacked in a November 12 letter. The general, in turn, sent an express to Governor Clinton with the "disagreeable Intelligence" about the raid, and requested that the governor forward it to General Washington as well, while he coordinated the American reaction to this latest attack. Brigadier General James Clinton wrote to his brother that Indians and Tories "Killed and Barbarous massacred" more civilians than soldiers at Cherry Valley. Forty-five of the prisoners had been permitted to return home, but of the prisoners carried off and still held by the enemy, most were civilians, primarily family members and servants of men who had been killed in their homes, and not militia post-ed for defense.[19] Unlike the attack on Wyoming, the "Cherry Valley Massacre" was not a description of hyperbole. An American officer accurately described it as "The most wonton destruction and horrid murders . . . committed by the Enemy."[20]

One of the freed captives returned to Cherry Valley carrying a letter from the enemy commander, Captain Walter Butler. Addressed to Major General Philip Schuyler, the ranger captain proposed an exchange of prisoners, specifi-cally civilian family members. Butler sought to exchange the wives, children, and servants of some leading Cherry Valley Patriots, including the family of Colonel John Campbell, in return for the safe passage of prominent Loyalist families to Canada. Butler was primarily concerned about his mother, who was left behind when he and his father, John Butler, fled to Canada with Guy Johnson in 1775. Mrs. Catherine Butler, along with her younger children, had been detained under house arrest by the Tryon County Committee of Safety ever since. Repeated requests for her to follow her husband to Canada were denied.[21]

Captain Butler indicated that his release of the forty-five captives was "induced by humanity lest the inclemency of the season, and their naked and helpless situation, might prove fatal to them." Colonel William Harper of the militia, however, saw an ulterior motive behind the "humanity." He believed that most of those freed were Loyalists who had been "captured" by Brant only to spare them from being murdered and scalped by the king's allies, and released when the Senecas marched away. Instead of accepting them in an exchange, Harper believed they should have been returned to Butler and Brant.[22]

Butler wrote that he expected the Americans to reciprocate and release an equal number of "our people," including his mother, to go to Canada. If the forty-five were not enough of a sign of his good faith, Butler proposed to exchange an equal number of the prisoners, taken by either rangers or warriors, still being held. He assured his adversaries that he had done everything in his power to "restrain the fury of the Indians from hurting women and children, or killing the prisoners" that fell into their hands. But he blamed the civilian loss-es, and his failure to prevent them, on the Americans. His Indian allies, he said, "were much incensed by the late destruction of their village" at Onaquaga. He then had the gall to say that he looked upon it "beneath the character of a sol-dier to wage war with women and children." Butler concluded by maintaining that he and his father had "no desire that your women or children should be hurt," but threatened that if the Americans persevered in detaining his father's family, the Butlers would "no longer take the same pains to restrain the Indians from prisoners, women and children, that we have heretofore done."[23]

After reaching Unadilla on November 17, 1778, Captain Walter Butler wrote to Colonel Mason Bolton that the British forces under his command and their Indian allies had burned the settlement of Cherry Valley and carried off prisoners and cattle. He admitted that many male inhabitants, who were not under arms, as well as women and children were among those killed in the attack. Butler praised Brant's and Captain Jacob's efforts for their Mohawks saving as many as they did by taking them as their prisoners for their own protection. Although Butler said that he "could not prevail with the Indians to leave the Women and children behind," Captain Johnston of the Indian Department convinced the Senecas to at least permit twelve Loyalists in their custody, along with those identified in Brant's and Captain Jacob's protection, to return to Cherry Valley. Curiously, he failed to mention his attempt at arranging an exchange of prisoners (hostages may be a more accurate description) with the Americans that would secure the release of his mother in return for some Patriot family members. The Provincial captain also said that the Indians were even "more incensed" that Colonel Dennison and the men who surrendered at Wyoming had violated their parole not to bear arms again against the Crown. Butler claimed that Dennison and other Wyoming Valley militia men had marched with Hartley's expedition and destroyed their towns at Tioga. With these charges, Butler ushered in a new phase of the border war, and stated that the Indians of the Six Nations allied with Britain "declared they would no more be falsely accused, or fight the Enemy twice; meaning that they would not in the future give Quarter."[24]

Joseph Brant was even less apologetic when he wrote to Colonel John Cantine of the Ulster County militia in December. He said it was "the Desire of the Seneca Chiefs and other Indians that [they] will Not in the Least trouble or moliest those People on the Delaware above Econack." Brant said, however, his men and their "Brothers the Senecas" were angry that the Rebels had burned their houses at Onaquaga while he and his warriors were gone. He failed to mention, however, that at that time they were raiding American settlements in Ulster and Orange counties. Brant's men and the Senecas, therefore, "Destroyed men, women and Children at Chervalle [Cherry Valley]" in retaliation for Lieutenant Colonel William Butler's attack on Onaquaga. Brant stated that the Indians wished to consider that all those living along the Delaware "about Shackaken" were brothers, and desired that the Americans would let them live in peace, "least you be worst delt with than the people of Cherry Valley." The militia colonel was warned that Americans along the frontier should not feel any more secure because of the changing seasons. Not even "hard winter would hinder war parties," according to Brant, because they had "Big Shouse" (snowshoes), and could reach any of the New York border settlements within a few days. Finally, Cherry

An Indian attack on a settler's home and family. Such a scene could have been enacted at Cherry Valley, where Britain's Indian allies killed unarmed men, as well as women and children. (*Library of Congress*)

Valley served as a reminder to the Americans that any counter stroke against Brant's people would lead to more bloodshed. Although Brant told Cantine that at that time his "face is another way," if the Americans destroyed an Indian village, "I will set my face again[st] you."[25]

When he learned of the raid, General Sir Henry Clinton, the British commander in chief for North America, thought the attack significant enough to report to Lord George Germain: "The Indians have again visited the Frontier and Surprized at Fort Alden, near Cherry Valley, part of two Regiments, thirty or forty were killed and Sixty taken prisoners, amongst them are the names of Field Officers. Our accounts are from Rebel papers and probably Softened, we therefore imagine they have Suffered a great deal."[26]

Colonel Klock, as he had agreed in the November 9 meeting with Brigadier General Hand, called out his regiment and was preparing to move on Cherry Valley to reinforce the garrison when he learned that the enemy had departed. Too late to assist the defenders, and without the necessary provisions and ammunition to mount an effective pursuit, Klock reluctantly dismissed his men. Hand alerted Colonel Van Schaick and his 1st New York Continental Regiment, which was quickly on the march toward Fort Plank on the Mohawk River to reinforce its garrison, that reports (which turned out to be false) said was also under attack.[27] At Hand's request, Brigadier General Abraham Ten Broeck ordered three regiments of his brigade to reinforce the post at Schoharie for fear it would also be attacked, and placed Colonel Abraham Wemple's militia regiment at Schenectady under Hand's orders until the crisis passed.[28]

In the meantime, there were false alarms and rumors that the enemy had again struck at and taken Fort Alden in Cherry Valley "by storm" and attacked Fort Plank on November 13.[29] Ten Broeck arrived in Schoharie with parts of the three militia regiments he had ordered out on Saturday, November 14. They quickly reinforced the garrisons of the three forts protecting that settlement, bringing them back to respectable numbers, since Lieutenant Colonel William Butler had marched his command, both the 4th Pennsylvania Regiment and the Rifle Corps, to the relief of Cherry Valley's garrison the previous day. But when Butler's column approached to within seven miles of Fort Alden, Major Whiting sent an express notifying him that the enemy had withdrawn the previous day (November 12) and was twenty miles away before dark. Butler countermarched back to Schoharie on Sunday. With the situation having stabilized at Cherry Valley, General Ten Broeck held a council of war with all the militia and Continental officers to plan for the defense of Schoharie, which had become the most important frontier settlement not yet attacked.

Ten Broeck's reinforcements continued to arrive, and before long, his units bolstered the garrisons at all three forts and had "Scouts who are kept out constantly." Together with Butler's Continentals, they were prepared to receive the enemy should they try one last attack before winter weather curtailed operations. By November 17, returning scouts reported seeing no enemy, but twelve inches of snow was on the ground in the woods. The weather continued to worsen. At last, the danger appeared to be over, prompting General Ten Broeck to write Governor Clinton with his assessment that "the season being so far advanc'd leads me to think they will hardly return from their Holes, to renew an Expedition replete with Fatigue and Danger."[30]

While Clinton commended Ten Broeck for his actions and directed him to continue supporting General Hand, enemy activity in other quarters of the frontier also needed attention. While the militia and Continentals north and west of Albany reacted to the attack on Cherry Valley, those in Ulster and Orange counties took precautions against Brant's reported intentions to stage attacks in the Cochecton area. Continental Army Colonel Philip Van Cortland and Militia Colonel John Cantine acted quickly. They moved reinforcements to Cochecton and strengthened the frontier guard posts. Soon, the situation along the Delaware south of the Catskills also seemed to turn quiet once again. With the rumors and alarms diminishing, and reports from scouting patrols confirming a reduction in enemy activity in the area, Colonel Van Cortlandt wrote to Governor Clinton that he was "not apprehensive of the Enemy attempting any thing further this Season." With the last alarm, one half of Ulster and Orange counties' militia men were then under arms, including those on actual service manning the guard posts.

Within a week of the Cherry Valley massacre, there was an increase in calls for a military expedition against the Indians. Governor Clinton personally wrote to General Washington and to Congress, the latter through Delegate John Jay. Cherry Valley was the seventh New York frontier settlement destroyed, and the most bloody in terms of the deliberate targeting of civilians. The experience showed that militia alone was too weak to prevent such depredations. The Tory rangers and their allied Indians could mass for an attack at any point, while the thinly stretched militia, even when reinforced by Continentals, could not be sufficiently strong anywhere. The loss of productive granaries such as Cherry Valley was sure to not only have an effect on the army and the war effort, but also cause hardship on the population. Governor Clinton recommended to both Washington and Congress that the sole means of effectively defending the frontier was "by Offensive Operations, thereby carrying the War into the Enemy's Country." He urged that if it were not possible that "a Competent Force can be detached from the Main Army without leaving it too Weak," he recommended that Congress consider raising one for the purpose.[31]

When Washington received Governor Clinton's letter on November 18, he answered with information that he was sending several units of Continentals to reinforce the efforts already under way on the frontiers of New York.[32] Cortlandt's 2nd New York Continental Regiment was instructed to take a post in the Rochester and Lauren Kill vicinity, and others were on the way. Brigadier General Count Casimir Pulaski was ordered to Minisink, where he took command of his own Pulaski's Legion,[33] joined by Colonel Charles Armand's 1st Partisan Corps,[34] Captain John Paul Schott's Independent Corps, and Colonel Oliver Spencer's Additional Continental Regiment.[35] As Washington had also informed the president of Congress two days before, the depredations against the frontier gave the general the most serious concern, and he "lament[ed] that we have not had it in our power to give them an effectual check." Although "perfectly convinced, that the only certain way of preventing Indian ravages is to carry the war into their own country," the commander in chief considered such an operation out of the question so late in the year. Instead, he believed that the only option was to "content ourselves for the present with defensive precautions." The general then reminded the president that, with the pending deployment of the rest of Brigadier General James Clinton's brigade of New York Continentals to Albany, "if anything offensive can possibly be undertaken, it shall be done."[36]

On November 20, 1778, General George Washington redefined the organization of Continental forces on the frontier so that they could deal with the enemy threat effectively with commands commensurate to two general officers, Brigadier Generals James Clinton and Edward Hand. Clinton was ordered to

Albany to assume command for all Continental troops "to the north and west," while Hand was ordered to Minisink to command the Continentals on the Delaware and Susquehanna. The two were to cooperate in protecting the frontier and executing offensive operations. Clinton's command included the two regiments of his own brigade at Albany, "Late Alden's" 6th Massachusetts at Cherry Valley, Lieutenant Colonel Butler's 4th Pennsylvania and Posey's Rifle Corps at Schoharie, and Colonel Seth Warner's "Green Mountain Boys" Additional Regiment on Otter Creek, in the Hampshire Grants, to the north. Hand exercised command over the forces that assembled under Pulaski's command at Minisink, Colonel Hartley's Additional Continental Regiment and two independent companies on the Susquehanna, and (although normally a part of Clinton's brigade) Colonel Van Cortlandt's 2nd New York Regiment posted at Rochester. Before the month was over, Washington ordered Colonel Baron Arendt's German Battalion[37] to Easton, Pennsylvania, and placed it under Hand's command as well. Governor George Clinton, due to his familiarity with the tactical situation and experience as a general officer in the Continental Army, retained authority for the best employment of his state's ranging companies in cooperation with both Hand's and Clinton's commands.[38]

In view of the deployment of Continentals and the diminished threat, there was not as great a need for militia to remain on active service through the winter. The classes of militia called out to meet the previous alarm were dismissed. Governor Clinton soon agreed with Colonel John Cantine's recommendation that the numbers of men on actual service as guards at the frontier posts of Ulster and Orange counties could be safely reduced or dismissed. Accordingly, on November 22, Clinton sent instructions for the militia colonel to consult with Colonel Van Cortlandt and General Hand about the minimum required to maintain only the most vital posts, and to send the rest of the troops home.[39]

After the attack on Cherry Valley, General Washington gave serious consideration to a western campaign. On November 21, 1778, Congress heard a letter from Washington describing the needs and outlining the measures he had taken to protect the frontier.[40] Recognizing that Congress had a "strong desire to undertake an Expedition against Canada," Washington set about the best means of execution. Any plans for a campaign under consideration by American forces would have to be dependent on what "Employment" the British "intend to give us on the Sea board next Campaign, on their strength in Canada, the State of our resources" and other logistical considerations. In a long letter to Major General Philip Schuyler, the commander in chief offered a number of possibilities and options, weighing advantages and disadvantages for each as he saw them, and asked for Schuyler's opinion.

Fort Niagara was among the prime targets. The choice seemed logical enough "For the more certain reduction of Niagara, and for the Peace and safety of the Frontiers of Pennsylvania and Virginia." The conceptual plan advanced a "body of Troops from Pittsburgh by the way of Alligany, la beauf (or French Creek) and Prisquile [Presque Isle]" to Niagara. Washington viewed this as a more realistic alternative than the expedition against Detroit that Congress had proposed and was still contemplating. The commander in chief reasoned that his move would be more practical, and keep the Indians' attention and "prevent them from affording succor to the garrison at Niagara," and therefore afford some protection to the Ohio frontier. Accordingly, the general gave orders for "Magazines of Provisions" to be gathered at Albany and on the Connecticut River to support a move against Canada from the either up the Mohawk to Lake Ontario or from the lower Coos in Vermont to Lake Champlain.[41] And while Generals Schuyler, Clinton, and Hand agreed, and advised Washington that a winter attack on the Indians was the best means of defending the frontier, other factors worked against it, primarily logistical deficiencies.[42]

By the end of November, Clinton and Hand reported to Washington that a winter campaign seemed impractical.[43] Schuyler answered with an "obliging letter" of sixteen pages of advantages and disadvantages for each option, along with his recommendation for the general's consideration. The commander in chief realized that the Continental Army's resources for supporting a winter campaign were "unequal to the preparations necessary for such an enterprise." Looking ahead to spring when a campaign might lead to the "emancipation of Canada and annexation to the United States, which Congress have much at heart," General Washington directed the Commissary General to stock large magazines of flour and salt provisions at Albany and other places, and the Quartermaster General to obtain and deliver materials for building boats, and stock forage and all classes of supply to support the intended expedition.[44] A spring campaign would make use of these boats and supplies, but it would not be the one Washington anticipated.

Chapter 10

WASHINGTON'S PLAN

D ESPITE the success of Provincial and Indian forces in terrorizing frontier inhabitants and keeping the Americans in a state of alarm along the borders, the American War for Independence had changed by 1779. With the entry of France and its allies into the conflict, North America was but one theater of a global war. General George Washington's Main Army had hounded the principal British field force of General Sir Henry Clinton in its withdrawal from Philadelphia, and successfully tested its new mettle at the Battle of Monmouth Courthouse in June 1778. That summer, on the Atlantic seaboard, redcoat armies held only Rhode Island in the northeast and the enclave around New York City in the middle colonies.

Late in the year, however, the forces of the Crown made two important moves. In the northwest, Lieutenant Colonel Henry Hamilton, lieutenant governor of Canada headquartered at Detroit, led a substantial part of his available forces to block Colonel George Rogers Clark's offensive at Vincennes in the Illinois territory. Sir Henry Clinton, commander in chief of British forces in North America, was ordered to invade the southern colonies and reestablish Crown authority there. Accordingly, he sent troops under the command of Lieutenant Colonel Archibald Campbell, supported by a fleet, to take Savannah, Georgia. In early 1779, the forces of Brigadier General Augustine Prevost, the British commander in East Florida, advanced north into Georgia and secured Savannah with Campbell's army.

To strengthen the numbers of men under arms, New York's Royal Governor, William Tryon, recommended to Lord George Germain, Secretary of State for the Colonies, that higher bounties be paid to recruits, and new military clothing sent from England to the commanders of the respective regiments and corps for issue to Provincial troops. Tryon also suggested "That the Indian Nations lying between Quebec and West Florida be let loose on the Frontiers of the revolted Colonies, unrestrained, excepting to Women and Children."[1]

As for the willingness of Indians to do so, John Butler wrote to governor and commander in chief of British forces in Canada, Lieutenant General Frederick

Haldimand, that with the exception of "the greatest part of the Oneidas . . . Indians in general have given the strongest assurances that they are determined to the last to persevere in the part they have taken, and never to come to terms with the rebels." Throughout the winter of 1778-1779, the Iroquois who were allied to the British had feared that the Americans would make another attempt to penetrate their territory. The Indian Department's officers were working hard to maintain the loyalty of their native allies by providing them firearms, gunpowder, and trade goods as gifts and signs of friendship. In February, Butler assured Haldimand that "Most of the Indians have been in to receive their clothing and presents."[2]

To prevent being surprised at Fort Niagara, the Provincial Rangers sent scouts out in every direction, while the main body was kept in readiness for immediate action, and prepared for the next campaign. In early February alone, members of Butler's Rangers and the Indian Department were conducting numerous patrols. There were two scouts on the Ohio, toward Fort Pitt and the areas adjacent to it. Two of his officers, Lieutenant Frederick Docksteder of Butler's Rangers and Captain William Johnson of the Indian Department were living with the Indians so that they would also have scouts out. One officer had a detachment at Chemung, and was sending scouts down the Susquehanna to Wyoming. Captain John Johnston of the Indian Department was posted with the Seneca. Some parties were scouting the area around Fort Schuyler, and the route between there and German Flats with hopes of intercepting American express carriers. Others, along with allied warriors, were scouting around Albany and Minisink to gain intelligence on the Americans' plans.[3]

On the American side, General George Washington outlined the strategic options the United States could pursue in the coming year. The first was conducting offensive operations, in conjunction with the French, "endeavoring to expel the enemy from their present posts in our front" at New York and Rhode Island, and remaining on the defensive elsewhere. The second involved "making an expedition against Niagara, to give effectual security to our Frontier and open a door to Canada," while remaining on the defensive at New York, Rhode Island and everywhere else. The third possible course was to remain entirely on the defensive, "except such smaller operations against the Indians as will be absolutely necessary to divert their depredations from us." Of these, the commander in chief favored an attack to recapture the city of New York. It would not only eject the enemy from that most important town, but would also compel them to abandon Rhode Island in order to reinforce their position. Washington favored an expedition against Niagara second. Potentially so expensive in men and material, however, it could prove to "exhaust our Strength and Resources in distant and indecisive Expeditions" while not significantly improving the "interior defense and absolute safety" of the states. With regret, Washington conceded that the only option that could realistically be implemented was the third, to stay on the defensive.[4]

In the northwest, Brigadier General Lachlan McIntosh's expedition against the Sandusky Indian towns stalled in the Tuscarawas Valley. With impending winter weather, McIntosh decided to construct a small fort, named Fort Laurens, along the Tuscarawas River, about 100 miles west of Fort Pitt, garrisoned by a small detachment commanded by Colonel John Gibson. General McIntosh planned to return to the fort in the spring to continue his offensive. After receiving Colonel Gibson's report on the state of activity at Fort Laurens, Washington was satisfied that the steps taken in the Western Department had "given at least a temporary relief to the inhabitants on the frontier," and looked forward for "pursuing a steady and properly concerted plan" in the next campaign. If nothing else, Washington believed the purpose of McIntosh's forces and the Indian commissioners was to "engage the friendship of the savages," and if that could not be accomplished, then to "reduce them to the necessity of remaining quiet" had been at least a partial success.[5]

Soon after Fort Laurens had been established, Indian scouts carried the news about the post to the Sandusky towns, where it was relayed to their British allies in Detroit. With Lieutenant Colonel Hamilton out leading a force to counter Colonel George Rogers Clark and his Virginia troops' expedition against Kaskaskia and Vincennes, Fort Laurens was not the major concern. Captain Richard Lernoult, who exercised command at Detroit in Hamilton's absence, was not prepared to commit what few British and Provincial forces he had against an isolated American post as long as Clark's force was still on the move. But Simon Girty, the militant agent and interpreter at the Sandusky towns, took matters into his own hands. Accompanied by seven Mingo warriors, he set out for the American fort on the Tuscarawas, intent on personally taking Colonel Gibson's scalp, and possibly Moravian missionaries at Coshocton or Lichtenau captive. In mid-January, missionary David Zeisberger learned about Girty's activities from some of his Delaware converts, and informed Gibson that the fort was likely to be attacked.[6]

Colonel Gibson, in turn, sought to inform General McIntosh. He sent a courier carrying the message containing the alarming news with the return trip of a convoy that had just brought supplies from Fort McIntosh. The letter also detailed the fort's weaknesses and precarious supply status. On January 22, the convoy departed, but after traveling about three miles from the post, it was ambushed. Captain John Clark and the men from his company of the 8th Pennsylvania providing the escort returned fire, and made a fighting withdrawal back to Fort Laurens. They suffered two killed, four wounded and one missing in the engagement. The soldier not accounted for was the courier carrying the sensitive correspondence to the general. He was captured, tortured and beheaded. His severed head was then displayed on the end of pole as a trophy back at one of the Sandusky towns. Although Girty did not grasp its significance, one of the other British Indian Department men realized what an intelligence boon the contents of the letter pouch contained, and rushed it to Detroit. When the convoy and escort tried again, they made it safely back to Fort McIntosh on January 29, and informed General McIntosh of the situation on the Tuscarawas.

Being at the end of long and tenuous line of communications, Fort Laurens proved difficult to keep supplied, especially after Girty's ambush in January. Through the winter of 1778-1779, convoys, work details, and soldiers sent to obtain supplies from traders living with the Delaware were harassed by small groups of Indians or attacked by war parties. Then in early February, Girty brought wampum belts from the Wyandot, Mingo, Shawnee, and Munsee to Detroit. He told his superiors that the allied nations were ready to field a force of 700-800 warriors, and were eager to strike a blow at the American fort on the Tuscarawas. Placed in an uncomfortable position, Captain Lernoult could not detach a large number of troops from his garrison without leaving Detroit vulnerable, nor could he do anything that might dampen the ardor or risk the continued loyalty of the Crown's Indian allies. The latter was a real possibility if they were restrained from taking action while the Americans kept a post so near their towns. When the chiefs of the major tribes gathered in Detroit for a council on February 7, they were read the contents of the dispatches captured by Girty and the appeal of the Six Nations. Captain Lernoult had no choice but to offer his support for an attack against Fort Laurens.

Captain Henry Bird, Lernoult's ranking subordinate, was assigned the mission. He had arrived in Detroit the previous autumn with a detachment of fifty men of the 8th Regiment of Foot from Fort Niagara to reinforce the Detroit garrison and assist in the construction of a new fortification. Bird selected ten volunteer redcoats, and went to join Girty's warriors on the expedition. When the captain reached the Sandusky towns, he found the warriors gathered there less numerous and not as eager for a fight as Girty had led him to believe. After Bird distributed ammunition, clothing, and other presents he brought them, about 180 Wyandot, Shawnee, Mingo, and Munsee stepped forward to join him. Undaunted, Captain Bird led the warriors, a few Loyalist volunteers and Indian Department men, and his ten redcoats on their expedition.

On February 22, Bird ordered his forces to prepare an ambush outside Fort Laurens. The next day, they surprised a fatigue party of nineteen soldiers that came out to gather wood and round up the horses. The attackers killed and scalped seventeen and took the remaining two men prisoner within sight of the fort. The combined British and Indian forces then showed themselves. In an effort to convince the Americans that an overwhelming force surrounded them, the enemy cleverly marched about in full battle regalia. Parties would then take turns withdrawing by concealed routes, and reappear in areas visible to the defenders. The ruse worked. Those in the garrison believed they were surrounded by more than 800 men.[7]

A supply convoy commanded by Major Richard Taylor of the 13th Virginia Regiment was attacked trying to reach Fort Laurens. It returned to Fort McIntosh on March 12, after suffering two men killed. Although the fort's supplies were running dangerously low, the besieging force was also short of provisions. By the middle of the month, runners brought the shocking news to Bird and the Indians that Lieutenant Colonel Hamilton had surrendered to Colonel Clark and his Virginians at Vincennes. The Wyandot warriors grew very worried and restless, and were soon determined to leave. On April 19, under the command of Major Frederick Vernon of the 8th Pennsylvania, a force of 300 Continentals and 200 Virginia and Pennsylvania militia, accompanied by a supply convoy, left Fort McIntosh. Although perhaps unaware of their approach, Bird lifted the siege the next day. Major Vernon arrived with fresh troops to relieve the beleaguered garrison after a four-day march. A detachment of three companies from his regiment, just over 100 men, took over the garrison from Gibson's weary troops, and Vernon assumed command of the post. Colonel Gibson led his men, the remainder of the relief column, and the now unburdened returning convoy on a six-day march toward Fort Pitt.[8]

At Continental Army headquarters, although concerned about the events at Fort Laurens, the commander in chief was developing a plan for a coordinated campaign against the Six Nations for the coming year. In January 1779, Washington outlined his campaign for his subordinate commanders and principal staff officers as they began the task of planning the two Indian expeditions Congress had resolved for the army to make in that year. First, he wanted to conduct the campaign when and where it was most favorable for "subsisting the army with ease and least Expence," Second, he wanted "To scourge the Indians at the proper season" that would do the most damage at the least risk to American forces. And third, he wanted to "rout the enemy from N York," should there be sufficient forces to do so.[9] In order to "scourge the Indians" properly, Washington envisioned an operation conducted by three divisions of substantial size marching into Iroquois country by different routes, preferably in June, or "at a season when their Corn is about half grown." Of the three divisions, he proposed that one would advance up the Allegheny River from Fort Pitt, one up the Susquehanna by way of Wyoming, and the third into Seneca country by the Mohawk River.

Although grand in terms of the resources committed, Washington envisioned the campaign's "only object should be that of driving off the Indians and destroying their Grain." Once accomplished, the expeditionary forces would return to their garrisons whether a major engagement was fought against substantial enemy forces or not. This was economic warfare, an attack on the enemy's ability to wage war. Success could be measured, in part, by forcing the Six Nations to become more of a burden on the already strained British logistics system in Canada. A victorious campaign against the Iroquois would also eliminate a threat to Washington's rear as he faced the entrenched British army around New York City, but would be a benefit in any case, "whether the Enemy continues in great or little force at N York."[10] Finally, Washington anticipated minimal participation from militia: "Continental Troops must be employed against the Indians or else the Work wont be half done."[11]

The commander in chief began directing the principal commanders that would be involved in the offensive to begin preparing their magazines to support the operations. He also ordered them to provide him with information on the nature of the terrain and enemy forces so that the operational concept could be translated into a realistic preliminary plan and the resources allocated. As a western expedition against Detroit had been part of the original intent of Congress, Washington wrote to Brigadier McIntosh asking about the state of readiness for the operation in the Western Department. He told McIntosh of his decision "to carry the War into the Indian Country" in the spring "as early as the Season and the State of our Magazines will admit." Although no particular plan had been formally adopted nor objectives for the attack fully determined, Washington was certain that one of the "principal places" from which the offensive would be launched was Fort Pitt. He therefore instructed McIntosh to begin his preparations by collecting intelligence on the "State of the Country, Waters, &ca over which we shall probably pass" on the way to Detroit. General Washington wanted information on the river system and requirement for bateaux or canoes, whichever was thought more suitable for transporting and supplying 1,000 to 1,200 troops on the western waters. Supplies, always a problem for the Continental Army, required the establishment of magazines to support a campaign of three to four months' duration. To ease the burden, Washington informed McIntosh that he was going to approach the Board of War for the formation of those magazines as early as possible.[12]

As a word of caution, the commander in chief told McIntosh that expeditions against both Detroit and the Six Nations were being considered. If the one against the Six Nations was preferred to one against Detroit or the Indians of the Ohio, the Western Department could be ordered to conduct a supporting operation. Therefore, Washington needed to know the same information about terrain, routes of advance, ease of troop and wagon movement or water carriage, and distances between Fort Pitt and the country of the Six Nations, especially that of the Senecas, "who are the most numerous and warlike and inimical of the whole." To preserve the element of surprise, Washington cautioned McIntosh not to disclose what the army was considering to any civilians or Indians that were inquired of or hired to furnish information.[13]

Protecting the flanks of the proposed force was also of vital importance. If the expedition was to be directed against the Six Nations, and the Indians of the Ohio country showed a "disposition for peace," McIntosh and his Indian Commissioner, Colonel George Morgan, were instructed to encourage them. It would, Washington said, be "bad policy to irritate them while we are employed another way." The general believed that if the expedition "can reduce or force the Six Nations into submission," it would have a beneficial effect on the "Western tribes, who tho' perhaps full as powerful in fact," would "not willingly offend a people who had chastised the most warlike Nation."[14] In short, defeating the Six Nations could quiet the Ohio Indians, Washington surmised.

If the Six Nations country proved to be the object of the campaign, Washington wanted McIntosh and his staff to inquire on what roads and passes led from the northwestern frontiers of Pennsylvania to Venango and other places on the Allegheny above it. He also wanted to know whether roads could accommodate marching troops and packhorse trains carrying supplies. Other logistical matters needed to be determined, such as the abundance of grass, and the best time that would have allowed it to have gained sufficient growth to subsist cattle and horses, which would preclude or reduce the army's need to carry forage and fodder. Likewise, knowledge of the depths of the rivers was of interest to determine which were navigable, and where they were fordable or could be passed without boats, and the navigability of French Creek, or la Beuf, to Presque Isle (present-day Erie). All this information was important to the planning of a coordinated campaign. Washington said that a proposed movement in the Northern Department would not commence until the Western Department was ready. Whether they were to cooperate with forces moving from Albany or along the Susquehanna, or acting "in a different quarter from them," the mutual benefit to all offensive movement commencing at the same time was sure to achieve the best result.[15]

The commander in chief sent similar directives to the other principal commanders facing the pending offensive into Indian territory. He ordered Brigadier General Edward Hand to seek information on the Susquehanna River approaches to Seneca country, the positioning of magazines, and the availability of boats. In order not to alert the enemy about their intentions, Lieutenant Colonel Zebulon Butler was not to start engaging in any preparations at Wyoming.[16] Militia Brigadier General James Potter was solicited for his advice on "the Routes of penetrating Indian Country" from western Pennsylvania.[17] Likewise, Brigadier General James Clinton was alerted to "secure a communication between Fort Schuyler and Schenectady" to support any expedition that might be mounted.[18]

Washington turned to one of his most trusted advisors on frontier warfare, Major General Philip Schuyler, on how best to approach Iroquois territory from the Northern Department. Schuyler had already provided the commander in chief with an extensive analysis of the situation and recommendations for the campaign against the Indians and Tories in that area. The principal target, or "capital object," was the country of the Seneca, whose warriors had caused the most destruction. Schuyler estimated a force of 3,000 men supported by light artillery would be adequate, and agreed that at least one division should move into Seneca country from the traditional invasion route of the Mohawk River. Schuyler further recommended that the expedition carry its provisions in trains of packhorses after the boats had carried them as far as possible. Some preparations, particularly the establishment of magazines and building of boats in Albany for the aborted invasion of Canada, could be used for the new expedition. Schuyler also advised that the plan include a feint from Coos on the Connecticut River by Colonel Seth Warner's Regiment of Green Mountain Continentals and militia, who had been rumored to be preparing an expedition, which could deceive the British and divert their attention.[19] Such a move, he believed, would cause alarm in Canada, and prevent the forces of the Crown from sending reinforcements to the Six Nations, Niagara, or Detroit.[20]

By mid-February, General Washington had decided on the basic concept of the operation. He notified Brigadier General McIntosh, "The more I contemplate on an Expedition from Fort Pitt, the more perswaded I am of the superior advantages that will result from its cooperation" with an offensive from the east. A move up the Allegheny would present the advantage of the greater use of water transportation, especially for the supply trains, and so McIntosh was directed to procure the necessary watercraft. With the objective determined to be the Seneca towns, McIntosh could concentrate on the intelligence necessary to begin planning in that direction. The commander in chief also instructed

McIntosh to give "as little trouble as possible with Militia next Campaign" to avoid expense, and to insure his "operations may be more governable and point-ed with respect to time." Instead of calling on militia, the department would rely on the "standing Forces" available as much as possible, primarily the 8th Pennsylvania and 13th Virginia regiments, along with the few independent com-panies of Continental or State Line troops, and the volunteer ranging compa-nies. In addition, Washington was going to order the Maryland Independent Corps, a unit of three companies under the command of Colonel Moses Rawlings, to join the department. Rawlings' officers were busily recruiting, try-ing to raise the corps from fifty or sixty men to the establishment strength of 100. As soon as Maryland militia relieved them from their duty of guarding German prisoners at Fort Frederick, they would march to Fort Pitt. Washington also took the necessary measures to place the Quartermaster Department's func-tions at Pittsburgh under McIntosh's direction, to facilitate logistical support.[21]

The commander in chief then turned to his Quartermaster General, Major General Nathanael Greene, to refine his instructions on logistical support of the pending campaign. The army's Commissary General, Colonel Jeremiah Wadsworth, was ordered to prepare a magazine with four months' provisions for 1,200 men at Fort Pitt, and another for 1,000 men at Sunbury on the Susquehanna River, exclusive of rations required for the daily subsistence of troops assigned in those areas. To cut the expense of transportation, the com-missary was to purchase supplies for the Fort Pitt magazines from the Virginia frontier, and for those at Sunbury, from west of the Susquehanna. Operations in Indian territory would rely on packhorses, instead of wagons, for transport-ing supplies over land. Magazines for forage also had to be established and filled. In addition, Greene was to stockpile items of equipment that were need-ed for the expedition at Easton, Pennsylvania, and obtain "in as secret a man-ner as the nature of the case will admit," a list of all the vessels the army had or could procure, with estimations of their carrying capacities, between Harris' Ferry (now Harrisburg) on the Falls of the Susquehanna and Wyoming.[22]

On February 25, the Continental Congress formally authorized General Washington to plan and execute an Indian expedition in 1779.[23] The com-mander in chief ordered his staff to begin planning in earnest, and requested his principal advisors and the pertinent department commanders to present their views on the proposed expedition against the Six Nations. At least part of the plan would send one division up the Susquehanna River against Chemung before advancing to join the divisions advancing from the Mohawk and Allegheny Rivers. Washington asked Brigadier General Schuyler to see if his fellow Indian Commissioners in the Northern Department, Reverend Samuel Kirkland and James Dean, could find out the locations of Indian towns and the numbers of warriors they could get in the field along the Mohawk River axis of advance from the friendly Oneidas.[24]

Schuyler also assumed responsibility for coordinating support in New York. After corresponding with Washington, he wrote Governor Clinton in early March that the contemplated plans to penetrate into Canada or even to reduce Fort Niagara had been deemed too ambitious. Instead, the expedition was to be prosecuted against the hostile tribes of the Six Nations, principally the Seneca. The earlier ideas were not entirely discarded, however. If the commander chosen to lead the expedition deemed it within the capability of the force at his disposal, he would be at liberty to take advantage of opportunities to move either into Canada or against Niagara. At the very least, it was envisioned that the Indian expedition could secure the western frontiers for the season, unless the enemy moved to destroy the border settlements before the Continental troops got there. American intelligence had received word from its informants in Canada that the enemy meant to "attack in every quarter this season," and a large body of Indians was expected to gather in Montreal in May.[25]

After digesting Schuyler's recommendation for the main effort of the campaign to advance against the Seneca country by the Mohawk River, Washington asked the opinion of another of his most trusted subordinates, Major General Nathanael Greene. Once he had studied Schuyler's recommendation, Greene voiced his opinion that the Susquehanna was the more advantageous avenue of approach to the enemy's territory. The Mohawk River avenue, by comparison, was more risky and therefore more expensive, and less certain of success, considering the objectives, the forces necessary, hazards to be encountered, time allowed for execution, the cost in manpower and materiel, and the certainty of execution.[26]

Greene pointed out that an advance along the Mohawk was perpendicular to the natural obstacles presented by the various lakes and rivers. That translated to a requirement for a larger expeditionary force that would also be exposed to more hazards as it traveled farther to reach its objectives than taking the Susquehanna River route. The movement of supplies and provisions was also more difficult. Supply trains of watercraft would have to move up the Mohawk River from Albany to Fort Schuyler, then portage into Wood Creek, and down the Creek into Oneida Lake. That would not only be slow and tedious, but after passing the lake and the Onondaga River, the force would still be as distant from the heart of the Seneca nation as it would be at Tioga.[27]

Greene also offered his view on the method of supplying the expedition. The construction of stockade forts along the line of march—a strategy often employed—was not worth the effort, he believed. The troops left to complete their construction and provide their garrisons would "considerably diminish" the combat strength of the committed force, while contributing little to the actual security of the stores deposited within the walls. Instead, concurring with General Schuyler, he recommended that after reaching the end of the watercourses, the easiest, most secure, and most efficient means of transporting the army's supplies was by packhorses traveling with the expedition. Also, if the army was to be defeated and its retreat along the rivers by which it entered the Seneca country cut off, it should carry sufficient provisions to move along with it in any direction it would be forced to take. Otherwise, the troops would risk starvation or surrender. Therefore, Greene did not believe the number of watercraft or packhorses estimated by Major General Schuyler to be adequate for an expedition from the Mohawk. Approaching the Seneca Nation from the Susquehanna, on the other hand, would require fewer packhorses and boats to keep the army supplied.[28]

There was also no point in attempting to surprise the enemy, according to Greene. The measures to maintain secrecy could only interfere with the plan and preparations of attack. By its nature, a conventional army conducting an expedition was too large and its movements too slow to surprise people who kept a good system of scouts and lookouts deployed in the forests with which they were intimately familiar. The Americans also had to anticipate the possibility that British forces would attempt to support their allies. If a large enemy force landed on the shore of Lake Ontario, as at Fort Oswego, after the American expedition was beyond the Onondaga River, they could cut the line of water communication and supply. American forces would have to either halt their advance to dislodge them, or risk the increased danger of continuing the advance while the supply routes "were so precarious and a retreat so insecure." Regardless, any halt would delay the expedition and reduce the prospects of success. If the expeditionary force was divided with one division addressing the threat on its flank, the army risked defeat in detail deep in enemy territory. Even if the expedition were successful in dislodging it, a British force on its flanks could easily retire to their ships on Lake Ontario. As soon as the American army attempted to move farther into Iroquois country, the British could return and "play the same game over again."[29]

Greene posed that if the "great object of the expedition" was to "give the Indians a severe chastising," anything less would not be worth the effort, much less the expense or use of resources that could be employed with more effect elsewhere. In Greene's opinion, a sufficient show of force might induce the Indians to agree to terms. But if that was the intended outcome of the offensive, he was not optimistic it could be achieved. "Unless their pride is broke down and they [are] sufficiently humbled," the expedition would gain little benefit from negotiations. Furthermore, as soon as the American forces were gone, the British were sure to "spirit them up to commit the same depredations again as they did in the last Campaign." Greene was therefore insistent that the plan of the expedition should be founded upon the principle of "chastising and humbleing the pride of the Indians and not trust to the uncertain advantages of a negotiation."[30] The Susquehanna route, he believed, was the avenue of advance that offered the best prospect of success at the least expense and risk.

Weighing the advice of Generals Schuyler and Greene, Washington formulated a preliminary plan for carrying the war into Indian territory, and forwarded his thoughts to those subordinates who were likely to carry it out. Brigadier Generals McIntosh and Hand were both asked for their comments, and for any intelligence they had or could obtain on the terrain, hostile Indians, and resources that could support the expedition.[31] Additionally, Washington wanted to determine whether the "principal settlements of the Indians of the Six Nations (particularly the Senecas) were most accessible by the Waters of the Susquehanna or by the Mohawk River." He therefore asked Hand to make inquiries of friendly Indians living in the border settlements and whites who had traveled into Indian territory, and three settlers who had recently escaped captivity by the Senecas.[32]

General Washington contacted Colonel William Patterson of the Pennsylvania militia to engage some "intelligent, active and honest Men" familiar with the Susquehanna, its tributaries, and the country from Chemung to Fort Niagara. After being told as little as possible why it was desired, they were sent "to obtain as minute and satisfactory information as possible" about the Indian towns of the Six Nations and their dependents, the readiness of the warriors and the garrison at Fort Niagara, and the suitability of roads and availability of forage along the way through observation and inquiry of the inhabitants. Patterson's spies were provided passes, and the commanders of the frontier posts at Fort Willis, Sunbury, and Wyoming were instructed to issue them with up to five days' rations and other assistance requested, and not to subject them to any delay or their canoes to the usual search.[33]

The commander in chief then approached General Potter and Joseph Reed, President of the Supreme Executive Council of Pennsylvania, and Governor George Clinton of New York about the forces their respective states could provide. Congress had voted on funds to pay five Pennsylvania and New York companies, and Washington requested that they be drawn from their states' "Corps of active Rangers who are at the same time expert marksmen and accustomed to the irregular kind of wood fighting practiced by the Savages." These men, "embodied under proper officers," were preferable to greater numbers of ordinary militia. Washington feared that the latter, "unacquainted with this species of war," would only consume provisions and ammunition from the limited supply in the magazines without performing any effective service before their terms expired, as so often had happened in the past. If the companies had to be raised, the commander in chief suggested they seek volunteers from "those inhabitants who had been driven from the frontier," who both possessed knowledge of the country over which they would likely march and were motivated toward exacting some retribution against the foe.[34]

Meanwhile at Fort Pitt, General McIntosh's abrasive style, which had not endeared him to the local people, was affecting his ability to command. In February, he lost the confidence of his principal subordinates, particularly Colonel Daniel Brodhead. The County Lieutenants of both Virginia and Pennsylvania distrusted him as an outsider instead of a mediator in resolving the border dispute between the two states. Before Washington instructed him to concentrate on a campaign up the Allegheny, he called a council of war to explore the resumption of the campaign against the Sandusky towns. Few subordinates or militia officers expressed their favor of his plans, and McIntosh reluctantly gave up the idea of attacking Detroit for good. At the beginning of March, with the approval of Congress, General Washington reassigned McIntosh to the Southern Department, where he had previously enjoyed some success, and replaced him as commander of the Western Department with Colonel Brodhead.[35]

Washington then turned his attention to selecting the commander of the expedition. In the letter offering the position, he outlined the mission to be undertaken. "The objects of this expedition will be effectually to chastise and intimidate the hostile nations, to countenance and encourage the friendly ones, and to relieve our frontiers from the depredations to which they would otherwise be exposed." To achieve these aims, "it is proposed to carry the war into the heart of the country of the Six Nations, to cut off their settlements, destroy their next year's crops, and do them every other mischief, which time and circumstances will permit."[36]

According to the intelligence collected, the estimated strength of the warriors of the Six Nations allied with the British and the Tories operating with them was about 3,000 men. It was possible that they could be reinforced by British and Provincial regulars, and receive other aid from the British garrisons on the frontiers and in Canada. Washington explained that about 4,000 Continental troops (rank and file fit for service) plus "such aids of militia as may be deemed absolutely necessary" were to be employed. The militia component was intentionally not large, as Congress was looking to pursue a plan "of strict economy," and calling out militia was always more expensive and less effective. The Continental supply system was strained, but the expedition was within its ability to support. Three thousand troops were to compose the main body, the remainder employed in other areas "to harass and distract the enemy, and create diversions in favor of the principal operation."[37]

Although he was not Washington's first choice, seniority and popularity among the delegates in Congress dictated that the post was first offered to Major General Horatio Gates. Accordingly, on March 6, Washington wrote to Gates and expressed his wish "that it may be agreeable" for him to "undertake the command of this expedition." Wanting the campaign to begin in May, Washington urged Gates to reply immediately. If he declined, Washington enclosed a letter with the same offer for Major General John Sullivan, along with the request that Gates forward it to that officer on making his decision.[38] In his March 16 reply from Boston, the fifty-year-old Gates wrote that "The Man who undertakes the Indian Service should enjoy Youth and Strength; requisites I do not possess." Saying it "Grieves me Your Excellency should Offer me The only Command, to which I am intirely unequal," Gates curtly declined and forwarded Washington's letter to Sullivan in Providence.[39] General Sullivan accepted.

Sullivan's military career to that point had been a series of highs and lows. He took command of the American troops who had failed in their invasion of Canada during the winter of 1775-76, and despite a pledge that they would not continue to retreat, Sullivan was forced to fall back. Joining Washington to face the British at Long Island in August 1776, Sullivan was captured by Hessian troops during the battle. Released in a prisoner exchange later that autumn, he returned to Washington's service and fought with tenacity and poise at the Battle of Trenton, capturing the bridge across Assunpink Creek to effectively cut off the enemy's retreat. He continued to lead troops alongside Washington in the Battle of Princeton. Despite this brief success, Sullivan complained to Washington about his command assignments. But after failing in an attempt to recapture Staten Island, he received the lion's share of blame for the defeat at the Battle of Brandywine, where his division was completely outflanked. In 1778, Sullivan was assigned to command the American forces in the failed attempt to capture Newport, Rhode Island, in conjunction with the French allies.

While waiting for Sullivan's acceptance, General Washington contacted Brigadier General Hand. The commander in chief alerted him that the troops under his command could be ordered to move on short notice for a march into enemy territory. Except for Colonel Van Cortlandt's regiment, which was to remain in place, Washington asked Hand to plan the best route of movement by his troops from Minisink to Wyoming.[40]

Washington next alerted Colonel Brodhead to prepare for an invasion of Indian territory from Fort Pitt, and to gather the information and supplies necessary. On the arrival of Colonel Moses Rawlings' Maryland Independent

Corps at Fort Pitt, Brodhead was to attach enough troops to bring Rawlings' command to 100 men, and issue them the necessary tools for building stockades, and send them to Kittanning. There, Rawlings was to establish security, "choose a good piece of ground," and erect a stockade fort for the security of convoys. After completing that post, Rawlings was to leave a small garrison and march with the remainder of his detachment to Venango to establish another post of the same kind for the same purpose.[41]

Colonel Gibson and the garrison at Fort Laurens was to join Brodhead at Fort Pitt "when matters are ripe for execution" of the campaign. Until it was time to move, Brodhead was instructed to keep the "intended removal from the Tuscarawas a profound secret." When the marching orders were received, Gibson was to abandon the fort as swiftly as possible. Colonel Brodhead was also urged to hasten the delivery and construction of the necessary watercraft. It was important that neither Indians nor anyone else be aware of the intended destination of the march until the movements themselves indicated the possible direction. Brodhead was encouraged to engage the assistance of as many friendly warriors as could accompany his force as scouts, and to procure good guides who knew the way from the "head of navigation of the Allegheny to the nearest Indian towns and to Niagara." Even after the movement began, Brodhead was to keep the objective a secret for as long as possible. He was to inform Washington by a "careful express" of his estimated time when he would be ready to begin, the time to march to Kittanning and Venango, then from there to the head of navigation of the Allegheny, and the distance and time required to reach the Indian towns. He was instructed to move as light as possible, with "only a few pieces of the lightest artillery." Accuracy of plans and reports were crucial, and the plan for cooperation with other movements had to "be perfectly formed."[42]

Through the winter, the Americans had tried to win allies among the Six Nations. Lieutenant Colonel Cornelius Van Dyck of the 1st New York Regiment, who was the commandant at Fort Schuyler, wrote to Brigadier General James Clinton in late December that Captain Peter Johnson of the British Indian Department was at Oneida Castle. Reportedly, Johnson was attempting to persuade the Oneidas to forsake their alliance with the United States and "join with their brother Indians" on the side of the Crown. In response, Van Dyck detached an officer with a party of soldiers to take Johnson prisoner and bring him back to the fort "to Enquire more Particularly into his Business." But the party returned empty-handed to report that the Indian Department officer had gone before they arrived.

In another meeting with the chiefs, the sachem Priest Peter informed Van Dyck that Captain William Johnson of the British Indian Department was at

Oneida Castle, claiming he had been sent by the Cayuga with a message for the Oneida and eight strings of black wampum painted with vermilion. Quoting Johnson, "They Expressed their sorrow that the Oneidas had separated themselves from the Confederacy and Joined its Enemies." By doing so, the Oneida had "Exposed themselves to the severe Resentment of the other tribes, but that they (the Cayugas) had hitherto Protected them from Insult."[43] Captain Johnson further warned the Oneidas that their "conduct" in carrying messages of intelligence on the Six Nations for the Americans "had proved them to be so Notoriously Disaffected to the Confederacy that it was neither their interest nor Indeed in their Power to protect them any Longer." They wanted the Oneida to "Reflect on the Consequences" of their separation from the Confederacy and urged them to "Reunite with their ancient friends & allies in a vigorous opposition against the Common Enemy," the Americans. If they would not actively join in fighting the Rebels, the Six Nations urged them to "at Least Strictly Observe those Solemn promises of Neutrality which they had Repeatedly made" to their brethren. If they could not comply with either request, the Cayuga threatened "they should not see another spring in peace." The events of the winter would determine their fate.[44]

A Frenchman, identified only as "Joseph," also entered the fort. He told Lieutenant Colonel Van Dyck that an Onondaga had informed him that the provisions destined for Fort Schuyler could not get through, and the bateaux were being held on the Mohawk. The Six Nations, Joseph said, were determined to capture the boats and cut the communications between the river settlement and the post. They intended to attack as soon as their people who had gone to Fort Niagara for a council with the British returned.[45]

In mid-January, the Onondaga met in council with representatives of the Oneida and Tuscarora to reach a resolution on the rift in the Iroquois Confederacy. The lack of consensus had caused the council fire to be ceremonially extinguished, symbolizing the disagreement. When the chiefs returned to Oneida Castle to inform their people, they explained that should any Oneida or Tuscarora choose to join the British, they were given "free liberty" to withdraw from the nations. The meeting resulted in a "unanimous resolution to stand by each other in defense of their lives and Liberty against any enemy that might be disposed to attack them." With that, they also unanimously agreed to answer the Cayuga message, saying, "That as they had ever behaved themselves in a quiet peaceable manner toward the Confederacy, they could not conceive their conduct was reprehensible by them." They had attempted to remain neutral and "utterly despaired of ever being able to effect reconciliation between the Confederacy and the United States." Their only hope was that their Iroquois brethren would "in time abandon the cause they had imprudently espoused."

The Oneidas and Tuscaroras said they would never violate the alliance with the Americans, nor would they be the aggressors or provoke any tribe to war, but would henceforth be on guard against any enemy.[46]

Seven Onondaga sachems who were considered neutral in the war were visiting Oneida on their way to Fort Schuyler. The Oneidas made them aware of the council proceedings and presented a large belt of black wampum to acquaint them with the results. The visiting Onondagas, it was said, were glad to hear of the resolution made by the Oneida and Tuscarora "children," although the heads of the confederacy's powerful tribes had declared themselves on the British side.[47]

With the Oneida and Tuscarora decision, the seven Onondagas, from the keepers of the council fire and holders of the tree of peace, said they "let go their hold of peace; extinguished the council fire, and sunk the tree of peace in the earth." These Onondaga emissaries then joined with the Oneida and Tuscarora in opposing any invader. They returned to Onondaga to "effect a final separation in their tribe, and insist that every one shall declare for one side or the other." Then they joined with the Oneida in requesting American troops to be sent for their protection and to furnish a supply of goods to trade at Fort Schuyler.[48] When he heard of the Oneida and Tuscarora declaration in late January, Brigadier General James Clinton ordered a fort to be built at Oneida Castle to aid in their defense against pro-British Iroquois.[49]

While campaign preparations and Indian negotiations were being carried out by the Americans, the British were not idle. When he learned that Lieutenant Colonel Hamilton had surrendered at Vincennes, the commander in chief and governor of Canada, Lieutenant General Frederick Haldimand, ordered reinforcements to Detroit. John Butler sent one company, about fifty men, under the command of Captain William Caldwell.[50] Then in early March, Butler notified Haldimand "that the Rebels have their Emissaries At work in Every Quarter, and are using Every act to intimidate the Indians and draw them to their Side." Some bands of the Onondaga, he warned, were "already in their Interest" and endeavoring to bring the rest. Butler feared that the Crown stood to lose "so many Friends" if the efforts of the American commissioners were successful. A letter from "Mr. Clinton" had arrived, inviting the Onondaga to a council to talk peace with the Americans. Butler convinced those remaining to use the absence of the rest of their chiefs as a pretext for not sending a positive reply. He was resolved not to let the Onondaga go, or to forward the Americans' wampum belt to the Ohio. He redoubled his efforts to keep them in the alliance, and kept the scouts from his ranger corps constantly busy on the frontier.[51]

Reports began to arrive at American headquarters that the enemy was planning something. Scouts patrolling near Fort Schuyler received intelligence that a large body of Indians and Tories was gathering at Fort Niagara and the Seneca towns to attack the Oneida. From there, they would continue their invasion down along the Mohawk Valley into the American settlements, and the Cayuga were allowing them free passage. The Oneida had information gathered by their own scouts that the "enemy intend very soon to attack the frontiers with a very considerable force." Militia and Continental officers soon requested supplies "to make a better stand," and asked their superiors to send more troops to protect the Mohawk River Valley settlements.[52]

It looked as if the British and their Indian allies were poised for a renewal of their terror campaign. Governor Clinton found it necessary to give the inhabitants of those areas "general Assurances of Protection" to prevent them from deserting their towns and farms. The New York General Assembly empowered the state to raise 1,000 levies.[53] Half of those would be available for frontier defense, providing the five companies Washington had asked for to support the Indian expedition. The rest would be used to temporarily bring New York's Continental battalions to the establishment strength as resolved by Congress. Congress readily acknowledged and approved of the New York legislature's action. Because the state had already suffered great hardship and distress caused by the "ravages committed by the Indians the previous fall" and because of the difficulty in manning posts to secure the frontiers, Congress also resolved to allow Continental pay and rations for the 1,000 levies.[54]

With the coming of spring, the enemy was becoming active and more aggressive. Continental and militia officers were again responding to reports that the enemy was sighted, especially in the Mohawk Valley of Tryon County. One scout of ten Indians was reported operating in the area of Fort Johnson and the now abandoned home of Colonel Daniel Claus on April 11, telling those civilians they encountered and took prisoner that enemy scouts were "spread all over." While in their custody, the scouts inquired of their prisoners on the locations of prominent Whigs and their families, and the state of readiness of the local militia. The scouts also questioned local inhabitants if they heard of any reports or rumors of Indians on the frontier, and whether they knew if the Continental Army was preparing to mount an expedition against Canada. Of the four men this party captured, one was released and one escaped.[55]

While the Tories and their Indian allies were conducting a new campaign of raids, the Americans received reports that the Onondagas were participating with most of the Six Nations on the side of the British. Others said that if not directly participating, they were at least providing a base from within their territory where the more hostile tribes were launching their bloody attacks on the frontier settlements. After receiving "repeated applications . . . daily and hourly . . . by the distressed Families from the Frontiers for Provisions," Brigadier

General James Clinton informed his brother that he was again compelled for "feelings of Humanity," exceeded his authority, and issued food to civilians. He also wrote to inform the governor that a secret mission, sanctioned by General Washington, was already under way. Colonel Goose Van Schaick was at that moment leading a detachment of 500 men against the Onondaga. The objective was to surprise and destroy Onondaga Castle, and carry away as many prisoners as possible to be used in exchange for American captives held by the Indians. As only the officers involved in the operation were informed of it, the general urged his brother to maintain the secrecy of the attack until its results were announced.[56]

At five o'clock in the evening of April 12, three artillery pieces fired a salute as six companies of Continental soldiers marched into Fort Schuyler. Some of them had been on the march since April 6, when one company of the 4th Pennsylvania and one from the Rifle Corps left the Fort Defiance at Schoharie. When they reached Cobleskill, they were joined by Captain John Johnson's company of the 5th New York marching from the Schoharie Lower Fort. Johnson assumed command of the detachment, and it proceeded to Canajoharie and Fort Plank, where they were provided wagons to carry the men's packs. When the three companies reached Fort Herkimer at German Flats on April 9, three more companies joined them, one each from "the late Alden's" 6th Massachusetts at Cherry Valley, and the 3rd and "Late Livingston's" 4th Regiments of New York. Captain Leonard Bleeker of the 3rd New York assumed command, and the detachment marched along the Mohawk River until it arrived at Fort Schuyler. The post was garrisoned by Colonel Van Schaick's 1st Regiment of New York Continentals and one company of Colonel John Lamb's 2nd Continental Artillery. For the next few days, four of the newly arrived companies camped on the fort's glacis, while the remaining two were billeted in two nearby houses, and prepared for the mission.[57]

Sixty-three Oneida warriors arrived with their women and baggage on April 15. They approached, firing their muskets, and three artillery pieces in the fort returned their salute. After a brief ceremony, the Indians established their camp about one quarter mile away. They were soon joined by twenty more Oneida and Tuscarora warriors the next day. The Oneida were there to conduct an expedition, and wished to cooperate with that which Colonel Van Schaick was preparing to lead. Without disclosing the objective of his own mission, the colonel issued the Indians provisions, and assigned a detachment under the command of Lieutenant Thomas McClellan, of Gansevoort's 3rd New York, to accompany them. Without issuing written orders to McClellan, Van Schaick instructed the Indian party to operate against Fort Oswego, and effectively screen the movement of his troops against the Onondaga. Leaving their sachems and women behind, the troops and about sixty Oneidas and Tuscaroras departed on a mission on April 18.[58]

After spending the day completing their own preparations, the soldiers were ordered to draw three days' rations and alerted to prepare to march in the morning. That evening, twenty-nine bateaux carrying stores arrived from Schenectady. After unloading supplies for the fort, the soldiers carried the bateaux over the portage to Wood Creek and reloaded with eight days' supplies and provisions. Although it had snowed, the troops were ready to march at daybreak on April 19.[59]

With Colonel Van Schaick commanding, and Lieutenant Colonel Marinus Willett acting as second in

John Sullivan. After experiencing both success and failure in his military career, Sullivan was selected to command the Indian Expedition of 1779. (National Park Service)

command, the force included three companies from Van Schaick's 1st, one each from the 3rd, 4th, and 5th New York, one each from the 4th Pennsylvania and 6th Massachusetts Regiments, and one from the Rifle Corps, for a total strength of 555 officers and men. After assigning one company to accompany the boats as guard while they moved down Wood Creek, the rest of the troops marched the twenty-two miles to join them at the end of Oneida Lake. After both had arrived, at about three o'clock in the afternoon, the troops boarded the boats and headed north on the lake. The next day, the troops disembarked. Leaving a detail to secure the boats, Van Schaick formed his command into two columns of four musket companies each, 100 yards apart, and posted one half of Lieutenant Elijah Evans' company of riflemen on each flank for security. The companies moved on line, two ranks deep, so they could file to right or left in the case of enemy contact, to quickly form a line of battle with the riflemen posted to the flanks. In this formation, they "Marched through the woods in greatest silence" toward the Onondaga towns eight or nine miles away.[60]

Having gone a short distance, they halted for the night, "lying on the arms" without fires and in the strictest of silence to preserve secrecy. Early on the morning of April 21, the battalion was on the move through the fog, heading for the southwestern end of Onondaga Lake. It crossed the 220-yard wide, four-foot-deep arm of Salt Lake, the men fording with cartridge pouches hung on fixed bayonets to keep their ammunition dry, and advanced to Onondaga Creek. Captain John Graham's light infantry company led the advance, and captured an unsuspecting Onondaga warrior who was out hunting. The prisoner provided the soldiers a good deal of information on the Onondaga towns, which extended for eight miles, as Graham's men secured the opposite bank. The main body of troops crossed the deep creek on a fallen log and reformed. Colonel Van Schaick then ordered Graham and his light infantry to push forward quickly to capture as many prisoners as he could in the nearest town. The rest of the battalion, divided into detachments, was ordered to advance by different routes to surround as many of the settlements as possible and do the same.[61]

Graham's men surrounded and entered the first settlement completely undiscovered by Indians. They killed one warrior, captured an Indian woman, two or three children, and one white man, but one or two Indians escaped to spread the alarm. Indians fled into woods, leaving behind everything of value. Major Robert Cochran of the 3rd New York, acting as third in command, led a detachment of two companies on a push to the next town where there was a brief engagement. Some Indians and Tories, including "a Negro who was their Dr.," were killed, and several were taken prisoner. The troops then plundered and set fire to the houses, and returned to the middle town where the prisoners were being gathered.[62]

The American troops took thirty-three Indians and one white man prisoner. About fifty dwellings and a large quantity of corn and beans were burned. Horses and other stock were killed. The troops seized about 100 firearms, including some rifles, and a considerable amount of ammunition. They discovered one swivel gun in the council house, plus "2 stand of Colors" and a number of scalps displayed as trophies. They left the council house standing, but extinguished the symbolic council fire. What plunder that could not be carried by the men was burned or destroyed with the captured ammunition, and the trunions of the swivel gun were damaged so it could no longer be used. The Americans moved back by the same route they had approached, in the same order of march, except for one company detailed to guard the prisoners placed between the two columns. After going two miles, about twenty warriors opened fire from concealment on the opposite side of the creek. The riflemen deployed from the flanks and quickly dispersed the enemy, who left the body of one of their dead comrades behind. The troops then crossed Onondaga Creek in two places and halted, "for fear the enemy would attack," but encountered no other interruption for the rest of the march.[63]

Americans burning an Indian village. Unlike that shown in the illustration, most of the towns destroyed in the Indian Expeditions of 1779 were established communities composed of traditional wooden longhouses, as well as log cabins and framed structures that were evacuated before the troops arrived.

After reaching the boats, by four o'clock, the Americans embarked for an island seven miles down the lake, where they camped for the night. On April 23, they were back in Wood Creek. Two companies guarded boats, while the rest marched back toward Fort Schuyler and encamped in the woods for the night. At noon the next day, April 24, the returning troops were saluted by three pieces of artillery at Fort Schuyler. The value of the plunder was divided among the captors, to supplement their pay. Colonel Van Schaick reported that in five and a half days, they had marched 180 miles, captured thirty-four prisoners, and killed twelve Indians, mostly warriors, and Tories without losing one man.[64]

As the Americans were making their way toward his people's towns, the Onondaga sachem Ostinoghiyata[65] declared his fidelity to the Crown. Through Captain John Johnston of the Indian Department he asked the British to "trust in him as a faithful friend ready to die in the cause and defense of the king." The pro-British Indian informed Johnston that he had attended the council called by the American commissioner, General Schuyler, with the Oneida, Tuscarora, and Onondaga in an attempt to turn them to the Rebel side. He affirmed that he would tell the Onondaga that Schuyler offered only "fair promises or threats." The old Onondaga leader then reaffirmed his alliance with the Seneca and British. As a show of solidarity, Johnston told his superior in the Indian Department, Lieutenant Colonel John Butler, that an Onondaga he called Aquandinoya requested four bags of paint for the warriors who he would bring into British service. Johnston asked his superiors to provide them with as much as could be spared, because it was "an article the Warrior wants for Encouragement."[66]

Although Ostinoghiyata had already spoken for them, there was little doubt that the Onondaga would now side with the British. The day after the attack on their towns, Johnston wrote to Colonel Butler to tell him that an Oneida named William informed him that the Rebels were on the march "on this side of the Onondaga," and had surrounded a number of women in a cornfield and took them prisoner. William told Johnston he saw one wounded Cayuga in the woods. The Indian Department officer asked Butler for "all the aid and assistance" he could send "with the greatest dispatch." Their Indian allies pleaded with him to ask Colonels Bolton and Butler to bring troops and warriors to fulfill their promises of assistance.[67]

On April 22, a runner from the Mohawk River settlements reported to Colonel Butler that the force that destroyed the Onondaga village returned immediately to Fort Schuyler carrying about thirty Onondaga and five or six Cayuga women and children as captives. The scout estimated that a force of about 700 men, 400 sent from Albany together with 300 from Fort Schuyler, "did the mischief." The scout said it did not appear the Americans were then headed for Oswego. Two weeks before, a "friend to Government" in Canajoharie told the spy a rumor was circulating that the Rebels intended to send 3,000 men against the Six Nations in the summer. Believing the reinforced garrison at Fort Schuyler represented the advanced guard of the invasion, Lieutenant Colonel Bolton ordered Butler to march with 400 rangers and Indian warriors to Canadesaga (Seneca Castle) to bolster the resistance of the Six Nations. From there, Butler's force was in a position to block that avenue, react against an American advance from the direction of either Fort Pitt or Wyoming, and screen the approach to Fort Oswego against an attack by the Oneidas.[68]

Butler's spy was unaware of Lieutenant McClellan's activities. In accordance with Colonel Van Schaick's verbal instructions, the lieutenant led a detachment of one other officer, a sergeant, a corporal, and thirty privates that accompanied sixty Oneida and Tuscarora warriors on their expedition against Fort Oswego. As soon as they arrived near the post on April 25, three Indians went to reconnoiter the garrison, and returned after capturing three British soldiers. Meanwhile, another party of Oneidas captured some Indians paddling a canoe on the river, and brought them back to be questioned as well. Both the redcoats and Indian prisoners provided corroborating information that the fort was garrisoned by only about forty soldiers commanded by a captain named Davis and a subaltern, and held only four cannons. The entire Oneida and American party moved closer to the garrison for a possible attack, and captured another British soldier, who verified the information gained earlier from the other prisoners.[69]

On closer inspection, it was apparent that even with the advantage of surprise, the raiders could not carry the fort by storm. The Oneida attempted to draw part of the garrison out for a fight with a small foray. When a detachment sallied from the gate to engage, the Oneida hoped to entice them into the woods for an ambush, and then rush the fort. Unfortunately, the Indians opened fire too soon, and the redcoats immediately retired into their works, leaving behind two dead. The Americans and their allies pursued their withdrawing foe to within sight of the fort, but the garrison covered them with "such a warm fire and musquetry" that the attackers were forced to retreat back into the woods. Frustrated, McClellan and his party marched seven miles away from the garrison and encamped for the night.[70]

The next morning, April 26, some Caughnawaga, or "French Mohawk," Indians friendly to the American cause approached to speak with Lieutenant McClellan and the Oneida leaders. One of them presented a letter written in French by Lafayette to the Canadians of Quebec, dated December 10, 1778, and offered to deliver it. As a show of good faith and to prove his friendly intentions to the Americans, he was willing to leave his son as a hostage. The American officers and Oneidas agreed, and requested that if he thought it safe to do so, proceed as far as Montreal and return by way of Saint John's, "taking particular notice of the Strength of the Enemy" along the way. The Caughnawaga "readily consented." They provided the Indian with what provisions they could spare, and he was off on his mission. Giving up the effort to capture Fort Oswego, Lieutenant McClellan led his detachment back to Fort Schuyler. They arrived on the last day of April, bringing back important information for the pending Indian expedition. The prisoners revealed that their commander had received a letter from Lieutenant General Haldimand at Quebec saying he could send no troops from Canada to fight against the Rebels in 1779, but believed he could send a large army the following year. They also revealed that the garrison at Fort Haldimand on Buck, renamed Carleton Island, consisted of only a few British regulars and Sir John Johnson's regiment, of Royal Yorkers, not more than 200 men in all. The Oneida insisted on taking the prisoners to their castle, but promised to deliver them after a few days.[71]

The Americans considered the short campaign from Fort Schuyler a success. Although Fort Oswego was not seized, the expedition collected some valuable intelligence. The strategic value of attacking the Onondaga, however, was questionable. Most of the Onondaga nation may have been sympathetic toward the

British, but some took the Americans' side. The Oneida worried that the raid would send the Onondaga entirely into the British camp. Nonetheless, in recognition, Washington commended the men who participated in the General Order for May 8, 1779. The general wrote, "The good conduct, spirit, secrecy and dispatch with which the enterprise" against the Onondaga "was executed do the highest honor to Colonel Van Schaick and the officers and men under his command and merit the thanks of the Commander-in-Chief."[72]

It was clear to both Washington and Congress that there would be no more use negotiating with the Six Nations to secure their neutrality. It was time to put Washington's plan for an expedition against the Iroquois into action.

Chapter 11

NOT MERELY OVERRUN, BUT DESTROY

HAVING failed to drive the British from their base on Rhode Island in August 1778, Major General John Sullivan was determined to succeed in his new assignment. Although it was bad luck—a storm made it impossible to land the seaborne French troops who were to support the Rhode Island offensive—rather than Sullivan's lack of planning or leadership that doomed the action, it was a bitter disappointment. Not the most aggressive of American general officers, he had at least proven to be reliable. In mid-April 1779 he had called a council of war to discuss the pending operation, and reviewed the materials General Washington had forwarded him, including the recommendations on the best route for the main effort from both Major Generals Philip Schuyler and Nathanael Greene.

He held no illusions that the campaign he was to lead would produce an easy victory. Sullivan described the enemy he was to face as "perfectly acquainted with the country, capable of seizing every advantage which the ground can possible afford, inured to war from their youth, and from their manner of living, capable of enduring every kind of fatigue." Sullivan expressed a grudging respect when he said they "are no despicable enemy," and realized that a two-to-one numerical advantage was no guarantee of success. Although confident, he was not overly so. The warriors of the Six Nations, even "when opposed to three thousand troops," were formidable. He held no unrealistic expectations from troops accustomed to conducting conventional operations against British regulars. Some of his Continentals were "totally unacquainted with the country and Indian manner of fighting, and who although excellent in the field," were "far from having the exactness with firearms or that alertness in a wooded country, which the Indians have." Inflicting destruction on the Six Nations would demonstrate the Continental Army's ability to carry war into their country. Sullivan was well aware that failure would give the enemy confidence, and possibly embolden them to increase the severity of their attacks against the frontiers.[1]

As Sullivan prepared to take command of the "Western Army," he studied the mission, the available intelligence on the enemy and terrain over which he and his men would march and fight. Brigadier General Hand was sent forward from his headquarters on the New York border at Minisink to Easton, Pennsylvania, with some of the troops in his command to establish posts and magazines, and prepare the way for the rest of the troops that were to be assigned to the expedition. Following a short leave to visit his family in Lancaster, Hand went to Wyoming to supervise the establishment of the expedition's forward operating base, and coordinate the gathering of intelligence between there and Chemung. To accomplish the mission, Washington assured Hand, the "proper measures have been taken with the commissary of ordnance and military stores to have the necessary supply of such articles," such as axes and pack saddles.[2]

With the main effort to move by way of the Susquehanna River to Tioga, the matter of the route for the division from the Mohawk was still being reviewed. Although he was convinced that the principal attack should proceed by way of Tioga, Major General Schuyler still saw merit to one division advancing along the Mohawk River by way of Fort Schuyler, while Washington favored an advance down the Susquehanna from Otsego Lake to a junction with the other division at Tioga. As the decision was being weighed, General Washington agreed that the forces that would approach from that direction under the command of Brigadier General James Clinton should assemble at Canajoharie. Doing so would "distract and perplex the enemy and keep awake different jealousies" as they were threatened in two directions simultaneously. From Canajoharie, Clinton's brigade could either move directly into Six Nations territory by the Mohawk, or quickly move southward to the Susquehanna and link up with General Sullivan at Tioga. The diversion presented by that option also offered the advantage of giving some protection to the northern frontier. In contrast, following the Mohawk River exclusively divided and thereby weakened the invasion force, increased the complexity of the operation, and, most important, risked defeat in detail. By fixing the rendezvous at Canajoharie while keeping the direction of advance and objective "a profound secret," bateaux and carriages could be assembled to support a move in either direction, thereby maintaining the diversionary value.[3]

Brigadier General Clinton was to originally have his brigade assembled and ready to move from Canajoharie on May 12. Clinton was directed to have bateaux of the lightest kind built, and wagons to convey them across country. For the expedition, the brigade would initially include the 3rd (Gansevoort's), 4th (Weisenfels' or Late Livingston's), and 5th (Dubois') New York, the 6th (Late Alden's) Massachusetts, 4th (Butler's) Pennsylvania Regiments, and (Morgan's) Rifle Corps. The riflemen were now under the command of the newly promoted Major James Parr, following the recall of Major Posey to his parent unit, the 7th Virginia Continental Regiment. The 1st (Van Schaick's) New York would remain in garrison at Fort Schuyler, and the 2nd (Van Cortlandt's) New York Regiment remained detached to Hand's command.[4]

Troops and stores were soon put in motion to their respective assembly areas at Wyoming for the main effort and Canajoharie for the northern wing. Although the expedition was sure to provide more security than the soldiers remaining in static posts, General Washington recognized that many frontier inhabitants would be concerned about their safety. As the Continental troops marched away, Washington asked Governors George Clinton of New York and William Livingston of New Jersey to call out militia to cover the vulnerable areas around Minisink in the absence of Hand's command.[5] Colonel Philip Van Cortlandt coordinated with Colonel John Cantine of the Ulster County militia about their knowledge of Indian country and the approach to Chemung by the Susquehanna. He also prepared to march with his 2nd New York Regiment to Easton. From there, they were detailed to widen and repair the road in order to facilitate the movement of troops and supply wagons to Wyoming.[6]

As early as the end of March, the Tories and Iroquois warriors were again making their presence felt at a very critical location. Their activities prompted American Lieutenant Colonel Zebulon Butler to send word to General Washington that a "Body of the enemy, consisting of Indians and others," had returned to the Wyoming Valley and raided a few farms. Concerned for both the safety of the inhabitants and the preparations for the Indian expedition, Washington directed Butler to keep active patrols and scouts out and to remain ever watchful for signs of enemy activity. As soon as General Hand arrived to assume command in the area and coordinate support for the expedition, Butler could concentrate on commanding and improving the post. In the meantime, reinforcements were on the way, and Butler was told to alert his commissaries to increase their supplies and stocks of provisions accordingly. The German Regiment, the infantry of Armand's Partisan Corps, and Schott's Independent Corps were the first ordered to leave their cantonments at Minisink and Easton for Wilkes-Barre. Before committing them to battle, Washington took the opportunity to mend some of the army's worn out or "broken" units. The under strength Additional Continental Regiments of Colonels Oliver Spencer and William Malcolm were consolidated to form the 5th New Jersey at Easton, while those of Colonels Thomas Hartley and John Patton were reconstituted as the 11th Pennsylvania Regiment under Lieutenant Colonel Commandant Adam Hubley when they reached Wyoming.[7]

In order to bolster the numbers of troops committed to the operation, General Washington approached the two states most affected by the previous year's Indian incursions, New York and Pennsylvania, for militia participation.

To allay their concerns about leaving their states' frontiers less protected during the expedition, Washington told them, "I am in hopes when the troops begin to operate, they will furnish too much employment to the Indians in their own Country to allow them to indulge their ravages in ours." The President of the Supreme Executive Council of Pennsylvania, Joseph Reed, was asked for 600 men, in addition to the rangers discussed previously, and who could remain in service through September. Instead of accompanying the expedition as the rangers would, they "must be posted on communication between Sunbury and the operating troops," to secure the logistical support base. Washington recommended that those who could not be ordered out for more than two months of continual service be immediately relieved by others as soon as their terms expired. To emphasize the importance of the militia to the logistics effort, the commander in chief explained, "it will make a most essential difference in our measures whether the aid of the militia I have requested be furnished or not."[8]

General Washington had wanted the expedition to begin as early as May, if possible, and concluded quickly rather than risk leaving the Main Army weakened by sizable detachments in the event Lieutenant General Henry Clinton led the principal British army out of New York for a general engagement. Furthermore, in Iroquois territory, where there were Indian trails but few good roads, the army had to leave its wagons behind. All of its necessary baggage, equipment, and supplies going overland had to be carried by packhorse, therefore it was essential that units committed to the Indian expedition travel light. General Washington drew the commanders' attention to a "general Order for the Officers to divest themselves of all superfluous baggage . . . [and] leave whatever will not be absolutely necessary for the Campaign" at their cantonments.[9]

On April 15, Sullivan wrote to Washington expressing his understanding of the mission and the necessary logistical support, and made a number of requests. In early May, General Washington ordered General Sullivan to "repair to Easton, in order to superintend and forward the preparations" for the "expedition to the Westward." It was an enormous undertaking, and Sullivan was instructed to make every necessary arrangement with the Quartermaster and Commissary General for the supplies, provisions, and stores needed, the conveying of cattle and pack animals, and all other manner of support to Wyoming.[10] The same day, Washington directed the army's Quartermaster General, Nathanael Greene, to "comply with his [Sullivan's] immediate requisitions for everything which falls under the providence" of his department.[11]

Sullivan had asked the commander in chief for the allocation of at least 3,000 troops to constitute the "fighting strength" of the expedition, after the two wings joined at Tioga. This number was exclusive of "the proper deductions for guards at the several posts, for boatmen, hospital guards, tenders, &c.," and the troops that would operate from the direction of Fort Pitt. Although he knew that Brigadier General James Clinton's brigade would constitute the northern wing of the expedition, Sullivan was not familiar with the fighting qualities of the New York soldiers. Brigadier General Edward Hand's command was also identified early for participation in the expedition. His composite force including the German Regiment, the various independent corps, and the remnants of Hartley's and Patton's regiments, would take part as a brigade-equivalent command. Sullivan had a less than favorable opinion of these units, for he believed the Pennsylvania regiments were too full of "old countrymen," or Europeans, generally "unacquainted with Indian warfare" and therefore not very useful on this campaign. Likewise, because he was not familiar with the independent corps and the nature of their usual mode of operations, he was wary of their ability to "act in a body with others." When the commander in chief identified Brigadier General Enoch Poor's New Hampshire and William Maxwell's New Jersey brigades, Sullivan was pleased with their selections. He described the New Hampshire soldiers, "who are all marksmen, and accustomed to the Indian mode of fighting," and the New Jersey troops, as "good."[12]

Washington did not want to concentrate the entire brigades "till the preparations are complete or nearly so to avoid consumption of provisions and stores necessary for the support of the expedition." He therefore ordered Generals Poor and Maxwell each to send one regiment to Easton for a fatigue detail to build a road from there to Wyoming. "It is essential," he told them, to get "the road opened without delay that the troops and supplies passing that way may meet with no obstruction." Brigadier General Hand was at Wyoming to accelerate transportation of stores and provisions up the river from Sunbury, and employ the troops at his command to "obtain the most precise intelligence of the enemy's situation and views." Overall, Washington instructed Sullivan "to employ every expedient to complete preparations for penetrating into Indian Country by way of Tioga, on the Susquehanna on the plan which has been already explained, and may be finally adopted" starting with these "preparatory instructions." There would be "more full and definite" directions when the "plan of operations is ultimately fixed and ready for execution."[13]

The plan was certainly not yet final. On April 21, Washington informed the Western Department commander, Colonel Daniel Brodhead, that he had "relinquished the idea of attempting a cooperation between the troops at Fort Pitt and bodies moving from other quarters against the Six Nations." This decision was prompted by the difficulty of acquiring supplies and obtaining intelligence on the routes and "nature of the country." Also, he did not believe "The uncertainty of being able to cooperate to advantage" and the "hazard" of an expedition by a relatively small number of Continentals to be worth the risks. In addition, such a plan as discussed would leave the frontier settlements vulnerable to incursions by the more western tribes. Instead, Washington directed the "post at Tuscarawas," or Fort Laurens, to "be preserved" and sufficiently garrisoned.

On the other hand, it was likely that success against the Six Nations could result in the availability of additional troops for an expedition in the Western Department, possibly for an attack on Detroit. In anticipation that the army would be able to "chastise the Western savages by an expedition into their country," Washington instructed Brodhead to continue preparing magazines and boats. In early May, Washington reiterated his decision not to invade the Six Nations from Fort Pitt. Instead, he directed Brodhead to maintain garrisons at Forts Laurens, McIntosh, and Hand, as well as the new posts under construction at Kittanning and Venango. These would afford protection to Westmoreland County, and the new posts would divert the Senecas' energies from Sullivan's offensive and cause them to not leave the Allegheny River approaches to their country undefended. Finally, Washington encouraged Brodhead to "Preserve the friendship of the Indians who have not taken up the Hatchet," because doing so would help keep the frontier quiet and reduce the need for military action.[14]

Back in New York, the 1,000 levies were being raised and posted to the frontier. When Congress resolved to pay for 1,000 men to fill the Continental regiments for the year's campaign and take part in the Indian expedition, it was not known that the New York brigade was to participate.[15] This fortunate occurrence allowed the state to employ half of the levies for frontier defense, since those destined for the New York Continental regiments would be on the campaign. As prescribed by the legislature, the militia officers drew the levies from voluntary enlistments before resorting to drafts from their regiments. Those from Albany County were formed into a temporary regiment commanded by a lieutenant colonel and were to join Clinton's brigade on the expedition. The men enlisted from Dutchess, Ulster, and Orange Counties were ordered to march to posts at Rochester, Lauren Kill, and Peenpack. The men from Tryon County joined the troops stationed at Fort Dayton and the other posts to provide security when the Continentals departed on campaign.[16]

As these preparations were progressing, an alarm went out that a war party of sixty Seneca and some Mohawks appeared at several locations in Tryon County at the end of April. They terrorized the Schoharie and Stone Arabia areas, killed and wounded several inhabitants, and confiscated a number of horses. Scouts from Fort Plank pursued one party of the raiders but were unsuccessful in catching up with them. Militia turned out "cheerfully" as the alarm spread throughout the county, but had it not been for the presence of his brigade, Brigadier General James Clinton expressed that the frontier could have been moved back to Schenectady in two days' time. Instead, he quickly responded to the raids and sightings of the enemy. Part of Gansevoort's regiment and the militia from Schenectady, about 200 men in all, marched toward Johnstown, where they joined with a large contingent of Tryon County militia to calm the panic.

The general established a post near Sacandaga to help restore some "tranquility" to the inhabitants of the area, and detailed Colonel Gansevoort to build a blockhouse on the road leading toward Sir William Johnson's Pleasure House, about ten miles from Johnstown on the road to Mayfield. He then posted a detachment from Dubois' 5th New York Regiment to the blockhouse, and the balance of the regiment at Johnstown.[17] When Fort Dayton was attacked on May 10, General Clinton told his brother, "you will see that the savages have not yet forgot their thirst for Blood." The militia was not called out. Instead, the levies from Tryon County assembled at Fort Dayton, and the detachment from the Mohawk Valley was ordered to the Sacandaga blockhouse to serve as guides to Colonel Dubois' regiment of Continentals.[18]

Ulster and Orange counties were also attacked by Indian raiders at the end of April. Colonel Van Cortlandt wrote to Governor Clinton that he would be happy when the "Draughts" arrived at the post in Kingston before he was ordered to leave on campaign. "I find all the Country is alarmed," which he believed "will frequently be the Case, until some Expedition is Carried on into the Country on the Delaware." Without Continental soldiers or standing militia posted in the neighborhood, he expressed the concern "for a few Tories may keep this Fruntier in Continual alarms."[19] On the morning of May 4, as his regiment marched out of Wawarsink, Van Cortlandt received news that thirty to forty of Brant's Indians attacked the town of Fantine Kill, burned several houses, and killed ten inhabitants, including women and children. He immediately marched to intercept, while Colonel Cantine quickly mustered some militia and marched to Lackawack, which he feared would be the next target. Although Van Cortlandt's men caught a glimpse of the enemy on two occasions as they pursued them up the side of a mountain, the Indians eluded attempts to surround them. The Continentals were able to engage only with some "long shots." As the invaders escaped, unwilling to risk an engagement with the soldiers, they released a woman they had seized as a captive.[20] When he was informed of the attacks, Governor Clinton called out one fourth of two militia regiments to reinforce the militia on active service with Colonel Cantine at the frontier posts in Orange County.[21] By Sunday, May 9, the Continentals loaded four wagon-loads of provisions and supplies into canoes and sent them down the Delaware before resuming their march to Fort Penn (present-day Stroudsburg). When they arrived two days later, they received orders to march and help Colonel Spencer's 5th New Jersey Regiment "Mend the road" from Easton to Wyoming for the transportation of the artillery.[22]

Out on the West Branch of the Susquehanna, the Tories and pro-British Indians had committed depredations all along the frontier during the spring. In April, they struck not only at Wyoming, but also in the neighborhoods of Fort Jenkins, on Fishing Creek, at Freeland's Mill, Fort Muncy, and Loyalsock. To offer some protection, Brigadier General Hand had kept Hartley's Additional Regiment in the area. Hartley had posted detachments at Fort Jenkins, Fort Muncy, and Sunbury. The Northumberland County militia also embodied one company of "nine-months men" under the command of Captain John Kemplen at Bossley's Mill, and detachments of militia were available at Fort Freeland and some other smaller posts in the area. In late June 1779, however, the remnants of Hartley's regiment were ordered to Wyoming for the buildup of forces to participate in the Indian expedition of General Sullivan.[23]

The expedition's preparations had taken their toll on the area's defense in several ways. The County Lieutenant of Northumberland County, Colonel Samuel Hunter, could call only one thirty-man company into "actual service" for two months to guard stores at Sunbury. Because so many local men were engaged as boatmen transporting supplies from the magazines at Sunbury to Wyoming, and were therefore temporarily exempt from militia duty, there was little prospect they could be replaced when their terms expired. To guard the frontier along the West Branch, Hunter had only small militia detachments, like those at Potter's Fort and Fort Freeland. Fort Freeland was the fortified home of Jacob Freeland and his family. When he and his neighbors returned to their homes after the panic of the "Great Runaway" subsided, Freeland sur-rounded his two-story log house with a wall of pickets. The stockade enclosed about one half-acre of ground, and through the winter had been home to thir-teen local families. It was also the rendezvous for the local militia when the frontier was under alarm.[24]

Despite the activity on the Susquehanna, the gathering of supplies was more difficult than had been anticipated. The planned May start of the offensive was postponed into June. The Quartermaster General, Nathanael Greene, was pushing the members of his department to do what they could to get everything ready for the expedition. While the road from Easton to Wyoming was being cut, supplies were moved by the easier overland route to Sunbury.[25] They were then transported upstream to Wyoming "under a proper guard." Major Richard Claiborne of the Quartermaster's Department at Sunbury reported back to Greene that they made the "utmost exertions . . . to have everything completed" at that post as soon as possible. "Not a moment's time is lost" in the boat-building operation at Sunbury, "as the men's anxiety pushes them forward in the business with all possible diligence."[26]

Assistant Quartermaster General Colonel John Cox wrote to Major General Greene in mid-May that the army had purchased 600 packhorses, but was finding forage scarce and the procurement of wagons difficult, which slowed the movement of supplies from Carlisle to Fort Pitt. Colonel Jacob Morgan, the Deputy Quartermaster General for Pennsylvania, was doing his best to recruit fifty "good active watermen" in and about the Reading area for the bateau service on the Susquehanna to support Sullivan's army. He told Greene that even when a sufficient number of boats was ready, they could not proceed up the river without a sufficient guard to protect them, as Assistant Quartermaster General Colonel Charles Pettit said no soldiers were available for that purpose. Colonel Robert Lettis Hooper, Jr., Deputy Quartermaster General, reported that Sullivan's troops were opening a road across the Great Swamp to Wyoming. When completed, he anticipated that the wagons carrying stores could pass "with Ease and tolerable expedition" from Easton, thereby requiring few pack saddles on that route.[27] In response, General Washington ordered Colonel Oliver Spencer's 5th New Jersey Regiment to "to open the road leading thro' the great Swamp to Wyoming and to make it fit for the passage of carriages &c., &c."[28] Colonel Van Cortlandt's 2nd New York Regiment joined the effort. He later reported to New York's governor that provisions and stores appeared to be reaching Wyoming by road and river with little interference from the Indians, although small parties were frequently seen near the fort and along the road they were cutting through the swamp known as "the Shades of Death."[29]

Despite Van Cortlandt's view, the logistical challenges to beginning the expedition continued to mount. On May 19, General Washington expressed his concern about the "deficiency of wagons, and the want of tents and other articles," of which Sullivan had complained to him, along with his desire for the Quartermaster General to address the problem to avoid "the embarrassment which our operations must experience" if not corrected.[30] The weather was also slowing the preparations and causing delays. Greene acted immediately, and Colonel Robert Cooper, Jr., reported that while heavy rain hindered work on the road, the amount of supplies and provisions being sent for the expedition was being increased, and an additional "brigade of teams" and wagons were ordered to support the effort between Easton and Wyoming.[31] Meanwhile, the Quartermaster Department was completing the manufacture of 1,500 pack saddles that would be carried on the campaign, and drawing tents from the magazine at Fish Kill to issue the men of Poor's New Hampshire brigade.[32]

In addition to informing General Washington on the difficulties he was experiencing with the support provided by the Quartermaster Department, Major General Sullivan was acting on his own behalf to prepare his army for marching, and even approached President Joseph Reed on his own authority about the possibility of impressing wagons and teams in Pennsylvania, causing some consternation.[33] Washington told Sullivan that the lack of supplies was one more reason for traveling as light as possible, and that success depended on "celerity."[34] To make his force more self-reliant, Sullivan requested the attachment of one company of artificers from the Quartermaster Department to repair equipment while on the march.[35] As Washington grew more impatient for the campaign to begin, there always seemed to be another cause for delay.

Sullivan assured the commander in chief he knew of "no Steps left untried" and "none shall be left unattempted."[36] Washington reminded his subordinate that every attempt to provide him the necessary support would be made, but the availability of supplies "are very unequal to the general wants of the army," and told him to "accommodate his arrangements" to the "low state of our Arsenals and Magazines."[37] Meanwhile, the troops continued to march to join the expedition at Wyoming. Washington expected Pennsylvania to send the 700 men of its independent companies to rendezvous at Sunbury. Despite all the effort to keep the details secret, intelligence reports indicated the British were aware of the expedition. Sullivan was told to expect them and their Indian allies to interfere with his preparations, and to strengthen his patrols and convoy escorts accordingly.[38]

The British were indeed aware of the American activities. A false alarm spread among the Cayugas that they were the next object of an American expedition from Albany, as the Onondaga had been. In response, Indian Superintendent John Butler moved some of his rangers and Seneca warriors to their defense. After the alarm was relaxed, Butler told Lieutenant General Frederick Haldimand that "appearing with the Rangers amongst them had Every good effect" on the Cayugas and other Iroquois. Likewise, the Indians expressed their satisfaction that the British were considering posting a larger force at Fort Oswego. Ultimately, the Indian Department deputy was pleased to inform his superior that the Six Nations "seem as much disposed as ever to exert themselves against the Rebels." Their war parties were out all along the frontiers, "as far up as Fort Pitt & beyond," and "seldom fail of success." Butler believed it was "probable the American Frontier Settlements will be almost entirely broken up" in the next campaign season.[39]

One party that had been raiding and scouting along the Allegheny returned with a prisoner who revealed that the settlers of the area had been encouraged not to flee their homes for help was on the way. He and his neighbors were told that 3,000 men were being sent on an expedition up the Susquehanna and that two regiments of Continentals, plus a "large Body of Militia," were being sent up the Allegheny to pacify the border areas. To support the move, ranger and Indian scouts' reports confirmed the Americans were preparing boats at Fort Pitt. On the Ohio, it appeared that the Rebels intended to make no new moves from Forts McIntosh and Laurens, but only keep the garrisons they had made the previous winter and "not to proceed any farther."[40] Scouts also confirmed that an overwhelming army was assembling on the Susquehanna, and raiding parties found that settlements everywhere were protected by chains of forts and blockhouses.

Butler believed the American attack on the Onondaga had served "further to confirm the Indians in their attachment to the Government," because most of those killed and captured were believed to be "chiefly in the Rebel Interest." The Six Nations' Superintendent had also heard even the Oneida were "much discontented" at the action, and according to his informants, threatened "to act with the rest of their Brethren" against the Americans. In the meantime, the Indian Department assisted Onondaga refugees in settling among the Seneca and establishing the Confederacy's council fire at Canadesaga, the principal Seneca town. Butler requested British provisions to distribute for their immediate subsistence while the Onondaga planted new corn.[41]

On May 22, Colonel Goose Van Schaick notified Brigadier General James Clinton that the still faithful Oneida had sent a party, along with one of his soldiers, to scout Buck Island. (The British renamed Buck Island as Carleton Island and the post there, Fort Haldimand.). The patrol had returned with three prisoners, members of Sir John Johnson's King's Royal Regiment of New York, on May 15. The prisoners revealed that no reinforcements had arrived at Buck Island during the spring, but the remaining seven companies of their regiment were expected to arrive and join the garrison any day. That addition, the scouts estimated, would increase the numbers of British on the island to 600 soldiers and 300 Indians. The prisoners had expected additional troops to come up the Saint Lawrence River, but had heard no more about them. The Royal Yorkers also revealed that besides four vessels on Lake Ontario, the enemy had two large vessels on the stocks ready to launch at the Buck Island naval station. The Indian Department leaders John Butler and Joseph Brant were also reported on the island on their way to "Colect the foreign [Canadian] Indians."[42] More intelligence came by way of Lieutenant Colonel Levi Pawling. After assuming command of the militia guarding the frontier, he told Governor Clinton in late May that he had learned "in a Private way" that "a large body" intended to oppose the American regulars preparing to move up the Susquehanna.[43]

Undeterred, the American buildup continued, albeit slowly. Major General Nathanael Greene's Quartermaster Department was obtaining boats, wagons, pack horses, and all classes of supply. After resolving the controversy caused by Sullivan's intimation of impressments, the officers of Greene's department applied to the government of Pennsylvania for wagons and teams from the county wagon masters according to the established procedure.[44] The army also procured new and reassigned its existing transportation assets as best it could to support the expedition, along with all its other commitments. Colonel John Davis reported to Greene that he was able to send 100 "wagon Horses" and 700 packhorses from Carlisle to the Main Army, and six brigades of wagons and one brigade of packhorses "westward" packed with supplies.[45]

As the days slipped by, the expedition continued to be delayed. At the end of May, General Washington wrote another very frank letter outlining his instructions to Major General Sullivan. The "immediate objects" of the operation was "the total destruction and devastation" of the settlements of the Six Nations, and the "capture of as many prisoners of every age and sex as possible." It was essential that their crops in cultivation be ruined and they be prevented from planting more in the same growing season.[46] The capture of prisoners was necessary as leverage in treaty negotiations, for prisoner exchange, and redeeming captives.

Clinton's New York brigade, then gathering at Canajoharie, was placed under Sullivan's command, and would either effect a juncture with the main body at Tioga or operate from the Mohawk, as Sullivan directed. The main body was to assemble at Wyoming, march to Tioga, and then take the "most practicable route into the heart of The Indian Settlements." Along the way, Sullivan was to establish intermediate posts to provide security for his supply convoys and his route of communication. Tioga would of necessity be the location of either a stockade fort or an entrenched camp, as it was the point where supplies carried by boat were transferred to packhorses. Washington recommended the erection of at least one post at the center of the Indians' country from which he could operate, by sending detachments throughout the rest of the enemy's territory "to lay waste all the settlements around with instructions to do it in the most effectual manner." Washington emphasized that "the country may not be merely *overrun*, but *destroyed*."[47]

As a general rule, Washington went on to caution Sullivan, his force was "to make rather than receive attacks, attended with as much impetuosity, shouting and noise as possible." The men were, "whenever they have an opportunity, to rush on with the war-whoop and fixed bayonet." Washington believed, perhaps from his experience fighting in the frontier twenty-five years before, "Nothing will disconcert and terrify the Indians more" than an aggressive attack carried out with audacity. If, after the thorough destruction of their settlements was complete, the Indians showed a "disposition for peace," Sullivan was instructed to encourage it on the condition that they provided evidence of their sincerity. One proof the Indians could offer was delivering into American custody some of those who instigated or led the attacks against the frontier settlements, like "the most mischievous of Tories, Butler and Brant, or any others in their power."[48] Sullivan was also authorized to offer "supplies of provisions and other articles of which they will stand in need" after agreeing to a treaty with the United States.

Knowing the treachery of which some Indian negotiators were capable, it was imperative that Sullivan receive explicit and substantial promises. The only security acceptable for such pledges was the delivery of hostages. Washington further instructed Sullivan to convince the Indians to surprise and capture Fort Niagara and British shipping on the Great Lakes as a condition for American friendship, but he was not given the authority to conclude a peace treaty. Instead, he was encouraged to negotiate the terms that would be submitted to Congress for ratification. "When we have effectually chastised them," Washington said, the Americans would "listen to peace. And endeavor to draw further advantages from their fears."[49]

Once the objects of the expedition as outlined had been accomplished, Sullivan was to rejoin "the main army, by the most convenient, expeditious and secure route." Washington reiterated how essential it was that the operation be conducted as rapidly as possible. Doing so would minimize the time the rest of the army faced the principal British army, and lessen the drain of provisions and other supplies from the already austere magazines and arsenals. Washington followed his instructions the next day with the order for Sullivan to "commence your operations the moment you have got yourself in readiness." There was no time to lose.[50]

Deputy Quartermaster General Colonel Robert Hooper, Jr., and General Sullivan inspected the nearly completed military road and thoroughly approved it.[51] Two weeks later, Major General Greene told Colonel Hooper,

"It is necessary to give dispatch to Gen Sullivan's motions." The expedition, Greene explained, had his "hearty concurrence and approbation" and expressed his wish to do everything in his power, "however inconvenient to the operations of this army, to insure its success."[52] Greene wrote to Sullivan, "The expedition you have the honor to direct will fix the Eyes of the whole Continent upon you." He went on to say that the "importance of the Object wings our expectation," and the people of the entire nation had high hopes for the success of his operation. A "disappointment," Greene said, "will be the more disagreeable." The Quartermaster General assured Sullivan that "Great preparations and great exertions have been made to pave the way" for his success. There had been nothing left undone, although the task of procuring laborers, scarce supplies, and provisions with depreciated Continental money rendered the task "Herculean."[53]

On June 18, after making preparation and continued arrangements for forwarding supplies, Major General Sullivan gave the order for those troops assembling at Easton, the brigades of Poor and Maxwell, the 4th Continental Artillery Regiment of Colonel Thomas Proctor with six cannon and two howitzers, and all the wagons and packhorses, to begin their movement over the Pocono Mountains along the newly cut road. The famous missionary and Indian commissioner Reverend Samuel Kirkland joined Sullivan's staff as chaplain and interpreter. The division trudged over mountains and through the great swamps, slowed by occasional broken wagons and tired horses. On June 23, after a march of fifty-eight miles, they arrived at Wyoming to join those sent ahead.

Sullivan expected to find stocks of adequate supplies waiting there, but was disappointed. Much of his salt meat was unfit to eat. Many of the cattle were in too poor a condition to walk. There was an inadequate supply of shoes and clothing for his troops. And, most crucially, the 700 volunteer rangers expected from Pennsylvania had not arrived. Despite the assurances from General Greene, Sullivan continued to complain about shortages of supplies to Washington and set his staff to obtain the necessary items and the means of transporting them. The task consumed the next six weeks, and resulted in some heated exchanges of correspondence among the principal general officers of the Army. The delays increased the impatience of the commander in chief, and there was even some danger that the expedition would be abandoned.

Up on the Mohawk, Brigadier General James Clinton received orders from Washington to be prepared to move either toward Wyoming on the Susquehanna, or up the Mohawk to form the junction where Sullivan decided, "on the shortest notice."[54] Shortly afterward, Sullivan sent his orders to join the two wings at Tioga. Clinton immediately prepared the brigade for movement from Canajoharie to Otsego Lake. Lieutenant Colonel William Butler's command, the 4th Pennsylvania Regiment and the Rifle Corps, was ordered to march from Fort Defiance in Schoharie to Schenectady on Friday, June 11, leaving behind a detachment of thirty men, plus officers and noncommissioned officers, for the safety of the community. Two days later, Butler's men began to escort thirty-six bateaux loaded with a "quantity of provisions" up the Mohawk to Canajoharie, where they arrived and unloaded the boats on Saturday, June 19.[55]

That same day, Colonel Van Schaick stopped at Canajoharie on his way to Albany to confer with Clinton. Van Schaick commanded the Continental forces left behind in the Northern Department during Clinton's absence on the expedition. In the course of the discussion, Van Schaick reported that some friendly Onondaga Indians had returned from another scout of Buck Island with two prisoners, who revealed no British reinforcements were expected from Canada that season. In the meantime, the 6th Massachusetts left Fort Alden in Cherry Valley for Otsego Lake, detaching a fatigue party at Springfield to repair the road from Canajoharie.[56]

Starting on Wednesday, June 16, the New York brigade began transporting its equipment and supplies overland from Canajoharie to the landing on the lake shore. Perhaps it was planned, but the route that took them near Springfield and Cherry Valley reminded the troops of the purpose for the campaign. As his regiment marched through on the way to Otsego, Lieutenant Erkuries Beatty remarked that Springfield was "a pretty little Settlement that had been destroyed by the Indians." In the first three days, 300 wagons, fifty-nine of them transporting bateaux, the remainder loaded with provisions, were rolling. Detachments of infantry were posted along the road for security, escorting them from fort to fort, and repairing the damage to the roads. More boats were expected to make their way from Schenectady, and after their arrival at Canajoharie, they too would be hauled to Otsego Lake. The movement spawned a flurry of activity that Lieutenant William McKendry, Quartermaster of the 6th Massachusetts, described as "Boats & provisions arrives at this Lake very fast 500 waggons going steady." By the end of the month, a general hospital and all its equipment arrived. The wagons halted at the landing on the lake shore. There, their cargoes were transferred to the boats, and moved to the south end of the lake, eight miles away.[57]

Out on the Ohio frontier, Colonel Daniel Brodhead was itching to get into a fight. He wrote to the Quartermaster General, Nathanael Greene, that he had only 429 "public horses" in the different brigades of the district.[58] Despite the difficulty in obtaining supplies, he said, "I should be much happier could I but act on the offensive" and mentioned a plan to Washington. He wished Sullivan great success against the "black Cardiff of the North (Iroquois)" and said that he would be happy to "meet him near the Heads of the Alleghany, and give the Senecas a complete flogging." Brodhead's patrols and friendly Delaware scouts told him there was very little game in the Mingo country, and "should their Corn be destroyed they will suffer as they deserve."[59]

Accordingly, Brodhead was not in favor of maintaining Fort Laurens. He said it provided only symbolic advantages, while it held many actual disadvantages. First, the post was constantly in danger of attack. Second, it was difficult to keep adequately supplied. Located at the end of a tenuous line of communication, convoys and relief parties always proceeded at great risk. Instead, Brodhead favored abandoning the isolated fort and conducting an offensive expedition up the Allegheny. Such a move could be directed either against the Seneca in conjunction with Sullivan, or as alternate route for another attempt to attack Detroit. Eventually, General Washington agreed with the Western Department commander, but directed that Fort Laurens be temporarily maintained. The fort's continued presence would give the hostile tribes of Western Indians cause to believe an attack on Detroit was still in the offing, and divert the enemy's attention from the campaign against the Six Nations. The British took that threat seriously, and continued to plan the reduction of the post on the Tuscarawas.[60]

On June 9, the redcoat Captain Bird wrote to Captain Lernoult that about 200 Indian warriors had gathered in the Upper Sandusky towns, and were ready to strike again at Fort Laurens. A reliable Delaware, known as Big Cat, informed Colonel Brodhead that the British, along with Wyandot, Shawnee, and Mingo allies, threatened to lay siege to the fort again. This time, the attackers claimed to have a cannon that could quickly reduce the fort's walls. Meanwhile, Brodhead ordered Major Frederick Vernon to strengthen the fort's defenses with an inner earthen wall. He had already approached Colonel Archibald Lochry, the County Lieutenant of Westmoreland County, Pennsylvania, to call out men with horses to cut a new road from Fort Pitt to Fort Laurens that would facilitate its relief. Instead, the threat to Fort Laurens greatly diminished after the Indians on the Upper Sandusky learned that their homes were in danger of invasion. After assembling 300 men at Harrodsburg, Colonel John Bowman, the County Lieutenant of Kentucky County, Virginia, led his troops across the Ohio, and ascended the Little Miami toward the Shawnee town of Chillicothe. The warriors hurried to protect their villages, and before they could concentrate to lay siege again, Fort Laurens was abandoned by its garrison.

As bad as the Americans' supply situation was, that of the British around Fort Niagara was at least as bleak. Lieutenant Colonel John Butler urged his Indian allies to plant more corn, and detailed members of his corps of rangers not on military missions to assist them in the area of Genesee. By early June, his stores were exhausted. Captain Walter Butler was sent toward Presque Isle, Venango, and the Ohio to scout, as well as to encourage the Indian allies there to "remain Vigilant and active." But before he could depart on his mission, his father had to request provisions and supplies for both his rangers and the Indians that would accompany them, as well as those who were sure to join him along the way. Lieutenant Colonel Butler even considered sending 300 men, excluding Indians, out of the Seneca country because of the supply situation. He informed Lieutenant Colonel Mason Bolton at Fort Niagara that he considered marching them from Canadesaga to Irondequot, so they could "beg" to be supplied from Fort Niagara. Butler also dispatched parties to bring back provisions from local suppliers with little success, because "every Resource in this country is exhausted & the Indians themselves starving." His battalion quartermaster, Jesse Pawling, attempted to purchase cattle, but only a few lean specimens could be found. In addition, the warriors were running low on ammunition, owing to their expending much of it in hunting birds to supplement their dwindling food supply. Butler lamented that the Iroquois would send out more war parties toward the frontiers "if they were certain the Enemy were not making preparations to attack them."[61]

By the third week of June, Butler's supply problems had eased, but not completely abated. He was able to procure some cattle, and had raiding parties of rangers and Indians out to drive some cattle off from the Whig settlements, and to collect intelligence on Rebel intentions while giving them "such annoyance." Gathering cattle and other provisions from the enemy increased the amount on hand in Butler's stores, and with parties out, the rate of consumption was reduced, resulting in an improvement of the supply situation. When Butler next wrote to Bolton, he still needed about "500 Cwt of Powder & 200 Cwt of Ball" ammunition (each hundredweight or "cwt" being 112 pounds), but he no longer considered it necessary to send his soldiers to Irondequot.

Lieutenant Peter Johnson of the Indian Department, with a party of recently recruited Mississauga, and Captain John McDonell's company of sixty of Butler's Rangers targeted the Mohawk Valley settlements. They returned after taking eighteen male captives and "a great many" women. According to Butler, the women were "all sent back unhurt" except for three the Mississaugas insisted on taking with them. Some of the prisoners told their captors that the Continental troops from Schoharie and German Flats had gone to Fort

Edward, leaving the settlements protected only by militia. Lieutenant Andrew Thompson, with a detachment of forty of Butler's Rangers and a band of fifty or sixty Wolf clan Delaware warriors under their chief, Captain Rowland Montour of the Indian Department, scouted on the Susquehanna toward Wyoming. Lieutenant Henry Hare led a ranger patrol reconnoitering toward Fort Hunter, and a war party of Cayugas scouted near the "Big Island" on the Susquehanna.[62]

At Wyoming, the troops continued to gather and establish camps until nearly 2,000 troops were encamped in the Wyoming Valley. Soon, the settlement that had been destroyed only the year before was bustling with activity. Fort Wyoming, built to replace the destroyed Fort Wilkes-Barre, was a small post, surrounded by abatis, with a "small redoubt to shelter the inhabitants in cases of an alarm" and a garrison 100 men, commanded by Lieutenant Colonel Zebulon Butler. The town consisted of about seventy structures, chiefly log buildings, plus "sundry larger ones erected by the army for the purpose of receiving stores, &c., and a large bake and smoke houses." Soldiers were amazed at the evidence of destruction caused by Butler's Rangers and their Iroquois allies that still remained. Many of them, like Lieutenant Colonel Commandant Adam Hubely of the 11th Pennsylvania Regiment, remarked that one could "not omit taking notice of the poor inhabitants of the town." Unlike the sensationalized newspaper reports of the year before, many soldiers appeared to have a more realistic perception of the destruction caused in 1778. Although there was no large-scale massacre of women and children, Hubely noted, "two thirds of them are widows and orphans, who, by the vile hands of the savages, have not only deprived some of tender husbands, some of indulgent parents, and others of affectionate friends and acquaintances, besides robbed and plundered of all their furniture and clothing." As a result, the victims were left completely dependent on the government or charity.[63]

To make sure they realized the importance of the mission on which they were to soon embark, Brigadier General Enoch Poor, commander of the New Hampshire Brigade, Lieutenant Colonel Henry Dearborn, commander of the 3rd New Hampshire Regiment, and "several other gentlemen" of the brigade rode out beyond the Plains of Abraham to view the field where the Wyoming militia had been defeated.[64] To the officers of the Continental Army whose troops were now assembling in the area, the town still exhibited a "melancholy scene of desolation in ruin'd Houses, wasted fields and Fatherless Children & Widows."[65]

As troops arrived and waited for General Sullivan to order the advance, the staff officers sought resolution to the various logistical problems and the soldiers

A carving on a contemporary powder horn accurately depicting artillerymen with a field piece, limber, and team of horses. (Harold J. Peterson Collection)

were kept busy conducting scouting patrols, escorting the wagon and boat convoys that arrived and departed daily, improving the roads, and strengthening the defensive works about their camps and at Fort Wyoming. They also trained and exercised the tactics they had adapted for fighting in the forest against Butler's Rangers and their Indians allies. The artillerymen of Colonel Thomas Proctor's 4th Continental Artillery Regiment also experimented with some of their field pieces on how to best support the infantry on the march to Tioga. They first tried arming a bateau with a 3-pounder "grasshopper" light field piece and demonstrated that it could fire both round shot and canister effectively. Next, they tried firing several shells from a 5 1/2-inch howitzer mounted aboard a bateau, with equal success.[66]

Out on the Ohio, Colonel Brodhead had been busy cultivating the "friendly disposition" of those Indian tribes that had previously caused trouble, but who potentially could be swayed back to neutrality, or even brought into an alliance with the Americans. He later reported to General Washington that he attempted to "inflame" the rivalry between the Wyandots and Mingoes to the Americans' advantage. The colonel was also chafing at the opportunity to act offensively, and approached the commander in chief to reconsider his department's participation in the pending Indian expedition. Brodhead was actively conducting reconnaissance and limited combat operations against those hostile Indians. In order to gain intelligence on their activities and intentions, and to retaliate for some of their depredations, Brodhead was sending out "light parties" of his own. These ranging operations, led by officers like the experienced Indian fighter Captain Samuel Brady of the 8th Pennsylvania, often accompanied by friendly Delaware warriors, were conducted by Continental soldiers dressed and painted like Indians. They greatly enhanced the efforts of the volunteer ranging companies in state service fielded by Westmoreland County and Bedford Counties, Pennsylvania, that were already patrolling the frontier. In late June, Washington urged Brodhead to continue his activities to encourage friends and intimidate enemies, and approved his conducting a "diversion in favor of the expedition of General Sullivan."[67]

Empowered with certain "discretion to act offensively against the Savages," Brodhead increased his preparations. The Army's Quartermaster General, Major General Nathanael Greene, directed Colonel Archibald Steele to personally supervise and coordinate his activities with Brodhead with regard to obtaining the necessary stores and supplies, and completion of the boats under construction, to aid the Western Department's logistical effort as much as possible.[68] By the second week of July, General Washington informed Brodhead he had applied to the Board of War to supply the Western Department with "articles to reward the Indians" who became favorable to the American cause. With the supply situation apparently resolved, the commander in chief reiterated his concurrence with Brodhead's plan to act against the Mingoes and "to make an expedition against the Seneca."[69]

The enemy, fully aware now that the expedition was poised to strike like a dagger into Iroquois country, attempted to distract the army from its preparations. Early in July, John Butler had learned from scouts, prisoners, and an American deserter that Hand's command had grown to 600 men, but a total of "nine Regiments and as many pieces of Cannon" were due to arrive under Sullivan's command. Joined by a second force coming down "from the Northward" and a third from Fort Pitt, they planned to "cut off the Indians as they came along, and then join their Forces to attack Niagara." A further indication of an attack, the British and their allies reported 600 pack horses gathered, and the Americans waiting for 400 more, along with "a great number of Boats laying in the River." Certainly, the strength and numbers surprised the British and alarmed the Indians. Butler had runners going off to the various Indian villages to collect warriors, and asked Lieutenant Colonel Bolton for an immediate supply of provisions, ammunition, "two gross of Knives and 50 lbs Paint."[70]

John Butler made an effort to further alleviate his supply problems, and cause the Americans enough grief to delay the start or dissipate the strength of the force set to conduct the Indian expedition. He turned to Captain Joseph Brant, who gathered twenty-eight of his Loyalist volunteers and sixty Indians and led them on a raid "in quest of provisions," and to gather intelligence along the New York frontier on the Delaware in the vicinity of Minisink. He also called on Captain McDonell to do the same on the West Bank of the Susquehanna. McDonell, leading a company of Butler's Rangers reinforced with a detachment of redcoats from the 8th Regiment of Foot, was joined by a Seneca war party commanded by a chief named Hioko, for a combined force of about 250 men. While he instructed the rest of his officers to keep out vigilant patrols to warn of the enemy approach, Butler remained at Canadesaga to bolster the spirits of the Indians, and continue the gathering of supplies.[71]

After leaving the rest of his followers at Chemung on July 8, Captain Brant reportedly ordered the eighty-eight that were going on the raid with him that "they Should not Kill any Women or Children" or Loyalists, and to take prisoner any who surrendered. But they should kill any person whom they saw running. Brant told them a force of sixty more Tories was waiting at Hallibarrack, ready to join them.[72] After stopping at Onaquaga and making preparations, Brant planned to strike at the settlement of Minisink before sunrise on Tuesday, July 22. His men were late in arriving, so after getting in position, Brant attacked at about noon. They rushed in, killing and taking a few inhabitants prisoner, as most of the alarmed townspeople made it to the safety of Fort Vanakan. Brant and his men surrounded that fort, and kept it under fire seeking an opportunity to penetrate the stockade. After about an hour, Brant ordered a halt to the attack. While some of his raiders kept the defenders occupied, the rest plundered the homes and searched for cattle, sheep, and horses. In the hours that his attack was delayed, it seemed that all the cattle had taken to the woods, and none were found close to the settlers' homes and barns where they could be gathered and driven off easily by Brant's men.[73]

While the raiders plundered the town and spent the night, the militia of the nearby communities mustered and the local commanders sent express messengers to Governor Clinton asking for help. The next morning, Brant and his men burned eleven houses and barns, some enclosed within small stockades, and the Dutch Reformed Church before withdrawing at about eight o'clock. According to his own report, Brant claimed his men "destroyed several small stockaded Forts, and took four Scalps & three Prisoners; but did not in the least injure Women or Children." He expressed his regret that he could not kill or take more Rebels prisoner, but there were "many Forts about the Place, into which they were always ready to run like ground Hogs." He was also disappointed at being unable to drive off cattle, which were desperately needed by Butler's forces in Canadesaga. He reported his own casualties in the attack as one killed and one wounded.[74]

While Brant and his men delayed their departure, a body of 150 militia men from Ulster and Orange counties and nearby communities in New Jersey mustered and marched in pursuit under the command of Lieutenant Colonel Benjamin Tusten. While Brant's men marched by a road along the river before camping for the night, the militia marched by a road leading through the woods, in an attempt to overtake their enemy before they crossed the

Lackawaxen ford. The next morning, Thursday, July 24, Brant sent two men to scout the second road, planning to ambush the American militia that was sure to pursue. The men failed to return to the Indian and Tory camp, so Brant was unaware American militia had already established an ambush not far from where his forces had camped for the night. The scouts, either through cowardice or by being captured, did not return before Brant was ready to move.[75] As his men began crossing the river, the militia opened fire, "so that the Rebels had fair play at us," according to Brant. The Mohawk captain was about 400 yards down the column when he heard the firing. While the men to the front scattered to return fire from along the river bank, Brant led forty of his men around a hill to attack the rear of the American militia ambuscade.[76]

The Rebels soon retreated to a rocky hill where they took a defensive posture. Brant's men, "employed & very busy," pressed their attack against the American force for four hard-fought hours, before driving them out of position. Brant claimed his men killed or wounded half of the 150 Americans they faced, and took "40 odd scalps and one prisoner." The prisoner, Brant said, was a captain. Brant reported his own losses as three dead and ten wounded (four mortally, he believed). Brant sustained a minor wound in the engagement himself. When the American survivors rallied to account for their men, they reported forty missing and believed killed or captured, including Lieutenant Colonel Tusten and three captains. This skirmish demonstrated just how lethal Joseph Brant and his forces were even when outnumbered and surprised. After arriving back at Onaquaga, Brant led eight men on a scout to the Mohawk to determine Americans' intentions or intelligence about the impending Indian expedition there, and sent the rest to Chemung with the cattle and plunder.[77]

Not all of Butler's scouts were successful in gathering intelligence. Lieutenant Henry Hare and Sergeant William Newberry were captured. Taken by militia, the two were observing Brigadier General James Clinton's troops and supplies moving along the Mohawk River and preparing for the campaign. Wearing civilian clothes when apprehended, the two were tried by court martial and hanged as spies.[78]

On hearing of the raid and receiving the appeals for help, Governor Clinton considered ordering the regiment of levies guarding the frontier to the area. Their commander, Lieutenant Colonel Albert Pawling, advised against it. He correctly pointed out to the governor that he was waiting for Sullivan's march order for the expedition, and believed those causing "mischief" were an "Inconsiderable Party" of enemy. Although they alarmed the inhabitants, he thought they would not continue their attack. Because Sullivan's "Army to Westward" was believed "at this Instant on their March from Wyoming to

Chemung," the enemy would be concerned about returning to defend their own settlements. Besides, the enemy would have done all the damage they could before leaving. Before any assistance arrived, the enemy would be gone. He offered to send one detachment toward Mamacating, which could rapidly rejoin the regiment if needed, as a precaution to counter a continued raid.[79] Governor Clinton recognized the wisdom of Pawling's recommendation, and ordered the levies to return to their stations and called out additional militia instead.[80]

The same week Brant struck Minisink, marauding Indians visited the West Branch settlements. On the morning of July 21, some men working in the cornfields near Fort Freeland were attacked by Indians. One managed to run back to the fort unhurt, but three of his companions were killed and scalped, and two men and a youth were taken prisoner. The militia of nearby towns mustered, but a relief force of Pennsylvania rangers sent from Sunbury arrived after the raiders had departed. There had been reports that on the same day, Indians had also attacked Fort Muncy, but that situation appeared to have calmed.

On July 27, "After a fatiguing march over mountains & through woods almost impenetrable," Captain McDonell's company of Butler's Rangers and Hioko's war party came upon the West Branch settlements. While a party of 100 warriors went to attack farms and drive off cattle, McDonell continued to march through the night with the troops and rest of the Indians. By daylight, McDonell's men "invested a small Place called Fort Freeland." Sensing no indication of trouble, early on Wednesday morning, July 28, Jacob Freeland, Sr., opened the gate of the stockade surrounding his home. Immediately he was struck by a musket ball and fell back inside. The twenty-one militia were quickly under arms, but just as fast they realized their fort was surrounded by about 150 enemy soldiers and Seneca warriors. Although willing to resist, the defenders were running low on ammunition. In the course of the siege, John Montour, one of the Indian Department officers serving with the warriors, rushed up to the picket wall to take an American scalp, when he received a minor bullet wound to the small of the back. After a two-hour fight and three summons to surrender, the Americans had suffered two men killed. With little hope of relief, or survival if they continued to resist, the garrison capitulated. Captain McDonell's terms offered to let their women, children, and elderly men go free, provided all the "men under arms" surrendered as prisoners of war.[81]

On hearing the sounds of an engagement at nearby Boone's Mill, thirty men of the local militia turned out under the command of Captain Hawkins Boone. While the Indian scouts that had been posted to warn of any approaching American relief columns were off capturing horses and pillaging houses, Captain Boone led his men forward to within sight of Fort Freeland, unaware that the garrison had given up. Boone quickly brought his men into action and opened a brisk fire. At first, the Indians retired, but soon rallied to attack the American left flank as the redcoats of the 8th Regiment and the rangers attacked them in front. The militia broke ranks and fled into the underbrush, leaving about half their number, including Captain Boone, dead on the field. In contrast, the British lost one Indian killed and one wounded.[82]

The Indians declined to pursue the retreating militia. Instead, they joined in plundering and burning the buildings and homes in and around the fort. The members of the garrison were marched into captivity, while the fifty-two women, children, and elderly men were allowed to travel safely to Sunbury. In the march back toward Indian territory, McDonell's force destroyed five forts and all the houses within thirty miles of "a close settled Country." Although most farms were found abandoned in their path, his men managed plunder them of goods, and collect about 116 cattle.

When the noncombatants arrived in Sunbury, Colonel John Cooke, a Deputy Quartermaster General, transmitted the news to General Sullivan. After relating the details of the attack on Fort Freeland, he said the Pennsylvania militia had only 150 men left to protect women and children, and expected another attack daily. He closed with an impassioned plea for assistance, for they were "the most frontier garrison & fear without some speedy Assistance, must fall a prey to Savage Tyrants." Sullivan, undeterred, refused to take the bait. He knew the effectiveness his expedition would have for the security of the frontier if it did not dissipate its strength or submit to distraction. Although he sent out small patrols to keep marauding Indians from damaging the army, he denied every request for assistance. When local leaders in Pennsylvania asked for assistance, he referred them to their state's council, which had reneged on its pledge to furnish men for the expedition.[83]

Washington was not the only one who was impatient at Sullivan's continued delay. Governor Clinton laid the responsibility for Brant's raid on Minisink at Sullivan's feet. He wrote, "The Source of our present Misfortune is the unaccountable Delay of General Sullivan at Wyoming." The expedition had drawn all the Continentals from the frontier. Pawling's regiment of levies, being in the pay of Congress, was answerable to the orders of General Washington, not Governor Clinton. The delay caused the realization of the fear that the expedition would weaken the border defenses, and leave the settlements exposed to enemy depredations. If Sullivan's army had been damaging the enemy's country, the outlook would have been different. As it was, with three brigades sitting at Wyoming and one at Otsego Lake, Sullivan's delay "has unavoidably left our Frontier more exposed than it otherwise would have been."[84]

Sullivan continued to delay the commencement of his expedition through the month of July, while waiting for more supplies to arrive. Every day, supply boats arrived from Sunbury to unload provisions and other stores. Hundreds of wagons and packhorses loaded with more equipment and head of cattle were driven over the mountains and through the swamps from Easton. As the end of July drew near, Sullivan still had not yet moved. He complained about the lack of supplies and the failure of the Quartermaster Department to deliver them to General Washington and to the Board of War. The board apologized "exceedingly [for] the delay of an expedition [whose] whole success greatly depended on Secrecy and Dispatch." The members of the Board agreed that Sullivan's complaints had "undoubtedly but too much foundation."[85] Sullivan then took his complaints about the lack of support he was receiving to Congress, possibly to lower the delegates' high expectations in the expedition, or to start absolving himself of blame early, should the expedition be defeated or fail to meet its objectives. Likewise, he criticized the state of Pennsylvania for not providing the 720 volunteer militia or rangers it had pledged to detach to the expedition.[86]

Brigadier General Clinton had moved his headquarters to Otsego Lake in the first week of July, but his brigade waited the better part of a month for orders from Sullivan to march. Enemy scouts were often seen, sometimes occasioned by brief exchanges of gunfire and casualties. In response, the Rifle Corps, sometimes reinforced by musket infantry, sent out a number of patrols to capture or drive the scouts away. In the meantime, Sullivan instructed Clinton to draw more supplies for his wing of the army to bring on the expedition. With the stores he had, Sullivan realized it was not enough to provision both the troops leaving Wyoming as well as those coming from Otsego Lake. When he wrote Brigadier General Clinton on July 11, he made it clear that if the New York brigade marched with only enough provisions to reach Tioga, and then depended on Sullivan's magazines, they "must all starve together." As the summer wore on, the water on the upper Susquehanna dropped to levels that would impede the movement of baggage and stores by boat. As a remedy, Clinton had his men construct an earthen dam across the mouth of the river at the foot of the lake to provide a headwater to float the heavily laden supply boats into the Susquehanna.[87]

With his brigade assembled, including twenty-five Oneida warriors to act as scouts, Clinton was anxious to march. The date of march was to be transmitted by Sullivan first to Governor Clinton, who would then forward it to Brigadier General Clinton at Otsego, and Lieutenant Colonel Albert Pawling. Timing was essential, so that Pawling's levies could join Clinton's brigade as it marched past Onaquaga, approximately seven days after leaving Otsego, and join with Sullivan within a day or two of his arrival at Tioga.[88]

Washington continued to chafe at about the delayed start to the campaign, and the commander in chief was filled with "inexplicable concern and apprehension of the worst consequence to the Expedition." He intended that the troops under Brigadier General Clinton were to stay at Canajoharie with boats ready to move up the Mohawk, or across country to Otsego, at Sullivan's choice. Once the expedition committed to one of the alternatives, however, it was essential that Clinton's brigade move "light, rapidly and undiscovered," with only enough stores to sustain the brigade on the march to the link up at Tioga, at which time both wings were to be supplied by Sullivan's supply train. Instead, Sullivan ordered Clinton to draw and transport enough stores and provisions to last for three months. By doing so, 200-300 bateaux needed elsewhere were "encumbered by useless supplies." In addition, the reason for remaining at Canajoharie was to conceal the expedition's destination from the enemy's scouts and spies "till the moment of execution." By the movement of such a ponderous train to the shore of Otsego Lake, only to sit there inactive, could serve no purpose but to telegraph the direction of movement, objectives, and possibly the entire plan to the enemy while waiting for Sullivan to issue the necessary orders. Furthermore, the size of the supply convoy threatened to weaken the combat strength of the brigade by drawing troops to defend it, and detailing soldiers to man the boats if enough boat men were not enlisted.[89] Clinton waited five weeks to march.

Out at Fort Pitt, Colonel Brodhead's preparations were nearing completion. Sullivan's delay probably worked to his advantage because he first had to shorten his supply lines and redistribute forces. On July 16, Lieutenant Colonel Richard Campbell of the 13th Virginia arrived at Fort Laurens with a force comprised of several companies of that regiment, and Rawlings' Corps, to deliver supplies and relieve the troops completing their tour of duty in the garrison. Campbell was to remain as commander of the post with the fresh garrison of seventy-five men after the rest returned to Fort Pitt, but it was to be a short tenure. The same day, Brodhead sent Campbell orders to abandon the fort he called the "hobby horse on the Muskingum." Captain Benjamin Harrison of the 13th Virginia was sent with a detail of guards and packhorses to bring back all the remaining provisions. By the end of the month, the now useless post was evacuated, but not before an enemy raiding party struck one last blow and killed two soldiers while the garrison was waiting to march. Back at Fort Pitt, sixty new boats were nearing completion. Colonel Brodhead felt he would be prepared to move a few days after the troops and supplies returned from Fort Laurens. Accordingly, he planned the start of his campaign for August 11.[90]

For all the effort to keep the object a "profound secret," Colonel John Butler continued to receive accurate intelligence. His Indian scouts and ranger patrols on the lower Susquehanna sent information that prompted Butler to remark, "It appears now without any doubt that the Rebels are firmly bent upon coming against the Six Nations with a large Body of men & have made all the necessary preparations." From the scouts lurking about Clinton's camp, he was aware of the American effort to dam Otsego Lake to raise the water level and flood the creek to float their supply-laden boats. His son, Captain Walter Butler, sent a runner from Canawagaras with word that there was a new Rebel post (Fort Armstrong) at Pine Creek, or Otego (Kittaning), about twenty-five miles upriver from Fort Pitt. The captain doubted the Americans would attack Detroit, and correctly deduced that the Americans were going to move against the Six Nations by way of the Allegheny instead.[91]

Finally, all was ready. Although not completely satisfied with the logistical support he had received, Sullivan realized it was time to execute the orders of General Washington in conforming to the resolutions of the Continental Congress, and requests of the states along the frontier. On Friday, July 30, 1779, a fatigue party of 600 men worked from six o'clock in the morning until nine o'clock at night loading boats and packhorses. A number of officers and soldiers penned their record of the order they had just received into their personal journals or letters home: "tomorrow we march." At his headquarters, Sullivan wrote that he "at length surmounted every obstacle." Duplicate messages were sent by different routes to Governor George Clinton in Poughkeepsie and Brigadier General James Clinton at Otsego Lake. Sullivan ordered General Clinton to begin the movement of his wing of the army down the Susquehanna on August 9. At long last, Sullivan sent the commander in chief the words he had waited for since assigning the mission: "I shall commence my March tomorrow morning."[92]

Chapter 12

THE SULLIVAN EXPEDITION

T HE morning of July 31, 1779, at Fort Wyoming began in the usual army way with the firing of the "morning gun." Soldiers were soon occupied with making their final preparations to march. This division of the Continental Army was poised to begin its long-awaited expedition to avenge the "depredations" committed by the British Provincial forces and their Iroquois allies over the previous two years. It was fitting, in more than strictly military terms, that the expedition started at Wyoming. Many men in the ranks had heard the news, especially over the past year or so, of numerous frontier settlements that had been destroyed. Some may have learned that their own homes were burned, and friends killed, neighbors severely wounded, or family members taken captive. Even if they had not, for several weeks they had been camping among the ruins of a once thriving but now devastated community, whose very name had become synonymous with the enemy's cruelty. For the men in the ranks of Spalding's company and the handful of militiamen, it must have been particularly poignant. Just across the river, about seventy of their fathers, brothers, and friends had been reverently interred in a common grave, but several score lay yet unburied where they fell.

At noon, Major General John Sullivan gave the order to advance. Lieutenant Colonel Zebulon Butler, commanding the 125 troops staying behind to garrison Fort Wyoming, ordered the artillery in the post to fire a thirteen-gun salute, as if to say, "give 'em hell." The artillery aboard the watercraft in the river returned the salute, acknowledging that the men of the expedition intended to do just that.[1]

Captain Jehoiakim Mothskin and his party of Stockbridge[2] Indian scouts were the first to move, taking the lead far in advance of the army to uncover any lurking enemy or find out which towns were still occupied. The wing of the army departing Wyoming numbered about 3,500 men and was organized into three brigades. The Third Brigade of Brigadier General Edward Hand, designated as the army's Light Corps, was first to march. Deployed into three columns, the brigade oriented its movement north on the single road leading from Wilkes-Barre along the eastern bank of the Susquehanna. Lieutenant Colonel Commandant Adam Hubley's 11th Pennsylvania Regiment "advanced by platoons from the center," initially in platoon columns, but was prepared to constrict into files, "as the country will admit." The German Regiment, commanded by Major Daniel Burchardt, and Schott's Independent Rifle Corps, commanded by Captain Anthony Selin, was similarly formed to their right.[3] A detachment of the 11th Pennsylvania's Light Infantry company and Schott's riflemen marched in file to provide security on the right flank. The third column, which consisted of most of Hubley's light company, commanded by Captain George Bush, and Spalding's Wyoming Independent Company, took its post in column on the left. Each of the three columns was joined by members of Captain John Franklin's detachment of Wyoming militia to act as guides, and had advanced guards deployed ahead to prevent the columns from being surprised by a concealed enemy.[4]

The main body followed less than one mile behind the Light Corps. Brigadier General William Maxwell's 1st Brigade, with Colonel Matthias Ogden's 1st, Colonel Israel Shreve's 2nd, Colonel Elias Dayton's 3rd, and Colonel Oliver Spencer's 5th New Jersey regiments, marched on the left. A detachment of sixty men, formed in two divisions under the command of a captain, provided security on the left flank. Brigadier General Enoch Poor's Second Brigade marched with Colonel Joseph Cilley's 1st, Lieutenant Colonel Commandant George Reid's 2nd, and Lieutenant Colonel Commandant Henry Dearborn's 3rd New Hampshire, and Colonel Philip Van Cortlandt's 2nd New York Regiments on the right. A detachment of 200 men, formed in two divisions and commanded by a field officer, provided the flank guard on the right. Every day, the brigades rotated the regiments in the order of march, and starting with Ogden's on July 31, each brigade detached "a regiment complete" on alternating days to provide security to the rear.

For the previous few weeks, while the army was assembled and waited for supplies, the troops had trained in the woods, defiles, swamps, and hills around the Wyoming Valley. In general, they trained to "act in as loose and dispersed a way as is consistent with a proper degree of government, concert, and mutual support." In particular, they rehearsed the preplanned actions they would take immediately to respond to enemy contact. If attacked in front, the Light Corps would deploy the 11th Pennsylvania and the German Regiment on line. The trailing brigades would move to extend that line, outflank the opposing force, and attempt to gain the enemy's rear. The regiment providing the rear guard would assume the role of the corps de reserve. If attacked to either flank, the brigade closest to the action would face the enemy and deploy on line, while

Hand's brigade and the rear guard regiment maneuvered on the enemy flanks, and the brigade farthest from the action assumed the role of reserve. If attacked in the rear, the trail regiment would face about as the two brigades extended the line to left and right and moving to outflank the foe, while Hand's brigade became the reserve. Thus, Sullivan's army was prepared to deny the enemy warriors and Tory rangers their greatest advantage when fighting in the forest—the element of surprise.[5]

Colonel Thomas Proctor's 4th Continental Artillery Regiment had nine pieces in its park: two 6-pounder and four 3-pounder field guns, two 5 1/2-inch howitzers, and a cohorn mortar. The guns, the traveling forge (a mobile blacksmith shop, usually found with artillery and cavalry units), artillery and infantry brigade ammunition wagons and carts were transported aboard the boats. Any elements of the artillery train traveling by land moved in the center when the army "formed to the right" in column, or followed Maxwell's brigade when compressed by the terrain. The packhorses and cattle were kept between the train of artillery and infantry brigades when permitted by unbroken ground, or followed Poor's brigade when the route was constricted.

Not counting the officers' mounts, there were about 1,200 horses on the expedition. They carried most of the flour and the baggage and provisions not transported by water. Each infantry brigade had its own train of 300 horses, Hand's corps and the artillery each had about 200, while 100 bore the "public stores." To provide the ration of fresh beef, about 800 head of cattle were driven along with the expedition. When the terrain and vegetation permitted marching in columns, the main body of Sullivan's army occupied about two miles of ground. When constricted, it stretched out to nearly six. The majority of the supplies, ammunition, and provisions were carried by boat. After the army reached Tioga Point the supplies on which it relied would be carried by pack animal into Iroquois country. Those needed for the return march to Wyoming would be stored at a fortified supply base at Tioga.

A flotilla of 120 boats and bateaux, manned by artillerymen and detachments from each of the infantry brigades and civilian boatmen, moved up the river under the command of Colonel Proctor. For mutual support and protection, the army tried to regulate its movements in order to keep abreast of the boats. Proctor had frequent signals sounded by horn to help maintain alignment, but the marching troops outpaced the watercraft on a few occasions. When that occurred, the troops encamped until the flotilla rejoined the army to land the necessary rations and supplies before the army continued its march.

A captain with a sixty-man detachment from Maxwell's brigade advanced ahead of the boats on west side to "scour the country and give notice of ambuscades." If attacked, an officer and twelve men moving in boats at the head of the flotilla could immediately reinforce them. If the enemy proved too strong to overcome quickly, the flankers would retreat across river in the light boats standing ready for their use. Proctor could then either maneuver the armed boats to their support or cover their retreat with artillery fire, and lead the officers and men manning the boats in executing the action he deemed appropriate. If the main body was attacked, Proctor was to await orders on how to maneuver his boats in support.[6]

As Sullivan's wing trudged along the east bank, it passed numerous abandoned settlements that been either voluntarily vacated or attacked and devastated by one side or the other in the course of the war. Heavy rains and difficult terrain slowed the march on occasion. After six days, the army marched through Wyalusing. The abandoned Moravian mission town of ninety log houses and a church was familiar to a number of the members of the 11th Pennsylvania, Spalding's company, and the Wyoming militia, as the scene of an engagement during Hartley's expedition the previous fall.

On Sunday, August 8, Proctor sent troops ashore on the west bank to burn the twenty-two buildings of Newtychanning, the first Iroquois town to be destroyed by the expedition. The terrain on the east bank varied from "level land and beautifully situated," to "high and steep mountains." The latter caused some packhorses to lose their loads and took the lives of others. On August 9, for example, the troops had to negotiate one of the many defiles in their path. Sergeant Major George Grant of the 2nd New York Regiment remarked that as the expedition inched along a narrow path, "where one man had scarce room to walk," for about half mile, three cattle and a few horses fell 120 yards down the steep embankment to their deaths. Fortunately, troops in the boats were able to retrieve some of them from where they fell in the river and dressed the carcasses, adding the fresh meat to the commissary stores. The men occasionally saw Indians shadowing the route, and a few tried to attack small parties of soldiers and drovers while they were out rounding up cattle and horses in the morning. The Americans knew they were being watched, but there was little serious opposition by the enemy.[7]

During the eighty-mile march to Tioga, Sullivan received an express from General Washington containing valuable intelligence about the Tory and Indian forces opposing him. American spies and scouts said—and Tory prisoners and deserters confirmed—that the enemy suffered from such a serious lack of supplies that Butler and the Indian war chiefs "were obliged to keep themselves in a dispersed state," and when concentrated, were not able "to remain long together" in the field. Sources also confirmed that the enemy might assemble a force of 1,500 "fighting men whites and Indians," at most. And while the enemy boasted they were equal to double their number of Continentals when fighting in the woods, John Butler's combined force currently amounted to no more than 300-400 at Canadesaga, and maybe 200-300 near Chemung. Washington warned Sullivan, "Chemung was appointed as the place of rendezvous where the Indians intended to give you battle." No reinforcements were expected from Canada, so if the enemy failed to stop the expedition there, Sullivan could expect them to retire toward Niagara, harassing the advance as much as possible "with small parties and ambuscades." The enemy's "principal strength," however, was in the Genesee towns. It was further believed that most of the pro-British Iroquois had already evacuated their old men, women, and children. The ones who doubted the American capability to launch such an offensive kept everyone at home.[8]

While the army approached Tioga on August 9, a fire was seen on a mountain to the west, possibly an enemy camp. The next day, Major General Sullivan ordered some field officers and one regiment from each brigade to go forward with him on a reconnaissance in force as far as the mouth of the Chemung River to locate a ford. The reconnaissance returned after finding a place to cross the Susquehanna below where the Chemung joined the Susquehanna. Indian scouts had watched them, and immediately sent runners back to Major John Butler with the news that the enemy "had been seen upon the Plains Six miles below Tioga." He and the chiefs sent out calls for "every Indian about Niagara" to immediately join him. He sent word for the Mississaugas to "march Night and Day" to do so, and requested that British authorities at Fort Niagara not issue provisions or anything else to Indian warriors not answering his call, and recommended that shirkers no longer be "looked upon as Friends." Butler pleaded for Lieutenant Colonel Bolton to send as much ammunition and as many redcoats as he could spare. Butler was aware that the Americans intended to construct a post after reaching Tioga, and hoped the resulting delay would allow enough time to "assemble a considerable Body before they advance."[9]

The Light Corps of Sullivan's army marched at 7:30 in the morning on August 11, and took post on the riverbank near the fording place. The main body followed one half hour later. Colonel Proctor landed his two 6-pounder field guns, and opened fire on the west bank with grape shot to "scour the woods and thickets" in order to harass any enemy that might be waiting there in ambush. After removing their overalls and boots, tying them about their necks, and hanging their cartouche boxes on their bayonets, the men of the Light Corps formed by platoons under cover of the flotilla. Then, each man grasped the hand of the comrade next to him. Supporting each other, they waded into the water, up to their armpits, against a strong current. To animate his brigade, General Hand dismounted from his horse, and waded across the river with his soldiers. The other brigades crossed in the same manner, followed by the packhorses and cattle. Within one half hour, the whole army—about 3,500 soldiers—was across without "Loss of Either Man or Horse, or any Baggage." Thomas Grant, one of the civilian surveyors accompanying the army to map the route, wrote, "The Sight was beautiful and pleasing, but must have been very Tarifying to the Enemy who, its very probable saw us from the Neighbouring hills which overlook the water."[10]

The expedition was in hostile territory within a half mile of Tioga, sometime marching in single or double files depending on terrain and vegetation. As a precaution, Colonel Proctor's artillerymen advanced two 3-pounders with the light infantry brigade. The army soon marched into open fields of high green grass in the area known as Queen Esther's Flats with "Drums beating, fifes playing, colors flying." After passing the ruins of Queen Esther's Town, the army briefly halted on the south bank of the Chemung River. Neither as deep nor as wide as the Susquehanna, the troops easily forded it in the same manner, with no difficulty, and marched to the ruins of the Munsee town, Tioga.

Many were astonished by the lack of opposition yet encountered. Surgeon Jabez Spencer of 5th New Jersey Regiment confided, "I verily wish these rusticks may be reduced to reason" and agree to remain neutral for the remainder of the conflict with Great Britain, as he did not wish to see them "suffering the extremes of war." The doctor reflected, "there is something cruel, in destroying the habitations of any people (however mean they might be) that I might say the prospect hurts my feelings." But diplomacy had failed to keep the Six Nations neutral. General Sullivan had his orders for the "total destruction and devastation" of the Settlements of the "Six Nations of Indians, with their associates and adherents" from the commander in chief. It was time for the army to avenge the losses inflicted on American settlements.[11]

Captain Jehoiakim Mothskin and his Stockbridge Indian scouts, mounted on horses they captured from the enemy, met the soldiers on their arrival. It was the first time the troops had seen them since leaving Wyoming. Jehoiakim told Sullivan that he believed the enemy was "collecting their whole force at Chemung," about twelve miles up the river, to give the Americans battle.[12] After establishing local security, the army prepared to encamp.

With Clinton's brigade marching down from Otsego Lake, Sullivan did not want to risk defeat in detail. Before detaching a sizable force from Tioga to meet and accompany Clinton's column the final several miles down the Susquehanna, he felt it prudent to address the threat before him. On the evening of the eleventh, Captain John Cummings of the 2nd New Jersey, accompanied by Captain John Franklin and Lieutenant John Jenkins, led five men from his regiment on a scout to Chemung in an "endeavor to make discoveries of the numbers of savages, and their situation, if possible." While patrols scoured the area around Tioga for skulking Indians or Tory rangers on August 12, fatigue parties started cutting timber to build blockhouses and raising earthworks for a fortification two and a half miles from the confluence of the Chemung and Susquehanna. The man-made fortification enhanced the natural defense offered by the long narrow neck of the peninsula, where the two rivers were separated by only about 190 yards of land. When General Clinton's brigade arrived, Tioga Point would be the army's forward logistical base, and include a magazine to store provisions for the return trip, supplies and stores, a hospital, and a landing for the supply boats that provided the line of communication back to Wyoming.[13]

Captain Cummings and his scout arrived near Chemung early in the morning. From a concealed position on a mountain overlooking the town, the members of the patrol observed both Indians and white Tories who were "busily employed," but were unable to tell whether they were preparing to fight or flee. At about noon, the captain gathered his scouts and headed back toward Tioga to inform the general. Deeper in Indian territory on the same day, runners brought Major John Butler reports that the Americans had begun building a fort at Tioga. With the enemy at the doorstep of the Six Nations, the major ordered his son, Captain Walter Butler, to request "four or five boats" and supplies from the British commander at Fort Niagara, and to "march immediately . . . with every man you have fit for Duty" and all the provisions they could carry to join him.[14]

Back at Tioga, American fatigue parties were hard at work building their defenses when Captain Cummings and his scouts returned at about three o'clock in the afternoon of August 12. Reporting to Sullivan, the captain told the general that the Tories and Indians in Chemung appeared to be in "great confusion," but could not determine their intentions. The scouts also collected two fresh scalps recently taken by the Indians.[15] General Sullivan immediately called a council of war, at which the assembled officers agreed with the decision to march immediately to reduce Chemung. With a view to moving fast and striking hard, Sullivan issued the necessary orders for "only the hardiest" troops to pack one day's cooked rations and be "light paraded" by six in the evening. Colonel Proctor would accompany the infantry, providing artillery fire support with a single cohorn mortar carried by hand and mounted on a "machine" devised by the artillery commander.[16]

General Maxwell, who was not feeling well, was ordered to remain at Tioga in command of a guard detachment of about 250 men. These were the "invalids," or soldiers who were not fit to make a difficult march with their units due to illness or injury sustained on the march, as well as the bulk of the artillerymen, whose services were not needed to operate or transport the cohorn. Until their regiments returned from Chemung, the stay-behind force was to safeguard the encampment, artillery park, boats, baggage, stores, cattle, and pack animals, as well as the noncombatant civilians who had accompanied the army.[17]

As in every nation's military in the era, the civilians who "belonged to the army," both male and female (and their children), paid and volunteer, free and slave, were collectively known as "camp followers." They provided necessary services to the troops, and represented both employees of the army, such as the Quartermaster agents and female hospital matrons, and private contractors, such as the cattle drovers and packhorse drivers. A number of the soldiers' wives (or other female relatives) found employment doing cooking and laundry. When the soldiers lined up on the infrequent paydays, the regimental paymaster deducted a fair price from each man's earnings, and divided it among the women appropriately. Generally, three or four women were allowed for each company-sized unit, and some were authorized to subsist "on the strength of the regiment." That meant a woman was not only issued rations, but space in the barracks when in garrison as well, if her husband's commander authorized her to do so. When the number of camp followers threatened to degrade the army's combat effectiveness, commanders could issue orders limiting the number of women who went on campaign.

At eight o'clock on the evening of August 12, leaving all of its baggage and pitched tents behind, the army was in motion. General Hand's brigade was in the lead. The main body followed. Poor's brigade marched "by the right," and Maxwell's, under the temporary command of Colonel Elias Dayton, marched in the rear "by the left." The "excessively dark" night made navigation and movement over "little used paths" through thick woods, "several considerable defiles," and a swamp very difficult. The troops "Marched very slowly on the whole night, sometimes setting down for a few minutes, and up again for eight or ten yards," as the guides, Captain Franklin and Lieutenant Jenkins, occasionally lost their way or took the wrong trails, "until daylight began to appear."[18]

After marching all night, the officers and guides realized the column had covered little more than half of the distance from Tioga to Chemung. The soldiers were ordered to quicken their pace, until they were running at the double quick. Their officers urged them on, hoping the heavy morning fog would conceal their approach from watching enemy scouts, and preserve the element of surprise. Finally, they arrived at and quickly surrounded a collection of Indian houses. Franklin and Jenkins soon realized, however, they had arrived at the partially abandoned village of "Old Chemung," not their objective. "New" Chemung, located on the riverbank and surrounded by agricultural fields, was the main Indian town in the area. The troops were quickly on the march again, and after going an additional mile, they arrived at their destination sometime between dawn and sunrise on August 13.[19]

New Chemung appeared deserted as well. Anticipating an enemy presence, Major General Sullivan intended to destroy, not just drive them off. The plan called for the town to be surrounded as the various regiments took up their posts on arrival. In order to prevent the enemy's escape, Sullivan sent Lieutenant Colonel George Reid with his own 2nd New Hampshire Regiment from Poor's brigade, and the German Regiment from Hand's, across the Chemung River and upstream, to block the enemy's likely avenue of escape over the water or along a path leading toward the next settlement. Hand was to lead an attack with the remainder of his Light Corps, the 11th Pennsylvania Regiment and the two independent companies, from the north side of the town. Poor's brigade was to advance on the town from the east. Sullivan, moving with the remainder of the army, was ready to support the operation with Proctor's cohorn and Maxwell's brigade from the "lower end." The latter, acting as the corps de reserve, would exploit any success or cover any failure by the maneuvering brigades. Operationally, the plan was simple. Hand's and Poor's brigades would converge in town to act as the hammer against Reid's anvil waiting outside.[20]

The troops advanced, according to Sergeant Moses Fellows of the 3rd New Hampshire Regiment, with "fixt bayonets and our Peaces [muskets] charged [loaded]." The soldiers saw only two or three warriors running for the concealment offered by the surrounding cornfields outside of town.[21] Lieutenant Colonel Hubley believed that the enemy "probably discovered our scouting party the previous day," and evacuated the town before the Americans arrived. The town was easily occupied, while Hand's brigade, minus the German Regiment, continued to advance.[22]

The town consisted of about fifty structures. Although there were a few log cabins, most were longhouse dwellings of split and hewn timber covered with bark, with neither wood floors nor chimneys. Two of the larger structures were thought to be "Publick" buildings. One was assumed to be a "council house," the other was "supposed to be a Chapple," one soldier said, which housed an "Idol, which might well enough be Worshipped." On entering the dwellings, the troops found the interiors "very dirty and smokey," but little in the way of furnishings except for a few baskets, kettles, buckets, ladles, plates, and animal skins and linens. The Indians had also driven their livestock away. Although the troops could hear the bells on some cattle off in the woods, they found no animals. The troops plundered the buildings of anything useful before they set fire to them.[23]

While the rest of the army remained in and about the town, Brigadier General Hand gained permission to move the 11th Pennsylvania Regiment and the two independent companies of his brigade forward to seek out any enemy forces in the area. Within a short time, Captain George Bush of the 11th Pennsylvania led his light infantry company on a reconnaissance of the road leading toward Newtown (near present-day Elmira, New York), the next Indian settlement about eight miles upriver. After going less than a quarter mile, the light infantrymen discovered a recently vacated camp. From the sleeping dogs, several still-smoldering campfires, and the number of deerskins and blankets lying about, Captain Bush estimated that forty warriors had camped there the previous night, presumably providing a rear guard during the evacuation. Bush sent a runner with word of his findings back to General Hand and waited for instructions.[24]

General Hand rode up and quickly assessed the situation. While waiting for the rest of the brigade to arrive, Hand sent Major Evan Edwards of Hubley's regiment to inform the commanding general of their findings and request permission to advance farther into enemy country. Sullivan ordered Hand "to endeavor, if possible, to make some discoveries" about enemy strength and intentions by proceeding a few miles up the path, and return. Hand ordered Captain Andrew Walker to command the van, or advanced guard, of twenty-four men from his company. The main body, the rest of Lieutenant Colonel Hubley's regiment and the two independent companies, marched in column along the Indian road with the river on their left. The forty men of Captain Bush's company provided flankers for security on the right.[25]

The advanced guard progressed about one mile when it negotiated the narrow passage between the river on the left and high ground on the right. Suddenly, the stillness was broken by the sound of musketry before a shroud of smoke from the ignited black powder hung across the ridge. Thirty Delaware warriors led by their chief Captain Rowland Montour reloaded their muskets behind a concealed breastwork. Walker's men coolly returned fire at the ambuscade as their comrades of the 11th Pennsylvania "formed a front" and deployed. With bayonets fixed, the Continentals "pushed up the hill with a degree of intrepidity seldom to be met with" while "under a severe fire from the savages." As soon as the Delawares initiated the ambush against the Walker's van, Captain Bush led his company up the spine of the ridge to try to outflank their breastwork line. Just before the light infantry could gain the enemy rear, and as Hubley's battle line advanced steadily uphill, the Indians and Tories abandoned their fortification, carrying off their dead and wounded.[26] Once dislodged, the retreating enemy disappeared in the dense undergrowth of the swampy low ground on the opposite side of the hill, where they knew every path. Unable to follow without great difficulty, the pursuing Continentals broke off the engagement. The American troops found no enemy bodies, and could only assume they inflicted some casualties by blood stains behind the deserted breastwork.[27]

With the enemy driven off the hill, the troops reformed and continued the advance "by the right" in company columns upriver in the direction of Newtown. General Sullivan arrived to investigate the cause of the firing. After allowing the men a brief rest halt, Sullivan ordered Hand to march his brigade back in the direction of Chemung to join the rest of the army. The brief engagement had cost eighteen casualties, all but two of whom were suffered by Hubley's regiment. Six of them, one sergeant, one drummer and four privates, were dead on the field. Twelve were wounded, including Captain Walker, the commander of the van, and the guide, Captain Franklin. All of the injured were expected to recover, except for the mortally wounded adjutant of the 11th Pennsylvania, Lieutenant John Huston.[28]

Back at Chemung, Poor's brigade had been alerted to reinforce Hand's, but was not needed. The troops remained engaged in destroying the large patches full of ripening beans, squash, potatoes, pumpkins, and other vegetables. Lieutenant Colonel Henry Dearborn estimated "about 40 acres fit to roast" were cut down and thrown "in heaps" in the fields or into the river. Colonel Joseph Cilley's 1st New Hampshire Regiment crossed over the Chemung River to destroy three or four cornfields. As they were laying waste to the last of them, Indians and Tories lurking in the woods of a nearby hill opened fire. One soldier was killed and four were wounded. Although the American troops returned fire and parties deployed to engage, the enemy withdrew without suffering apparent loss.

With the destruction of the town complete, General Sullivan reassembled the three brigades on the afternoon of August 13. Surgeon Ebenezer Elmer of the 2nd New Jersey Regiment estimated that the troops destroyed a total of 200 acres under cultivation, leaving one large field on the left bank standing at the lower end of town, to be used when they marched through again later in the campaign. To carry them back to Tioga for interment, and to deny the enemy an exact knowledge of the American losses, the troops "fixed" the bodies of the dead on the backs of horses. The brigade was soon on the march, and returned to their encampment after dark, with the troops "much fatigued."[29] The next day, while they waited for Clinton's brigade to arrive before pushing deeper into enemy country, they cleaned weapons, repaired equipment, and improved the fort that would secure the men and materiel left behind while they waited for Clinton's brigade to arrive before pushing deeper into the wilderness.

Brigadier General James Clinton's brigade of Continentals had been on the march from Otsego Lake since Monday, August 9. Knowing it would take him about seven days of marching to reach Onaquaga, he requested his brother, Governor George Clinton, to send orders for Lieutenant Colonel Albert Pawling's regiment of levies from the New York militia to join the brigade there. General Clinton made it clear he would not wait at Onaquaga longer than August 17 before resuming the march to Tioga. Clinton's men had spent most of the day on August 8 loading the boats with supplies and provisions and preparing to march. That evening, a sluiceway was broken in the earthen dam to flood the river sufficiently to float the boats to the main channel of the Susquehanna. The next morning, drums sounded the "General" at six o'clock, and the troops began striking their tents. In two hours, the 1,600 men of Clinton's Fourth Brigade were ready to begin their movement to Tioga.[30]

Three days before he marched, Clinton had detached the light infantry companies from all the regiments of the brigade, along with the two companies of Major Parr's Rifle Corps, and formed them into a single battalion of about 300 men under the command of Lieutenant Colonel Commandant William Butler. They constituted Clinton's Light Corps, and along with an advanced party of boats, were the first to march at eight o'clock. The battalion companies detached enough soldiers to provide each of the 210 supply-laden boats and bateaux with a crew of three. Soldiers not assigned to watercraft marched as flank or rear guards on the east bank of the Susquehanna. The boats and marching detachments followed the same order of movement. In the event of enemy opposition, the boats would turn toward the bank so the troops could disembark and quickly form in their regiments. The cattle and packhorses drivers moved their animals along the shore between the boats and the marching units.

When they pulled into the river, the boats supporting the light infantry came first in the van, followed by General Clinton's headquarters, and those assigned to the three companies detached from the 2nd (Lamb's) Continental Artillery. The first artillery boat was armed with a light 3-pounder cannon mounted on a four-truck carriage.[31] The boats manned by soldiers from Lieutenant Colonel Butler's 4th Pennsylvania, Lieutenant Colonel Frederic Weisenfels' 4th New York, and Major Daniel Whiting's 6th Massachusetts Regiments followed next. The rest of the artillery, the trailing boat of which was armed with the second cannon, followed the boats transporting the military hospital. The boats manned by soldiers of Colonel Peter Gansevoort's 3rd New York Regiment brought up the rear.[32]

Few hostile warriors or Tory rangers were encountered, except for the occasional scouts, or those attacking individual drivers who wandered outside the picket lines while rounding up cattle and horses that strayed from the main herds. The riflemen in the lead occasionally came across signs of recent occupation by Indian scouting parties, as well as the location of a camp near Otego Creek with evidence that it had apparently been used by Brant's men on their way to attack Cherry Valley the previous winter. Clinton sent a detachment to investigate the Scotch-Tory settlement of Albout, on the east bank of the river about five miles upstream from Unadilla. They found the town abandoned and set it on fire. The next day, Friday, August 13, while Sullivan's division was attacking Chemung, Clinton's brigade reached Conihunto and Unadilla, the Indian settlement and Tory stronghold that had been destroyed by Lieutenant Colonel Butler's expedition the previous fall. In one more day, the brigade arrived at Onaquaga, where Brigadier General Clinton planned to rendezvous with Lieutenant Colonel Pawling's levies. After the troops established security and an encampment, Clinton ordered the destruction of Onaquaga completed. Any buildings not burned, or rebuilt since the preceding fall, were set on fire, and the cornfields and orchards destroyed.[33]

Each day while the brigade was encamped and waiting for the militia, Clinton ordered his artillery to fire a morning and evening gun. He hoped the levies were close enough to hear the report and realize the army was waiting for them at the rendezvous. He assumed Pawling would then speed their march and send a messenger with the news that they were on the way. At noon on Monday, August 16, Major Thomas Church led the 4th Pennsylvania on a march of five or six miles in search of Pawling's command, but they returned in the evening having encountered no sign of the militia. As planned, the brigade resumed its march on Tuesday morning. Before halting for the night, the brigade reached Chenango, a Tuscarora town burned by the Indians themselves when they evacuated. It was evidently the town belonging to the band of Tuscaroras that sided with Brant's Mohawks and the British. While scouting about the area, Parr's riflemen found the body of a dead white man. He had apparently been "lately taken" prisoner, tortured, and executed. Not far from the corpse, the troops discovered a war post with markings that indicated the number of houses destroyed, and scalps and prisoners taken on a recent raid, possibly at Minisink. There was also a "ledge of rock" on the left bank where the Indians had painted the image of a bateau to warn the inhabitants of the danger coming down the river.[34]

At Pittsburgh on August 11, the day Sullivan's wing arrived at Tioga, and two days after Clinton's wing began its move from Otsego Lake, Colonel Daniel Brodhead's command began its march up the Allegheny River. In a month of preparation, Brodhead and the staff of the Army's Western Department and the Continental Army's Quartermaster Department had succeeded in obtaining a barely adequate amount of supplies, provisions, packhorses, and watercraft for him to mount an offensive against the Indians of the Upper Allegheny. The best troops available, the Continentals of the 8th Pennsylvania and 9th Virginia Regiments[35] and Rawlings' Maryland Independent Corps, could together provide few more than 700 troops. Inadequate for both an offensive operation and the security guard of the settlements while on campaign, Brodhead called on Virginia and Pennsylvania for militia and volunteer reinforcements. Two volunteer ranging companies from Westmoreland County and units of common militia joined the expedition. Enough Pennsylvania and Virginia militia responded to ensure sufficient troops manned the garrisons of the various posts to secure the settlements while the army was away. As a result, Brodhead was able to take the field with a mobile force of nearly 700 Continentals, militia, volunteers, and some friendly Delaware warriors, plus boatmen, cattle drovers, and packhorsemen.[36]

Brodhead also benefited from the services of John Montour, the well-known and highly educated trader and statesman of mixed French, Iroquois, and Delaware ancestry who was adopted into the Wyandot nation. Earlier in the war, like his namesake serving in the British Indian Department, Montour had supported the Crown. More recently, however, he had swung to backing the Americans. Not only had he convinced the Wyandot, along with other western Indians, to abandon their participation in the war on the British side, but Montour also volunteered to accompany Brodhead as a guide.

Through great effort, the logistical support system of the Continental Army managed to provide enough provisions to sustain the soldiers on the expedition for thirty days. Barrels of flour, dried salted meats, whiskey, and other provisions were readied for transport or placed at the upriver forts to replenish the expedition's stores as it moved away from Fort Pitt. Most of the remaining stores were loaded aboard a small flotilla of bateaux and keelboats, while the rest, packaged in "half loads," was put on the backs of about 400 packhorses. As the army marched, some 100 troops were detached to provide escort for the boatmen aboard the watercraft, and the rest marched along the west bank of the Allegheny, followed by the packhorses and some 400 head of beef cattle.

Stopping to encamp opposite Fort Crawford on the Kiskiminitas River and Fort Armstrong at Kittanning to replenish the supplies already consumed along the way, the expedition pushed ahead. But instead of heading along the traditional Indian trail up the river toward the fort at Venango, near the mouth of French Creek, Brodhead's force forded the Allegheny, and encamped on the left bank flats near the abandoned Indian town of Mahoning. Following a delay of four days because of heavy rains and the need to gather stray cattle and horses, the stores and provisions were landed from the boats and loaded on the packhorses. The expedition struck cross-country along an Indian path for the Delaware settlement of Cushcushing, about fifteen miles upriver from Venango. On reaching the Allegheny again, Brodhead's troops crossed to the right bank, and resumed the march toward the Indian town of Conewago.[37]

Knowing that Sullivan's force was encamped at Tioga, and while Clinton's wing descended the Susquehanna from Otsego Lake, and Brodhead's expedition ascended the Allegheny from Pittsburgh, British Lieutenant Colonel Mason Bolton met in council for three days with the leaders of the king's Indian allies at Fort Niagara. From Bolton's point of view, the situation was dire. He wrote to Governor-General Frederick Haldimand in Quebec that the Indians' "behavior all together was very different" from that he had ever seen in them. The arrival of such a large American force at Tioga alarmed and put them in a "disagreeable situation." Afraid that the Rebels were determined to "oblige" the king's allies "to observe a Neutrality," Bolton was determined to reassure the Indians of British support, but felt that his commander in chief did not share the same sense of urgency. Bolton tried to convince him of the gravity of the situation.[38]

Bolton informed Haldimand that a major cause of the Indians' discomfort was the perceived failure of the British government to honor its promises. Knowing of the poor harvests and lack of game in the Iroquois country in the preceding several months, and convinced by British officers that there were large quantities of provisions in Quebec, the chiefs demanded "to know the Reasons why the Great King their Father did not assist them in their time of Distress." To prevent revealing the strain under which the British logistics support system operated, as Butler and his rangers knew all too well, Bolton was left no alternative but to supply them "everything they wanted in Clothing, Provisions &c" he had on hand at Niagara.[39]

Some of the sachems also began to question the British commitment to the defense of Indian territory. The failure to post forces in a sufficient garrison at Fort Oswego had been a source of consternation since 1777. According to their own scouts as well as those sent out by Captain Joseph Brant and Major John Butler, the Americans were "advancing from all Quarters" against them. The Indians were "at a loss which way to go." They feared that without British help,

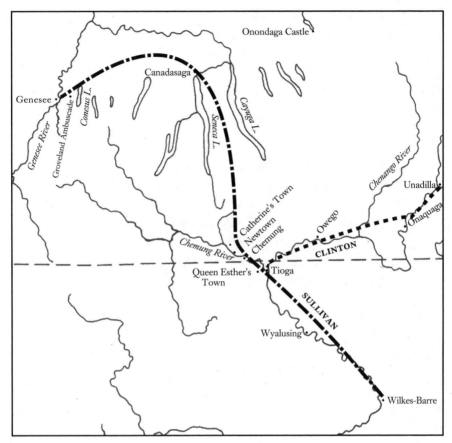

General advance of the Sullivan and Clinton expeditions.

their "Villages would be cut off," and then "they could no longer fight the King's battles." Seneca war chief Kayashuta requested "100 soldiers might be sent with him to attack 600 Rebels and 100 Delaware," whom his runners had reported were "15 miles this side of Venango." To underscore the necessity the Indians placed in sending British troops to their aid, after being informed that no redcoats could be spared, out of 200 assembled warriors at the council, Bolton "could only prevail on 44 to set off" with Kayashuta. Bolton then concluded in a letter to Haldimand, "if Major Butler should be defeated," he was convinced the Six Nations "would follow the example of their Brethren at Detroit" and revert to neutrality.[40]

Back at the Allegheny River after their overland trek, Colonel Brodhead reorganized his force for moving along the restrictive terrain by the river. Lieutenant John Hardin of the 8th Pennsylvania Regiment's Light Infantry Company led the advanced guard of fifteen soldiers and eight friendly Delaware scouts. With flankers deployed to its left and the Allegheny River on the right, the rest of the expedition followed in the narrows between the river and a high hill. The terrain was extremely rugged and the movement difficult. Men and animals inched along, sometime drawn out single file over several miles. After marching about twenty miles, still ten miles short of their objective, Conewago, the men of the advanced guard sighted seven canoes carrying about forty warriors paddling downstream. The warriors, who noticed the soldiers at the same time, immediately beached their canoes, stripped off their shirts and prepared to fight. Lieutenant Hardin gave the order for an immediate attack.[41]

When Brodhead heard the musketry up ahead, he deployed his command in the narrows between the river and high hill, and except for the rear guard and the flankers, "immediately prepared to receive the enemy." The colonel advanced to the sound of the firing to determine his next move, but found that the brief skirmish had already ended. Five enemy warriors lay dead, and the rest had fled. Brodhead counted six enemy retreating across the river without their weapons. The rest withdrew into the woods on the near bank, helping their wounded escape, but leaving canoes, blankets, shirts, provisions, and firearms behind. Two soldiers and one Delaware scout, the young chief named Nanowland, received minor wounds. After taking the necessary precautions to prevent a surprise attack, Brodhead gave the order to encamp for the night.[42]

The next morning, the expedition marched into the abandoned Indian town of Buckaloons at the mouth of Brokenstraw Creek. After halting, Colonel Brodhead ordered the men to construct a breastwork of felled timber and fascines to secure the baggage and stores, and posted a captain in command of forty men to guard it. The remainder of his force, lighter and more agile than it had been, continued its march. On reaching Conewago, they found the town had been abandoned by its occupants for some time, possibly for as long as two years. At this point, there was some apprehension among the troops, because they would soon be in Seneca country without guides who were familiar with the area.[43]

Avoiding a narrow seven-mile long gorge of the Allegheny, the expedition followed a well-traveled Indian trail up to high ground, and proceeded another twenty miles. The cautious troops then descended into a land of abundant cornfields and the recently evacuated "Upper Seneca towns." The inhabitants had obviously fled when they learned of the soldiers' approach, many having left just before the advanced guard arrived. So hasty was their departure that they left behind packs of deer skins, recently bundled for the trading post. When the advance guard came to a war post, which was painted with an image and clothed in a dog skin, John Montour told Colonel Brodhead they had reached Yoghroonwago, a large Seneca settlement of eight towns. Estimating that he was forty miles from the Genesee, or Little Beard's Town, Colonel Brodhead took the opportunity to send two couriers with an express toward Tioga, requesting instruction from Major General Sullivan on coordinating their next moves. The troops remained in the area for three days, destroying cornfields and buildings (with some detachments possibly ranging as far as Salamanca and Olean, in present-day New York). Altogether, there were 130 longhouses, large enough to accommodate three or four Indian families each, and some 500 acres of ripening vegetables. The colonel ordered the troops to load as much of the harvest as could be carried back to Pittsburgh as plunder of war. There it could be sold, and the proceeds divided for the benefit of the troops.[44]

Back in Tioga, on Saturday, August 14, those who fell in the fighting at Chemung were interred with full military honors, with the exception of firing the volleys. Otherwise, the troops recovered from the exertion of the short but strenuous mission, and cleaned their weapons and equipment. On Sunday, fatigue parties drawn from each of the three brigades continued to work on the four blockhouses, as the troops waited for the arrival of General Clinton's brigade. On the flat of land between the foot of the mountain and the west bank of the Chemung River, directly opposite the encampment of the Light Corps, some unsuspecting cattle drovers and packhorse drivers were tending their grazing animals.[45]

A number of Delaware warriors slowly advanced, cautiously creeping up to the herds. At about two o'clock in the afternoon, the otherwise bucolic scene was shattered by the report of twelve or fifteen musket shots. One civilian packhorse driver fell dead. Another was wounded, but made his escape. Hearing the gunfire in the camp, detachments were quickly under arms from the 11th Pennsylvania Regiment in the Light Corps' "upper camp," and from two New Jersey regiments in the "lower camp." The soldiers forded the river, and swept across the meadow in search of the raiders, who made off with a few horses but caused little other damage. The Continentals ascended the mountain, and then marched along the summit in an attempt to gain their rear. "All possible means were used to catch up with them," but they had too much of a head start. After scouring the mountain and valley beyond, their officers realized the enemy had escaped, and broke off the pursuit. The soldiers recovered the corpse of the dead driver as they made their way back to camp, "much fatigued" from the exertion.[46]

The next morning, Brigadier General Poor, accompanied by Hand, led a force of 900 "picked" men with two artillery pieces to make contact with and escort Clinton's brigade back to Tioga. The men, drawn from each of the brigades, carried rations and drove enough cattle for fresh beef for eight days.

Back in camp, so as to prevent more raids like the one the day before, each brigade was ordered to detach a sergeant with a corporal and twelve privates to scout around the mountains in order to ambush any Indians attempting to infiltrate the camp. One bold party of Indians approached undetected and killed some cattle. As soon as it was discovered, Captain John Holmes led a company from the 1st New Jersey Regiment out after them. After spending much of the day and night looking for Indian raiders without success, the captain and his men mounted guard over the herds at the flats, and prevented the horses and cattle from straying into the mountains.[47]

Throughout much of August 17, the troops continued to prepare equipment for marching after the arrival of Clinton's wing. Late in the afternoon, a group of six soldiers from the German Regiment asked for and were granted permission to retrieve their missing horses. Not long afterward, the sound of firing was heard about 500 yards in front of the advanced pickets of the light corps. The soldiers returned fire and retreated back toward camp, but two fell before they could reach safety. Lieutenant Colonel Hubley, in temporary command of the brigade in General Hand's absence, sent a detachment of fifty men to investigate. They found one of the two missing troops with a severely wounded arm, and the scalped body of the other. Early the next morning, Captain James Broderick of the 5th New Jersey led his company on an early morning scout in an attempt to intercept any Indian raiding parties. Hubley sent out three scouts from the Light Corps, each composed of a subaltern with twenty men, "in order to entrap the savages who keep sneaking about the encampment." One was posted on the mountain opposite the camp of the light troops. A second took its position on a small island about a half-mile upstream on the Chemung River. The last was posted about one mile in front of the Light Corps encampment.[48]

Meanwhile, on the same day, after marching about eighteen miles up the Susquehanna from Tioga, General Poor's detachment halted at the "remains" of the deserted Indian town of Choconut. The crops were destroyed and the fifty or sixty buildings burned. Although the officers worried that Clinton's progress had been impeded, as the troops prepared to encamp for the night, they heard the report of the evening gun fired at Clinton's encampment in the distance. The artillerymen answered the signal by firing a blank cartridge from the cohorn. The detachment was up again at five o'clock, and in motion by eight on the morning of August 19. The column had not marched very far when the advanced guard encountered a sergeant leading a scout of nine men and carrying a message from Clinton informing Poor that he expected to arrive at Choconut by mid-morning. Consequently, Poor ordered his men to countermarch back to their recently vacated camp site, and they arrived just before the boats of Clinton's brigade came into view. After linking up, the 4th Brigade and its escort marched to Owego.[49]

The combined force reached the large town of Owego at sunset. Despite its pleasant appearance and abundant fields, Lieutenant William McKendry of the 6th Massachusetts Regiment knew it as the town where the enemy took Sergeant Hunter's patrol after capturing them just before the attack on Cherry Valley. The troops of his regiment felt no remorse in putting the town to the torch.[50]

As the anticipation rose, the work in preparation for marching intensified. When the Commissary officers noticed that there were not enough sacks to load sufficient amounts of flour onto the packhorses, details of troops cut tents to make more. The four blockhouses neared completion. As the two detachments moved on to Tioga, one of the boats from Clinton's advanced guard arrived at camp on August 20. Lieutenant Thomas Boyd and ten men from the Rifle Corps reported to General Sullivan that both Clinton's wing of the army and Poor's escort were on their way. It would not be long before the entire "Western Army" was ready to move into Iroquois country.[51]

Two days later, Sunday, August 22, the men of Clinton's wing of the army entered Tioga, completing their 160-mile journey from Otsego Lake. As the boat carrying the brigadier general passed the encampment of the Light Corps, the rest of the army saluted his brigade's arrival. The park of artillery fired a salute of thirteen rounds, the 4th Continental (Proctor's) Artillery Regiment's "band of musick" played alternately with the fifes and drums of the infantry. The "light corps being likewise drawn up and received them in proper form," and troops from all the brigades along the river gave "three huzzahs" for the arriving comrades. As they rounded the point into the Chemung, the troops from upriver proceeded to their places in the encampment.[52]

The British commanders closest to action, Major John Butler and Captain Joseph Brant, were worried about the deteriorating tactical situation and the seeming reluctance of their allies to fight in greater numbers. Butler informed Lieutenant Colonel Bolton that chiefs were requesting that he send men and supplies from Fort Niagara for their assistance. Brant, who had arrived in Chemung just after the skirmish there on August 13, wrote in a letter to Lieutenant Colonel Bolton that he was "a little afraid we shall have hard work to drive the enemy back, for our friends are too slow in joining us." Brant had assembled a force of 300 men, and knew it was not enough. Scouts had reported the movement of Poor's command, and he was puzzled about the Americans' intentions. The Cayuga chiefs, fearing a raid was being mounted against their territory from the east, were reluctant to send Brant more forces when so many of their warriors were with him already. Although his army was few in number, he assured Bolton that "most of the Chief Warriors" were "in high spirits & not discouraged," and confident that they would "beat the enemy."[53]

While waiting for Major Butler and Sayenqueraghta to arrive with the rangers and Seneca warriors, Brant had "to watch the Enemy's motions." Because he had too few men, he lamented, "it is impossible to be everywhere." He was unaware that Clinton's brigade had struck its camp at Otsego Lake and was heading to meet Poor on the way to Tioga. Nonetheless, he expected the Americans to move "in two or three days," and that there would be an engagement, which, he believed, would prove decisive. "If we beat the Rebel Army," he said, "they will never invade our country again." In view of the need for the Six Nations to face Sullivan's army, Brant suggested that Bolton convince all the Iroquois warriors near Fort Niagara to make their way to Chemung. In order to divert the Americans' attention, he also recommended that the Canadian Indians be enlisted to send war parties on raids toward Fort Stanwix [Fort Schuyler] and the Mohawk River valley settlements, "which will be of great service."[54]

Before leaving to join forces with Brant, Major John Butler was attempting to coordinate the acquisition of supplies, assemble reinforcements, and gather intelligence on the Americans' intentions. As with Brant, the departure of Poor's detachment had puzzled him. Butler thought the move signaled either a junction between the two wings of an invasion against Indian country, the establishment of two strong fortified posts to limit Indian and Tory freedom of action, or perhaps both. As hard as his men and their Indian allies might try, intelligence was proving difficult to obtain. He had "Scouts constantly at their Camp," but they had managed only to drive off a few horses and take "two or three scalps," but no prisoners from whom to extract information on enemy plans. Contrary to what Bolton may have been told by other sources, Butler did not face the hastily assembled militia or ill-trained levies and volunteers that his rangers and Indians had easily defeated before. From the accounts he had gained from spies or militia and civilians taken in recent raids on the back settlements, they were up against "some of the best Continental Troops commanded by the most active of the Rebel Generals, and not a Regiment of Militia among the whole."[55]

Butler heard that Lieutenant Colonel Commandant Sir John Johnson and his King's Royal Regiment of New York were on their way to Fort Oswego. If Butler, Brant, and their Indian allies could not stop the American invasion, Fort Niagara would be in danger of attack. Therefore, the major requested that

Bolton have Sir John march his regiment, with as many provisions as they could possibly move, to the head of Cayuga Lake. If Butler and his command were defeated in an engagement in the Chemung area, they intended to retreat in that direction, and were sure to be in great need of reinforcements and resupply when they arrived.[56]

On August 23, at Tioga, Major General Sullivan reviewed his campaign plans with his subordinate commanders and reorganized his army in preparation for marching to Tioga. Lieutenant Colonel William Butler's 4th Pennsylvania Regiment, Major James Parr's Rifle Corps, and the four light infantry companies

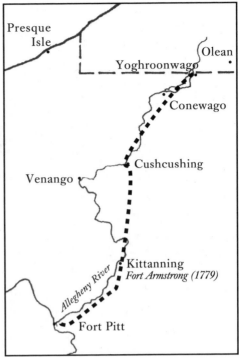

General advance of the Brodhead expedition.

from Clinton's brigade were transferred to Brigadier General Hand's brigade, or Light Corps. Major Daniel Whiting's, or "Late Alden's," 6th Massachusetts Regiment joined Brigadier General Enoch Poor's New Hampshire Brigade. Colonel Philip Van Cortlandt's 2nd New York Regiment was ordered from Poor's back to Clinton's brigade. The three companies of the 2nd (Lamb's) Continental Artillery joined Colonel Proctor's 4th Continental Artillery as the army's "park of artillery."[57]

The next morning the troops were paraded and inspected to insure that all was in readiness. The army still experienced a "want of bags" for transporting flour, and more tents were cut up to make them. Due to the recent Indian raids to steal horses, and others wandering off while grazing, the army also found it did not have enough pack animals to carry the twenty-seven days of provisions required to execute its plan. In consequence, officers' baggage was unloaded and moved to the fort, while the packhorses were loaded with mission-essential stores and provisions. When it was unloaded from the boats and inspected, much of the salted meat transported by Clinton's brigade was spoiled. The army would take what was left, but the garrison of the fort at Tioga would have to send boats to Wyoming for fresh provisions for themselves and for the army's return.

The soldiers of the light infantry and flanking and covering parties "took their foot" and refreshed their training for action on enemy contact. After the troops had spent much of August 24 making final preparation, it was time. At the signal of a gun at five in the afternoon, the troops struck their tents and loaded their baggage. The various regiments moved some distance to form in the prescribed order of march. Units being transferred to other brigades joined their new commands. At seven o'clock, a second fired the signal to pitch tents and encamp. The army was set to move the next day.[58]

Those elements staying behind, such as the Flying Hospital and Quartermaster Department personnel remaining with the stores, moved into the fort. Colonel Israel Shreve of the Second New Jersey Regiment was ordered to take command of the post, now named Fort Sullivan by the officers in honor of their commanding general. Shreve commanded a garrison of 200 men, "properly officered," drawn from all the regiments on the expedition, including two companies of artillery with two 6-pounder cannons. The colonel was also responsible for all the sick and lame patients in the hospital, the civilian boatmen, and the women and children belonging to the army. Two days after the army marched, a convoy of sixty boats left Tioga for Wyoming. The boats carried Reverend William Rogers, whose services were needed elsewhere with Pennsylvania troops, other "supernumerary" officers, sick and wounded "invalids," and all the women (and their children) deemed "Not Absolutely Necessary as Nurses in the Hospital, or to Wash for the troops," or to "take Charge of the Baggage or any other Necessary Purpose."[59]

Heavy rain on the morning of August 25 and a shortage of horses postponed the start of the campaign. While the troops waited and details were out collecting stray horses, a party of three Oneida Indian "men of integrity and sobriety," arrived to offer their services as scouts to General Sullivan, which were gladly accepted. Their captain, called Hanyost, or Hanyerry, held a lieutenant's commission in the Continental Army from Congress. The two runners sent by Colonel Brodhead from the Upper Allegheny arrived with a letter to General Sullivan suggesting they join forces for an attack aimed at Genesee.[60]

As day broke on Thursday, August 26, 1779, the army was still not yet "perfectly ready." The time to march was changed from eight o'clock, as originally planned, to eleven. One piece of artillery fired a blank round to signal the advance, followed by the horn relaying the order to the riflemen and light infantry. The men of Parr's Rifle Corps dispersed "considerably in front" to "reconnoiter mountains, defiles and other suspicious places" to prevent the enemy from surprising them in ambush. The rest of Hand's brigade formed in six columns of two, each separated by 200 to 300 yards and proceeded at a set distance by a company of light infantry. Lieutenant Colonel William Butler commanded the division on the right, Lieutenant Colonel Adam Hubley, that on the left. Captain Anthony Selin commanded a detachment of pioneers, composed of details from each brigade and his own independent corps, that followed the six columns. The duty of the pioneers was to prepare fords, fell trees, break down steep embankments, fill ditches, repair roads or trails, and clear a path sufficiently wide for the artillery and supply wagons that followed to pass. Colonel Proctor's artillery park was next in the order of march. It came on with six light 3-pounder guns, two 5 1/2-inch howitzers and a cohorn, nine pieces in all. The rest of the artillery train, a traveling forge and three ammunition wagons, followed the guns.[61]

The main body of the army moved in a "hollow square" formation, with Poor's brigade marching in a column of platoons, aligned with the right of Hand's brigade, and Maxwell's arrayed the same on the left. Each brigade detailed about 200 men from its regiments to provide flankers, or security on its respective side along the line of march. General Clinton's brigade moved in six columns, mirroring the deployment of Hand's brigade, at the back of the square. For security, Clinton detailed the 2nd New York Regiment to gather and escort the stray cattle forward while it provided the rear guard. Inside the square, the army's 1,200 packhorses marched in two columns along the center, under the burden of supplies and provisions planned to last twenty-seven days. The drovers herded 800 head of beef cattle between the pack train in the center and brigade columns on the outside flanks of the square, when the terrain permitted. Moving along the Chemung, four boats loaded with supplies followed the progress of the marching columns. When the rear guard of Clinton's brigade finally moved at noon, the entire "Western Army" was on the march.[62]

Chapter 13

THE BATTLE OF NEWTOWN

MAJOR John Butler was just a few miles up the Chemung River, preparing his rangers and Indian allies to meet the invasion, when one of his scouts reported that the American army was "upon the March toward us in great Force."[1] Previously, scouts had determined that Sullivan's army encamped at Tioga had been reinforced by Clinton's brigade from Otsego Lake, and that Poor's detachment had returned. By all indications, they appeared ready to move against the Indian towns. Butler had arrived at Newtown with his battalion of rangers the day before, August 26. Out of five companies, about 200 men were fit for service, to add to the 300 Captain Joseph Brant had gathered since arriving about two weeks before. Sayenqueraghta came in with another 300 Iroquois, mostly Seneca, warriors. After establishing camp west of Newtown, the leaders met in council.[2]

Realizing that the size of the assembled force was inadequate "to engage the Enemy with a probability of success & aware of the bad consequences of a Defeat," Major Butler tried to persuade the Indians to retreat to a more "Advantageous situation." He believed that they could do more damage to the enemy if they positioned "strong Parties out along the Heights to harass the Enemy upon their March & keep them in perpetual alarms." Captain Brant vainly tried to convince the chiefs of the wisdom of Butler's plan, but they would not hear of it. The Delawares were emphatic, and "pointed out a Place where they said the Enemy ought to be opposed." The Senecas and other Iroquois present were "obstinately determined" to meet the Americans "in a Body," and Butler was left no choice but to comply with their decision.[3]

Major Butler sent his sick and lame off to Catherine's Town with the corps' baggage, and went to reconnoiter and occupy the ground on which the Indians elected to make a stand, about a mile from the encampment. On the right there was a ridge, about one half mile in length, beyond which was a plain of land that bordered the river and terminated in a narrow pass between the end of the ridge and the water. If the Americans came that way, the advantageous position afforded a relatively small force the ability to subject the attackers to a

264

withering fire. A steep, wooded mountain stood on the left, parallel to the ridge. Between the hill and ridge, one could face the trail from Chemung and see where it emerged from a swamp into a large open area before it crossed a steep defile with a large creek.

It was perfect for an ambuscade. A relatively small force, like that at Butler's command, could surprise an unsuspecting foe by opening fire from concealed positions, and hold them in front while Indian warriors swept down around their flank from the foothills, and assaulted through the woods. If the Indians gained the rear of Sullivan's army, they could cause great confusion, possibly stampede the cattle, and inflict casualties disproportionate to their numbers. At the very least, a few companies massing their musket fire could get off one or two good shots without risking very many casualties before they yielded the field to the much larger enemy army. Butler's men dug ditches, disassembled the buildings of a small village near their line for its wood, chopped down trees, and "threw up some Logs one upon the other by way of a Breastwork," and concealed it from enemy view by bushes and other foliage.[4]

The semicircular disposition offered Butler and the Indians the advantage of interior lines, where reinforcements could be sent to meet a threat from any part of the line not heavily engaged. Most of the warriors were posted to the foot of the mountain. Captain John McDonell with sixty rangers, and Captain Brant with thirty Loyalists and Mohawks, took position on the ridge. The detachment from the 8th Regiment of Foot, the rest of Butler's Rangers, and the remaining Indians manned the center at the breastwork overlooking the creek. In order to give his attention to the Indians and coordinate the combined effort, Major Butler placed his son, Captain Walter Butler, in command of the rangers. As the inhabitants evacuated their town, the defenders remained in the position, converted a few buildings to makeshift blockhouses, and improved the breastwork from noon until sunset on August 27. When scouts reported that the Americans had camped below Chemung, Butler and the chiefs had their men return to camp to "dress a few ears of corn" and rest.[5]

For the Americans, the first day's march was not a long one. The leading elements proceeded to the upper end of Tioga flats, only four miles from Fort Sullivan, before they were ordered to halt. The army encamped on the flat land along the river, where a broad meadow afforded plentiful wild grass for grazing the horses and cattle. The established procedure for the army to march was marked by the firing of three cannons. The first conveyed the order to strike tents. The second was the signal to load baggage. The third gun was the order to march. On Friday, the morning gun sounded at six o'clock, and the men dutifully struck and stacked their tents. While the rest of the army prepared to march, the Rifle Corps advanced several miles ahead of the army to reconnoiter, and cover the pioneers as they cut and mended the road through the first two defiles, or narrows, along the march route. Meanwhile, after the second gun fired at seven, the drums beat "Assembly," and the troops loaded the baggage onto the packhorses. Due to some delay, the third gun, the signal to march, was not fired until half past eight.[6]

The terrain proved to be the "most disagreeable" that the troops of Sullivan's wing had seen since they left Wyoming. The slow work of the pioneers as they cleared the road for the artillery and ammunition wagons "much impeded" the army's progress "threw thick woods and Difficult Defiles." The rugged terrain "Broke two wagons, [and] overset a traveling forge and one of the [artillery] pieces," and caused additional delays for repair halts, one of which lasted seven hours. Although Hand's, Poor's, and part of Clinton's brigades remained on the high ground, the "country through which they had to pass being extremely mountainous and rough," slowed the progress of men, cattle and pack animals considerably. It could not compare to the ordeal of the rest of the army. Proctor's artillery, Maxwell's, and part of Clinton's brigades and baggage had to cross the swollen Chemung twice to avoid one "very bad Defile." Some baggage and flour was lost while crossing the "Waist Deep and Very rapid" water. Every time a gun or wagon was upset or became mired, infantrymen were called to help right or extract it with "Such Cursing, Cutting and Digging," which was "not to Be Seen Every Day."[7]

The Light Corps arrived near the last narrows at the lower end of Chemung at about seven o'clock in the evening, with the main body about a mile behind. Delayed by the river crossings and problems with the artillery and wagons, the last of Clinton's brigade caught up to the rest of the army around ten o'clock at night. The infantrymen placed the blame for the hard march with a "Universal cry against the artillery."[8]

Between the Light Corps and main body lay "some very extensive" fields. On Saturday morning the soldiers were ordered to substitute corn and other vegetables from the standing gardens for one day's ration. The army's Indian scouts, who had been sent out the night before, returned from their reconnaissance of Newtown, about eight miles up the Chemung River. They had heard the sounds of the chopping and digging, and reported that "a body of men were fortifying a pass about six miles in front" of the army. The scouts had also located a large encampment with "a great number of fires" on an "extensive piece of ground," which they supposed belonged to a "very formidable" enemy force that meant to give battle. On the way back, the friendly Indians "discovered four or five small scouting parties" of the enemy on the way to reconnoiter the American army.[9]

After feasting on vegetables, the troops laid waste to the eighty acres the army left standing on its earlier raid. As they were doing so, the "general and principal officers" went forward to reconnoiter before giving the order to advance to Chemung. The defile before them was "excessively narrow," and "almost impracticable" for the artillery, wagons, pack animals, and cattle to pass. Two suitable fords were located, and the army marched at about three o'clock in the afternoon. The Rifle Corps, Maxwell's brigade, and the left flanking division crossed and covered the movement of the vehicles and animals to the west bank. That wing of the army then marched one and a half miles up river, and recrossed to the east side. They were met by the Light Corps, Poor's and Clinton's brigades, and the right flanking division, who had ascended the high hill on the east side, advanced along the summit, and descended onto the Chemung flats by about six o'clock. While on the hill, the officers' attention was drawn to clouds of smoke in the distance, which they assumed came from the enemy encampment the scouts had reported earlier.[10]

Reunited, the army was ordered to encamp and turn the animals out to graze on the rich grasses of the flats. Chemung, in the words of Lieutenant Colonel Hubley, was considered the enemy's "principal magazine" and "chief rendezvous, whenever they intend to go to war" due to its key position in relation to the New York and Pennsylvania frontiers. General Sullivan therefore ordered the troops to complete the destruction of the town and its agricultural fields. Earlier in the day, a party of warriors had fired on a group of soldiers who crossed the river to burn some Indian buildings. The enemy withdrew after firing, and inflicted no casualties on the troops, all of whom returned to the army safely. Some time after the army halted for the day, a scout of four or five Indians came down to the riverbank and shot at the boatmen from across the water. Although none were hurt, the incidents indicated that the enemy was active and observed the army's every move.[11]

Back at Newtown, Major Butler and the chiefs had their men on their line since early Saturday morning, August 28. While the American forces slowly bypassed the Chemung defile and leveled the town and cornfields, the rangers and warriors waited and improved their positions. When his scouts reported that the enemy had advanced no farther than Chemung, Butler ordered the men to retire to camp once more. Back on the line again at daybreak on Sunday, they waited, "Exposed to the heat of the Sun without refreshment of any kind" for the Americans to appear.[12]

Meanwhile, the American army at Chemung prepared for the day's march on August 29. With Lieutenant Colonel William Butler in command, the advanced guard moved out at about eight o'clock. Leading the way, the riflemen advanced "well scattered in front of the Light Corps who moved with the greatest precision and caution." When they approached the high ground where the engagement of August 13 had been fought, the van discovered Indians to the front. The riflemen exchanged shots with the warriors, who only fired and fled. The rest of the army proceeded more slowly, between nine and ten o'clock, following the pace set by the pioneers as they cleared the way for the artillery and baggage.[13]

The further the riflemen and light infantrymen advanced, the bolder the Indian skirmishers became. They still did not stand and fight, but ran off into the woods before the riflemen's advance. After they entered some marshy ground, which "seemed well calculated for forming ambuscades," the light troops cautiously advanced as more Indian warriors fired and retreated. Major James Parr suggested to Brigadier General Hand that the situation was too dangerous to proceed without further reconnaissance, lest the warriors lure them into a trap. The major ordered one of his men to climb up a tree in order to "make discoveries" of the enemy up ahead. From that vantage point, after some time, "he discovered the movements of several Indians, which were rendered conspicuous by the quantity of paint on them." The rifleman described the enemy as "laying behind an extensive breastwork, which extended at least half a mile, and most artfully concealed with green boughs and trees." As the Americans viewed it, the line was situated on high ground, with the left flank secured by a mountain and the right by the river. To assault the works directly, the Americans had to cross marshy ground, ford a difficult stream, and advance uphill through a cleared field 100 yards wide.[14]

Immediately after Major Parr informed him of the enemy disposition, General Hand advanced the Light Corps to within 300 yards of the enemy's breastworks and formed a line of battle. The Rifle Corps continued to advance under cover as far as the creek and "lay under the bank" within 100 yards of the enemy. After he was informed, General Sullivan came forward for a look, and sent for the rest of his subordinate commanders to join him for a council of war while waiting for the army to move up.[15]

The enemy's fortifications "were very extensive, tho' not impregnable." Because the Americans did not want to merely drive the Tories and Indians out of their defenses, Sullivan presented a plan to turn their flank in order to "bring them to a fair and open action." The Rifle Corps and light infantry would continue to "amuse" the enemy, and keep their attention fixed in front. Colonel Matthias Ogden, with the 1st New Jersey Regiment and the rest of the left flanking division, would form on the Light Corps' left flank, and if the opportunity presented itself, turn the enemy's right. Colonel Thomas Proctor was to move the six 3-pounders, two 5 1/2-inch howitzers, and cohorn of his artillery in front and centered on the regiments of the Light Corps, immediately opposite the enemy breastwork, to support by fire. The guns would remain concealed until all was ready. General Maxwell's brigade, minus the left flanking division, was to "remain some distance to the rear" as the corps de reserve. The brigades of Poor and Clinton, along with the right flanking division, were to gain the enemy's left flank and rear, and cut off their retreat along the road through Newtown toward Catherine's Town. For the plan to succeed, it was imperative that the units making the flank attack were in position to take the enemy in the rear when the artillery cannonade commenced. The Rifle Corps and light infantry would then advance on the breastwork.[16]

At about one o'clock, the diversion began. Tory Major John Butler recalled, "A few of the Enemy made their appearance at the skirt of the wood to our Front." The riflemen then went into action, when, according to the Continental Lieutenant Colonel Adam Hubley, "A heavy fire ensued between the rifle corps and the enemy, but little damage was done." At the same time, the artillery filed off to the right, and was "carried to an advantageous piece of ground" about a quarter mile from the Tory breastwork. Generals Poor and Clinton then ordered their brigades to "march by column from the right of regiment by files." The troops passed through a very thick swamp overgrown with bushes. For nearly a mile, the "Columns found great difficulty in keeping their order." But by General Poor's "great Prudence & good conduct," experienced officers like Lieutenant Colonel Henry Dearborn remarked, the brigade "proceeded in much better order than I expected we possibly could have done." After negotiating the swamp, the columns inclined to the left and crossed the creek, which ran in front of the enemy's breastwork farther down. As they did so, the soldiers noticed about twenty recently built but yet unoccupied buildings, which curiously had no land cleared nearby for cultivation. Some of the men assumed these were to be used for magazines to supply raiding parties heading for the frontier settlements. Once across, the troops began to ascend the spur of the mountain that defined the enemy's left.[17]

After the American riflemen had "amused" his troops and warriors facing them across the open field for about two hours, the Tory commander suspected that the Americans were not taking the bait he had dangled in front of them. Unlike the militia he had faced at Oriskany or Wyoming, these regulars were not lured into the defile where his men could blaze away at them from behind their breastwork. When it became apparent that the Americans were probably deploying to bring their overwhelming numbers to bear, Butler considered a retreat. While the Rifle Corps occupied their attention to the front, however, the Indians were reluctant to leave their fortification. Brant and the Cayuga chief left their position on the right to meet with Butler, and recommended withdraw before they became decisively engaged in a losing battle.[18]

At about three in the afternoon, the American artillery was ordered to advance to the high ground on the near side of the defile, about 200 yards from the enemy position. The six guns, two howitzers, and cohorn opened fire on the breastworks as "the rifle and light corps . . . prepared to advance and charge." The storm of round and grape shot soon "obliged" the defenders to leave their log fortification. When howitzer and cohorn shells began bursting behind them, many of the Indians believed the Americans had surrounded them with artillery. Many of the warriors were "So startled & confounded" that a "great part of them run off" in panic. Butler led his rangers and a number of the Indians toward the hill that marked the left of their line in order to retreat.[19]

The swamp and thickets had delayed the progress of Poor's and Clinton's brigades, so that they were not yet in position when they heard the artillery cannonade begin. After ascending halfway up the hill, the Continentals were "saluted by a brisk fire" and war whoops from a body of Indians posted to keep them from turning the flank of the breastwork. As the riflemen of the right flanking detachment kept up a "scattering fire," the rest of Poor's brigade quickly formed the line of battle.[20] Though much fatigued by the difficult march and climb under the burden of heavy packs in the oppressive heat, the troops pressed up the hill. With their lines dressed and bayonets fixed, the disciplined Continentals advanced rapidly in the face of enemy fire and, without returning a shot, drove the enemy "from tree to tree" before them. On reaching the summit, the command was given, and Poor's soldiers leveled their muskets and fired a full volley that broke the resistance of the Indians to their front and sent them flying. Clinton's New York brigade, following Poor's up the hill by a quarter mile, "pushed up with such ardor" that a number of soldiers fainted from heat exhaustion. As they closed on the crest, Clinton's brigade extended to the right and endeavored to block the enemy's retreat through the defile along the river.[21]

When they heard the musketry of Poor's battle on the hill, Major Butler and the other rangers and redcoats realized the Americans had gained the high ground on their flank, and threatened to completely surround them. At the same moment, Hand's Light Corps attacked and swarmed over the breastworks as the last of the British, Tories, and Indians abandoned them in flight. In desperation, the remnants of Butler's command turned west. Nearly surrounded, the warriors, rangers, and redcoats made their escape as best they could, carrying many of their dead and wounded. Some kept along the hill, skirmishing with the pursuing American light infantry for over a mile. Others crossed the

During the Battle of Newtown the attempted ambush of the advancing American column nearly resulted in the destruction of the force of British redcoats, Provincial Rangers, Tory volunteers, and allied Indian warriors. This scene is a representation of the attack on the Indian left flank by the Continental brigade of General Enoch Poor.

Chemung River or took to canoes to avoid capture. Most rangers headed for a village about five miles away where Butler had told them to rendezvous. Many warriors, however, crossed the mountain in an attempt to return to their respective homes.[22]

Meanwhile, on the hill, although most regiments of Poor's brigade remained on line, Lieutenant Colonel Reid's 2nd New Hampshire "was more severely attacked" and prevented from advancing as far as the rest. Lieutenant Colonel Henry Dearborn, commanding the 3rd New Hampshire Regiment on Reid's right, saw what was happening. Reid's unit had become separated from the rest of the brigade by a distance of "more than a gun shot." Dearborn therefore "thought it proper" to "reverse the front" of his unit and go to Reid's assistance. A large number of warriors attempted to attack the American rear by going around the left of Poor's brigade, but Reid's regiment stood in the way. They clashed on the slope of the hill and the Indians were in the process of surrounding the Continentals. Reid "was reduced to the necessity" of ordering either a retreat back down or a desperate bayonet charge up the mountain. He chose the latter, and had no sooner given the order to execute the move when Dearborn's regiment arrived and fired a full volley that broke the Indian attack. The enemy now left the scene of action "in great precipitation & confusion," leaving nine dead warriors on the field.[23]

Soldiers of Hand's Light Corps pursued the enemy beyond the breastwork and along the mountain until they made contact with the flanking brigades.

The rifle and light infantry companies continued to pursue for another mile or so before returning to join the rest of the army in Newtown at about six o'clock, where they encamped on the same ground the enemy had. Three Americans were killed and thirty were wounded, one of them mortally. During the night, Lieutenant Nathaniel McCauley of the 1st New Hampshire Regiment, whose wounded leg had required amputation, died. He and the three other soldiers killed in the battle were interred near Newtown the next day.

The rout of the enemy had been complete. The enemy's former positions were littered with brass kettles, packs, blankets, and other articles dropped in their haste to carry off their dead and wounded in the escape. Some of Poor's men scalped the Indian corpses, as others searched for lurking warriors who could still be in the area. Two prisoners, "a white and a Negro," were taken. The white Tory had feigned death until an officer noticed that there were no wounds on his body. After being struck with the side of a sword and ordered to get up, the man pleaded for mercy. The black prisoner was taken by Hand's light troops after he had became "separated from his company" during the retreat. Both revealed the enemy's strength at 200 Butler's Rangers, 14 British redcoats, and about 500 warriors, "all the Indians that could be mustered from the five Nations." In his report to his British superiors, Major Butler reported the loss of five dead and three wounded rangers, and five dead and nine wounded Indians.[24]

While encamped about Newtown, the American troops set fire the settlement's approximately forty buildings, and destroyed some 150 acres of corn and other vegetables. Parties of soldiers combed the area searching for plunder and the bodies of dead Indians. Some accounts told of soldiers finding as many as nineteen Indian bodies hidden in the woods, possibly increasing the number of battle deaths.[25]

After consulting with his staff, General Sullivan came to the realization that the army's slow movement to this point had consumed more supplies than had been planned. In addition, due to the supply problems that had plagued the expedition from the start, and unavoidable losses of packhorse loads and beef cattle by wandering off or drowning during river crossings, there were not sufficient provisions to supply the men with a full ration of meat and flour per day for the length of time estimated to "effect the destruction of Indian territory." The day after the battle, August 30, Sullivan assembled the troops. He praised them for their conduct in the campaign thus far, and reminded them of the important mission they had come to perform. He asked the soldiers to voluntarily accept a reduction to half rations, supplementing them with fresh vegetables from the Indian gardens. The general promised to ask Congress that the soldiers be paid for the cost of the rations that were sacrificed for the cause. The troops accepted with an almost universal cheer of three "huzzahs."[26]

To facilitate the movement of the army, Sullivan elected to proceed with only the four bronze light 3-pounder guns and cohorn for artillery support. All the necessary ammunition for both the infantry and artillery was then loaded on packhorses. After all the supplies were unloaded from the boats and redistributed onto packhorses, wounded soldiers, wagons, and the heavy 5 1/2-inch howitzers and iron 3-pounders were loaded aboard, and sent down the river back to Fort Sullivan at Tioga.[27]

On or about the same day as the battle of Newtown, having received no reply from to his message to General Sullivan, Colonel Daniel Brodhead began his march back down the Allegheny. Stopping at the mouth of Brokenstraw Creek, his men recovered the supplies and wounded they had left at the breastwork fort and completed the destruction of the Seneca and Delaware towns of Conewago, Buckloons, and Mahusquechikoken. Instead of completely retracing his steps, Colonel Brodhead ordered his command to march to Venango, at the mouth of French Creek, then south along the right bank of the Allegheny. The Brodhead expedition arrived back in Pittsburgh on September 14 having suffered no fatalities or the loss of any packhorses.[28]

Just north of Newtown, at Catherine's Town, two days after the battle, Major John Butler was trying to regroup and rally his forces. Holding council with the Indians, he urged them to join his force and fight. When the women protested that they should remain in the village and submit to American generosity, Butler told them that the Rebels would take them hostage in order to negotiate better terms. The warriors agreed to fight, but only after they evacuated their families into the surrounding mountains. Butler gathered all the boats in the area, and sent his wounded and sick down Seneca Lake to Canadesaga.[29]

Dashing off a letter to Lieutenant Colonel Mason Bolton in Niagara with his usual plea for supplies and reinforcements, Butler gave his version of the battle at Newtown. He blamed the loss on "some officious Fellow" among the Indian chiefs repositioning men on the flank, and the poor turnout of Delaware warriors. Notwithstanding any shortcomings of the Indians, he admitted to Bolton that the American army "moved with the greatest caution & regularity and are more formidable than you seem to apprehend." The major warned of the serious consequences that would follow if his rangers and Indian warriors were unable to stop them. If there was not "speedily a large Reinforcement," Butler was certain that after the Indians' villages and corn were destroyed, the refugees would flock to Fort Niagara, where they would burden the already strained supply system by consuming the limited provisions meant for the king's forces.[30]

If Bolton was unable to obtain reinforcements from the Governor-General of Canada, perhaps Colonel Guy Johnson could. The superintendent of Indian Affairs had finally returned to Montreal after an absence of almost four years. Backed by the powerful Lord George Germain, Johnson finally convinced Haldimand to order his brother-in-law's regiment, the KRRNY, to Butler's aid, and to take the reestablishment of the post at Fort Ontario "under contemplation." Johnson wrote Germain to say that both actions, long requested by the Indians and Butler, "could have been undertaken sooner." Johnson realized that helping the Iroquois to prevent Sullivan from taking Niagara was vital to maintaining control of lake navigation and friendship of the other Indian nations.[31]

On August 31, Sullivan's army marched toward Catherine's Town with the right division along the hills and left and artillery along the river. The movement over "chiefly plains & flats" proved much quicker and they covered more ground than the strained and difficult march to Chemung. On the way, the familiar pattern was repeated. As the army marched through, every Indian town was burned and agricultural fields laid waste. Frequently, detachments were sent to discover and destroy towns not directly along the line of march. On the first day, it was Konowhola. Every opportunity to engage the enemy was also sought. When the advanced guard sighted a group of Indian canoes heading upstream into one of the tributaries of the Chemung, General Sullivan sent Colonel Elias Dayton with his own 3rd New Jersey Regiment and a detachment of riflemen to see if they could engage. Although they returned having made no contact, now flushed with victory, the army was intent in bringing on a fight. The favorable terrain allowed the army to halt and camp in its "hollow square" formation, providing more security and reducing the number of stray cattle and packhorses.

The next day, General Sullivan intended to take Catherine's Town, and possibly catch Butler there. While the main body took a route through a low ground morass, Hand's Light Corps ascended the mountains and moved along the ridgelines. Although the terrain over which they marched was rugged, the riflemen approached to reconnoiter the settlement just before sunset. As the rest of the corps stood ready with fixed bayonets, they found the town deserted. Burning cook fires indicated that Butler's rear guard or scouts had "scampered off" just as the American patrol arrived. When the rest of Hand's brigade moved up to consolidate and encamp, there was little to do but wait for the rest of the army.[32]

For the main body, the second day of the march from Newtown was a nightmare. The army plunged into the thickly wooded and "most horrid" Twelve-mile Bear Swamp. Nestled in a defile, the morass was covered by bogs and deep mud, cut by streams and gullies, clogged with windfalls, thick undergrowth, "and every obstacle to impede artillery." Movement was extremely fatiguing. Cannons bogged down repeatedly. Several horses went lame or lost their loads. The pioneers did their best to clear a road and build bridges for the artillery and animals, but the confusion increased as the sun went down. Major Jeremiah Fogg recalled, "The whole night was a disagreeable scene of confusion and the darkness was almost perfect." The men built bonfires to mark the way, and kept at the task. If the enemy had chosen the morass for an ambuscade, the result could have been disastrous for the expedition. The leading elements finally emerged from the swamp into Catherine's Town near midnight. Clinton's brigade spent the night in the mud, and did not complete the move until the next day. Major John Burrows of the 5th New Jersey Regiment later wrote, "We never had so bad a days march since we set off, but what will not men go through to be free."[33]

The rest of the army made it into Catherine's Town in the morning, and the troops spent the rest of the day recovering lost packhorse loads, cleaning their clothing and equipment, destroying cornfields and orchards, and setting the thirty buildings on fire. Looking for plunder, some soldiers uncovered a recently dug grave in which lay two warriors dead of gunshot wounds. The soldiers surmised that they had been carried off the Newtown battlefield a few days before. While searching the town and nearby woods, some soldiers found an elderly woman named Madam Sacho. She was taken to the general's marquee tent and made comfortable. The Oneida scouts were able to communicate with her, and she provided them with intelligence about Butler's force, including how their morale suffered as a result of the Newtown battle. She had been left behind when the warriors had evacuated the rest of the women and children, before leaving to join Butler's Rangers in Canadesaga. Shortly thereafter, a lame middle-aged woman was found and brought into town. Although the rest of the houses had been destroyed, the Oneida scouts and a few soldiers placed the women in a shelter with provisions enough to last until their people returned.[34]

The army left Catherine's Town and moved up the east side of Seneca Lake. In contrast to the Bear Swamp, the open woods with little underbrush afforded what Major Burrows described as the "best marching we have had yet." Along the way, General Sullivan sent two of the Oneida carrying messages. One went to Colonel Brodhead in reply to that officer's letter. The other was taken to the chief warriors of the Oneida requesting additional scouts "who have a perfect knowledge of the country."

When the riflemen in the advanced party approached Candaia, or Appletown, on Sunday, September 5, they encountered a white man who had escaped from Indian captivity. Luke Swetland was taken captive at Nanticoke, in the Wyoming Valley, during the Tory-Seneca invasion in the summer of 1778 and adopted into the tribe, but had looked for an opportunity to escape ever since. He was "overjoyed at meeting some of his acquaintances from Wyoming" who were in the army. One of them was Lieutenant John Jenkins. With some satisfaction, he shared that several of their former neighbors, who were serving in Butler's Rangers, "looked very much ashamed when they returned from Newtown."[35]

Swetland provided intelligence on the strength, morale and intentions of Butler's Rangers and their warrior allies. The Indians, he told them, "were distressed for food," and were looking forward when the corn in the fields would be "fit to eat," after last year's poor yield. Swetland also related that the warriors were "much alarmed and dejected at being beat at Newtown," and heard that the British believed that the object of Sullivan's army was the capture of Fort Niagara, not the destruction of Indian towns and crops. Butler had passed through the town the preceding Thursday with an estimated 300 Tories and 500 Indians heading for Canadesaga, where he intended to give battle again.[36]

Swetland may have somewhat overestimated Butler's numbers, but apparently not the Indians' increasing hesitation to fight. Up ahead, at Canadesaga, the Indians were "much alarmed" at the size of the invasion, and Butler anticipated only a "small Body of them" would be willing to fight. After he evacuated the sick, "who are many," he assured Lieutenant Colonel Bolton he would "endeavor to harass them on the march with the Indians & the Remainder of the Rangers, & stop them if possible" before they reached the Canadesaga.[37]

Sullivan's army approached Canadesaga with caution, expecting to be attacked or ambushed along the march. In mid-afternoon, Hand's and Maxwell's brigades made a "circuitous march & by a different route" surrounded the town while Poor's and Clinton's waited. Just before sundown on Tuesday, the artillery took position as a precaution that "the enemy were still in possession," and the scouts went forward to reconnoiter. They found that town, like all the others, had been evacuated not long before their arrival. The men could not help but notice the trophies, six scalps of white people, on display in the town. The soldiers discovered a boy of about three years of age, who had apparently been taken captive in a raid on one of the frontier settlements. He could speak Seneca, and could only understand but not speak English. Captain Thomas Machin, of the 2nd (Lamb's) Continental Artillery, cared for the child and adopted him after his return from the expedition.[38]

Canadesaga was a large town with more than forty buildings, surrounded by cornfields and orchards. The next morning, fatigue parties of troops were out laying the fields to waste, chopping down fruit trees and setting the buildings on fire. An old fort, built under the direction of Sir William Johnson during the French and Indian War with a stockade and blockhouse, was among the structures. What was not dismantled for firewood was destroyed. Detachments were sent to other nearby towns to level them. The Rifle Corps went on a two-day foray to destroy the town of Gothseungquen, for example, and the company of volunteer rangers from Tryon County, commanded by Captain John Harper, toward Schoyer on Cayuga Lake. Another, under the command of Lieutenant Colonel William Smith of the 5th New Jersey Regiment, destroyed a large town on the west shore of Seneca Lake.[39]

On Wednesday morning, September 8, the commissary officers examined the state of the provisions already issued and the balance remaining. As a consequence, Sullivan called his principal commanders and staff officers to a council of war. Given the remaining provisions, he asked them, how much further into Six Nations territory would the expedition carry? The officers concurred that the army should proceed as far as the largest Seneca town, Genesee, also called Little Beard's Town, before turning back toward Tioga. The order was given for the army to march in the morning.[40]

Before the army moved on September 9, a "properly officered" detachment of fifty "able-bodied" men under the command of Captain John Reed of the 6th Massachusetts Regiment was sent as an escort to conduct the sick and lame soldiers, and packhorses too weak to carry cargo, back to Tioga. The rest of the army was ordered to march at noon. Before going more than a few miles, however, the soldiers encountered a very thick and deep swamp that consumed their energies for the rest of the day and resulted in two gun carriages being broken. Fortunately, the army reached an "eminence" of high ground that rose like an island from the swamp, and was "Clear of timber & filled with high grass." Encamping for the night, and after artificers repaired the broken gun carriages, the army moved back into the swamp in the morning. The trudging continued a few more miles in the sticky morass until the troops emerged into open country that afforded easier movement to the recently evacuated lakeside town of Canandaigua, where the army halted. Once encamped, the soldiers went about the work of destroying the crops and putting the buildings to the torch.[41]

The army was on the move again early on the eleventh. After a full day of good marching, the riflemen in the advanced guard approached Honeoye, a town situated on an area "of clear intervale near a small lake of the same name." The riflemen caught a glimpse of a few fleeing Indians as they entered the evacuated town. When the main body arrived, the orders were given to pitch camp. The settlement had eleven houses, several cornfields, and a creek of "very good water." To enable the army to quickly push on to its last objective, General Sullivan decided to establish a magazine.

While soldiers went about destroying the town and fields, a fatigue detail was ordered "to fix one of the houses in such a manner as to defend it." A fortification "by way of palisade" was fashioned from boxes, kegs and sacks of flour, and the post was soon completed. All baggage, supplies, provisions and ammunition in excess of what was essential for the army to fight and march the twenty-five miles to Genesee and back were unloaded. A detachment of artillerymen with a 3-pounder field gun and a "proper guard" of fifty foot soldiers provided the garrison, commanded by Captain John Cummings of the 2nd New Jersey Regiment. Before the army returned from Genesee, the post was improved with loopholes and embrasures in the walls, and sharpened pickets and an abatis using the local apple trees. His fellow officers dubbed the post "Fort Cummings" after their friend. All the soldiers too infirm for the pending march, which the officers described as "the sick, lame and lazy," along with the "worst" packhorses, their drivers, and excess beef cattle, were left behind.[42]

Having failed to make a stand at Canadesaga, the Iroquois war chiefs assured Major John Butler that they had "determined to collect all the force they can and meet them" at Canawaugus,[43] northwest of Conesus Lake. With Captains Walter Butler and Rowland Montour keeping out scouts to monitor every move the Rebel army made, Major Butler continued to ask for assistance from Lieutenant Colonel Bolton. Likewise, Butler sent Captain John Powell of the Indian Department, carrying "some strings of Wampum" from the chiefs, to the Indians living around Niagara, hoping to "bring off" as many warriors he could gather, and those Bolton had "fitted out." Despite the odds, the major claimed that the Indians were in better spirits than they had been before the battle at Newtown, but added that with "any succour from Niagara," they could be persuaded to attack the Rebels on their march. Captain Brant went a little further, and suggested to Bolton, "a few Troops from Niagara would be of the greatest service," and timely, without weakening the garrison. Brant pointed out that Bolton could always summon reinforcements from Carleton Island.[44]

The Seneca war chief Garganwahgah (Cornplanter), and Captain Brant met with the Iroquois and Delaware chiefs that had assembled at Genesee on Friday, September 10, the same day the Americans destroyed Canandaigua. In the council, the two war chiefs encouraged their counterparts to "exert themselves with Spirit and Resolution." With the enemy approaching and the situation desperate, Butler had reconsidered Bolton's offer of two 3-pounder "Grasshopper" field guns. The terrain and vegetation about Conesus Lake and Genesee Castle was open, and more favorable for the use of artillery, than that between Newtown and Catherine's Town. But it was a race against time. Butler had to collect a sufficient number of horses to move the guns and ammunition, but those items, like the Indian reinforcements, had yet to arrive.[45]

A heavy thunderstorm hit the American encampment at Honeoye on Saturday night, and the rain lasted through mid-Sunday morning. When the weather finally cleared, the troops struck their tents, drew four days' rations, and moved out for Genesee at about noon. After crossing the defile and fording the outlet of Honeoye Lake, the army formed in line of march. The troops made good progress over ground that was "hilly but not difficult" to traverse. As usual, the riflemen and advanced guard of light infantry led the way, traveling northwest by west. Aware they were being watched by enemy scouts and rangers, Lieutenant Erkuries Beatty of the 4th Pennsylvania Regiments remarked, the "Enemy kept just a head of us." The soldiers, Beatty continued, "could discover their tracks very fresh and the water muddy where they had crossed" the streams. When night fell, Hand's brigade had covered almost half the distance to Genesee, but was half a mile short of the day's march objective, a small Seneca town of Conesus.[46] The Light Corps was ordered to halt and camp in the woods, with the main body of the army following about one mile to their rear.[47]

Knowing that they were close to the objective, Major General Sullivan sought information that would enable the army to surprise any defenders before they had time to offer an effective defense or flee. He ordered Brigadier General Hand to send an officer with three or four riflemen and an Oneida chief to reconnoiter Genesee, thought to be seven miles away. The Oneida was Hanyost Thaosagwat, or Hanyerry, a veteran of the battle of Oriskany whom Lieutenant Colonel Adam Hubley described as "remarkable for his attachment to this country, having served as a volunteer since the commencement of the war." Lieutenant Thomas Boyd of the Rifle Corps was selected to lead the mission. Boyd's patrol included the Oneida chief, eighteen "Riflemen" from his own corps, and eight "Musket men" from the 4th Pennsylvania Regiment. Traveling in the dark, Boyd's twenty-seven-man patrol "went on without any Interruption," from about eleven at night until daybreak, when it arrived at the town of Gathtsegwarohare, which they presumed to be their intended objective. Boyd advanced with a small scout, and confirmed the town had been evacuated, and was not defended. Boyd then sent two runners back to inform the general, and said he would keep the town under observation until the army arrived. With any luck, they might capture a prisoner or two. The patrol moved into the woods where they could watch from concealed positions.[48]

On the same morning that Sullivan's army marched toward Conesus, scouts brought Major Butler news that the enemy had camped at Honeoye, on the road to Genesee, the night before. At a hastily called council, the Indian chiefs proposed to attack the Americans before they reached Genesee. Not waiting for the boats of supplies or reinforcements Bolton had promised, 400 Butler's Rangers and allied warriors marched in the afternoon for another unevenly matched battle. After reconnoitering for a suitable ambuscade, they decided on a large hill overlooking a ravine where there Indian trail leading toward Genesee emerged from a sizable morass. It was their intent to let part of the American army cross the swamp and attack when the rest would not be able to support them. The rangers and warriors then "took Possession of the ground" where they intended to "Surprise the Enemy early in the next morning." Instead of fighting as two divisions, the Indian chiefs requested Butler to deploy his rangers "intermixt" among the warriors. As they prepared their positions and waited for the invaders to move through Conesus, the rangers and Indians were unaware that Boyd's patrol had passed around their right flank in the night, and was now behind them.[49]

The American army held reveille early on the chilly morning of September 13, struck tents and began marching northward at six o'clock, through fields covered in heavy dew. After halting at Conesus, a town of about fifteen structures, the troops built cooking fires and started breakfast, while enough cattle were butchered to issue every man a three-day ration of beef, albeit at half allowance. By noon, Boyd's messengers arrived and told General Sullivan that Genesee was empty and the patrol was waiting for them there. Ahead of the army, however, lay the inlet to Conesus Lake, a "very bad morass & Creek" that was impossible for artillery and horses to cross. It would be hours before the army could move. Riflemen and light infantry crossed the swamp to provide security on the far bank, while the pioneers improved the road and built a bridge. The rest of the army cut down corn, and placed the stalks in the longhouse buildings, where it was burned.[50]

Back near Gathtsegwarohare, as Boyd's patrol watched the town for signs of enemy activity, four warriors rode into town on horseback. The lieutenant sent Sergeant Timothy Murphy with five men to take them by surprise. Shots were fired. One warrior fell dead, but the rest, one of whom had been wounded, fled. The scout returned to Boyd with their victim's scalp, horse, saddle, and bridle. Boyd feared that the gunfire alerted the enemy to their presence, and sent two more runners to discover the cause for the army's delay. They had not traveled far when they sighted five Indians, and ran back to tell Boyd. The lieutenant "thought it proper to return with his party to the Army," and expected to meet them on the way. After moving about two miles, the patrol encountered the same five Indians. Choosing to fight through them, Boyd's men opened fire. As the Indians ran, the soldiers came on slowly, pausing to fire and reload as they went. One of the warriors fell dead, and one of Boyd's soldiers went to scalp him.[51]

As Boyd was trying to head back, Major Butler's Rangers and Indians "were waiting with impatience for the Enemy to begin to pass their Bridge." A party of surveyors from the American army was taking readings in front of one of the Indian positions. Absorbed in their work, the party under the direction of Captain Benjamin Lodge had progressed about a half mile beyond the sentries guarding the pioneers building the bridge. When the Indians heard the scattered gunfire from Boyd's running fight in the distance, and believing the ambush had been initiated, they opened fire on the surveyors. One of the "chain men," a corporal named Calhoun, was mortally wounded. The surveyors dropped their instruments and fled back toward the sentinels, with warriors in close pursuit. The Indians gave up the chase and retreated when the soldiers opened fire. The American camp was alarmed, and the drums called Assembly.[52]

From where he was, Boyd heard the gunfire and drums, and thought safety was within reach. He and his men soon realized a large enemy force stood between them and their comrades. The Indians and Tories who were waiting to ambush the army turned their weapons on these Americans who "had fallen into the Right of our Line" instead. Boyd "formed his men for Action and began a heavy fire," but were greatly outnumbered. Two of his flankers became separated, but found their way back to camp to inform General Sullivan that the patrol was attempting to return. Major Butler was "allarmed by a firing above us to the Right," and after it had continued for some time, heard the Indians calling out that they were surrounded. Gathering all available forces, they "pushed for the place where the firing was."[53]

Boyd's troops "fought them for some considerable time," but were soon "obliged to attempt a retreat." Alternating loading and firing, and running from tree to tree, the soldiers attempted to break contact. In the confused firefight, seven more of Boyd's men evaded the Indians and rangers that were swarming around the patrol, but the enemy was too numerous for all to make it. The rest retreated to a grove of trees that stood in an otherwise cleared field, and were soon completely surrounded. Determined "to sell themselves as dear as possible," they fought until only two men had not been killed and scalped. The wounded Lieutenant Boyd and Sergeant Michael Parker were captured and taken by the Indians to Genesee Castle. According to Butler, Boyd's move resulted in Butler revealing his own force's position, and "frustrated our Designs of surprising them." With no hope of inflicting any real hurt on the invaders,

Butler maintained that the Indians insisted on retreating to Genesee, leaving him no alternative but to agree.[54]

With the sound of heavy firing ahead, and the first of Boyd's stragglers arriving, General Sullivan ordered the light infantry to reinforce the ill-fated patrol. Major Parr and the Rifle Corps led the way, but the Indians ran off at their approach. The rest of General Hand's brigade and the right flanking division ascended the hill and formed a line of battle, but they were too late. They arrived to see the Indians and Tories retreat, leaving behind "at least a wagon load" of hats, packs, blankets, and other baggage, most of which appeared to belong to Butler's Rangers, in their haste. One of Boyd's patrol who evaded capture, although wounded, rejoined his comrades of the 4th Pennsylvania, and told them what had happened. A short while later, Sergeant Murphy of the Rifle Corps rejoined his unit. Although the men of the Light Corps found only one enemy body, the two survivors recalled watching from concealment as the Indians and Tories carried their casualties away and "killed . . . tomahawked and scalped six" of their comrades.[55]

By noon, after four hours of labor, the bridge was completed, and the army marched, heading for the Indian town of Gathtsegwarohare, seven miles away. General Sullivan received intelligence that the enemy "were paraded and ready to fight" in the woods on the opposite side of the town. When the advanced guard saw five Indians in the village, the army halted and deployed. The artillery was drawn up in front. Maxwell's brigade was posted on the left with the left flanking division to turn the enemy right. Poor's brigade was on the right. Two regiments from Clinton's brigade and the right flanking division were poised to move around Poor's brigade and assail the enemy left. The Light Corps was in the center, and ready to push on in front supported by the rest of Clinton's brigade. When they received the signal, the line advanced and took the abandoned town without opposition. They saw only a few of the "enemy flying before us across" Canaseraga Creek, "a branch of the Genesee where it was impossible to follow." In the approaching darkness, "the most disagreeable time for fighting," the three 3-pounders were drawn up and "fired all together with round shot to scour the woods" as a precaution. As the troops prepared to encamp, they built fires from wood pulled from the town's twenty-five buildings, and one or two more survivors from Boyd's patrol rejoined their units.[56]

Butler and his allies retreated to Genesee, while his scouts reported the Americans "had followed us closely" before they halted and encamped. He therefore posted a thin screen of scouts to watch the enemy's next move as he and the rest of the Tory and Indian leaders decided what to do next. But his Indian allies were "uneasy and in great distress." He told Colonel Guy Johnson that keeping a large force of warriors together was impossible after Newtown. Since hearing of the approach of Sullivan's army, the Seneca women had also been pleading for their warriors to sue for peace so they could remain at home and benefit from the coming harvest. They had been living on green corn since spring, and were questioning the Indian Department's promises. They faced the "greatest terror and confusion," and many realized that if their crops and homes were destroyed, the British government could not keep them adequately housed and supplied. Now, with the invaders only a few miles away, many Iroquois blamed Butler for deceiving them into this ruinous war. One Indian, allegedly, attempted to shoot the superintendent. Having none of it, Butler persuaded the chiefs to send the women and children to Canada, and to join him at Niagara with their warriors. With that, "all the Indians, except about 60, moved off" in a "Great hurry and confusion."[57]

Although Boyd and Parker told Butler that the American army would proceed no farther than Genesee, Butler insisted that Sullivan intended to lay siege to Niagara. The Tory major then gave the prisoners over to the Indians "for Satisfaction for the damages that were done to them." Boyd and Parker were tied to trees, stripped naked, and ritually tortured to death. The next morning, when scouts reported that Sullivan's army was moving, Butler and Brant "left the place in a great hurry."[58]

On the morning of September 14, General Sullivan's army completed the destruction of Gathtsegwarohare and the cornfield where they had encamped. In the afternoon, the order was given to cross the creek and move toward Genesee. The terrain opened up, and soon the army was crossing mostly cleared fields in its open square marching alignment. When the thick grass reached a height of nearly eight feet, mounted officers followed their troops' progress only by watching the gun barrels move along the sea of green. In late afternoon, the first units of the advanced guard reached Genesee Castle. With more than 100 "mostly large and very elegant" longhouses, the principal Seneca town stood amid miles of extensive fields growing corn "and every kind of vegetable that can be conceived."[59]

After marching 136 miles from Tioga, the expedition had finally reached Genesee, the intended limit of its advance; eighty miles short of Niagara, where the British thought it was going, but farther than it could have gone, had additional provisions not been secured along the way. By mid-September, the delayed start of the campaign that had so irked the impatient General Washington proved providential since crops and vegetables were ripe and in abundant supply. Surgeon Jabez Campfield of the 5th New Jersey Regiment remarked, "The army must have dropped the prosecution of this expedition long ago, had it not the corn, beans, &c., which it found from place to place, subsisted it." Reflecting on the soldiers' voluntary acceptance of half rations after the battle of Newtown, Campfield put true credit where it belonged, and continued, "The virtue of this army must exceed any yet exhibited."[60]

On entering Genesee, the soldiers found the mangled bodies of Boyd and Parker, which more than one described as "a most horrid spectacle to behold," and which taught the men the necessity of "fighting to the last moment rather than fall into their hands alive." The two were buried with full military honors. The troops noticed that one of the longhouses had curiously been set on fire by the Indians before they left. On inspecting the ruins, troops noticed charred human remains, and assumed the Indians placed the warriors killed in the ambush of Boyd's patrol in the structure and burned it instead of burying them. The soldiers also found quantities of corn the Indians had already gathered. Some of it was husked and hung to dry, while some was lying in heaps. General Sullivan's Indian Expedition had reached the "Western Door" of the Six Nations the same day that Colonel Brodhead's returned to Pittsburgh.[61]

The next morning, the entire army was "turned out" at six o'clock to destroy Genesee. The riflemen, one regiment from each brigade, and the artillery were posted for security, while the rest went to work. The men took particular delight in destroying the fields that had been cultivated by Butler's Rangers for their own magazines, to be used for rations in their raids on the frontier. Soldiers picked 15,000 bushels of corn and other vegetables, and threw them in the river. Produce was also placed inside kilns or longhouses that were set on fire, or piled in heaps on bonfires of wood from dismantled structures. Fruit trees were chopped down. What few cattle that had been left behind by the inhabitants were killed. Mary Jemison, a woman who had been taken captive in the French and Indian War and assimilated into the Seneca nation, later said the American troops "left nothing but bare soil and timber." Sullivan explained that the town and its agriculture were destroyed "so that the enemy might not reap the least advantage from it."[62]

While the troops were busy at the task, a woman carrying her small child approached the army. Lieutenants Obadiah Gore and John Jenkins recognized her as the wife of John Lester, a neighbor from the Wyoming Valley town of Westmoreland. She and her baby were taken captive in a raid the previous year, as her husband and son were killed and scalped before her eyes. She had escaped in the confusion of the evacuation, and wanted to go home.[63]

By about three o'clock in the afternoon on September 15, "the business was finished." Genesee, which means "beautiful valley," was in flames. General Sullivan announced in General Orders to "this brave and resolute army that the immediate objects of this expedition are accomplished; total ruin of the Indian settlements, and the destruction of their crops, which were designed for the support of those inhuman barbarians, while they were desolating the American frontiers." The army then formed, executed a "right about face," and headed back toward Tioga in the reverse order of march. An advanced guard commanded by Major Robert Cochrane of the 3rd New York Regiment went in front, followed by the cohorn and rest of Clinton's brigade in four columns. Poor's and Maxwell's brigades on the flanks, "marched by the right," in the "advance by the left," formation. Hand's brigade "fetched up the Rear." Two guns trailed, and Parr's riflemen came "in the rear of the whole."[64]

As it retraced its tracks, the army completed the destruction of towns and fields that was left undone or bypassed. On halting near the scene of fighting on the thirteenth, Captain William Henderson of the 4th Pennsylvania Regiment led a detail of sixty men to recover and bury the bodies of those slain. Including the six that were found immediately after the fight ended, the men found the corpses of thirteen scalped and "badly mangled" soldiers, and the particularly mutilated body of the faithful Oneida chief, Hanyerry, where they had fallen "near together." They were "buried as decently as we could in the situation," according to Lieutenant Jenkins. The final cost of the ambush was sixteen of Boyd's twenty-seven men, and one member of the survey party killed, making September 13 the deadliest day of the campaign for the Americans.[65]

The day after Sullivan's army did its "right about face," the situation could not have appeared more desperate at Fort Niagara. On September 16, Lieutenant Colonel Bolton penned a message to Governor-General Haldimand that he expected Sullivan's 5,000-man army at Genesee and Brodhead's 1,500 men at Venango to move and attack him. Against them, he had only a weak garrison. Butler's Rangers were reduced by sickness to 150 effective men. With their towns destroyed, Bolton expected little help from the Indian warriors. He had alerted commanders of the smaller posts in the area, Forts Schlosser and Erie, "to hold themselves in readiness" to bring their troops to Niagara to reinforce him, and expected detachments from Detroit and Carleton Island to arrive daily. Despite the outlook, Bolton assured Haldimand that Niagara "will be defended with spirit."[66]

Unknown to Bolton, Brodhead's much smaller force, and carrying provisions for only thirty days, had already returned to Pittsburgh. Sullivan felt that his expedition had advanced as far as necessary and was already beyond the limits his supplies could normally be expected to support. With numerous Seneca towns bypassed, and those of the Cayugas and Mohawks yet to be visited, Sullivan intended to accomplish the task General Washington had given him.

In "high spirits," the soldiers were "willing to make great marches," knowing they were heading home after a successful campaign, and quickened the pace. When the men returned to Honeoye, they were relieved to find the stores and supplies necessary for the remainder of the march safe. There had been some apprehension following the ambush of the thirteenth, but "Fort Cummings" had been made quite formidable. No longer needed, it was dismantled, the stores repacked, and the soldiers who had garrisoned it returned to their units.[67]

Before leaving Honeoye, the soldiers' ration of flour was increased, leading Lieutenant Erkuries Beatty of the 4th Pennsylvania Regiment to remark, "we can now sit down and eat a hearty meal's victuals with a clear conscience" after weeks on reduced rations. The army's packhorses began to give out, and many had to be put out of their misery before reaching Tioga. On the evening of September 19, the army camped on the same fields it occupied on its previous halt at Canadesaga. While moving in, a three-man express from Tioga brought the news that Spain had declared war on Great Britain. Just outside Canandaigua, four Oneida warriors, including a sachem, joined the army in response to General Sullivan's letter. Although saddened by the death of Hanyerry, they "seemed much rejoiced at our great success against the Seneca." They also wanted to intercede for the Cayugas. Sullivan called a council of war the next morning. The Oneidas told the Continental officers that although the Cayuga had acted with the Senecas in alliance with the British, they now desired to make peace with the United States. The council of officers, however, determined that no treaty should be offered, and the Cayuga would be attacked as the Seneca had. Sullivan also issued orders to destroy those Seneca towns that the army had bypassed or which were not along its route of march on the way to Genesee.[68]

While Sullivan led the main body of the army between Seneca and Cayuga Lakes, four detachments fanned out to widen the path of destruction. Lieutenant Colonel William S. Smith of the 5th New Jersey Regiment led 290 men down the west side of Seneca Lake to complete the destruction of Kershong and the other towns located there, before rejoining the main body at Catherine's Town.

Lieutenant Colonel William Butler of the 4th Pennsylvania Regiment led 600 members of the Light Corps, including Major Parr's riflemen, to the east side of Cayuga Lake. The Oneida warriors accompanied him in an attempt to persuade the Cayugas to "deliver themselves up as prisoners." But on entering the villages of "those pretended neutral Cayugas," the soldiers and Oneidas discovered a number of trophy scalps that appeared to have recently been taken from American frontier settlements. The Oneidas were satisfied by the evidence

This depiction shows Lieutenant Boyd and Sergeant Parker being questioned by John Butler before being turned over to the Indians to be tortured and executed. A nineteenth century illustration, the British characters appear to be more appropriate to the War of 1812. (*New York State Library*)

that the Cayuga remained enemies of the United States, and Butler's men destroyed the nation's five principal towns, a number of scattered houses, and 200 acres of "excellent corn with a number of fruit trees." On September 21, Lieutenant Colonel Henry Dearborn of the of the 3rd New Hampshire Regiment led 200 men to west side of Cayuga Lake to burn settlements, destroy cornfields, and intercept those Indians fleeing before Butler's Light Corps. Dearborn's detachment burned six towns including one left partially standing on the army's previous visit.[69]

Colonel Peter Gansevoort of the 3rd New York Regiment led 100 "such soldiers as were at that place" to recover the baggage of those regiments that began the campaign in the frontier districts of Tryon County, New York. The men were also instructed to destroy the Lower Mohawk Castle. Since 1778, the few Mohawks who remained on Schoharie Creek had constantly given intelligence to the enemy and supported their scouting parties during their incursions against the frontier settlement. They were now going to have to pay for their actions. Gansevoort's men were to capture those Mohawks "left to answer such a purpose." The colonel was cautioned that the Upper Castle was now inhabited by Oneidas, friends of the United States, and was "not to disturb" them.[70]

Gansevoort's detachment marched through the ruins of the capital town of the Onondaga nation, which had been destroyed during Colonel Van Schaick's expedition the previous spring. When it arrived at the Tuscarora town of Canaseraga, the detachment was greeted by the inhabitants with presents of "boiled corn & eels" and congratulated for "the success of our arms" against the Seneca. The scene was repeated as they marched through Oneida Castle the next day on the way to Fort Schuyler. In another reminder of why they had been ordered on the campaign, Gansevoort's men "passed the place where Gen. Herkimer's battle happened" in 1777, and saw "the skulls & bones of many of the unfortunate victims are still to be found" at Oriskany. The men arrived in German Flats the next day, September 26. The baggage was collected and troops were sent to "carry off the remainder of the Mohawk tribe that lived near Canajoharie on Schoharie Creek." After the prisoners were turned over to Indian Commissioner James Dean and the baggage put aboard ship for transport, the soldiers of Gansevoort's detachment marched to the headquarters of the Main Army at New Windsor to await the arrival of their regiments.[71]

Meanwhile, the main body halted at Catherine's Town on September 23. The next morning, after reveille, the light infantry covering force moved into Bear Swamp, as the pioneers cleared the way and repaired the bridges. The troops slogged through, although not quite as excruciatingly as before. But the struggle was too much for many of the packhorses, and a number of them had to be killed after the army emerged from the morass.[72]

A few miles after resuming the march, Sullivan's advanced party was saluted by a thirteen rounds of artillery, which were answered by the cohorn and three cheers from the troops. General Sullivan had ordered a magazine to be established at Conowalohala, to be ready to issue the troops with plenty to eat when they arrived. Captain John Reed executed the command after escorting the convoy of invalids from Canadesaga. With a two-hundred-man detachment from Tioga, he established a fortification, and waited with 100 head of cattle and enough flour and spirits to issue every man six days' provisions. When they reached "Fort Reed," every soldier was issued "one Jill of Whiskey," their first spirits in over a month, and "likewise a full allowance of Beef for the first time."[73]

The army encamped there for five days to rest, await the arrival of the detachments, and dispatch others to the nearby countryside to locate and destroy other Indian settlements in the vicinity. After the exhausting march, the encampment at Fort Reed had an air of celebration. The army was paraded to fire a "Feu de Joy," or a running fire of muskets from right to left. Not satisfied with the first attempt, General Sullivan ordered it be done again. The second "Feu de Joy," Sullivan said, "went like a hallelujah," along with a thirteen-gun artillery salute, and a rousing three cheers to Congress, for resolving to pay the troops in money for their shortened rations, and the king of Spain, the new ally. Each brigade was issued a large bullock, and the soldiers feasted on roast beef.

Over the next three days, detachments under Lieutenant Colonels Dearborn and Butler rejoined the army, while Colonel Philip Van Cortlandt of the 2nd New York Regiment led 300 men for nine miles up a branch of the Chemung, accompanied by boats, to find and destroy settlements and cornfields. They returned with nine boatloads of corn. During the period, Colonel Elias Dayton led a force to sweep the south side of the Chemung, and Captain Samuel Spalding and his Westmoreland Independent Company led a detachment of light troops up the Tioga to burn a Tory settlement. On September 28, orders were given to march the next morning. The army lightened its burden. Most of the stores, baggage, artillery ordnance stores, and sick troops were transported to Tioga by boat. The lame were mounted on horses too weak to carry heavy loads of supplies, and Fort Reed was demolished.[74]

On September 29, the army marched the short distance to Chemung and encamped on the same ground they had on the night before the battle at Newtown. The next day, the army negotiated the narrow defile below the town, and marched to within one mile of Tioga before halting at nine o'clock in the morning. The word went out for the "Musick & Colours." As the fifes and drums and Proctor's regimental band assembled, the officers "found the men in proper line of March." The "Western Army" of Major General John Sullivan "then march'd on with Musick playing and Colours flying." The returning troops moved "in the greatest order," and Colonel Shreve was ready. As the troops passed Fort Sullivan, the paraded garrison presented arms, and a "salute with 13 Pieces of Cannon regularly fired." The expedition's artillery of the park returned the honor. The cheers and "lively martial music" continued as the various regiments and corps marched to the campgrounds they had occupied before marching for thirty-five days and 136 miles, in each direction. The officers spent the evening in "grand entertainment" with an elegant dinner, and the soldiers had their own festivities in their messes, and shared "Myrth and Joy" having finished the campaign "Gloriously."[75]

Conclusion

THEIR SETTLEMENTS MUST EVER BE IN OUR POWER

B UTLER's RANGERS and their allied Indian warriors had been driven in disarray before the Continentals for 136 miles through Iroquois country until "compelled to retire to Niagara after the Rebels took possession of Genesee." By the time Sullivan's army was passing back through Canadesaga, the British realized that the important post at Fort Niagara was no longer in immediate danger.[1] But there was no disguising the fact that Britain's Indian allies had suffered a catastrophic blow. It was not enough that the Iroquois Confederacy was punished so completely, but with all its might, the British Empire seemed powerless to offer any meaningful assistance to the Six Nations.

In contrast to the situation when Butler encouraged them to attack a vulnerable settlement like Wyoming Valley, the pro-British Iroquois were never able to rally a credible force of warriors to oppose the Sullivan's invasion. Major Butler and Lieutenant Colonel Bolton attributed that failure to the lack of timely reinforcement from other forces at the disposal of Lieutenant General Frederick Haldimand, the commander in chief of his majesty's forces and royal governor of Quebec. Without reinforcement, Butler remarked, the Rebels' "superior strength & numbers made all our efforts to stop their progress of small avail."[2] Bolton added that had there even been enough new recruits for Butler's Rangers to take the field with an effective strength of 500 men, "there is no doubt that instead of 300, at least a thousand Warriors would have turned out" to oppose Sullivan's expedition. In consequence "the Indians not being supported as they expected, thought of nothing more than carrying off their families."[3]

Butler had repeatedly requested reinforcements of Haldimand, either directly or through Bolton, without satisfaction. It was not until Colonel Guy Johnson, the Crown's Superintendent of Indian Affairs, was back in the province that the governor-general gave the requests serious consideration. But since they did not arrive while there was still time to effectively oppose "the numbers & Designs of the Enemy," Butler told the governor, "The Reinforcements Your Excellency is sending are too late to save the Country of the Five Nations from being Destroyed."[4] Those reinforcements consisted of

290

the 140 men of King's Royal Regiment of New York, commanded by Lieutenant Colonel Sir John Johnson, with a detachment of the 34th Regiment of Foot, and a number of Canadian Indians, including Caughnawaga, or "French Mohawks."

While still waiting for transport at Fort Haldimand on Carleton Island, Sir John proposed an attack to dislodge Fort Sullivan, the post the Americans had established at Tioga. Johnson said that if the Six Nations approved plan "and join us immediately together with the Rangers under the command of Major Butler," he could bring six weeks' provisions enough for 1,500 men. To batter the walls of the American stockade and blockhouses, Johnson had an artillery detachment with "two Brass Six-Pounders," and requested Bolton to attach either two cohorns or one cohorn and a howitzer. However, Johnson needed Bolton to provide an "officer and proper number of men to work the artillery," plus enough horses to move the guns, ammunition, and provisions on the expedition.[5]

Bolton voiced the opinion that such a British plan "to follow them is too late to be of any great consequence." In addition, Johnson's proposed expedition "would be attended with many difficulties," not the least of which was the transporting of provisions, given the shortage of horses at Niagara. Ironically, the Americans abandoned and demolished Fort Sullivan on their way back to Wyoming, while the British were still considering the plan to dislodge it. Bolton, however, began to believe that the Americans' campaign objective in 1779 had been to cut a road as far as Genesee in preparation for laying siege to Fort Niagara in the spring. With that in mind, he advised posting Johnson's regiment in the area and reinforcing the "upper posts."[6] Although late in the campaigning season, if Haldimand considered it necessary that "something should be done in order to return the visit" Sullivan's army had "paid the Six Nations," Bolton would support it. The Six Nations, he believed, would, join Sir John Johnson's troops in an expedition against the Oneidas, "for they have given no quarter to those of that nation who have fell into their hands."[7]

Butler attempted to show that they had not been beaten. "Notwithstanding the losses the Indians have suffered by the Destruction of their Corn and Villages," he wrote to Haldimand, "they seem still unshaken in the attachment to His Majesty's cause & declare as soon as they placed their women & Children in security they will go take Revenge on the Enemy."[8] Bolton was likewise impressed, observing that the Iroquois "bear this misfortune with more patience than I could possibly expect, & are determined to take revenge when an opportunity offers." But scarcity of provisions and loss of the corn crop made taking any action "impracticable" before winter.[9] The warriors returned to the warpath in 1780 alongside Butler's Rangers and Johnson's Royal Yorkers to terrorize American and Oneida settlements.

Governor-General Haldimand was a critic of the Indian Department's expenses before the invasion began. Major John Butler, who as deputy for the Six Nations had managed the Indian Department in the absence of its superintendent, Colonel Guy Johnson, took it personally. Butler assured Haldimand that while "all the Economy possible had been used," the expenses could not be lessened. Adding, that because Haldimand was late in sending reinforcements to stop the Sullivan expedition, the department's expenses would surely have to be increased "by the distrest situation to which the Indians under my charge are now reduced in being driven from their Country and having everything destroyed."[10]

As he had warned, the number of Indians living around Fort Niagara swelled with refugees as a consequence of Sullivan's unstoppable advance. By the time Butler's scouts reported that the Americans had left Genesee, there were 5,036 men, women, and children at Niagara. Although many were sent to other places of refuge, Bolton reported that 3,678 were still there at the beginning of October.[11] The strain was great. Bolton was "extremely alarmed, for to support such a multitude I think will be absolutely impossible." To alleviate the problem, Governor-General Haldimand hoped that, despite their late arrival, Johnson's reinforcements would reassure the Indians of Great Britain's continued support and assistance. He further directed Major Butler to encourage those Indians whose villages were destroyed to spend winter in Montreal, and those "who have not suffered by the Enemy that they must return home, & take care of their Corn."[12] Haldimand failed to grasp the extent to which the invasion had laid cornfields to waste, and how few cornfields were left to tend.

In another attempt to alleviate the supply problems at Fort Niagara, Indian Department officers were instructed to encourage the Seneca to return to Genesee, "where they can so easily receive assistance from Niagara," or to send "the greatest part of their women and children to Quebec." Despite the assurances representatives of the Crown had given the Indians in return for their alliance and loyalty when they went to war in 1777, Haldimand remarked, "they cannot be so unreasonable as to suppose it possible that a sufficiency of provisions to maintain them all can be transported to Niagara." At the same time, he curtailed plans to reinforce Niagara with Sir John Johnson's regiment for the season.[13] In the meantime, the Indians faced a winter that Mary Jemison described as "the most severe I have witnessed since my remembrance." According to Jemison, the Indians were reduced "almost to a state of starvation," while, "many of our people barely escaped with their lives, and some actually died of hunger and freezing."[14]

On the American side, Major General John Sullivan reported the accomplishments of his army included the destruction of forty towns in all, and an estimated 160,000 bushels of corn "with a vast quantity of vegetables of every kind." Colonel Daniel Brodhead reported that his expedition burned 165 houses, destroyed 500 acres of corn and other vegetables, and took an estimated $30,000 worth of produce in plunder. In the true classical definition of economic warfare, Sullivan and Brodhead literally

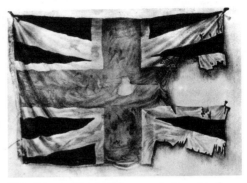

This flag, or King's Color, was believed to have been carried by Butler's Rangers during the Revolutionary War and taken as a trophy when American forces plundered the home of John Butler during the War of 1812. It is now in the collection of the U.S. Military Academy Museum, West Point, New York.

forced the enemy to bear the cost of supporting their invading armies when the troops supplemented their rations with Indian produce. The destruction of the Iroquois and hostile Delaware food supplies also forced the British to assume the burden for their allies' subsistence through the winter.[15]

Although it would have been satisfying to draw out and defeat the warriors of the "hostile tribes" of the Six Nations in a decisive engagement, General Sullivan's campaign achieved the strategic objective General George Washington specified in his operational instructions of May 31, 1779. Sullivan was not expected to capture Fort Niagara, as the British believed, but to destroy Indian towns and cornfields. The strategy was intended to "chastise," or present the Six Nations with a choice between two equally unpleasant consequences for their decision to actively support, or at least countenance, the cooperation of their war parties with the British since the "Year of the Hangman." If the Indians allied themselves closer to the Crown, becoming even more dependent, they would further strain the British army's logistical system and increase Britain's financial costs for carrying on the war. As an alternative, the Indians could have agreed to enter into a treaty with the United States. In return for the Indians choosing latter, Sullivan was authorized to promise them the assistance of American provisions and supplies to survive the winter and beyond.[16] American foodstuffs would have been more plentiful and readily available, since the rich agricultural backcountry that produced them would have been secure from Indian raids. As a condition for American friendship, and to demonstrate their sincerity, the Six Nations would have been expected to turn against their former British allies and deliver Fort Niagara to the United States' hands. The Indians chose the first of the two alternatives, but either outcome was of greater benefit to the American cause than allowing the Tory rangers and Iroquois warriors to continue raiding the vulnerable frontier unchecked.

Likewise, the Iroquois Campaign was not expected to completely put an end to raids along the frontier if the Six Nations did not choose to enter into a treaty with the United States. In his March 6, 1779, letters offering the command to both Gates and Sullivan, Washington explained that one of the purposes of the expedition was to "relieve our frontiers from the depredations to which they would otherwise be exposed."[17] With an American army wreaking havoc in Iroquois country, it was hoped that the warriors would be too busy contending with the dangers to their own towns to threaten those on the borders of New York and Pennsylvania for a third consecutive year. Regardless of which alternative the Iroquois chose in response, the summer expedition served to secure the 1779 harvest in the frontier districts, thus achieving another of its intended objectives.

With view to postwar national expansion, Sullivan reported, "Every creek and river has been traced," by the survey party attached to his headquarters, and "the whole country explored in search of Indian settlements." The general added his belief that the enemy nations "would never think of settling again in a country once subdued, and where their settlements must ever be in our power." If the hostile nations of Iroquois became more attached to the king through their dependency on the British, the Oneida emerged more attached to the Americans because of Sullivan's campaign. The sachems requested that the Continental Congress grant the Oneida "liberty to hunt in the country of the Five Nations." General Sullivan referred the ally's request to Congress in consideration of their friendly conduct, along with his recommendation to "grant them every advantage that would not interfere with our settlement."[18]

If Sullivan's expedition failed to bring the pro-British Iroquois and Delaware to terms, Colonel Brodhead's expedition significantly improved the military and diplomatic situation with regard to the western Indians. He was confident that the counties of Westmoreland, Bedford, and Northumberland (Pennsylvania), "if not the whole Western Frontiers will experience good effect of it." At every Seneca and Munsee "Warrior's camp on the path" his troops marched past, they found the "pairings of scalps and the hair of our Countrymen." These sights provided such "new inducements for Revenge" that Brodhead sought General George Washington's permission to make occasional "excursions against any of the Indian nations who may hereafter prove inimical to us." Brodhead also expressed the willingness to lead an expedition against Detroit, taking the Shawnees in his way, in the next campaign season, if the money and troops were available.[19]

Not long after he returned from the Upper Allegheny, thirty Delaware warriors arrived to volunteer to go to war on the American side. Before he could take them into service, Brodhead sought goods, or the money to obtain them, to use as presents "to engage the Delaware to harass the enemy frequently." The chiefs of the Delaware approached the commander of the Continental Army's Western Department asking not only for peace with the Americans, but their protection from the British and Mingoes. In response, the colonel sent a detachment of troops to build them some blockhouses at Coshocton.[20]

Brodhead was aware that Colonel George Rogers Clark was conducting peace talks with the Indians at Vincennes. He therefore requested guidance from General George Washington, so the two colonels would not work at cross purposes. Brodhead feared the "worst consequences" should one of them enter into a treaty that the other broke. The "Chief of the Wyandot, and the King of the Maquichee tribe of Shawanese" came to Fort Pitt to enter into treaties with the United States. In response, Brodhead "promised them peace provided they take as many prisoners, and scalps, from the Enemy as they have done from us," to which they agreed.[21]

The Continental Congress passed resolutions that thanked General Washington "for directing and to Major General Sullivan, and the brave officers and soldiers under his command, for effectually executing an important expedition against such of the Indian nations as, encouraged by the councils and conducted by the officers of his Britannic majesty, had perfidiously waged an unprovoked and cruel war against these United States, laid waste many of their defenceless towns and with savage barbarity slaughtered the inhabitants thereof."[22] The Congress also thanked "Colonel D. Brodhead and the brave officers and soldiers under his command, for executing the important expedition against the Mingo, and Munsee Indians, and that part of the Senecas on the Allegheny river, by which depredations of those savages, assisted by their merciless instigators, subjects of the king of Great Britain, upon the defenceless inhabitants of the western frontiers, have been restrained and prevented."[23]

As the result of George Washington's campaign against the Iroquois, the Six Nations were no longer as militarily powerful, nor as politically united as they had been before 1777. Its warriors could not strike against American border settlements without fear of reprisal, as they had done for two years. The disagreements between most of the Oneida and Tuscarora siding with the Americans on one side against the majority of Seneca, Mohawk, Onondaga, and Cayuga with the British on the other seemed irreparable. Although the latter would continue to send war parties to raid the American frontier settlements, they could neither field a military force large enough to defend their country nor impose their will over the Indian nations they once considered their dependents.

The Revolutionary War continued for almost four more years, 1779 through 1783, and while many other tribes reverted to neutrality or sought the friendship of the United States, the fighting Iroquois remained faithful allies of the king even following the war's conclusion. They continued to battle alongside Butler's Rangers and the Indian Department well after the British field armies retired into fixed fortifications following Cornwallis' surrender at Yorktown. When the Treaty of Paris was signed in 1783, however, the king's commissioners neglected to include the Iroquois in the settlement. When the United States gained sovereignty over their country, many of the Iroquois moved north into Canada. Such was the legacy of the Year of the Hangman for the Six Nations of Iroquois.

A Contemporary American View of the Wyoming "Massacre"

The following is an account of the Tory and Indian attack on the Wyoming settlement that appeared in the *New York Gazette*, dateline Poughkeepsie, on July 20, 1778. It was reprinted in numerous other newspapers shortly thereafter, and continued to be quoted in historical but uncritical narratives of the battle for two centuries. On August 10, 1778 Continental Congress Delegate Roger Sherman of Connecticut wrote to Governor Jonathan Trumbull Sr. that "The Indians and the more barbarous Tories have desolated our Settlements at Westmoreland." Although the enemy had committed some barbarous acts, he and others realized that many of the reports about the murder of unarmed civilians may have been exaggerated. He confided to Trumbull, "The account given in a Poughkeepsie paper is said to be much beyond the truth."[*]

Since our last many of the distressed refugees from Wyoming settlement on the Susquehannah, who escaped the general massacre of the inhabitants, have passed this way, from whom we have collected the following account, viz.

On the 1st instant (July) the whole body of the enemy, consisting, it is supposed of near 1600, (about 300 of whom were thought to be Indians under their own Chiefs, the rest Tories painted like them, except their officer, who were dressed like regulars) the whole under the command of Colonel John Butler, (a Connecticut Tory, and cousin of Colonel Zebulon Butler, the second in command in the settlement) came down near the upper fort, but conceded the greatest part of the number; here they had a skirmish with the inhabitants, who took and killed two Indians, and lost ten of their own men, three of whom they afterwards found killed, scalped, and mangled in the most inhuman manner.

Thursday, July 2. The enemy appeared on the mountains, back of Kingston, where the women and children then fled into the fort. Most of the garrison of Exeter fort were Tories, who treacherously gave it up to the enemy. The same night, after a little resistance, they took Lackawanna fort, killed 'Squire Jenkins and his family, with several others, in a barbarous manner, and made prisoners of most of the women and children; a small number only escaped.

Friday, July 3. This morning Colonel Zebulon Butler, leaving a small number to guard the fort (Wilkesborough) crossed the river with 400 men, and marched to Kingston fort. The enemy sent in a flag, demanding a surrender of the fort in two hours. Colonel Butler answered he should not surrender, but was ready to receive them. They sent in a second flag, demanding an immediate surrender, otherwise the fort should be stormed, plundered and burnt, with all its contents, in a few hours—and said that they had with them 300 men. Colonel Zebulon Butler proposed a parley, which being agreed to, a place in Kingston was appointed for the meeting, to which Colonel Zebulon Butler repaired with 400 men, well armed; but finding no body there, he proceeded to the foot of the mountain, where at a distance he saw a flag, which as he advanced, retired, as if afraid, twenty or thirty rods; he following, was led into an ambush, and partly surrounded by the enemy, who suddenly rose and fired upon them. Notwithstanding the great disproportion of 1600 to 400, he and his men bravely stood and returned the fire for three quarters of an hour, with such

---

[*](Roger Sherman to Gov. Jonathan Trumbull Sr., letter dated Philadelphia, August 10, 1778, *Letters of Delegates to Congress*: Volume 11, 799.)

briskness and resolution, that the enemy began to give way, and were upon the point of retiring —when one of Colonel Zebulon Butler's men, either through treachery or cowardice, cried out that the Colonel ordered a retreat—This caused a cessation of their fire, threw them into confusion, and a total route ensued. The greatest part fled to the river, which they endeavored to pass, to Fort Wilkesborough, the enemy pursued with the fury of devils, many were lost or killed in the river, and no more than about 70, some of whom were wounded, escaped to Wilkesborough.

Saturday morning, July 4. The enemy sent 196 scalps into Fort Kingston, which they invested on the land side, and kept up a continual fire upon it. Colonel Nathan Dennison went, with a flag, to Exeter fort, to know of Colonel John Butler what terms he would grant on a surrender. Butler answered the hatchet. Colonel Dennison returned to Fort Kingston, which he defended till Sunday morning, when his men being nearly all killed or wounded, he could hold out no longer, and was obliged to surrender at discretion. The enemy took away some of the unhappy prisoners, and shutting up the rest in the houses, set fire to them, and they were all consumed together. These infernals then crossed the river to Fort Wilkesborough, which in a few minutes surrendered at discretion. About 70 of the men, who had inlisted in the Continental service to defend the frontiers, they inhumanly butchered, with every circumstance of horrid cruelty; and then shutting up the rest, with the women and children, in the houses, they set fire to them, and they all perished together in the flames.

After burning all the buildings in the fort, they proceeded to the destruction of every building and improvement (except what belonged to some tories) that come within their reach, on all these flourishing settlements, which they have rendered a scene of desolation and horror, almost beyond description, parallel, or credibility; and were not the facts attested by a number of the unhappy sufferes, from different quarters of the settlement, and unconnected with each other, it would be impossible to believe that human nature could be capable of such prodigious enormity. When these miscreants had destroyed the other improvements, they proceeded to destroy the crops on the ground, letting the cattle and horses to the corn, and cutting up as much as they could, or what was left. Great numbers of the cattle they shot and destroyed; and cutting out the tongues of many others, left them to perish in misery.

Key Personalities

British and Loyalists

Sir William Johnson (1715–1774)

Longtime British Superintendent for Indian affairs, Sir William was a hero of the French and Indian War, a major general of Provincial forces, and successful businessman and land speculator. With his first wife, Catherine Weisenberg, he had three children, Ann, John, and Mary. Ann married Christian Daniel Claus and Mary married her father's nephew Guy Johnson. After Catherine's death in 1759, he married Caroline, or Catherine, Peters, the niece of Mohawk chief King Hendrick. She bore him one son, William, and two daughters. After Catherine died, Sir William married his third wife, "Molly Brant," Joseph Brant's older sister. That marriage produced eight surviving children, including a son, Peter. Sir William Johnson died on the eve of the Revolutionary War, on July 12, 1774.

Sir John Johnson (1742–1830)

John was Sir William's eldest son by his first wife, Catherine Weisenberg. Sir John served in Pontiac's War and was knighted in 1765, and inherited his father's Baronetcy on the latter's death. He married Mary, or "Polly," Watts, the daughter of a prominent family. An ardent Tory and member of the New York Provincial Assembly, he fled from his Tryon County, New York, home in early 1776 to avoid imprisonment by Continental authorities and local Whigs. After arriving in Canada, he was commissioned a lieutenant colonel of Provincial forces and authorized to raise the King's Royal Regiment of New York, the "Royal Yorkers." In 1782 he replaced Guy Johnson as Superintendent of Indian Affairs.

Guy Johnson (1740–1788)

Guy was Sir William Johnson's nephew as well as his son-in-law by virtue of marrying Sir William's daughter Mary. He was picked to succeed Sir William as Superintendent of Indian Affairs in the Northern Department upon his uncle and mentor's death. After leaving Tryon County to avoid capture by local Whigs, he established the Indian Department in Canada, but immediately came into conflict with Governor-General Carleton over his authority and method of employing Indian warriors. After traveling to England to strengthen his political clout, he returned to North America, but was content to direct his department from British headquarters in New York until 1779. He returned to Canada in the summer of 1779, and directed his department from Fort Niagara.

Joseph Brant, or Thayendanegea (1743–1807)

A member of the Wolf Clan of the Mohawk, Brant was a veteran of the French and Indian and Pontiac's Wars. As he was the younger brother of Sir William Johnson's Mohawk wife, Molly, the Indian Superintendent took an interest in Joseph and became his mentor. After receiving an English education at Eleazar Wheelock's (later known as Moor's) Indian School, the predecessor of Dartmouth College, Brant became a valuable member of the Indian Department, first as a translator and rising to the post of secretary with the military rank of captain by the Revolutionary War. Although not a sachem, he acquired a reputation for military skill and bravery that earned him a reputation as a chief warrior among the Iroquois. Together with his captaincy in the Indian Department, he was considered one of the most influential Indian leaders on the British side.

Mary, or "Molly," Brant, or Koñwatsi'tsiaiéñni (1736–1796)

An Indian woman reputed to have married Sir William Johnson, his third wife, according to Mohawk rites, although some described the marriage as "common law," bearing him eight children. After Sir William's death, she returned to the Mohawk settlement of Canajoharie. In 1777, when the message to her brother resulted in the ambush of American militia at Oriskany, Molly fled to British protection, and was housed on Carleton Island. As a tribal matron, she had considerable influence within the Iroquois Confederacy, and was instrumental in gaining and maintaining their support for Great Britain during American Revolution. Following the Treaty of Paris in 1783, she joined many Iroquois relocating in Canada.

Christian Daniel Claus (1727–1787)

Married to Sir William Johnson's daughter Ann, Claus was a protégé of the Indian Superintendent. Appointed the Deputy Superintendent for the Seven Nations of Canada after the fall of New France in the French and Indian War, he was displaced when Governor-General Carleton appointed a Superintendent for Canadian Indians on his own authority in a dispute with Guy Johnson. After the battle of Oriskany, he served as the Deputy Superintendent for the Caughnawaga, or "French Mohawks."

John Butler (1728–1796)

Loyalist leader in Tryon County, New York, John Butler served as William Johnson's second in command during the capture of Fort Niagara in the French and Indian War. He rose to the rank of lieutenant colonel, and second in command, in Guy Johnson's pre-war militia regiment. Butler also served in the Indian Department with the rank of lieutenant colonel as the Deputy Superintendent for the Six Nations under Guy Johnson. He fled his home with his son Walter, Guy Johnson, and Daniel Claus in 1775 when Patriot sentiment became dominant in Tryon County. He assumed the duties of acting superintendent during Johnson's long absence, answering to the direction of Governor-General Carleton. He received a commission as a major of Provincial forces and authorization to raise a battalion of rangers while continuing to serve as Indian Superintendent with department rank of lieutenant colonel. In 1780 he was promoted in Provincial service to the equal rank when the ranger battalion reached its full complement. He was active in the establishment of the Tory settlement around Niagara after the war, and served as the Commissioner of Indian Affairs from 1784 until his death in 1796. He married Catherine Bradt, daughter of a prominent Loyalist family, who spent much of the war under house arrest and unable to join her husband, after he left her in Tryon County in 1775.

Walter Butler (1752–1781)

Loyalist leader Walter Butler was the son of John Butler. After fleeing Tryon County with his father in 1775, he secured a commission in the 8th King's Regiment of Foot. After the battle of Oriskany, he volunteered for service in Butler's Rangers, and was captured while leading a mission appealing to Loyalists of the Mohawk Valley to join the rangers or Sir John Johnson's regiment. Although he was sentenced to hang, the punishment was commuted to imprisonment. The "young Butler" escaped in 1778. He led the rangers in the attack on Cherry Valley in November 1778, was present at Newtown and Groveland in 1779, and was killed in the battle of Battle of Jerseyfield, also called West Canada Creek, in October 1781.

Sir Henry Clinton (1730–1795)

Sir Henry Clinton, along with Sir William Howe and John Burgoyne, was one of the three major generals who arrived in Boston in May 1775. He was a veteran of the Seven Years War in Europe. After promotion to the local rank of lieutenant general, he served as second in command to Sir William Howe when the latter ascended to the post of commander in chief for North America. He received a knighthood and promotion to lieutenant general in the regular establishment before replacing Howe on the latter's resignation in 1778. He remained commander in chief of British forces in North America until 1782. A distant cousin of George and James Clinton of the U.S. Army, he was the son of a career naval officer and onetime Royal Governor of New York, also named George Clinton.

Guy Carleton (1724–1808)

As a major general, he was appointed Governor of Quebec, and subordinate to General Thomas Gage in military matters until Sir William How was named Commander in Chief of British Forces in North America in October 1775, when Commander in Chief of British forces of Canada became an independent command. He served until June 1778 when he was replaced as Governor-General of Canada by Frederick Haldimand. Carleton was appointed Commander in Chief in North America, replacing Sir Henry Clinton, in February 1782, and oversaw the evacuation of New York City in November 1783.

Sir Frederick Haldimand (1718–1791)

As a major general, he served as second in command of British forces in North America to General Thomas Gage from 1773 to 1775. After some time serving as an observer and advisor on the war in America to Lord George Germain, he was promoted to lieutenant general, and in June 1778, and appointed to succeed General Guy Carleton as Royal Governor of Quebec and Commander in Chief of British forces in Canada, until 1784. Returning to England, he was knighted in that year.

Henry Hamilton (1734?–1796)

A veteran of the French and Indian War, he served with the rank of lieutenant colonel as commandant of Fort Detroit and lieutenant governor of Canada. Known as the "hair buyer" by the Americans for allegedly paying allied warriors for enemy scalps, he supervised Indian Department officers Alexander McKee and Simon Girty in encouraging and supporting the Indians of the "Old Northwest" to attack American border settlements. He surrendered to George Rogers Clark at Vincennes in 1779, and was taken to Williamsburg in irons as a prisoner for inciting the Indians. After the war, he returned to his post as lieutenant governor of Canada, and was later appointed the royal governor of Bermuda and Dominica.

AMERICAN INDIANS

Note: there are numerous variations of the spellings of Indian names.

Sayenquerachta, or Old Smoke, or Old King (c. 1700-1786)

A Seneca chief warrior, he was a veteran of the French and Indian War, and was considered the primary war chief of the Six Nations of Iroquois during the Revolutionary War. Although at an advanced age, he took part in the battle of Oriskany in 1777 and the attack on Wyoming in 1778.

Garganwahgah, or Cornplanter (1732-1836)

A veteran of the French and Indian War, he was also a leading warrior of the Seneca, and was considered the second in command of the forces of the Six Nations of Iroquois during the Revolutionary War. He came to support the United States after the Revolution, and was instrumental in bringing New York and Pennsylvania Iroquois into the War of 1812 on the American side.

Kayashuta (1725-1794)

A veteran of the French and Indian War, he was a Seneca war chief, as well as a diplomat to the Ohio Indians on behalf of the Six Nations, and spoke for the Mingo at the Council Fire at Onondaga. He attended numerous councils with both deputies of the British Indian Department and the Continental Board of Commissioners for Indian Affairs, and led war parties against American border settlements.

Keigh-tugh-qua, or Cornstalk (1720-1777)

A veteran of the French and Indian War, on the side of the French, and Pontiac's War, Cornstalk led his people against the Virginia colonial army during Dunmore's War, and negotiated the Treaty of Camp Charlotte that ended it. He and his people remained neutral in the Revolutionary War until 1777, when they agreed to join the British side. When Indians killed a militiaman while the chief was visiting the Continental officers at Fort Randolph to inform them of his tribe's decision to go to war, the man's friends blamed the deed on Cornstalk, and murdered him.

PATRIOTS

Daniel Brodhead (1736–1809)

He began the war as the Deputy Surveyor General of Pennsylvania, a post held since 1773, before being commissioned a lieutenant colonel in the 2nd Pennsylvania Rifle Battalion of the Continental Line in 1776. He rose to the rank of colonel, and took command of the 8th Pennsylvania Regiment in 1777. After being ordered to Pittsburgh with his regiment in 1778, he eventually assumed command of the Army's Western Department in 1779. He remained in command of the department, and was brevetted to the rank of brigadier general by the end of the war. After the war he returned to the post of Surveyor General of the state, holding it for eleven years.

William Butler (?–1789)

A veteran of Pontiac's War, he was one of four brothers who served as officers in the Continental Army, and rose to the rank of lieutenant colonel commandant. He commanded the 4th Pennsylvania Regiment in the 1778 defense of Schoharie, the attack on Unadilla and Onaquaga, and the 1779 Sullivan's expedition.

Zebulon Butler (1731–1795)

A veteran of the French and Indian War, he was one of the leading settlers in the establishment of the Connecticut community in the Wyoming Valley, and during the resulting dispute with Pennsylvania authorities called the Yankee-Pennamite War. At the beginning of the Revolutionary War he served as a colonel of Connecticut militia until he received a commission as a lieutenant colonel in the Continental Army in 1777. Home on furlough, he commanded the American forces in what became known as the Wyoming massacre in 1778. He returned to the valley to command the garrison, remained at that location during the Sullivan expedition, and was later reassigned to the Main Army.

George Clinton (1739–1812)

A brigadier general in the Continental Army, George Clinton served as a delegate to the Second Continental Congress, and was elected as the first governor of New York in 1777 following adoption of that state's constitution. After serving six terms as governor, Clinton served as vice president to Thomas Jefferson (1804-1809) and James Madison (1809-1812), until his death in office.

James Clinton (1733–1812)

The brother of Governor George Clinton, he was also a veteran of the French and Indian War, served as a delegate to the Provincial Congress in 1775, and was an officer in the Continental Army. He served in the Sullivan expedition of 1779 in the rank of brigadier general, and commanded a brigade.

Edward Hand (1744–1802)

A physician by profession, he came to America as the surgeon's mate of a British regiment stationed on the frontier in 1767. After ascending to an ensign's commission, he resigned in 1774 to practice medicine in Philadelphia. Commissioned as a lieutenant colonel in the Continental Army from Pennsylvania in 1775, he was promoted to colonel in 1776, and brigadier general in 1777, with the assignment as commander of the Army's Western Department. The following year he was reassigned to command the Army's Northern Department, and commanded a provisional brigade on the Indian Expedition of 1779. The following year he assumed command of a new brigade of light infantry, and was brevetted to major general before the end of the conflict. He resumed his medical practice after the war.

Philip John Schuyler (1733–1804)

A veteran of the French and Indian War, as the scion of an old aristocratic Dutch family, he entered both politics and the Patriot movement early. He served in the Second Continental Congress, and was among the first of the major generals appointed in the Continental Army in 1775, and assumed command of the army's Northern Department. He was a gifted strategist, tactician, and logistician, but had a number of political foes who blamed him for the British capture of Fort Ticonderoga as a pretext for removal, but a court martial cleared his reputation in 1778. Although he did not hold an official position from 1777 on, he continued to serve as an advisor on military matters to General George Washington and Governor George Clinton, and was active on the Board of Commissioners for Indian Affairs through the end of the Iroquois Campaign of 1779. He returned to a seat in Congress, continuing a life of public service.

John Sullivan (1740–1795)

An attorney by profession, he served in the pre-war New Hampshire militia, and was a delegate to the First and Second Continental Congress. In May 1775, he was appointed as a brigadier general in the Continental Army. Captured at the battle of Long Island in 1776, he was exchanged, and eventually promoted to major general and given command of a division. Although described as having courage and a sense of organization, he was not a particularly gifted tactician. He was placed in command of the attempt to capture Newport from the British in 1778, where his lack of success was attributed to poor coordination with the French more than any tactical errors. The following year, he was entrusted to command the expedition against the Iroquois, one of the Continental Army's largest independent operations in the entire conflict. He resigned from the army in November 1779. He returned to the Continental Congress, and later served in state government, completing his public service as a judge.

George Washington (1732–1799)

A veteran of the French and Indian War, he served in the Virginia House of Burgesses and as a delegate to both the First and Second Continental Congress before he was appointed commander in chief of the Continental Army in June 1775. He served in that capacity until the war was over and the last British forces evacuated New York City in 1783, after which he resigned his commission to Congress, which was then meeting in Annapolis, Maryland. Although technically holding the rank of a major general, other officers in the Continental Army usually referred to him as "the General." In 1789 the newly formed Electoral College unanimously elected him the first President of the United States. He served two terms until 1797.

Chronology

1773

March 18	Virginia House of Burgesses suggests a committee of correspondence
May 10	Parliament passes the Tea Act
December 16	Boston Tea Party

1774

January	General Assembly of Connecticut formally annexes Wyoming
January 27	Virginia troops occupy Fort Pitt and rename it Fort Dunmore
March 31	Parliament passes the Coercive Acts
May 12	General Thomas Gage arrives in Boston to be royal governor; dissolves the colony's representative assembly; the Massachusetts General Court continues to meet illegally
	Virginia House of Burgesses grants Governor Dunmore funds to prosecute "Dunmore's War" against Indians on the Ohio River
May 20	Parliament Passes the Quebec Act
May 24	Virginia Burgesses call for a "Day of Fasting, Humiliation and Prayer" in support of the Massachusetts Bay colony
May 26	Dunmore dissolves the House of Burgesses
June 1	Britain closes the port of Boston
June 17	Massachusetts Whigs call for a Continental Congress
July 10	Governor Dunmore departs on a military expedition for the Ohio Valley
July 12	Sir William Johnson, Superintendent of Indian Affairs, dies during an Indian council
August 1-6	First Virginia Convention meets in Williamsburg
September 5	First Continental Congress convenes
October 10	Battle of Point Pleasant, Dunmore's War
October 17	Dunmore's War ends with Treaty of Camp Charlotte
October 18	Continental Association formed
October 26	First Continental Congress adjourns

1775

March 23	Second Virginia Convention meets in Richmond, resolves to raise an independent militia
April 3	Loyalist-dominated New York Assembly meets for the last time
April 19	Battles of Lexington and Concord
April 20	Whig-dominated New York Provincial Convention meets
May 10	Second Continental Congress convenes
	New England Rebels capture Ticonderoga
June 1	Virginia House of Burgesses convenes
June 8	Lord Dunmore seeks refuge aboard HMS Fowey
June 14	Congress creates the Continental Army
June 15	Congress appoints George Washington commander in chief
June 17	Battle of Bunker Hill
July 5	Congress sends the Olive Branch Petition to the King
August 23	King George III proclaims the American colonies in rebellion
August 28	American invasion of Canada begins
October 10	Sir William Howe replaces Gage as British commander in chief
October 19	Continental Commissioners and Indian leaders meet at Fort Pitt
November 7	Lord Dunmore proclaims martial law in Virginia and offers freedom to slaves who fight the rebellion

December 22	Parliament passes Prohibitory Act on trade and declares the colonies beyond the protection of the Crown

1776

March 17	British evacuate Boston
June 2	Virginia Convention passes Declaration of Rights and new Constitution
June 7	American forces retreating from Canada defeated at Trois Rivières
June 19	New Pennsylvania Conference overthrows old government
June 24	Congress declares Loyalist property may be confiscated
July 2	Howe's British army lands at Staten Island
July 4	Continental Congress declares Independence
August 27	Battle of Long Island
September 15	British occupy New York City
September 16	Battle of Harlem Heights
October 11	Battle of Valcour Island on Lake Champlain
October 28	Battle of White Plains
November 18	Capture of Fort Washington
December 8	British occupy Rhode Island
December 26	Battle of Trenton

1777

January 3	Battle of Princeton
April 20	New York Provincial Convention adopts a constitution
June 23	John Burgoyne begins invasion of New York from Canada
July 6	Burgoyne captures Fort Ticonderoga
July 7	Battle of Hubbardton
July 9	George Clinton declared the first governor of New York
July 23	Sir William Howe begins campaign to capture Philadelphia
August 6	Battle of Oriskany
August 16	Battle of Bennington
September 1	Attack on Wheeling and Fort Henry
September 11	Battle of Brandywine
September 19	Battle of Freeman's Farm
September 20	Paoli Massacre
September 26	British occupy Philadelphia
September 30	Continental Congress convenes in York, Pennsylvania
October 4	Battle of Germantown
October 6	Henry Clinton's forces take Forts Montgomery and Clinton in the Hudson Highlands
October 7	Battle of Bemis Heights
October 17	Burgoyne surrenders at Saratoga
November 15	Congress adopts Articles of Confederation and submits to states
December 5	Battle of Whitemarsh
December 19	American Main Army encamps at Valley Forge

1778

February	Hand's "Squaw Campaign" on the Ohio
February 5	France and United States sign treaty of amity and military alliance
May 8	Henry Clinton replaces Howe as British commander in chief
May 30	Joseph Brant destroys Cobleskill
June 18	British evacuate Philadelphia
	Joseph Brant destroys Springfield (New York)

June 19	Joseph Brant destroys Andrustown
June 28	Battle of Monmouth
July 3	John Butler's Rangers and Indians destroy Wyoming Valley
July 4	George Rogers Clark captures Kaskaskia
August 29	Battle of Rhode Island
September 17	Brant's and Butler's forces destroy German Flats
September 21– October 5	Thomas Hartley leads expedition against Queen Esther's Town and Tioga
October 2	William Butler leads expedition against Unadilla and Onaquaga
November 4	Lachlan McIntosh leads expedition from Pittsburgh to attack the Sandusky towns; halts on the banks of the Tuscarawas River to build Fort McIntosh
November 11	Brant's and Butler's forces destroy Cherry Valley
December 29	British capture Savannah

1779

January 29	British capture Augusta, Georgia
February 25	George Rogers Clark captures Vincennes
April 12	Franco-Spanish treaty brings Spain into war
April 21	Goose Van Schaick attacks Onondaga
July 15	Battle of Stony Point
July 22	Joseph Brant attacks Minisink
July 31	Sullivan's expedition marches from Wyoming
August 9	James Clinton's brigade marches from Otsego Lake to join Sullivan's army at Tioga
August 11	Sullivan's army reaches Tioga
	Daniel Brodhead's expedition marches from Pittsburgh
August 13	Sullivan's army attacks and destroys Chemung
August 22	Clinton's brigade join's Sullivan's army at Tioga
August 26	Sullivan-Clinton army marches from Tioga
August 29	Battle of Newtown
September 13	Groveland ambuscade
September 14	Sullivan-Clinton army reaches Genesee
September 16	Brodhead returns to Pittsburgh
September 30	Sullivan-Clinton army returns to Tioga
October 25	British evacuate Rhode Island

1780

April 2	Brant raids Harpersfield
April 24	Second raid of Cherry Valley
May 12	British capture Charleston, South Carolina
May 22	Brant raids Caughnawaga
June 23	Battle of Springfield (New Jersey)
	Sir John Johnson raids Johnstown
July 10	French army lands at Newport, Rhode Island
August 1	Brant raids Canajoharie
August 16	Battle of Camden
October 7	Battle of King's Mountain
October 15-19	Sir John Johnson raids Schoharie, Canajoharie, and Stone Arabia
October 19	Battle of Klock's Field

1781

January 17	Battle of Cowpens
March 1	Congress ratifies Articles of Confederation
March 15	Battle of Guilford Courthouse

April 25	Battle of Hobkirk's Hill (or Second Battle of Camden)
May 9	Spanish forces take Pensacola
May 22-June 5-	Americans recapture Augusta, Georgia
May 22-June 19-	Siege of Ninety-Six
July 6	Battle of Greenspring
July 9	John Doxtader raids Currytown
July 10	Battle of Sharon Springs Swamp
August 22	Battle of Wawarsing
September 5-7	Battle of the Chesapeake Capes
September 8	Battle of Eutaw Springs
	Benedict Arnold burns New London
September 28- October 19	Siege of Yorktown
October 19	Cornwallis surrenders at Yorktown
October 25	Battle of Johnstown
October 30	Battle of Jerseyfield/ West Canada Creek

1782

July 4	Battle of Sandusky/Crawford's Defeat
July 11	British evacuate Savannah
August 14	Indians raid Hannah's Town
August 15	Battle of Bryan's Station
August 19	Battle of Blue Licks
September 11-13	Second Siege of Fort Henry/Wheeling
December 14	British evacuate Charleston

1783

April 19	Congress proclaims the end of the war
September 3	Treaty of Paris signed
November 23	Congress disbands the Continental Army
November 25	British evacuate New York City
December 23	Washington resigns his commission

Orders of Battle

ORISKANY (AUGUST 6, 1777)

American Forces

Tryon County (New York) Militia Brigade
Brig. Gen. Nicholas Herkimer
        Oneida War Party—Hanyerry (or Hanyost Thaosagwat)
        First or Canojoharie District, Battalion—Col. Ebenezer Cox
        Second, or Palatine District, Battalion—Col. Jacob Klock
        Third, or Mohawk Valley District, Battalion—Col. Frederick Visscher
        Fourth, or Kingsland-German Flats District, Battalion—Col. Peter Bellinger

British Forces (Tory and Indians)

Lt. Col. Commandant Sir John Johnson
        Light Infantry Company—Capt. Stephen Watts
        Lieutenant Colonel's Company—Capt.-Lt. John McDonell
        Loyalist Volunteers and Mohawk Warriors—Capt. Joseph Brant
        Iroquois War Party (mostly Seneca)—Sayenqueraghta
        Detachment of King's Royal Regiment of New York (KRRNY)
        Detachment of Indian Department Rangers—Lt. Col. John Butler

IROQUOIS CAMPAIGN OF 1779

American Forces

I. Northern Department (Van Schaick Expedition, April 1779)

Brigadier General James Clinton
Provisional Battalion—Colonel Goose (or Gosen) Van Schaick
        Detachment (one company), (Morgan's) Rifle Corps
        Detachment (three companies), 1st New York Regiment
        Detachment (one company), 3rd New York Regiment
        Detachment (one company), 4th New York Regiment
        Detachment (one company), 5th New York Regiment
        Detachment (one company), 4th Pennsylvania Regiment
        Detachment (one company), 6th Massachusetts Regiment
Reconnaissance in Force/Diversion against Fort Oswego
Lieutenant Thomas McClellan
        Oneida-Tuscarora War Party
        Detachment from 3rd New York Regiment

II. Western Army (Sullivan-Clinton Expedition, August–September 1779)

Major General John Sullivan, Commander-in-Chief
        Stockbridge Indian Scouts—Captain Jehoiakim
        Oneida Indian Scouts—Hanyerry (or Hanyost Thaosagwat)
(Represents order of battle on departing Tioga, August 27, 1779)
First (New Jersey) Brigade
Brigadier General William Maxwell
        1st New Jersey Regiment—Col. Matthias Ogden
        2nd New Jersey Regiment—Col. Israel Shreve
        3rd New Jersey Regiment—Col. Elias Dayton
        5th New Jersey Regiment—Col. Oliver Spencer

Second (New Hampshire) Brigade

Brigadier General Enoch Poor

      1st New Hampshire Regiment—Col. Joseph Cilley

      2nd New Hampshire Regiment—Lt. Col. George Reid

      3rd New Hampshire Regiment—Lt. Col. Henry Dearborn

      6th ("Late Alden's") Massachusetts Regiment—Maj. Daniel Whiting

Third Brigade (Light Corps)

Brigadier General Edward Hand

      (Morgan's) Rifle Corps (two companies)—Maj. James Parr

      (Schott's) Independent Rifle Corps (two companies)—Capt. Anthony Selin

      Wyoming (Connecticut) Independent Company—Capt. Simon Spalding

      4th Pennsylvania Regiment—Lt. Col. William Butler

      11th Pennsylvania Regiment—Lt. Col. Adam Hubley

      "German" (8th Maryland) Regiment—Maj. Daniel Burkhardt

      Detachment, Wyoming Militia—Capt. John Franklin

Fourth (New York) Brigade

Brigadier General James Clinton

      2nd New York Regiment—Col. Philip Van Cortlandt

      3rd New York Regiment—Col. Peter Gansevoort

      4th ("Late Livingston's") New York Regiment—Lt. Col. Frederick Weissenfels

      5th New York Regiment—Col. Lewis Dubois

      Tryon County Volunteer Company—Capt. (Col.) John Harper

      1st New York Regiment (Fort Schuyler garrison)—Col. Gosen Van Schaick

Artillery

Chief of Artillery—Col. Thomas Proctor

      4th Continental (Proctor's) Continental Artillery

      Detachment (three companies) 2nd Continental (Lamb's) Artillery

III. Western Department (Brodhead's Expedition, August–September 1779)

Colonel Daniel Brodhead

      Delaware Scouts—War Chief Nanowland

      Rawlings' (Maryland) Independent Corps—Col. Moses Rawlings

      8th Pennsylvania Regiment—Lt. Col. Stephen Bayard

      13th Virginia Regiment—Col. John Gibson

      Independent Virginia Companies (two)

      Westmoreland County (Pennsylvania) Volunteer Ranging Companies (two)

      Detachments—Pennsylvania (Westmoreland County) Militia

      Detachments—Virginia (Augusta and Ohio Counties) Militia

British Forces (Tory and Indians)

(Battle of Newtown, August 28, 1779)

Sayenqueraghta and Major John Butler

      Butler's Rangers—Capt. Walter Butler

        Detachment of 8th "King's" Regiment of Foot

      Brant's Volunteers—Capt. Joseph Brant

      Six Nation's Warriors— Sayenqueraghta

      Delaware Warriors—Capt. Rowland Montour

Notes and References

Chapter 1

1. Smith, *An Account of the Remarkable Occurrences*, 94, 172.

2. Parker, *The Constitution of the Five Nations*.

3. Smith, *An Account of the Remarkable Occurrences*, 119.

4. Ibid., 161-162.

5. Ibid., 169-170.

6. Ibid., 17.

7. Sullivan, ed., *The Papers of Sir William Johnson* (hereafter *Johnson Papers*), 1: 60-61.

8. Return of Officers &c in the Department of Colonel Guy Johnson Superintendent of Indian Affairs, dated New York, October 4, 1776, Great Britain, Public Record Office, Headquarters Papers of the British Army in America, PRO 30/55/10209.

9. Henry Fox, Secretary of State for the Southern Department, to Sir William Johnson, Letter, Whitehall, March 13, 1756, in O'Callaghan, ed., *Documents Relative to the Colonial History of the State of New York* (hereafter *DCHNY*), 7: 76-77.

10. Proclamation of Instructions to Colonial Governors, October 7, 1763, O'Callaghan, *DCHNY*, 7: 478-479.

11. O'Callaghan, *DCHNY*, 8: 2, 35-36, 55-56.

12. O'Callaghan, *DCHNY*, 7: 224-244, 548-562.

Chapter 2

1. Aeneas Mackay to Arthur St. Clair, letter dated Pittsburgh, January 14, 1777, in Smith, ed., *The St. Clair Papers: The Life and Public Services of Arthur St. Clair*, 1: 271-273.

2. Ibid., 1: 10-11.

3. Siebert, *The Tories of the Upper Ohio*, 1.

4. Tryon County Committee of Safety, *The Minute Book of the Committee of Safety*, 1-4.

5. Unless otherwise stated, information on Dunmore's War is found in Reuben Gold Thwaites, and Louise Phelps Kellogg, eds., *Documentary History of Dunmore's War, 1774* and Virgil Lewis, *History of the Battle of Point Pleasant*.

6. Ibid.

7. Ibid.

8. Ford, ed., *Journals of the Continental Congress: Edited from the Original Manuscripts in the Library of Congress 1774-1789* (hereafter, *Jour. Cont. Cong.*), 2: 174, 175, 183, 251; and Kennedy, ed., *Journal of the Proceeding of the House of Burgesses of Virginia, 1773-1776*, from Session beginning June 1, 1775.

9. Lewis, *History of the Battle of Point Pleasant*, 57, 61.

10. *United States Statutes at Large*, 9: Section 1, 13-14.

11. Kennedy, *Journal of the Proceeding of the House of Burgesses of Virginia*, Session beginning June 1, 1775.

12. Abernathy, *Western Lands and the American Revolution*, 142, 167.

13. Ibid, 167.

14. Tryon County Committee of Safety, *Minute Book*, 1-4.

15. State of New York, *Calendar of Historical Manuscripts Relating to the War of the Revolution*, 1: 4.

16. Ibid, 1: 5.

17. Col. Guy Johnson, Journal, *DCHNY*, 8: 658.

18. Francis Parkman, "A List of the Different Nations and Tribes of Indians in the Northern District of North America, with the Number of their Fighting Men &c. In the Year 1778," Parkman Papers, MSS, Massachusetts Historical Society, volume 27, 454-455.

19. General Thomas Gage to Lord Dartmouth, letter, Boston, June 12, 1775, in Force, ed., *American Archives: A Collection of Authentick Records, State Papers, Debates, and Letters and other Notices of Publick Affairs: forming a Documentary History*, 4th series, 2: 967.

20. Lord Dartmouth to Guy Johnson, letter, Whitehall, July 24, 1775, *DCHNY*, 8: 596.

21. Stone, *Life of Joseph Brant-Thayendanega*, 1: 89.

22. Sir Guy Carleton to Lord Dartmouth, letter, Quebec, August 14, 1775, Canada Archives, State Papers, Q, (Ottawa), Volume 11, 222.

23. Joseph Brant to Lord George Germain, letter, London, May 7, 1776, *DCHNY*, 8: 678.

24. Siebert, *Tories of the Upper Ohio*, 2-3.

25. *Jour. Cont. Cong.*, 2: 174.

26. Records of the Albany Council, August 31, 1775, *DCHNY*, 8: 622.

27. *Jour. Cont. Cong.*, 2: 174.

28. Ibid, 2: 175, 183, 251.

29. *Jour. Cont. Cong.*, 12: 1125-1127; Siebert, *Tories of the Upper Ohio*, 3-4.

30. Col. Guy Johnson, Journal, *DCHNY*, 8: 658.

31. Johnson, Lieut. Colonel Commandant of the King's Royal Regiment of New York, Memorial to the Right Honorable the Lords Commissioners of the Treasury, Great Britain, Public Record Office, Treasury, class I, volume 547, folio 388.

32. General William Howe was formally appointed Commander in Chief of the British Army in the Thirteen Colonies in April 1776, while Major General Guy Carleton was named Commander in Chief in Canada.

33. Curtis, *The British Army in the American Revolution*, 68-69; General Guy Carleton to Sir Barrington, letter, dated Chambly, July 8, 1776, Great Britain, Public Record Office, War Office, class 1, volume 2, folio 315.

34. Force, *American Archives*, 5th series, 1: 36-37.

35. Records of the Albany Council, August 31, 1775, *DCHNY*, 8: 688-90

36. Ibid.

37. *Jour. Cont. Cong.*, 4: 394.

38. *Jour. Cont. Cong.*, 5: 452.

39. Conference with Indians at Fort Pitt, July 6, 1776, Force, *American Archives*, 5th series, 1: 36-37.

40. Stone, *Life of Joseph Brant–Thayendanega*, 2: 3.

41. Quoted in Harvey, *A History of Wilkes-Barre*, 2: 935.

42. Joseph Brant to Lord George Germain, letter dated London, May 7, 1776, *DCHNY*, 8: 678.

43. Cruikshank, *The Story of Butler's Rangers and the Settlement of Niagara*, 33-34.

44. Gov. Guy Carleton to Lt. Gov. Hamilton, letter dated Quebec, October 6, 1776, *Frederick Haldimand Papers*, BM 121: 3, Archives Canada copy.

Chapter 3

1. *Jour. Cont. Cong.*, 7: 21, 22.

2. Wright, Jr., *The Continental Army*, 290-291.

3. Abernethy, *Western Lands and the American Revolution*, 188.

4. *Jour. Cont. Cong.*, 8: 494.

5. Lord George Germaine to General Sir Guy Carleton, letter dated Whitehall, February 19, 1777, William L. Clements Library, University of Michigan, *Sir Henry Clinton Papers*, volume 26, item 32.

6. Lord George Germain to Gov. Guy Carleton, letter dated Whitehall, March 26, 1777, *Frederick Haldimand Papers*, BM 21: 698; Archives Canada copy.

7. Ibid.

8. Cruikshank, *Story of Butler's Rangers and the Settlement of Niagara*, 34.

9. Gov. Clinton to Committee of Safety of Schenectady, dated Poughkeepsie, June 18, 1778, in Hastings, ed., *Public Papers of George Clinton, First Governor of New York* (hereafter, *Clinton Papers*), 3: 467-468.

10. Col. Guy Johnson to Lord Germain, letter dated New York, June 8, 1777, *DCHNY*, 8: 711.

11. Lyman Draper, Draper Manuscripts, Series U, *Frontier War Papers*, (Unpublished manuscript in the State Historical Society of Wisconsin, Madison), 11: 196-197.

12. Cruikshank, *Story of Butler's Rangers and the Settlement of Niagara*, 37.

13. Daniel Claus, Esqr. late a Captain in the 60th Regimt. (& Appointed to Command a band of Indians the last Campaign), to Col. Guy Johnson, letter dated Montreal, November 12, 1777, *Sir Henry Clinton Papers*, volume 26, item 32.

14. Maj. Gen. Guy Carleton to Maj. John Butler, Beating Order, dated Quebec, September 15, 1777, *Register of Letters from Sir Guy Carleton to Various Persons, 1777-1778*, British Library, Sloane and Additional Manuscripts (Add MSS) 21700.

15. Remarks of the Beating Orders and Pay Lists for the Corps of Rangers, no date, Great Britain, Public Record Office, War Office, class 28, volume 4, p. 17.

16. Siebert, *The Tories of the Upper Ohio*, 5.

17. *Jour. Cont. Cong.*, 9: 942; and, Siebert, *The Tories of the Upper Ohio*, 5.

18. Thwaites and Kellogg, eds., *Frontier Defense of the Upper Ohio, 1777-1778*, x, 14, 21-24, 33-42, 46, 51-68, 70, 142.

19. *Jour. Cont. Cong.*, 9: 831.

20. Siebert, *Tories of the Upper Ohio*, 6

21. McKnight, *Our Western Border, Its Life, Forays, Scouts, Combats, Massacres, Red Chiefs, Adventures, Captivities, Pioneer Women, One Hundred Years Ago*, 516-517.

22. Ibid., 517.

23. Ibid., 519.

24. Ibid., 519-20.

25. Ibid., 520.

26 Ibid., 349-350.

27. Ibid., 520-21.

28. Return of a Corps of Rangers to Serve with the Indians Commanded by Major John Butler, dated Niagara, February 3, 1778, Great Britain, British Library, Additional MSS, 21,765, folio 15.

29. Hastings, ed., *Clinton Papers*, 3: 204.

30. Col. Daniel Claus to Col. Guy Johnson, letter dated Montreal, November 12, 1777, *Sir Henry Clinton Papers*, volume 26, item 32.

31. Col. Daniel Claus to Secretary William Knox, letter dated Montreal November 6, 1777, in O'Callaghan, ed., *DCHNY*, 8: 724.

32. Kercheval, *A History of the Ohio Valley of West Virginia*, 200.

33. *Jour. Cont. Cong.*, 9: 942-944.

34. *Jour. Cont. Cong.*, 7: 213, 252.

35. Maj. John Butler to Gen. Guy Carleton, letter dated Fort Niagara, February 2, 1778, *Frederick Haldimand Papers*, BM, Add. MSS 21, 756-1, 96: 117, Archives Canada copy.

36. Siebert, *Tories of the Upper Ohio*, 6.

37. George I. Denniston to Gov. George Clinton, letter dated Fort Schuyler, February 20, 1778, *Clinton Papers*, 2: 781-782. *Jour. Cont. Cong.* 4: 394.

38. Maj. John Butler to Gen. Guy Carleton, letter dated Fort Niagara, February 2, 1778. Although Washington was officially commissioned in the rank of lieutenant general by the Continental Congress, he was universally referred to as 'the General.' by his officers; *Jour. Cont. Cong.* 5: 452.

39. Ibid.

40. Ibid.

41. Return of the Corps of Rangers to serve with the Indians, and Maj. John Butler to Gov. Guy Carleton, letter dated Fort Niagara, February 2, 1778.

42. Col. George I. Denniston to Gov. George Clinton, letter dated Fort Schuyler, February 20, 1778, *Clinton Papers*, 2: 781-782.

Chapter 4

1. Gov. George Clinton to Maj. Gen. Marquis de Lafayette, letter dated Poughkeepsie, March 8, 1778, *Clinton Papers*, 3: 3-4.

2. Maj. John Butler to Gov. Guy Carleton, letter dated Fort Niagara, February 2, 1778, *Frederick Haldimand Papers*, BM 21, 756-1, 96: 117, Archives Canada copy.

3. Col. George Denniston to Gov. George Clinton, letter dated Fort Schuyler, April 2, 1778, *Clinton Papers*, 3:118.

4. Maj. John Butler to Gen. Guy Carleton, letter dated Fort Niagara, April 10, 1778, *Frederick Haldimand Papers*, BM 21, 756-1, 105: 27, Archives Canada copy.

5. Brig. Gen. Philip Schuyler to Gov. George Clinton, letter dated Albany, March 16, 1778, *Clinton Papers*, 3:44-45.

6. Col. John Williams to Gov. George Clinton, letter dated Albany, March 14, 1778, *Clinton Papers*, 3:39-40.

7. Benjamin Dickson to Gov. George Clinton, letter dated Albany, April 4, 1778, *Clinton Papers*, 3:126-127.

8. Peenpeck Mamacotten Committee of Safety to Gov. George Clinton, letter dated Mamacotten Precinct, April 19, 1778, *Clinton Papers*, 3:192-193.

9. Ibid., 3:193-194.

10. Inhabitants of the Northern Towns to Gov. George Clinton and reply, letter dated Poughkeepsie, April 24, 1778, *Clinton Papers*, 3:209-212.

11. Gov. George Clinton to Col. John Cantine, letter dated Poughkeepsie, May 1, 1778, *Clinton Papers*, 3:250.

12. Col. Jacob Klock to Gov. George Clinton, letter dated Palatine, May 1, 1778, *Clinton Papers*, 3:251.

13. James Dean to Maj. Gen. Philip Schuyler, letter dated Oneida, May 25, 1778, *Clinton Papers*, 3:358.

14. Charles Thompson, Secretary of the Board of War, to Brig. Gen. John Stark, letter dated In Congress, April 17, 1778, *Clinton Papers*, 3:178.

15. Maj. Gen. Horatio Gates to Brig. Gen. John Stark, dated York, April 17, 1778, *Clinton Papers*, 3:179.

16. Maj. Gen. John Stark to Capt. William Patrick, letter dated Albany, April 20, 1778, in Stark, ed., *Memoir and Official Correspondence of General John Stark, with notices of several other officers of the Revolution*, 142-143.

17. Lt. Col. Mason Bolton to Gen. Guy Carleton, letter dated Fort Niagara, April 8, 1778, *Frederick Haldimand Papers*, BM 21, 756-1, 96: 195, Archives Canada copy.

18. Pay List of Butler's Rangers December 24, 1777, to October 24, 1778, *Frederick Haldimand Papers*, BM 21,765, 105: 58-78, Archives Canada copy.

19. Maj. John Butler to Gen. Guy Carleton, letter dated Fort Niagara, April 10, 1778, *Frederick Haldimand Papers*, BM 21,756-1, 105: 27, Archives Canada copy.

20. Abraham Yates to Gov. George Clinton, letter dated Albany, April 21, 1778, *Clinton Papers*, 3:203-204.

21. Lt. Col. John Butler to Gov. Guy Carleton, May 15, 1778, Kanadasaga, *Frederick Haldimand Papers*, BM 21,765, 105: 39, copy from Archives Canada.

22. Brig. Gen. Abraham Ten Broeck to Gov. George Clinton, letter dated Albany, June 27, 1778, *Clinton Papers*, 3:504-506.

23. Lt. Col. John Butler to Gov. Guy Carleton, letter dated Kanadasaga, May 15, 1778, *Frederick Haldimand Papers*, BM 21,765, 105: 39, Archives Canada copy.

24. Ibid.

25. Maj. John Butler to Gen. Guy Carleton, letter dated Fort Niagara, April 10, 1778, *Frederick Haldimand Papers*, BM 21,756-1, 105: 39, Archives Canada copy.

26. Moses Van Campen, "An Inch of Ground to Fight On," in Drimmer, ed., *Captured by the Indians: Fifteen Firsthand Accounts, 1750-1870* ; reprinted from *Scalps and Tomahawks: Narratives of Indian Captivity*, 106.

27. Ibid., 106-107.

28. Rev. Samuel Kirkland to Maj. Gen. Philip Schuyler, letter dated May 4, 1778, *Jour. Cont. Cong.*, 11: 536.

29. Henry Laurens to John Houston, letter dated in Congress, June 1, 1778, in Smith, ed., *Letters of Delegates to Congress*, 10: 9.

30. James Dean to Maj. Gen. Philip Schuyler, letter dated Oneida, May 25, 1778, *Clinton Papers*, 3: 356-358.

31. Ibid.

32. Robert Benson to Col. Jacob Klock, letter dated Poughkeepsie, May 30, 1778, *Clinton Papers*, 3: 379-380.

33. Simms, *Frontiersmen of New York*, 153.

34. Ibid., 154-155

35. Simms, *Frontiersmen of New York*, 154.

36. Lt. Col. Christopher Yates to Col. Abraham Wemple, letter dated Schoharie, May 30, 1778, *Clinton Papers*, 3: 378.

37. Brig. Gen. John Stark to Maj. Gen. Horatio Gates, letter dated Albany, May 31, 1778, 3: 379-380.

38. Mayor John Barclay and Brig. Gen. Abraham Ten Broeck to Gov. George Clinton, letter dated Albany, May 31, 1778, *Clinton Papers*, 3: 380-381.

39. Col. Jacob Klock to Brig. Gen. Abraham Ten Broeck, letter dated Canajoharie, May 31, 1778, *Clinton Papers*, 3: 382.

40. Col. Abraham Wempel to Brig. Gen. Abraham Ten Broeck, letter dated Schoharie, June 2, 1778, *Clinton Papers*, 3: 383.

41. Return of Troops under the command of Coll. Wempell at Present at Schoharie, June 2, 1778, *Clinton Papers*, 3: 383.

42. Fernow, ed., *Documents Relating to the Colonial History of the State of New York*, 15: 30-34.

43. *Jour. Cont. Cong.*, 187-189.

44. Ibid.

45. Ibid.

46. Judge William Dietz to Brig. Gen. John Stark, letter dated Schoharie, May 30, 1778, *Clinton Papers*, 3: 377-378, 382.

47. Col. Jacob Klock to Brig. Gen. Ten Broeck, letter dated Caghnawage, June 6, 1778, *Clinton Papers*, 3: 414-416.

48. Mayor John Barclay to Gov. George Clinton, letter dated Albany, June 7, 1778, *Clinton Papers*, 3: 424-425.

49. Col. Jacob Klock to Gov. George Clinton, letter dated Canajoharie, June 22, 1778, *Clinton Papers*, 3: 475.

50. Robert Jones Disposition to Henry Wisner, Esq., at Menecinct, July 10, 1778, *Clinton Papers*, 3:542.

51. Gov. George Clinton to Mayor and Corporation of Albany, letter dated Poughkeepsie, June 2, 1778, *Clinton Papers*, 3: 387.

52. Brig. Gen. Abraham Ten Broeck to Gov. George Clinton, letter dated Albany, June 4, 1778, *Clinton Papers*, 3: 421-423.

53. Ibid.

54. Col. Abraham Wemple to Brig. Gen. Ten Broeck, letter dated Schoharie, June 6, 1778, *Clinton Papers*, 3: 413–414.

55. Col. Jacob Klock to Brig. Gen. Ten Broeck, letter dated Caghnawage, June 6, 1778 (11:00 A.M.), *Clinton Papers*, 3: 414-415.

56. Col. Jacob Klock to Gov. George Clinton, letter dated Palatine, Tryon County, June 5, 1778, 3: 402-404.

57. *Jour. Cont. Cong.*, 11: 589-590.

58. James Duane to Gov. George Clinton, letter dated Albany, June 6, 1778, *Clinton Papers*, 3: 418-419.

59. Gov. Clinton to Brig. Gen. Ten Broeck, letter dated Poughkeepsie, June 11, 1778, *Clinton Papers*, 3: 447-448.

60. Gov. Clinton to Brig. Gen. Starke, letter dated Poughkeepsie, June 11, 1778, *Clinton Papers*, 3: 448.

61. *Jour. Cont. Cong.*, 11: 589-90.

Chapter 5

1. Deposition of Robert Jones, dated Minisink, July 10, 1778, *Clinton Papers*, 3: 542.

2. Gov. Clinton to Committee of Safety of Schenectady, letter dated Poughkeepsie, June 18, 1778, *Clinton Papers*, 3: 467-468.

3. Colonel Jacob Klock to Governor George Clinton, letter dated Canajoharie, June 22, 1778, from Canajoharie, *Clinton Papers*, 3: 475.

4. Deposition of James Armitage to Abraham Ten Broeck, dated Albany, July 6, 1778, *Clinton Papers*, 3: 525-528.

5. Pay List of Butler's Rangers, December 24, 1777, to October 24, 1778, *Frederick Haldimand*

Papers, BM 21, 765, 105: 58-78, Archives Canada copy.

6. Lossing, *Pictorial Field Book of the Revolution*, 1:340.

7. The title "half king," or its translation, further reinforced the subordination of the Delaware sachem to those of the Iroquois Confederacy.

8. Unless otherwise cited, the descriptions of Wyoming Valley and the battle of July 1778 are drawn from several secondary sources, mainly Jewell, *A History of Wilkes-Barre, Luzerne County, Pennsylvania* and Miner, *History of Wyoming, in a Series of letters from Charles Miner, to his son William Penn Miner, Esq.*

9. *Colonial Records of Connecticut*, 15: 152.

10. *Jour. Cont. Cong.*, 3: 439-440.

11. *Colonial Records of Connecticut*, 15:197.

12. *Jour. Cont. Cong.*, 3: 452-453.

13. S. P. Meandor, S. P., "The First American Soldier," *Journal of American History*, Volume 1 (1907), 120.

14. The term "rank and file" in eighteenth- century usage described the "bayonet strength" of an infantry company: i.e., the corporals and privates, but excluding the company officers, sergeants, and musicians.

15. *Colonial Records of Connecticut*, 15: 12, 43.

16. Ibid., 15: 152.

17. Ibid., 15:197.

18. *Jour. Cont. Cong.*, 5: 698-699.

19. Ibid.: 914.

20. *Jour. Cont. Cong.*, 2: 406.

21. *Records of the State of Connecticut*, 1: 264-265.

22. Wintermute, or "Wintermoot."

23. Lossing, *The Pictorial Field-Book of the Revolution*, 1: 351.

24. Reynolds, *Report of the Commission to Locate the Site of the Frontier Forts of Pennsylvania*, 1: 438-439.

25. Ibid., 443.

26. The site is in what is now West Pittston Borough.

27. Reynolds, *Report of the Commission to Locate the Site of the Frontier Forts of Pennsylvania*, 1: 446-448.

28. Ibid., 449-450.

29. Ibid., 450-451.

30. Col. Nathan Dennison to Brig. Gen. Oliver Wolcott, Jr., letter dated Westmoreland, September 20, 1777, *Oliver Wolcott Jr. Papers*, (hereafter *Wolcott Papers*), 1: Folder 1.8, 29.

31. *Records of the State of Connecticut*, 2: 58.

32. *Jour. Cont. Cong.*, 10: 261-2.

33. *Susquehanna Settlers*, Mss, Series 2, 1771-1797, 1: 29

34. *Records of the State of Connecticut*, 2: 57.

Chapter 6

1. *Jour. Cont. Cong.*, 11: 634.

2. Gen. George Washington to the Board of War, letter dated Camp near Coryels, June 22, 1778, Fitzpatrick, ed., *The Writings of George Washington from the Original Manuscript Sources, 1745–1799* (hereafter *George Washington Papers*), Letter Book 3: 354.

3. *George Washington Papers*, Letter Book 3: 354-355.

4. *Jour. Cont. Cong.*, 11: 635-636.

5. Ibid., 634.

6. Unless otherwise stated, the descriptions of the July 3, 1778 battle are based largely on Zebulon Butler, "Correspondence of Col. Zebulon Butler, Wyoming, June–December, 1778." Proceedings of the Wyoming Historical and Geological Society, 7 (1902): 131-150; supplemented with Harvey, *A History of Wilkes-Barre, Luzerne County, Pennsylvania*, and Miner, *History of Wyoming, in a Series of letters from Charles Miner, to his son William Penn Miner, Esq.*

7. Maj. John Butler to Lt. Col. Mason Bolton, dated Lacuwanack (PA), July 8, 1778, *Frederick Haldimand Papers*, BL Add. MSS 21,760, folios 31-34, Archives Canada copy.

8. Ibid.

9. Richard, McGinnis, Journal, "Loyalty and Order Triumph over Confusion and Treason," in Commager and Morris, eds., *The Spirit of Seventy Six: The Story of the American Revolution as Told by Participants*, 1006.

10. Maj. John Butler to Lt. Col. Mason Bolton, letter dated Lacuwanack (PA), July 8, 1778, *Frederick Haldimand Papers*, Archives Canada copy.

11. McGinnis, Journal, 1006.

12. Maj. John Butler to Lt. Col. Mason Bolton, letter dated Lacuwanack (PA), July 8, 1778, *Frederick Haldimand Papers*, Archives Canada copy.

13. Col. John Butler to Lt. Elisha Scovell, letter dated Westmoreland, July 5, 1778, *Clinton Papers*, 3: 520-521.

14. McGinnis, Journal, 1006.

15. John Butler and Zebulon Butler were not relatives, although some accounts have incorrectly described them as being cousins.

16. Maj. John Butler to Lt. Col. Mason Bolton, letter dated Lacuwanack (PA), July 8, 1778, *Frederick Haldimand Papers*, Archives Canada copy.

17. Ibid.

18. McGinnis, Journal, 1007.

19. Quoted in Harvey, *A History of Wilkes-Barre*, 2: 1014.

20. Maj. John Butler to Lt. Col. Mason Bolton, letter dated Lacuwanack (PA), July 8, 1778.

21. Taken from *The Manual Exercise as Ordered by His Majesty in 1764 Including the Fundamentals of Marching and Maneuvering.* The most widely used manual by the prewar militia, and early war militia and Continentals. Although it is possible another manual was used, or Butler had ordered massed battalion volleys, I believe the "firings in the advance" was more likely employed.

22. McGinnis, Journal, 1007.

23. Quoted in Harvey, *A History of Wilkes-Barre*, 2: 1014.

24. Maj. John Butler to Lt. Col. Mason Bolton, dated Lacuwanack (PA), July 8, 1778, *Frederick Haldimand Papers*, Archives Canada copy.

25. McGinnis, Journal, 1007.

26. Ibid.

27. Maj. John Butler to Lt. Col. Mason Bolton, dated Lacuwanack (PA), July 8, 1778, *Frederick Haldimand Papers*, Archives Canada copy.

28. Crèvecoeur, *Sketches of Eighteenth-Century America*, 197–206, quoted in Henry Steele Commager and Richard B. Morris, eds., *The Spirit of Seventy Six: The Story of the American Revolution as Told by Participants*, 1007. Crèvecour, who lost his wife in an Indian raid on his home, was reporting what others told him; he was not an eyewitness.

29. Ibid., 1008-9.

30. There is some disagreement over whether this event actually occurred, or whether Queen Esther was present. The men of the Continental Army who kept journals recorded the story as they heard it from local inhabitants while waiting to conduct the punitive Indian expedition the following summer.

31. Crèvecoeur, *Sketches of Eighteenth-Century America*, 1009.

32. Ibid.

33. McGinnis, Journal, 1007.

34. Maj. John Butler to Lt. Col. Mason Bolton, dated Lacuwanack (PA), July 8, 1778, *Frederick Haldimand Papers*, Archives Canada copy.

Chapter 7

1. Maj. John Butler to Lt. Col. Mason Bolton, dated Lacuwanack (PA), July 8, 1778, *Frederick Haldimand Papers*, Archives Canada copy.

2. Cruikshank, *The Story of Butler's Rangers and the Settlement of Niagara*, 48.

3. Maj. John Butler to Lt. Col. Mason Bolton, dated Lacuwanack (PA), July 8, 1778, *Frederick Haldimand Papers*, Archives Canada copy.

4. *Frederick Haldimand Papers*, BM 21, 756-1, 96: 117, Archives Canada copy.

5. Cruikshank, *Story of Butler's Rangers and the Settlement of Niagara*, 50.

6. Richard McGinnis, Journal, "Loyalty and Order Triumph over Confusion and Treason," in Commager and Morris, eds., *The Spirit of Seventy Six*, 1007.

7. A List of Cattle taken from the Company of Lt. Elisha Scovell, dated Westmoreland, July 5, 1778, *Clinton Papers*), 3:521.

8. Richard McGinnis, Journal, "Loyalty and Order Triumph over Confusion and Treason," in Commager and Morris, eds., *The Spirit of Seventy Six*, 1007.

9. Maj. John Butler to Lt. Col. Mason Bolton, dated Lacuwanack (PA), July 8, 1778, *Frederick Haldimand Papers*, Archives Canada copy.

10. Ibid.

11. Cruikshank, *The Story of Butler's Rangers and the Settlement of Niagara*, 51

12. Citizens of Goshen to Gov. George Clinton, letter dated Goshen, July 5, 1778, *Clinton Papers*, 3: 522-523.

13. Gov. George Clinton reply, Poughkeepsie, July 6, 1778, *Clinton Papers*, 3: 523-525.

14. Captain Cuddeback's statement, Minisink, July 10, 1778, *Clinton Papers*, 3:541-542.

15. Pennsylvania Archives (hereafter PA), (Series 5), III, 308.

16. PA (Series 1), VI, 666.

17. PA (Series 5), III, 309.

18. PA (Series 5), III, 309, 737.

19. *Boston Gazette*, August 3, 1778, original edition in the collection of Alan Shields of Oliphant, Pennsylvania.

20. Roger Sherman to Gov. Jonathan Trumbull, Sr., letter dated Philadelphia, August 10, 1778, *Letters of Delegates to Congress*, 10: 799.

21. Gen. George Washington to Judge John Cleve Symmes, letter dated Paramus, July 10, 1778 *Writings of George Washington*, 12: 332

22. Brig. Gen. Abraham Ten Broeck to Gov. George Clinton, letter dated Albany, July 11, 1778, *Clinton Papers*, 3: 536-537.

23. Gov. George Clinton to Col. Levi Pawling, and to be forwarded to Col. Cantine, letter dated Poughkeepsie, July 11, 1778, *Clinton Papers*, 3: 538-539.

24. Col. Peter Gansevoort to Maj. Gen. Philip Schuyler, letter dated Fort Schuyler, July 10, 1778, Gansevoort Military Papers, IV, NYPL.

25. Col. Gansevoort to Gov. Clinton, letter dated Fort Schuyler, August 12, 1778, *Clinton Papers*, 3: 24-25; and Col. Gansevoort to Gen. Washington, August 18, 1778, *George Washington Papers*.

26. Gov. George Clinton to Col. Levy Pawling, and to be forwarded to Col. Cantine, letter dated Poughkeepsie, July 11, 1778, *Clinton Papers*, 3: 538-539.

27. Brig. Gen. Abraham Ten Broeck to Gov. George Clinton, letter dated Albany, June 20, 1778; and, Col. Jacob Klock to Gov. George Clinton, letter dated Canajoharie, June 22, 1778, *Clinton Papers*, 3: 473-474, 475-476.

28. Lt. Col. Jacob Ford to Brig. Gen. Abraham Ten Broeck, letter dated Cherry Valley, July 18, 1778, *Clinton Papers*, 3: 555-557.

29. Brig. Gen. Abraham Ten Broeck to Gov. George Clinton, letter dated Albany, June 20, 1778; and, Col. Jacob Klock to Gov. George Clinton, letter dated Canajoharie, June 22, 2778, *Clinton Papers*, 3: 473-474, 475-476.

30. Col. Jacob Klock to Gov. George Clinton, letter, June 22, 1778 from Canajoharie, *Clinton Papers*, 3: 475.

31. Lt. Col. Jacob Ford to Brig. Gen. Abraham Ten Broeck, letter dated Cherry Valley, July 18, 1778, *Clinton Papers*, 3: 555-557.

32. Lt. Col. Jacob Ford to Col. Jacob Klock, letter dated Cherry Valley, July 19, 1778, *Clinton Papers*, 3: 563-564.

33. Lt. Col. Jacob Ford to Brig. Gen. Abraham Ten Broeck, letter dated Cherry Valley, July 18, 1778, *Clinton Papers*, 3: 555-557.

34. Lt. Col. Jacob Ford to Brig. Gen. Abraham Ten Broeck, letter dated Cherry Valley, July 19, 1778, *Clinton Papers*, 3: 558.

35. Brig. Gen. Abraham Ten Broeck to Gov. George Clinton, letter dated Albany, July 19, 1778, *Clinton Papers*, 3: 558.

36. *Clinton Papers*, 3:563-564.

37. Col. Jacob Klock to Brig. Gen. Ten Broeck, dated Palatine, Tryon County, July 19, 1778, *Clinton Papers*, 3: 559.

38. Brig. Gen. Philip Schuyler to Gov. George Clinton, letter dated Albany, July 20, 1778, *Clinton Papers*, 3: 565.

39. Gov. George Clinton to Gen. George Washington, letter dated Poughkeepsie, July 21, 1778, *Clinton Papers*, 3: 570-571.

40. Gen. George Washington to Congress, letter dated Haverstraw, July 18, 1778, *Writings of George Washington*, 12: 214.

41. Gen. George Washington to Brig. Gen. John Stark, letter dated Haverstraw, July 18, 1778, *Writings of George Washington*, 12: 190.

42. Gov. George Clinton to Brig. Gen. Philip Schuyler, letter dated Poughkeepsie, July 21, 1778, *Clinton Papers*, 3: 565-566. Clinton to Schuyler, not Washington—just confirming it's the right source

43. Gov. George Clinton to Gen. Washington, letter dated Poughkeepsie, July 21, 1778, *Clinton Papers*, 3: 570-571.

44. Gov. George Clinton to Brig. Gen. Ten Broeck, letter dated Poughkeepsie, July 21, 1778, *Clinton Papers*, 3: 573-574.

45. Militia officers and Committee of Safety of German Flats to Gov. Clinton, dated German Flats, July 22, 1778, *Clinton Papers*, 3: 581-583.

46. Col. Peter Vrooman to Brig. Gen. Abraham Ten Broeck, letter dated Schoharie, July 24, 1778, *Clinton Papers*, 3: 583-584.

47. Maj. Joseph Baker to Brig. Gen. Abraham Ten Broeck, letter dated Schoharie, July 29, 1778, *Clinton Papers*, 3: 594-595.

48. Col. Peter Livingston to Gov. George Clinton, letter dated Manor Livingston, July 28, 1778, *Clinton Papers*, 3: 591-592.

49. Return of the Detachment of Rifle Men Under the Command of Capt. Commandant Thomas Posey, dated Albany, July 28, 1778, *Clinton Papers*, 3: 588; Return of the State of the 4th Pennsylv'a Regim't Commanded by Wm. Butler Esqr. Lieut't Colonel, dated Albany, July 28, 1778, *Clinton Papers*, 3: 589.

50. Lt. Col. William Butler to Gov. George Clinton, letter dated Albany, July 29, 1778, *Clinton Papers*, 3: 595-596.

51. Ibid.

52. Brig. Gen. Abraham Ten Broeck to Gov. George Clinton, letter dated Albany, August 1, 1778, *Clinton Papers*, 3: 599-600.

53. Lt. Col. William Butler to Gov. George Clinton, letter dated Schoharie, August 13, 1778, *Clinton Papers*, 3: 630-632.

54. Ibid.

55. Ibid.

56. Col. William Butler to Gov. Clinton, letter dated Schoharie, Aug 31, 1778, *Clinton Papers*, 3: 710-712.

57. Col. William Butler to Gov. Clinton, letter dated, Albany, Sept 1, 1778, *Clinton Papers*, 4: 104.

58. Gen. George Washington to Brig. Gen. John Stark, letter dated Fishkill, October 8, 1778, *George Washington Papers*, Series 3, Subseries 3, Letter Book 2, 306.

Chapter 8

1. Lt. Col. Berent Staats to Brig. Gen. Ten Broeck, letter dated Cherry Valley, September 9, 1778, *Clinton Papers*, 4: 15-16.

2. Unless otherwise stated, the information on the German Flats raid is based on the following letters found in *Clinton Papers*: Col. Jacob Klock to Col. Frederick Fisher, letter dated Palatine, September 16, 1778, 4: 39; Col. Klock to Gov. George Clinton, letter dated German Flats, September 17, 1778, 4: 47; Col. Peter Bellinger to Gov. Clinton, letter dated German Flats, September 19, 1778, 4: 47-50; Col. Klock to Col. Fisher, letter dated Palatine, September 16, 1778, 4: 39; Brig. Gen. Abraham Ten Broeck to Gov. Clinton, letter dated Albany, September 18, 1778, 4:53-54; Gov. Clinton to Brig. Gen. Ten Broeck, letter dated Poughkeepsie, September 20, 1778, 4:54-55; Gov. Clinton to Gen. George Washington, letter dated Poughkeepsie, September 24, 1778, 4: 78-79; Brig. Gen. Ten Broeck to Gov. Clinton, letter dated Albany, September 24, 1778, 4: 79-81; Col. Abraham Wemple to Brig. Gen. Ten Broeck, letter dated Caughnewaga, September 20, 1778, 4: 82-83.

3. Capt. Caldwell to Maj. Butler, letter dated September 21, 1778, Archives Canada, B105, p. 56.

4. Colonel Jacob Klock to Gov. George Clinton, letter dated German Flats, September 17, 1778, Volckert P. Douw to Gov. George Clinton, letter dated German Flats, September 17, 1778, *Clinton Papers*, 4: 47.

5. Capt. Caldwell to Maj. Butler, letter dated September 21, 1778, PAC, B105, p. 56; and Volckert P. Douw to Gov. George Clinton, *Clinton Papers* 4: 130-133;

6. Gen. George Washington to Brig. Gen. John Stark, letter dated Fishkill, October 8, 1778, *Washington Papers*, Letter Book 2, 306; and Gen. George Washington to Gov. George Clinton, letter dated Fredericksburg (N.Y.), October 16, 1778, *Writings of George Washington*, 13: 87-88.

7. Gov. Clinton to Brig. Gen. Ten Broeck, letter dated Poughkeepsie, September 20, 1778, *Clinton Papers*, 4: 54-55.

8. Gen. George Washington to Gov. George Clinton, letter dated, Head Quarters, Fredericksburg, October 19, 1778, *Writings of George Washington*, 13: 108-109.

9. Col. Thomas Hartley to Supreme Executive Council, dated Sunbury, September 1, 1778, PA (1), VI, 730.

10. *Proceedings and Collections of the Wyoming Historical and Geological Society* (hereafter *WHGS*), 7: 128.

11. Col. Hartley to Supreme Executive Council, dated Sunbury, September 1, 1778, PA (1), VI, 730.

12. Col. Hartley to Lt. Col. Butler, letter dated Sunbury, September 10, 1778, *WHGS*, 7: 140.

13. Ibid.

14. Ibid.

15. PA (1), VII, 5.

16. Ibid.

17. PA (1), VII, 5, 6.

18. Capt. John Johnston to Maj. John Butler, letter dated Canadesaga, September 30, 1778, *Frederick Haldimand Papers*, BM 21,765, B. 105, 53, Archives Canada copy; and Cruikshank, *The Story of Butler's Rangers and the Settlement of Niagara*, 54.

19. Cruikshank, *The Story of Butler's Rangers and the Settlement of Niagara*, 54.

20. Col. Thomas Hartley to Pennsylvania Supreme Executive Council, letter dated Sunbury, October 8, 1778, PA (1), VII, 3-9.

21. Ibid.

22. Ibid.

23. Ibid.

24. *WHGS*, 7: 120; and, PA (1), VII, 7-8.

25. PA (I), VII, 3.

26. Unless otherwise noted, the information is taken from Col. Thomas Hartley to Congress, dated Sunbury, October 8, 1778, Papers of the Continental Congress, item 78, vol. 11, 341-352, and PA (1) VII, 5-9.

27. PA (1), VII, 8.

28. Col. Thomas Hartley to Congress, dated Sunbury, October 8, 1778, Papers of the Continental Congress, item 78, vol. 11, 341-352 and PA (1) VII, 5-9.

29. *WHGS*, 7: 142; Col. Butler to Board of War, October 30, 1778. <where is this letter from?>

30. October 28, 1778 Returns, *WHGS*, 7:129, 30.

31. *Jour. Cont. Cong.*, 12: 1131-1132; and Henry Laurens to Gen. George Washington, letter dated Philadelphia, November 15, 1778, *Letters of Delegates*, volume 11 October 1, 1778-January 31, 1779, 341-52; and, PA(1), VII, 81-82

32. PA (1), VII, 86-87.

33. PA (5), III, 737-738.

34. Col. John Cantine to Gov. George Clinton, letter dated Marbletown, September 28, 1778, *Clinton Papers*, 4: 113-116.

35. Return of the Detachment of Foot, Commanded by Wm. Butler Esqr. Lt. Col. Comm'd't at Schohary, *Clinton Papers*, 4: 229-230. Unless otherwise noted, all strength totals include field,

company, staff and civil officers, staff noncommissioned officers, sergeants, musicians, as well as the "rank and file," or corporals and privates.

36. Lt. Col. William Butler to Gov. George Clinton, letter dated Schohary, October 28, 1778, *Clinton Papers*, 4: 224.

37. Although the numbers of horses and drivers are not specified in the returns or Butler's report, two drivers were usually assigned to every ten packhorses.

38. Return of the Detachment of Foot That Was at Onohogwage Under the Com'd of Wm. Butler, Esqr. Lt. Col., dated Schohary, October 1778, *Clinton Papers*, 4: 231.

39. Lt. Col. William Butler to Gov. George Clinton, letter dated Schohary, October 28, 1778, *Clinton Papers*, 4: 224.

40. Ibid.

41. Ibid., 225.

42. Ibid., 225-226.

43. Ibid., 226.

44. Ibid., 226-227. Continental regiments were not officially organized with a "grenadier" company, although some commanders created their own.

45. Ibid., 227-228.

46. Ibid., 228.

47. Ibid., 222-223.

48. Gov. George Clinton to Gen. George Washington, letter dated Poughkeepsie, October 15, 1778, *Clinton Papers*, 4: 163.

49. Gen. George Washington to Gov. George Clinton, letter dated Fredericksburg (NY), October 16, 1778, *Writings of George Washington*, 13: 87-88.

50. Gov. George Clinton to Gen. George Washington, letter dated Poughkeepsie, October 17, 1778, *Clinton Papers*, 4: 167-168.

51. *Clinton Papers*, 4: 158-161, 163-167.

52. *Clinton Papers*, 4: 158-161, 164-167.

53. Lt. Col. John Hardenbergh to Gov. Clinton, letter dated New Hurly, October 16, 1778, *Clinton Papers*, 4: 166.

Chapter 9

1. Lt. Col. Sir John Johnson to Col. John Carleton, letter dated October 6, 1778, *Frederick Haldimand Papers*, Archives Canada copy, B 100: 60.

2. Brig. Gen. Abraham Ten Broeck to Gov. George Clinton, letter dated Albany, November 8 and 13, 1778, *Clinton Papers*, 4: 254-255 and 266-267, respectively; and Col. Lewis Van Woert to Brig. Gen. Abraham Ten Broeck, letter dated Cambridge, November 11, 1778, *Clinton Papers*, 4: 268.

3. Kayontwakon is another Anglicized spelling of Cornplanter's Indian name. Some sources also place the names of the following lesser chiefs or head warriors on the raid: Half Town, Little Beard, Little Billy, Farmer's Brother, Jack Berry, Twenty Canoes, Wundunohteh, Hiadeoni, Conneuesut, Souetdo, Hohnogwus, and Onoongadaka.

4. Gov. George Clinton to Col. John Cantine, letter dated Poughkeepsie, October 21, 1778, *Clinton Papers*, 4: 181-182.

5. Gov. Clinton to Col. Van Cortlandt, letter dated October 27, 1778, *Clinton Papers*, 4:210; and Col. Mason Bolton to Maj. Gen. Frederick Haldimand, letter dated Fort Niagara, November 11, 1778, *Frederick Haldimand Papers*, Archives Canada copy, B 100:69.

6. Cherry Valley Citizens to Brig. Gen. Edward Hand, letter dated Cherry Valley, November 9, 1778, *Clinton Papers*, 4: 259-261.

7. *Clinton Papers*, 4: 267.

8. Unless otherwise stated, the account on Cherry Valley is based on: Capt. Walter Butler to Lt. Col. Mason Bolton, letter dated Unadilla, November 17, 1778, *Frederick Haldimand Papers*, BL Mss. No. 21, 760, folios 77-80, and B100, 82-88, Archives Canada copy; and Major Daniel Whiting to Brig. Gen. Edward Hand, letter dated Fort Alden, Cherry Valley, Nov. 13, 1778, *Clinton Papers*, 4:286-287.

9. Ibid.

10. Ibid.

11. Stone, *The Life of Joseph Brant–Thayendanega*, 2: 380-390.

12. Ibid.

13. Ibid.

14. Ibid.

15. Ibid.

16. Colonel William Harper to Gov. George Clinton, letter dated Mohawk District, Tryon County, December 2, 1778, *Clinton Papers*, 4: 410-414; and, Major Daniel Whiting to Brig. Gen. Edward Hand, letter dated Fort Alden, Cherry Valley, Nov. 13, 1778, *Clinton Papers*, 4: 286-287.

17. Brig. Gen. James Clinton to Gov. George Clinton, letter dated Albany, November 28, 1778, *Clinton Papers*, 4: 337-338.

18. Brig. Gen. Abraham Ten Broeck to Gov. George Clinton, letter dated Schoharie, November 17, 1778, *Clinton Papers*, 4: 289-292.

19. Col. William Harper to Gov. George Clinton, letter dated Mohawk District, Tryon County, December 2, 1778, *Clinton Papers*, 4: 410-414.

20. Ibid.

21. Ibid.

22. Capt. Walter Butler to Lt. Col. Mason Bolton, letter dated Unadilla, November 17, 1778, *Frederick Haldimand Papers*, Archives Canada copy, B 100:82.

23. Joseph Brant to Col. John Cantine, letter dated December 13, 1778, *Clinton Papers*, 4: 364.

24. Sir Henry Clinton to Lord George Germain, letter dated New York, January 11, 1779, *Clinton Papers*, 4: 480-482.

25. Brig. Gen. Edward Hand to Gov. George Clinton, letter dated Schenectady, Nov. 15, 1779, *Clinton Papers*, 4: 284-285; and Cal. Wash. Cor., 2: 844; and, transmitted through Clinton to Washington, Schenectady, November 15, 1778, *Clinton Papers*, 4:284-285.

26. Brig. Gen. Abraham Ten Broeck to Brig. Gen. Edward Hand, letter dated Albany, November 12, 1778, 5 p.m., *Clinton Papers*, 4: 285-286.

27. *Clinton Papers*, 4: 284-288, 293.

28. Brig. Gen. Abraham Ten Broeck to Gov. George Clinton, letter dated Headquarters, Schoharie, November 17, 1778, *Clinton Papers*, 4:290-292.

29. Gov. Clinton to John Jay, letter dated Poughkeepsie, November 17, 1778, *Clinton Papers*, 4: 289-290.

30. Gen. George Washington to Gov. Clinton, letter dated Headquarters, Fredericksburgh, November 18, 1778, in *Writings of George Washington*, 13: 275-276.

31. Pulaski's Legion was an independent corps consisting of one troop of lancers, two troops of dragoons, one company of riflemen, and a two company battalion of light infantry under the command of Brigadier General Casimir Pulaski.

32. Col. Charles Armand Tuffin, known as Armand, commanded Armand's, or the 1st Partisan Corps, consisting of two companies of riflemen and two companies of light infantry, recruited largely of foreign volunteers. In 1780 it was designated Armand's Legion with the addition of mounted troops.

33. Col. Philip Van Cortlandt to Gov. George Clinton, letter dated Rochester, November 15, 1778; and, Gov. George Clinton to Brig. Gen. Abraham Ten Broeck, letter dated Poughkeepsie, November 15, 1778, *Clinton Papers*, 4: 276-277 and 277-278, respectively; and, Gen. George Washington to Brig. Gen. Casimir Pulaski, letter dated Headquarters, Fredericksburgh, November 24, 1778, *Writings of George Washington*, 13: 322-323.

34. Gen. George Washington to Pres. Henry Laurens, letter dated Headquarters, Fredericksburgh, November 16, 1778, *Writings of George Washington*, 13: 263-264.

35. Gen. Washington to Maj. Gen. Philip Schuyler, letter dated Headquarters, Fredericksburgh, November 16, 1778, *Writings of George Washington*, 13: 264-265.

36. Gen. George Washington to Brig. Gen. Edward Hand, letter dated Headquarters, Fredericksburgh, November 16, 1778, *Writings of George Washington*, 13: 267-268.

37. The German Battalion, or Regiment, was originally raised in 1776, equally by both Pennsylvania and Maryland from their German communities. First designated as a regiment of Pennsylvania Continentals, in 1778 it was officially recognized as Maryland's eighth regiment in Continental service, but was seldom called by any name other than the German Regiment.

38. Gen. George Washington to Brig. Gen. James Clinton, and to Brig. Gen. Edward Hand, letters dated Head Quarters, Fredericksburgh, November 20, 1778, and to the President of Congress dated November 24, 1778, *Writings of George Washington*, 13: 292-293 and 316-318, respectively.

39. Gov. George Clinton to Col. John Cantine, letter dated Poughkeepsie, November 22, 1778, *Clinton Papers*, 4: 305.

40. *Jour. Cont. Cong.*, 12:1149; and Washington to the President of Congress, November 21, 1778, *Writings of George Washington*, 13: 305-307.

41. Gen. George Washington to Maj. Gen. Phillip Schuyler, letter dated Headquarters, Fredericksburgh, November 20-21, 1778, *Writings of George Washington*, 13: 297-305.

42. Cal. Wash. Corr. 2: 865 Washington to Schuyler.

43. Wash. Corr. Nov 28 - 2: 869 Clinton and Hand to Washington.

44. Gen. George Washington to Maj. Gen. Philip Schuyler, letter dated Headquarters, Middlebrook, December 18, 1778, *Writings of George Washington*, 13: 429-433.

Chapter 10

1. Royal Gov. William Tryon to Lord Germain, letter dated Out Post King's Bridge, December 24, 1778, in *DCHNY*, 8: 756.

2. Lt. Col. John Butler to Gen. Frederick Haldimand, letter dated Fort Niagara, February 14, 1779, *Frederick Haldimand Papers*, Archives Canada copy, B: 105: 92.

3. Cruikshank, *The Story of Butler's Rangers and the Settlement of Niagara*, 61-62.

4. Gen. George Washington to the Committee of Conference, letter dated Philadelphia, January 13, 1779, *Writings of George Washington*, 4: 3–13.

5. Gen. George Washington to Brig. Gen. Lachlan McIntosh, letter dated Philadelphia, January 31, 1779, *Writings of George Washington*, 14: 58-62.

6. Rev. David Zeisberger to Brig. Gen. Lachlan McIntosh, letter dated February 18, 1779, *George Washington Papers*, Series 3, Subseries B, Letterbook 7. Unless otherwise stated, much of

the information on Fort Laurens is based on the narrative found in: Thomas I. Pieper, and James B. Gidney, *Fort Laurens, 1778-1779: The Revolutionary War in Ohio* (Kent, Ohio: Kent State University Press, 1976).

7. Col. John Gibson to Brig. Gen. Lachlan McIntosh, letter dated February 13, 1779, *George Washington Papers*, Series 3, Subseries B, Letterbook 7.

8. Brig. Gen. Lachlan McIntosh to Maj. Richard Taylor, letter dated February 8, 1779; Maj. Frederick Vernon to Brig. Gen. Lachlan McIntosh, letter dated March 28, 1779; Col. John Gibson to Brig. Gen. Lachlan McIntosh, letter dated February 13, 1779; Brig. Gen. Lachlan McIntosh to Gen. George Washington, letters dated March 12, March 19, 1779, *George Washington Papers*, Series 3, Subseries B, Letterbook 8.

9. Maj. Gen. Nathanael Greene to Gen. George Washington, letter dated Philadelphia, January 5, 1779, in Richard K. Showman, ed., *The Papers of General Nathanael Greene*, 3: 144.

10. Ibid., 145.

11. Ibid.

12. Gen. George Washington to Brig. Gen. Lachlan McIntosh, letter dated Philadelphia, January 31, 1779, *Writings of George Washington*, 14: 58-62.

13. Ibid.

14. Gen. George Washington to Brig. Gen. Lachlan McIntosh, letter dated Philadelphia, January 31, 1779, *Writings of George Washington*, 14: 58-62

15. Ibid,

16. Gen. George Washington to Brig. Gen. Edward Hand, letter dated Head Quarters, Philadelphia, January 25, 1779, *Writings of George Washington*, 14: 74-75.

17. Gen. George Washington to Brig. Gen. James Potter, letter dated Head Quarters, March 2, 1779, *Writings of George Washington*, 14: 175-176.

18. Gen. George Washington to Brig. Gen. James Clinton, letter dated Head Quarters, February 11, 1779, *Writings of George Washington*, 14: 98.

19. Gen. George Washington to Maj. Gen. Philip Schuyler, letters dated Philadelphia, January 25, and Middlebrook, February 11, 1779, *Writings of George Washington*, 14: 44-46, and 94-98; Brig. Gen. Phillip Schuyler to Washington, Albany, February 4, March 1 and 8, 1779, Cal. Wash. Corr. 2: 931 and 930; *Clinton Papers* 4: 602-604.

20. Maj. Gen. Phillip Schuyler to Gov. George Clinton, letter dated Albany, March 2, 1779, *Clinton Papers*, 4: 602-605.

21. Gen. George Washington to Brig. Gen. Lachlan McIntosh, letter dated Head Quarters, Middle Brook, February 15, 1779, *Writings of George Washington,* 14:114-118.

22. General George Washington to Maj. Gen. Nathanael Greene, letters dated Head Quarters, Middle Brook, February 24, and March 2, 1779, *Writings of George Washington*, 14: 142-143, 176-178.

23. *Jour. Cont. Cong.*, February 25, 1779, 13: 251.

24. Gen. George Washington to Maj. Gen. Philip Schuyler, letter dated Head Quarters, Middle Brook, February 26, 1779, *Writings of George Washington*, 14: 149-51.

25. Maj. Gen. Philip Schuyler to Gov. George Clinton, letter dated Albany, March 2, 1779, *Clinton Papers*, 4: 602-605.

26. Maj. Gen. Nathanael Greene to Gen. George Washington, letters dated Middlebrook, between March 10-17, 1779, *Greene Papers*, 3: 346-349.

27. Ibid.

28. Ibid., 347.

29. Ibid., 346-7.

30. Ibid., 346.

31. Gen. George Washington to Brig. Gen. McIntosh, letters dated January 31, 1779, February 15 and March 31, 1779, Cal. Wash. Corr., 2: 912; and *Writings of George Washington* 14: 59; and Gen. George Washington to Brig. Gen. Edward Hand, letter dated February 28, 1779, Wash. Corr. 2: 928.

32. Gen. George Washington to Brig. Gen. Edward Hand, letters dated Headquarters, Middle Brook, March 16 and 21, 1779, *Writings of George Washington*, 14: 251-252, and 273-274.

33. Gen. George Washington to Col. William Patterson, and Col. Zebulon Butler, letters dated Head Quarters, March 1 and 2, 1779, *Writings of George Washington*, 14:168-169, 170, and 174.

34. Gen. George Washington to Brig. Gen. James Potter and Pres. Joseph Reed, letters dated Head Quarters, March 2 and 3, 1779, *Writings of George Washington*, 14: 175-6, and 186-188; and to Gov. George Clinton, dated March 6, 1779, *Clinton Papers*, 4: 615-617.

35. Gen. George Washington to Brig. Gen. Lachlan McIntosh, letter dated March 5, and Col. Daniel Brodhead, letters dated February 15 and March 5, 1779, *Writings of George Washington*, 14: 193-194; and 119-120 and 194-196, respectively.

36. Gen. George Washington to Maj. Gen. Horatio Gates, letter dated Head Quarters, Middle Brook, March 6, 1779, *Writings of George Washington*, 14: 198-200.

37. Ibid.

38. Ibid.

39. Maj. Gen. Horatio Gates to Gen. George Washington, letter dated Boston, March 16, 1779, *George Washington Papers*, 6: 189; and Gen. George Washington to Maj. Gen. John Sullivan, letter dated Head Quarters, Middle Brook, March 6, 1779, *Writings of George Washington*: 14: 201-202.

40. Gen. George Washington to Brig. Gen. Edward Hand, letters dated Headquarters, Middle Brook, March 16 and 21, 1779, *Writings of George Washington*, 14: 251-252, and 273-274.

41. Gen. George Washington to Col. Daniel Brodhead, letter dated Middlebrook, March 22, and to Col. Moses Rawlings, letter dated March 21, 1779, *Writings of George Washington*, 14: 278-281, and 276.

42. Ibid.

43. Lt. Col. Cornelius Van Dyck to Brig. Gen. James Clinton, Fort Schuyler, December 23, 1778, *Clinton Papers*, 4: 417-418.

44. Ibid.

45. Ibid..

46. Lt. Col. Cornelius Van Dyck to Brig Gen James Clinton, Fort Schuyler, letter dated Fort Schuyler, January 18, 1779, *Clinton Papers*, 4: 492-494.

47. Ibid.

48. Ibid.

49. Brig. Gen. James Clinton to Gov. George Clinton, letter dated Albany January 31, 1779, *Clinton Papers*, 4: 528-529.

50. Cruikshank, *The Story of Butler's Rangers and the Settlement of Niagara*, 62.

51. Col. John Butler to Lt. Gen. Frederick Haldimand, letter dated Niagara, March 8, 1779, *Frederick Haldimand Papers*, Archives Canada copy, B 105: 113.

52. Maj. Gen. Philip Schuyler to Gov. George Clinton, letters dated Albany, March 7 and 8, 1779, *Clinton Papers*, 4: 620, and 624-625.

53. Levies were soldiers drafted from designated classes of militia to serve active duty terms, usually for the duration of one campaign or as much as one year.

54. April 1, 1779, *Jour. Cont. Cong.*, 13: 402; and, President John Jay to Gov. George Clinton, Philadelphia, April 4, 1779, *Clinton Papers*, 4: 689-690.

55. Depositions of Albert H. Vather and Andres Rodingburg to William Harper, Esq. (Justice of Tryon County), *Clinton Papers*, 4: 714-717.

56. Brig. Gen. James Clinton to Gov. George Clinton, letter dated April 8, 1779, *Clinton Papers*, 4: 702-704.

57. Unless otherwise stated, based on Brig. Gen. James Clinton to Gov. George Clinton, letter dated Albany, April 8, 1779, *Clinton Papers*, 4: 702-704; and the journals of Capt. Thomas Machlin and Lt. Erkuries Beatty, in Cook, ed., *Journals of the Military Expedition of Major General John Sullivan against the Six Nations of Indians in 1779* (hereafter *Journals of the Military Expedition*), 192-193, and 16-18.

58. Unless otherwise stated, based on sources in note 57 and Lt. Thomas McClennan to Brig. Gen. James Clinton, letter dated Fort Schuyler, April 30, 1779, *Clinton Papers*, 4: 804-807.

59. Gen. James Clinton to Gov. George Clinton, letter dated Albany, April 8, 1779, *Clinton Papers*, 4: 702-704; and the journals of Thomas Machlin and Erkuries Beatty in *Journals of the Military Expedition*, 192-193, 16-18.

60. Ibid.

61. Ibid.

62. Ibid.

63. Ibid.

64. Ibid.

65. Capt. Johnston spelled the name "Asdondanoya" in his correspondence to Lt. Col. Butler.

66. Capt. John Johnston to Lt. Col. John Butler, letter dated Cunnutarage, April 21, 1779, *Frederick Haldimand Papers*, Archives Canada copy, B 100: 135.

67. Capt. John Johnston to Col. John Butler, Cannadasago, April 22, 1779, 1779, *Frederick Haldimand Papers*, Archives Canada copy, B 100 139.

68. Lt. Col. John Butler to Lt. Col. Mason Bolton, [late] April 1779, *Frederick Haldimand Papers*, Archives Canada copy, B 100: 134; and Cruikshank, *The Story of Butler's Rangers and the Settlement of Niagara*, 62-63.

69. Lt. Thomas McClennan to Brig. Gen. James Clinton, letter dated Fort Schuyler, April 30, 1779, *Clinton Papers*, 4: 804-807.

70. Ibid.

71. Ibid.

72. General Orders for May 8, 1779, *Writings of George Washington*, 15: 27, 54.

Chapter 11

1. Maj. Gen. John Sullivan to Gen. George Washington, letters dated Mill Stone, April 15 and 16, 1779, In Hammond, ed., *The Letters and Papers of Major General John Sullivan, Continental Army*, 3: 1-5, 5-9.

2. Gen. George Washington to Brig. Gen. Edward Hand, letters dated Headquarters, Middle Brook, April 4, 9, and 30; to Gov. George Clinton, April 5 and May 3; and to President Joseph Reed, April 19 and 27, 1779, *Writings of George Washington*, 14: 336, 337-338, 340-341, 354-355, 405-406, 448-455, 465-466, 476-478.

3. Gen. George Washington to Maj. Gen. Philip Schuyler, and to Brig. Gen. James Clinton, letters dated Middle Brook, April 19, 1779, *Writings of George Washington*, 14: 407-409 and 414-416.

4. Ibid.

5. Gen. George Washington to Gov. George Clinton and William Livingston, letters dated Head Quarters, Middle Brook, April 19; and to Gov. Clinton, April 5 and 17, 1779, *Writings of George Washington*, 14: 337-338, 340-341, 397-398 and 414-417.

6. Gen. George Washington to Col. Philip Van Cortlandt, letters dated Head Quarters, Middle Brook, April 13 and 19, 1779, *Writings of George Washington*, 14: 374-375, and 417.

7. Gen. George Washington to Brig. Gen. Edward Hand and Lt. Col. Zebulon Butler, letters dated Head Quarters, Middle Brook, April 1; and to Hand, dated April 9, 1779, *Writings of George Washington*, 14: 323-324 <check pages here> 1, 321-322, and 354-355.

8. Gen. George Washington to Brig. Gen. Edward Hand, letters dated Headquarters, Middle Brook, April 4 and 9; to Gov. George Clinton, April 5 and May 3; and to President Joseph Reed, April 19 and 27, 1779, *Writings of George Washington*, 14: 336, 337-338, 340-341, 354-355, 405-406, 448-455, and 476-478.

9. Gen. George Washington to Col. Philip Van Cortlandt, letters dated Head Quarters, Middle Brook, April 13 and 19, 1779, *Writings of George Washington*, 14: 374-735, and 417.

10. Gen. George Washington to Maj. Gen. John Sullivan, letter dated Middle Brook, May 4, 1779, *Writings of George Washington*, 14: 402-403.

11. Gen. George Washington to Maj. Gen. Nathanael Greene, letter dated Middle Brook, May 4, 1779, *Writings of George Washington*, 14: 493-494.

12. Maj. Gen. John Sullivan to Gen. George Washington, letters dated Mill Stone, April 15 and 16, 1779, *Sullivan Papers*, 3:1-5, and 5-9.

13. Gen. George Washington to Maj. Gen. John Sullivan, letter dated Middle Brook, May 4, 1779, *Writings of George Washington*, 14:402-403.

14. Gen. George Washington to Col. Daniel Brodhead, letters dated Middle Brook, April 21 and May 3, 1779, *Writings of George Washington*, 14:421-422 and 480; and Brodhead's replies, dated Fort Pitt, May 6, 1779, in *George Washington Papers*, 242, 367.

15. Gov. George Clinton to Gen. George Washington, letter dated Poughkeepsie, April 25, 1779, in *Clinton Papers*, 4: 755-757.

16. Gov. George Clinton to Maj. Van Benscoten, letter dated Poughkeepsie, April 27, 1779, *Clinton Papers*, 4: 764-767.

17. Brig. Gen. James Clinton to Gov. George Clinton, letter dated Albany, April 28, 1779, *Clinton Papers*, 4: 770-771.

18. Brig. Gen. James Clinton to Gov. George Clinton, letter dated Albany, May 13, 1779, *Clinton Papers*, 4: 811.

19. Col. Philip Van Cortlandt to Gov. George Clinton, letter dated Kingston, April 29, 1779, *Clinton Papers*, 4: 777-778.

20. Col. Philip Van Cortlandt to Gov. George Clinton, letter dated Warwasink, May 4, 1779, *Clinton Papers*, 4: 798-799.

21. Gov. George Clinton to Col. Philip Van Cortlandt, letter dated Newburgh, May 54, 1779. *Clinton Papers*, 4: 799.

22. Col. Philip Van Cortlandt to Gov. George Clinton, letter dated Great Swamp Wilderness, May 26, 1779, *Clinton Papers*, 4: 851-852.

23. Buckalew, *The Frontier Forts within the North and West Branches of the Susquehanna River*, 1: 11-17; Bell, *History of Northumberland County, Pennsylvania*, 125-130.

24. Ibid.

25. *Greene Papers*, 4: 38.

26. Maj. Richard Claiborne to Maj. Gen. Nathanael Greene, letter dated Easton, May 17, 1779, *Greene Papers*, 4: 37.

27. Col. John Cox to Maj. Gen. Nathanael Greene, letter dated Bloomsbury (N.J.), May 18, 1779, *Greene Papers*, 4: 44.

28. Gen. George Washington to Col. Oliver Spencer, letter dated Middlebrook, May 7, 1779, *Writings of George Washington*, 15: 16-17.

29. Col. Philip Van Cortlandt to Gov. George Clinton, Great Swamp Wilderness, May 26, 1779, *Clinton Papers*, 4: 851-852.

30. Gen. George Washington to Maj. Gen. Nathanael Greene, letter dated Middlebrook, May 19, 1779, *Writings of George Washington*, 15: 107.

31. A brigade of teams consisted of twenty-nine wagons drawn by two horses each.

32. Col. Robert Cooper, Jr., to Maj. Gen. Nathanael Greene, letter dated Easton, May 23, 1779, *Greene Papers*, 4: 45.

33. Maj. Gen. John Sullivan to Pres. Joseph Reed, letters dated Easton, May 11 and 21, 1779, *Sullivan Papers*, 3: 19, 28.

34. Gen. George Washington to Brig. Gen. James Clinton, letter dated Head Quarters, Middle Brook, May 18, 1779, *Writings of George Washington*, 15: 77.

35. Maj. Gen. John Sullivan to Maj. Gen. Nathanael Greene, letter dated Easton, May 23, 1779, *Greene Papers*, 4: 72.

36. Maj. Gen. John Sullivan to Gen. George Washington, letter dated Easton, May 23, 1779, *Sullivan Papers*, 3: 33-34.

37. Gen. George Washington to Maj. Gen. John Sullivan, letter dated Headquarters, Middlebrook, May 28, 1779, *Writings of George Washington*, 15: 171-173.

38. Ibid.

39. Lt. Col. John Butler to Lt. Col. Mason Bolton, letters dated Genesee, May 13, and Canadasaga, May 21 and 28; to Lt. Gen. Frederick Haldimand, dated Canadasaga, May 28; and Capt. Walter Butler to Lt. Gen. Haldimand, dated Niagara, May 20, 1779, *Frederick Haldimand Papers*, Archives Canada copy, B 100, 140, 157, 180, and B 105, 129, 135.

40. Ibid.

41. Ibid.

42. Col. Goose Van Schaick to Brig. Gen. James Clinton, letter dated Fort Schuyler, May 22, 1779, *Clinton Papers*, 4: 843-844.

43. Lt. Col. Levi Pawling to Gov. Clinton, letter dated Marbletown, May 24, 1779, *Clinton Papers*, 4: 845-846.

44. *Greene Papers*, 4: 88.

45. Col. John Davis to Maj. Gen. Nathanael Greene, letter dated Carlisle, May 30, 1779, *Greene Papers*, 4: 109.

46. Gen. George Washington to Maj. Gen. John Sullivan, letters dated Head Quarters, Middlebrook, May 28 and 31, 1779, *Writings of George Washington*, 15: 171-173.

47. Ibid., 171-173, 189-193.

48. Ibid.

49. Ibid.

50. Ibid., 171-173, 189-193, 203.

51. Col. Robert L. Hooper, Jr. to Maj. Gen. Nathanael Greene, letter dated Easton, Pennsylvania, May 31, 1779, *Greene Papers*, 4: 111.

52. Maj. Gen. Nathanael Greene to Col. Robert L. Hooper, letter dated Smith Tavern, Clove, N.Y., June 15, 1779, *Greene Papers*, 4: 162.

53. Maj. Gen. Nathanael Greene to Maj. Gen. John Sullivan, letter dated Camp Smith's Cove, N.Y., June 21, 1779, *Greene Papers*, 4: 175.

54 . Gen. George Washington to Brig. Gen. James Clinton, letter dated Head Quarters, Smith's Cove, June 10, 1779, *Clinton Papers*, 15: 256-258.

55. Brig. Gen. James Clinton to Gen Washington, letter dated Camp Canajoharie Creek, June 19, 1779, *George Washington Papers*; and Lieut. Erkuries Beatty, *Journals of the Military Expedition*, 18.

56. Brig. Gen. James Clinton to Gen. George Washington, letter dated Camp Canajoharie Creek, June 19, 1779.

57. Ibid.; Lieut. William McKendry, *Journals of the Military Expedition*, 199. Lieut. Erkuries Beatty, *Journals of the Military Expedition*, 18.

58. Col. Daniel Brodhead to Maj. Gen. Nathanael Greene, dated Pittsburgh, May 26, 1779, *Greene Papers*, 4: 81-83.

59. Ibid.

60. Gen. George Washington to Col. Daniel Brodhead, letter dated Middle Brook, May 21, 1779, *Writings of George Washington*, 15: 119-121.

61. Lt. Col. John Butler to Lt. Col. Mason Bolton, letters dated Canadasaga June 5, and 18, 1779, *Frederick Haldimand Papers*, Archives Canada copy, B 100, 184, 187.

62. Lt. Col. John Butler to Lt. Col. Mason Bolton, letter dated Canadasaga, June 24, 1779, *Frederick Haldimand Papers*, Archives Canada copy, B 100, 210.

63. Lt. Col. Adam Hubely, Journals, 146.

64. Lieutenant Colonel Henry Dearborn, Journal; Cook, ed., *Journals of the Military Expedition of Major General John Sullivan Against the Six Nations of Indians in 1779* (hereafter, *Journals of the Military Expedition*), 64.

65. Captain James Norris, Journal, *Journals of the Military Expedition*, 224.

66. Rev. William Roger, Journals, 250, 252.

67. Gen. George Washington to Col. Daniel Brodhead, letters dated Head Quarters, New Windsor, June 23 and July 13, 1779, *George Washington Writings*, 15: 302-304, and 418-419.

68. Maj. Gen. Nathanael Greene to Col. Daniel Brodhead, and Col. Archibald Steele, letters dated New Windsor, July 6, 1779, *Greene Papers*, 4: 207, 208-209.

69. Gen. George Washington to Col. Daniel Brodhead, letters dated Head Quarters, New Windsor, July 13, 1779, *Writings of George Washington*, 15: 418-419.

70. Lt. Col. John Butler to Lt. Col. Mason Bolton, letter dated Canadasaga, July 3, 1779, *Frederick Haldimand Papers*, Archives Canada copy, B 100, 200.

71. Unless otherwise stated, the account of the engagement at Fort Freeland is based on: Capt. John McDonell to Lt. Col. John Butler, letter dated Camp, Tioga Point, August 5, 1779, *Frederick Haldimand Papers*, Archives Canada copy, B 100, 223; Capt. James Norris and Rev. William Rogers, Journals, 227, 255; Buckalew, *Frontier Forts Within the North and West Branches of the Susquehanna River*, 1: 11-17; and PA 1 (VII), 321, 344, 408.; Bell, *History of Northumberland County*, 125-130.

72. Unless otherwise noted, the account of the engagement at Minisink is based on: Capt. Joseph Brant to Lt. Col. Mason Bolton, letter dated Oghwage, July 29, 1779, *Frederick Haldimand Papers*, Archives Canada copy, B 100, 212; Lt. Col. Levi Pawling to Gov. George Clinton, letter dated Marbletown, July 22, 1779, *Clinton Papers*, 5: 150; Gov. George Clinton to Lt. Col. Albert Pawling, letters dated Poughkeepsie, July 22 and 24, 1779, *Clinton Papers*, 5: 150-151, 160-161; Dr. Nathan Ker to Gov. George Clinton, letter dated Goshen, July 29, and reply Gov. George Clinton to Dr. Nathan Ker dated Poughkeepsie, July 30, 1779, *Clinton*

Papers, 5: 162-166; Gov. George Clinton to Brig. Gen. James Clinton, letter dated Poughkeepsie, August 5, 1779, *Clinton Papers*, 5: 180; Gov. George Clinton to Col. Goose Van Schaick, letter dated Poughkeepsie, August 27, 1779, *Clinton Papers*, 5: 217; and Gov. George Clinton to Maj. Gen. Philip Schuyler, letter dated Poughkeepsie, August 27, 1779, *Clinton Papers*, 5: 218.

73. Ibid.

74. Ibid.

75. Brant said the "rascals" became afraid and fled, but one of Brant's men, an American deserter, fell into American hands. One of the men told his American captors he turned himself in voluntarily, but it was believed he merely lost his way.

76. Ibid.

77. Ibid.

78. Parker Journal; *Journals*, Lieut. William McKendry, 199; Cruikshank, *The Story of Butler's Rangers and the Settlement of Niagara*, 65. Brig. Gen. James Clinton to Mrs. Mary Clinton, letter dated Camp at South end of Otsego Lake, July 6, 1779, *Clinton Papers*, 5: 122.

79. Gov. George Clinton to Lt. Col. Albert Pawling, letter dated Poughkeepsie, July 22, 1779, *Clinton Papers*, 5: 150-151.

80. Gov. George Clinton to Lt. Col. Albert Pawling, letter dated Poughkeepsie, July 24, 1779, *Clinton Papers*, 5: 160-61.

81. Ibid.

82. Ibid.

83. Maj. Gen. John Sullivan to John Cook, and Col. Samuel Hunter, letters dated Wyoming, July 30, 1779, *Sullivan Papers*, 3: 88-89.

84. Gov. George Clinton to Dr. Nathan Ker, letter dated Poughkeepsie, July 30, 1779. *Clinton Papers*, 5: 164-166.

85. Board of War to Maj. Gen. John Sullivan, letter dated Philadelphia, July 1, 1779, *Sullivan Papers*, 3: 78-79.

86. Maj. Gen. John Sullivan to John Jay, letter dated Wyoming, July 21 and 26, 1779, *Sullivan Papers*, 3: 84, 86.

87. Maj. Gen. John Sullivan to Brig. Gen. James Clinton, letter dated Wyoming, July 11, 1779, *Clinton Papers*, 5: 149.

88. Brig. Gen. James Clinton to Gov. George Clinton, letter dated Camp Lake Otsego, July 20, 1779, *Clinton Papers*, 5: 148. Brig. Gen. James Clinton to Mrs. Mary Clinton, letter dated Camp at South end of Otsego Lake, July 6, 1779, *Clinton Papers*, 5: 122.

89. Gen. George Washington to Maj. Gen. John Sullivan, letter dated New Windsor, July 1, 1779, *Writings of George Washington*, 15: 348-351.

90. Col. Daniel Brodhead to Maj. Gen. Nathanael Greene, letter dated Fort Pitt, August 2, 1779, *Greene Papers*, 4: 292.

91. Lt. Col. John Butler to Lt. Col. Mason Bolton, letter dated Canadasaga, August 3, 1779, *Frederick Haldimand Papers*, Archives Canada copy, B 100, 220.

92. Maj. Gen. John Sullivan to Gen. George Washington, Gov. George Clinton, and Brig. Gen. James Clinton, letters dated Wyoming, July 30, 1779, *Clinton Papers*, 5: 177-178, 180.

Chapter 12

1. Unless otherwise stated, the narrative of the expedition is based on Maj. Gen. John Sullivan to Gen. George Washington, letter dated Tioga, August 15, 1779, the *Papers of the Continental Congress*, No. 160, folio 298, Library of Congress, Washington, D.C.; Maj. Gen. John Sullivan to

John Jay, President of Congress, letter dated Tioga, September 30, 1779, *Papers of the Continental Congress*, No. 160, folio 302; Cook, *Journals of the Military Expedition of Major General John Sullivan against the Six Nations of Indians in 1779.*

2. These were Christianized Mahican Indians from the mission community of Stockbridge, Massachusetts.

3. Scott's Rifle Corps was detached from Major Count Nicholas Ottendoerf's Corps, also known as Armand's Legion, when the parent regiment was ordered back to the Main Army from Wyoming in May 1779.

4. *Journals of the Military Expedition*, Rev. William Rogers 255; Lt. Col. Henry Dearborn, 68.

5. Ibid. Gen. George Washington to Maj. Gen. John Sullivan, letter dated Head Quarters, Middlebrook, May 31, 1779, *Writings of George Washington*, 15: 189-193.

6. *Journals of the Military Expedition*, Rev. William Rogers, 253.

7. *Journals of the Military Expedition*, Lieut. William Barton, 5-6; Sgt. Maj. George Grant, 138.

8. Gen. George Washington to Maj. Gen. John Sullivan, letter dated Headquarters, West Point, August 1, 1779, *Writings of George Washington*, 16: 29-31.

9. Lt. Col. John Butler to Lt. Col. Mason Bolton, letter dated Canadasaga, August 10, 1779, Canadian Archives, *Canadian State Papers*, Q 16-2, 364.

10. *Journals of the Military Expedition*, Lt. Col. Henry Dearborn, 54; Sgt. Maj. George Grant, 109; Rev. William Rogers, 260; Thomas Grant, 139.

11. *Journals of the Military Expedition*, Dr. Jabez Campfield, 54. Gen. George Washington to Maj. Gen. John Sullivan, letter dated headquarters, May 31, 1779, *Writings of Washington*, 15: 189-193.

12. Maj. Gen. John Sullivan to Gen. George Washington, letter dated Tioga, August 15, 1779, *Papers of the Continental Congress.*

13. *Journals of the Military Expedition*, Lt. Col. Adam Hubley, 151-152.

14. *Journals of the Military Expedition*, Maj. John Butler to Capt. Walter Butler, letter dated August 12, 1779; Canadian Archives, State papers, Q 16-2, 367.

15. *Journals of the Military Expedition*, Rev. William Rogers, 261.

16. Although no details are provided, cohorns were usually mounted on two-wheeled gun carriages.

17. Unless otherwise stated, the descriptions of the operation against Chemung is drawn from a combination of: Maj. Gen. John Sullivan to Gen. George Washington, letter dated Tioga, August 15, 1779, and Maj. Gen. John Sullivan to John Jay, President of Congress, letter dated Tioga, September 30, 1779, *Papers of the Continental Congress*; and *Journals of the Military Expedition.*

18. *Journals of the Military Expedition*, Lieut. William Barton, 6.

19. *Journals of the Military Expedition*, Lt. Col. Henry Dearborn, 71; Col. Adam Hubley, 151.

20. Ibid.

21. *Journals of the Military Expedition*, Sgt. Moses Fellows, 87.

22. *Journals of the Military Expedition*, Lt. Col. Adam Hubley, 151.

23. Ibid.; Major James Norris, 229.

24. *Journals of the Military Expedition*, Lt. Col. Adam Hubley, 151

25. Ibid.

26. American reports and journals said enemy losses were unknown; Brant and Butler both reported their losses at one warrior killed.

27. *Journals of the Military Expedition*, Lt. Col. Adam Hubley, 151. Capt. Joseph Brant to Lt. Col. Mason Bolton, letter dated Chemung, August 19, 1779; Maj. John Butler to Lt. Col. Mason Bolton, letter dated Chucknut, August 26, *Frederick Haldimand Papers*, Archives Canada copy, B 100, 229 and 229, respectively.

28. *Journals of the Military Expedition*, Lt. Col. Adam Hubley, 151.

29. *Journals of the Military Expedition*, Lt. Col. Henry Dearborn, <add page no.>; Lieut. Thomas Blake, 20, Dr. Ebenezer Elmer, 85.

30. Brig. Gen. James Clinton to Gov. George Clinton, letter dated Lake Otsego, August 5, 1779; Gov. Clinton to Lt. Col. Albert Pawling, letter dated Poughkeepsie, August 5, 1779, *Clinton Papers*, 5:182-183.

31. More suitable for use aboard a vessel than the two-wheeled field carriage, two four-truck carriages, which were usually employed in forts or aboard ships, were obtained from the garrison of Fort Schuyler.

32. Robert Parker, "Journal of Lieutenant Robert Parker of the Second Continental Artillery, 1779," Thomas R., Bard, ed., *Pennsylvania Magazine of History and Biography*, 27 (1904), 12-25. *Journals of the Military Expedition*, Lieut. Erkuries Beatty, 22; Lieut. William McKendry, 201; Lieut. Rudolphus Van Hovenburgh, 277.

33. *Journals of the Military Expedition*, Lieut. Ebenezer Beatty, 22-23.

34. *Journals of the Military Expedition*, Lieut. William McKendry, 202.

35. Ibid.

36. Unless otherwise stated, the account of the Brodhead or Upper Allegheny Expedition is based on Col. Daniel Butler to Gen. George Washington, letter dated Pittsburgh, September 16, 1779, and Col. Daniel Brodhead to Maj. Gen. John Sullivan, letter dated Headquarters, Pittsburgh, October 10, 1779, PA (1): 12, 155 and 165; William Young Brady, "Brodhead's Trail up the Allegheny, 1779," *Western Pennsylvania Historical Magazine*, 37 (1954-1955), 19-31; Col. Daniel Brodhead to President Joseph Reed, letter dated Headquarters, Pittsburgh, June 24, 1779, PA (1) (VII): 505.

37. Ibid.

38. Lt. Col. Mason Bolton to Lt. Gen. Frederick Haldimand, letter dated Fort Niagara, August 16, 1779, Canadian Archives, State Papers, Q 16-1, 360.

39. Ibid.

40. Ibid., and Capt. Joseph Brant to Lt. Col. Bolton, letter dated Chemung, August, 19, 1779, *Frederick Haldimand Papers*, Archives Canada copy, B 100, 229.

41. Col. Daniel Butler to Gen. George Washington, letter dated Pittsburgh, September 16, 1779, and Col. Daniel Brodhead to Maj. Gen. John Sullivan, letter dated Headquarters, Pittsburgh, October 10, 1779, PA (1): 12, 155, 165; Brady, "Brodhead's Trail up the Allegheny, 1779."

42. Col. Daniel Brodhead to Gen. George Washington, letter dated Pittsburgh, September 16, 1779, and Col. Daniel Brodhead to Maj. Gen. John Sullivan, letter dated Headquarters, Pittsburgh, October 10, 1779, PA (1): 12, 155, 165; Lieut. John Docksteder to Lt. Col. Mason Bolton, letter dated September 1, 1779, *Frederick Haldimand Papers*, Archives Canada copy, B 100, 234. Adler, ed., *Chainbreaker's War*, 99-101; William Young Brady, "Brodhead's Trail up the Allegheny, 1779," *Western Pennsylvania Historical Magazine*, 37 (1954-1955), 19-31.

43. Ibid.

44. Ibid.

45. Gore, Jr. *The Revolutionary War Diary of Lieut. Obadiah Gore, Jr.* (hereafter, *Gore Diary*), 181.

46. Maj. John Butler to Lt. Col. Mason Bolton, letter dated Chucknut, August 26, 1779, *Frederick Haldimand Papers*, Archives Canada copy, B 100, 232; *Journals of the Military Expedition*, Lt. Col. Adam Hubley, 152, Thomas Grant, 139; *Gore Diary*, 182.

47. *Journals of the Military Expedition*, Thomas Grant, 139; Lt. Col. Adam Hubley, 152; Lieut. John Jenkins, 171; Rev. William Rogers, 262.

48. *Journals of the Military Expedition*, Sgt. Maj. George Grant, 109; Lt. Col. Adam Hubley, 152.

49. *Journals of the Military Expedition*, Dr. Jabez Campfield, 55; Lt. Col. Henry Dearborn, 71; Maj. Jeremiah Fogg, 93; Sgt. Maj. George Grant, 109.

50. Journals, Lieut. William McKendry, 202.

51. *Gore Diary*, 181; *Journals of the Military Expedition*, Lt. Col. Adam Hubley, 153.

52. *Journals of the Military Expedition*, Dr. Jabez Campfield, 55; Lt. Col. Henry Dearborn, 71; Lt. Col. Adam Hubley, 152; Rev. William Rogers, 262; Sgt. Maj. Nathaniel Webb, 286.

53. Capt. Joseph Brant to Lt. Col. Mason Bolton, letter dated Chemung, August 19, 1779; Maj. John Butler to Lt. Col. Mason Bolton, letter dated Chucknut, August 26, 1779, *Frederick Haldimand Papers*, Archives Canada copy, B 100, 229 and 232.

54. Ibid.

55. Maj. John Butler to Lt. Col. Mason Bolton, letter dated Chucknut, August 26, 1779, *Frederick Haldimand Papers*, Archives Canada copy, B 100, 229.

56. Ibid.

57. *Journals of the Military Expedition*, Lieut. William Barton, 7; Lt. Col. Henry Dearborn, 71; Lt. Col. Adam Hubley, 153; Capt. Daniel Livermore, 185.

58. *Gore Diary*, 181; *Journals of the Military Expedition*, Lieut. Erkuries Beatty, 26; Lieut. Thomas Blake, 39; Sgt. Maj. George Grant, 110; Maj. John Burrows, 48; Lt. Col. Adam Hubley, 154.

59. Garrison Orders, Fort Sullivan, August 27 and 28, 1779, German Regiment Orderly Book, June 25, 1779 to March 29, 1780, Library of Congress Manuscript Division, Washington, D.C.; James Fairlie, "Journal," (hereafter *Fairlie Journal*) typewritten and transcribed manuscript, notes by W. R. Brock, New York State Library, Albany; *Journals of the Military Expedition*, Dr. Jabez Campfield, 55; Rev. William Rogers, 203.

60. *Journals of the Military Expedition*, Lieut. Erkuries Beatty, 26; Lieut. Thomas Blake, 39; Lt. Col. Henry Dearborn, 71; Maj. Jermiah Fogg, 94; Rev. William Rogers, 264.

61. Parker, "Journal," 12-25; *Journals of the Military Expedition*, Maj. Jeremiah Fogg, 94; Lt. Col. Adam Hubley, 154. *Fairlie Journal* <or Journal?>

62. *Fairlie Journal*; *Journals of the Military Expedition*, Lieut. Erkuries Beatty, 26; Lt. Col. Adam Hubley, 154.

Chapter 13

1. Maj. John Butler to Lt. Col. Mason Bolton, letter dated Shechquago, August 31, 1779, *Frederick Haldimand Papers*, Archives Canada copy, B 100, 242.

2. Capt. Joseph Brant to Lt. Col. Mason Bolton, letter dated Chemung, August 19, 1779; Maj. John Butler to Lt. Col. Mason Bolton, letter dated Chucknut, August 26, *Frederick Haldimand Papers*, Archives Canada copy, B 100, 229 and 229.

3. Ibid.

4. Maj. John Butler to Lt. Col. Mason Bolton, letter dated Shechquago, August 31, 1779, *Frederick Haldimand Papers*, Archives Canada copy, B 100, 242.

5. Ibid.

6. *Journals of the Military Expedition*, Lieut. Erkuries Beatty, 26; Maj. John Burrows, 44-45; Lt. Col. Henry Dearborn, 71.

7. *Journals of the Military Expedition*, Dr. Jabez Campfield, 55; Sgt. Moses Fogg, 94; Lt. Col. Adam Hubley, 154.

8. *Journals of the Military Expedition*, Sgt. Moses Fogg, 94.

9. *Gore Diary*, 181; Robert Parker, "Journal of Lieutenant Robert Parker of the Second Continental Artillery, 1779" (hereafter *Parker Journal*), Thomas R. Bard, ed., *Pennsylvania Magazine of History and Biography*, 27, (Harrisburg, Pa., 1904), 12-25; *Fairlie Journal*; Brig. Gen.

James Clinton to Gov. George Clinton, letter dated New Town, August 30, 1779, *Clinton Papers*, 5: 224-27; *Journals of the Military Expedition*, Dr. Jabez Campfield, 55; Lt. Col. Henry Dearborn, 71; Sgt. Moses Fogg, 94.

10. *Journals of the Military Expedition*, Dr. Jabez Campfield, 55; Sgt. George Grant, 110; Thomas Grant, 140.

11. *Gore Diary; Fairlie Journal; Journals of the Military Expedition*, Lt. Col. Adam Hubley, 155; Dr. Jabez Campfield, 55; Lieut. Erkuries Beatty, 26.

12. Maj. John Butler to Lt. Col. Mason Bolton, letter dated Shechquago, August 31, 1779, *Frederick Haldimand Papers*, Archives Canada copy, B 100, 242.

13. *Journals of the Military Expedition*, Lt. Col. Adam Hubley, 155; Lieut. William Barton, 7; Maj. John Burrows, 44.

14. *Journals of the Military Expedition*, Lt. Col. Adam Hubley, 155; Maj. John Burrows, 45; Lieut. John Jenkins, 172.

15. *Journals of the Military Expedition*, Lt. Col. Adam Hubley, 155.

16. Brig. Gen. James Clinton to Gov. George Clinton, letter dated New Town, August 30, 1779, *Clinton Papers*, 5:224-27; *Journals of the Military Expedition*, Lt. Col. Adam Hubley, 155-56.

17. Ibid.; *Journals of the Military Expedition*, Lt. Col. Henry Dearborn, 71; Maj. Jeremiah Fogg, 84.

18. Maj. John Butler to Lt. Col. Mason Bolton, letter dated Shechquago, August 31, 1779, *Frederick Haldimand Papers*, Archives Canada copy, B 100, 242.

19. *Parker Journal*; Maj. John Butler to Lt. Col. Mason Bolton, letter dated Shechquago, August 31, 1779, *Frederick Haldimand Papers*, Archives Canada copy, B 100, 242; *Journals of the Military Expedition*, Lt. Col. Adam Hubley, 156.

20. Brig. Gen. James Clinton to Gov. George Clinton, letter dated New Town, August 30, 1779, *Clinton Papers*, 5: 224-27; *Journals of the Military Expedition*, Lt. Col. Henry Dearborn, 72; Capt. Daniel Livermore, 186; Maj. James Norris, 231-32.

21. Maj. John Butler to Lt. Col. Mason Bolton, letter dated Shechquago, August 31, 1779, *Frederick Haldimand Papers*, Archives Canada copy, B 100, 242.

22. *Journals of the Military Expedition*, Lt. Col. Henry Dearborn, 72; Capt. Daniel Livermore, 186; Maj. James Norris, 231-32.

23. Brig. Gen. James Clinton to Gov. George Clinton, letter dated New Town, August 30, 1779, *Clinton Papers*, 5: 224-27; T. Barton to Gov. George Clinton, letter dated Newtown, August 30, 1779, *Clinton Papers*, 5: 242; Maj. John Butler to Lt. Col. Mason Bolton, letter dated Shechquago, August 31, 1779, *Frederick Haldimand Papers*, Archives Canada copy, B 100, 242; *Journals of the Military Expedition*, Lieut. William Barton, 8; Maj. John Burrows, 44; Maj. James Norris, 232.

24. *Journals of the Military Expedition*, Lieut. William Barton, 8; Ens. Daniel Gookin, 105-6; Lieut. Rudolphus Van Hovenburgh, 279.

25. *Journals of the Military Expedition*, Maj. Gen. Sullivan's Report to John Jay, dated Tioga, September 30, 1779, 297; Lt. Col. Adam Hubley, 156-57.

26. Ibid., and Lieut. Erkuries Beatty, 31; Sgt. Maj. George Grant, 110; Lt. Col. Henry Dearborn, 72-73.

27. Col. Daniel Brodhead to Gen. George Washington, letter dated Pittsburgh, September 16, 1779, PA 1 (VII): 12, 155.

28. Maj. John Butler to Lt. Col. Mason Bolton, letter dated Shechquago, August 31, 1779; *Journals of the Military Expedition*; Lieut. William Barton, 9; Maj. John Burrows, 45; Lt. Col. Henry Dearborn, 73; Lt. Col. Adam Hubley, 158.

29. Maj. John Butler to Lt. Col. Mason Bolton, letter dated Shechquago, August 31, 1779, *Frederick Haldimand Papers*, Archives Canada copy, B 100, 242.

30. Col. Guy Johnson to Lord George Germain, letter dated Montréal, September 5, 1779, *DCHNY*, 8:775.

31. *Journals of the Military Expedition*, Lt. Col. Adam Hubley, 158.

32. *Parker Journal; Fairlie Journal; Journals of the Military Expedition*, Lieut. William Barton, 9; Sgt. Moses Fellows, 89; Maj. Jeremiah Fogg, 96; Lt. Col. Henry Dearborn, 73; Maj. John Burrows, 45.

33. *Parker Journal; Journals of the Military Expedition*, Lieut. William Barton, 9; Lieut. Erkuries Beatty, 28; Maj. John Burrows, 45; Dr. Jabez Campfield, 57; Jeremiah Fogg, 96.

34. Maj. Gen. John Sullivan to the Oneida Chiefs, Papers of the Continental Congress, No. 160, folio 328; *Gore Diary; Journals of the Military Expedition*, Lieut. John Jenkins, 173; Lt. Col. Henry Dearborn, 73; Lieut. William McKendry, 205.

35. Ibid.; *Journals of the Military Expedition*, Sgt. Moses Fellows, 89; Lieut. William Barton, 10; Maj. Jeremiah Fogg, 96.

36. Maj. John Butler to Lt. Col. Mason Bolton, letter dated Canadesaga, September 3, 1779, *Frederick Haldimand Papers*, Archives Canada copy, B 100, 252.

37. *Gore Diary; Journals of the Military Expedition*, Sullivan's Report, 299; Lieut. William Barton, 10; Dr. Jabez Campfield, 57; Maj. John Burrows, 45; Maj. James Norris, 233; Lt. Col. Adam Hubley, 157.

38. *Journals of the Military Expedition*, ibid.

39. *Parker Journal; Journals of the Military Expedition*, Maj. John Burrows, 45; Maj. Jeremiah Fogg, 96.

40. *Parker Journal; Journals of the Military Expedition*, Lt. Col. Henry Dearborn, 73; Sgt. Moses Fellows, 89; Dr. Jabez Campfield, 57; Maj. Jeremiah Fogg, 96.

41. *Gore Diary; Parker Journal; Journals of the Military Expedition*, Sullivan's Report, 299; Lieut. Erkuries Beatty, 31; Maj. John Burrows, Burrows, 47; Dr. Jabez Campfield, 59; Lt. Col. Henry Dearborn, 74; Maj. Jeremiah Fogg, 97; Sgt. Maj. George Grant, 112.

42. Maj. John Butler to Lt. Col. Mason Bolton, letter dated Canawaugas, September 10, 1779, *Frederick Haldimand Papers*, Archives Canada copy, B 100, 262.

43. Ibid.

44. *Parker Journal; Journals of the Military Expedition*, Lieut. Erkuries Beatty, 31; Maj. Jeremiah Fogg, 98; Lt. Col. Adam Hubley, 161.

45. *Parker Journal; Journals of the Military Expedition*, Sullivan's Report, 299; Lieut. Erkuries Beatty, 31; Lieut. Rudolphus von Hovenburgh, 280.

46. Maj. John Butler to Lt. Col. Mason Bolton, letter dated Canawaugas, September 10, 1779, *Frederick Haldimand Papers*, Archives Canada copy, B 100, 262; Maj. John Butler to Lt. Col. Mason Bolton, letter dated Canawaugas, September 14, 1779, Canadian State Papers, Q, 16-2, 607; *Journals of the Military Expedition*, Lieut. Erkuries Beatty, 31.

47. *Gore Diary; Parker Journal; Journals of the Military Expedition*, Sullivan's Report, 299; Lieut. William Barton, 11; Lieut. Erkuries Beatty, 31; Lieut. Thomas Blake, 41; Maj. John Burrows, 47; Dr. Jabez Campfield, 59; Lt. Col. Henry Dearborn, 74; Sgt. Moses Fellows, 90; Maj. Jeremiah Fogg, 97; Sgt. Maj. George Grant, 111-12; Lieut. John Hardenbergh, 125; 74; Thomas Grant, 142; Lt. Col. Adam Hubley, 161-62; Lieut. John Jenkins, 174-75; Maj. James Norris, 234-35; Lieut. Rudolphus Van Hovenburgh, 277.

48. Ibid.

49. Maj. John Butler to Lt. Col. Mason Bolton, letter dated Canawaugas, September 14, 1779, Canadian State Papers, Q 16-2, 607; ibid.

50. *Gore Diary, Parker Journal, Journals of the Military Expedition*, Sullivan's Report, 299; Lieut. William Barton, 11; Lieut. Erkuries Beatty, 31; Lieut. Thomas Blake, 41; Maj. John Burrows, 47; Dr. Jabez Campfield, 59; Lt. Col. Henry Dearborn, 74; Sgt. Moses Fellows, 90; Maj. Jeremiah Fogg, 97; Sgt. Maj. George Grant, 111-12; Lieut. John Hardenbergh, 125; 74; Thomas Grant, 142; Lt. Col. Adam Hubley, 161-62; Lieut. John Jenkins, 174-75; Maj. James Norris, 234-35; Lieut. Rudolphus Van Hovenburgh, 277.

51. Ibid.

52. Ibid.

53. Ibid.

54. Ibid.

55. Maj. John Butler to Lt. Col. Mason Bolton, letter dated Canawaugas, September 14, 1779, Canadian State Papers, Q 16-2, 607; *Gore Diary, Parker Journal, Journals of the Military Expedition*, Sullivan's Report, 302; Lieut. William Barton, 11; Lieut. Erkuries Beatty, 31; Dr. Jabez Campfield, 60; Lt. Col. Henry Dearborn, 75-76; Sgt. Moses Fellows, 91; Maj. Jeremiah Fogg, 99; Sgt. Maj. George Grant, 112; Lieut. John Hardenbergh, 133; Thomas Grant, 142; Lt. Col. Adam Hubley, 162-163; Lieut. John Jenkins, 175; Capt. Daniel Livermore, 188; Lieut. William McKendry, 206-207; Maj. James Norris, 235; Lieut. Samuel Shute, 272; Lieut. Rudolphus Van Hovenburgh, 281.

56. Ibid.

57. Ibid.

58. Ibid.

59. Seaver, *A Narrative of the Life of Mrs. Mary Jemison, the White Woman of Genesee*, 105.

60. *Gore Diary, Journals of the Military Expedition*, Sullivan's Report, 302; Lieut. William Barton, 11; Lieut. Erkuries Beatty, 31; Lt. Col. Henry Dearborn, 75-76; Sgt. Moses Fellows, 91; Maj. Jeremiah Fogg, 99; Sgt. Maj. George Grant, 112; Lieut. John Hardenbergh, 133; Lt. Col. Adam Hubley, 162-63; Lieut. John Jenkins, 175; Lieut. William McKendry, 206-7; Maj. James Norris, 235; Lieut. Rudolphus Van Hovenburgh, 281; Lieut. John Jenkins, 175.

61. Ibid.

62. Ibid. Major Butler reported that his men killed twenty-two of Boyd's men in the ambush.

63. Lt. Col. Mason Bolton to Gov. Gen. Frederick Haldimand, letter dated Niagara, September 16, 1779, *Frederick Haldimand Papers*, Archives Canada copy, B 100, 269.

64. *Journals of the Military Expedition*, Sullivan's Report, 302; Lt. Col. Henry Dearborn, 75-76; Sgt. Moses Fellows, 91.

65. *Journals of the Military Expedition*, Sullivan's Report, 302; Lieut. William Barton, 12; Maj. Jeremiah Fogg, 100; Lt. Col. Adam Hubley, 164.

66. *Journals of the Military Expedition*, Sullivan's Report, 303-5; Lt. Col. Henry Dearborn, 76; Maj. Jeremiah Fogg, 100; Lt. Col. Adam Hubley, 164.

67. *Parker Journal, Journals of the Military Expedition*, Sullivan's Report, 302.

68. *Journals of the Military Expedition*, Sullivan's Report, 302; Lieut. William Barton, 12; Lieut. Erkuries Beatty, 32-33; Maj. John Burrows, 49; Lt. Col. Henry Dearborn, 76; Maj. Jeremiah Fogg, 99; Sgt. Maj. George Grant, 112; Lt. Col. Adam Hubley, 164; Lieut. John Jenkins, 175; Lieut. William McKendry, 207; Maj. James Norris, 237.

69. Ibid.

70. *Parker Journal*; *Journals of the Military Expedition*, Sullivan's Report, 303-5; Lieut. William Barton, 12; Lieut. Erkuries Beatty, 33; Lieut. John Hardenbergh, 134; Lieut. William McKendry, 207; Lieut. Rudolphus Van Hovenburgh, 281.

71. Ibid.

72. *Journals of the Military Expedition*, Sullivan's Report, 303-5; Lieut. William Barton, 13-14; Lieut. Erkuries Beatty, 35; Lt. Col. Henry Dearborn, 78; Maj. Jeremiah Fogg, 101; Sgt. Maj. George Grant, 114; Lieut. John Hardenbergh, 134; Lt. Col. Adam Hubley, 166; Lieut. John Jenkins, 177; Capt. John Livermore, 189; Lieut. William McKendry, 209; Lieut. Charles Nukerk, 219; Maj. James Norris, 237; Lieut. Rudolphus Van Hovenburgh, 283.

73. *Journals of the Military Expedition*, Sullivan's Report, 303-5; Lieut. Erkuries Beatty, 33-34; Maj. John Burrows, 49-50; Dr. Jabez Campfield, 61; Lt. Col. Henry Dearborn, 78; Maj. Jeremiah Fogg, 100; Sgt. Maj. George Grant, 112-113; Lieut. John Hardenbergh, 134; Lt. Col. Adam Hubley, 164-165; Lieut. John Jenkins, 125; Capt. John Livermore, 188-189; Lieut. William McKendry, 2079; Lieut. Charles Nukerk, 218-219; Lieut. Samuel Shute, 273; Lieut. Rudolphus Van Hovenburgh, 281.

74. Ibid.

75. Ibid.

Conclusion

1. Lt. Col. Mason Bolton to Lt. Gen. Frederick Haldimand, letter dated Niagara October 2, 1779, *Frederick Haldimand Papers*, Archives Canada copy, B 100, 284.

2. Maj. John Butler to Sir Frederick Haldimand, letter dated Niagara, September 20, 1779, *Frederick Haldimand Papers*, Archives Canada copy, B 105, 179.

3. Lt. Col. Mason Bolton to Lt. Gen. Sir Frederick Haldimand, letter dated Niagara, October 2, 1779, *Frederick Haldimand Papers*, Archives Canada copy, B 100, 284.

4. Maj. John Butler to Sir Frederick Haldimand, letter dated Niagara, September 20, 1779, *Frederick Haldimand Papers*, Archives Canada copy, B 105, 179.

5. Lt. Col. Sir John Johnson to Lt. Col. Mason Bolton, letter dated Fort Haldimand, September 29, 1779, *Frederick Haldimand Papers*, Archives Canada copy, B 100, 281.

6. Lt. Col. Mason Bolton to Major John Nairne Niagara September 22, 1779; *Frederick Haldimand Papers*, Archives Canada copy, B 100, 274.

7. Lt. Col. Mason Bolton to Lt. Gen. Frederick Haldimand, letter dated Niagara October 2, 1779, *Frederick Haldimand Papers*, Archives Canada copy, B 100, 284.

8. Maj. John Butler to Sir Frederick Haldimand, letter dated Niagara, September 20, 1779, *Frederick Haldimand Papers*, Archives Canada copy, B 105, 179.

9. Lt. Col. Mason Bolton to Major John Nairne, letter dated Niagara, September 22, 1779, *Frederick Haldimand Papers*, Archives Canada copy, B 100, 274.

10. Maj. John Butler to Sir Frederick Haldimand, letter dated Niagara, September 20, 1779, *Frederick Haldimand Papers*, Archives Canada copy, B 105, 179.

11. Lt. Col. Mason Bolton to Lt. Gen. Frederick Haldimand, letter dated Niagara, October 2, 1779, *Frederick Haldimand Papers*, Archives Canada copy, B 100, 284.

12. Lt. Col. Mason Bolton to Lt. Gen. Frederick Haldimand, letter dated Niagara, October 2, 1779, *Frederick Haldimand Papers*, Archives Canada copy, B 100, 284.

13. Lt. Gen. Sir Frederick Haldimand to Lt. Col. Mason Bolton, letter dated Quebec, October 6, 1779, *Frederick Haldimand Papers*, Archives Canada copy, B, 104, 73.

14. Seaver, *A Narrative of the Life of Mrs. Mary Jemison, the White Woman of Genesee*, 105.

15. *Journals of the Military Expedition*, Sullivan's Report, 303-5; Col. Daniel Brodhead to Gen. George Washington, letter dated Pittsburgh, September 16, 1779, Pennsylvania Archives (1), 12, 155; Col. Daniel Brodhead to Maj. Gen. John Sullivan, letter dated Pittsburgh, October 10, 1779, PA I (12) 165.

16. Gen. George Washington to Maj. Gen. John Sullivan, letter dated Head Quarters, Middlebrook, May 28 and 31, 1779, *Writings of George Washington*, 15: 171-173, 189-193.

17. Gen. George Washington to Maj. Gen. Horatio Gates, letter dated Head Quarters, Middle Brook, March 6, 1779, *Writings of George Washington*, 14: 198-200; Gen. George Washington to Maj. Gen. John Sullivan, letter dated Head Quarters, Middle Brook, March 6, 1779, *Writings of George Washington*, 14: 201-2.

18. *Journals of the Military Expedition*, Sullivan's Report, 303-5.

19. Col. Daniel Brodhead to Gen. George Washington, letter dated Pittsburgh, September 16, 1779, PA (1), 12, 155; Col. Daniel Brodhead to Maj. Gen. John Sullivan, letter dated Pittsburgh, October 10, 1779, PA (1), 12, 165.

20. Ibid.

21. Ibid.

22. *Jour. Cont. Cong.*, 15:1170.

21. Ibid, 1212-1213.

Bibliography

ARCHIVAL AND DOCUMENTARY SOURCES

Boston Gazette. August 3, 1778. Original issue in the collection of Alan Shields of Olyphant, Pennsylvania.

British Military and Naval Records: 1767-1899, RG 8, 1, C Series, Library and Archives Canada, Ottawa, Ontario.

Carleton, Sir Guy. British Headquarters Papers, New York City 1774-1783. Library and Archives Canada (MG 23 B1), Microfilm copies from photostatic copies of original documents presented to the Queen in 1957, Sir Guy Carleton Manuscripts Collection, Class 30/55, courtesy of the Public Record Office, London.

Clinton, Sir Henry. Sir Henry Clinton Papers, Volume 26, item 32, Copies at the University of Michigan, William L. Clements Library.

Documents Relative to the Colonial History of New York, O'Callaghan, E. B., ed., 15 Volumes, Albany, NY: 1853-87.

Draper, Lyman, Draper Manuscripts, Series U, Frontier War Papers, Vol. 11, unpublished manuscript in the State Historical Society of Wisconsin, Madison.

Fairlie, James. Journal. Typewritten and Transcribed Mss, notes by W. R. Brock. New York State Library, Albany.

Gansevoort, Peter. Peter Gansevoort Military Papers, Tss, New York State Archives. Albany, New York. Manuscript Collection #AO131:D20616. [These papers were transcribed, under authorization of the 1895 State Legislature and recorded in Chapter 393, from the original manuscripts which were destroyed in the New York State Library Fire of 1911]. Copies courtesy of the New York State Archives.

Goring, Francis. Francis Goring Correspondence, Mss, MG 24, D 4, Public Archives Canada, Ottawa, Canada.

Great Britain. Colonial Office Papers, America and West Indies, 1606-1807, Military Correspondence 1775-1783, Library and Archives Canada, (MG 11), copied from Manuscripts Class 5, (C.O. 5) 5:92-103, in the Public Record Office, London.

——. Treasury Board Papers, 1775-1783, Treasury Correspondence, Library and Archives Canada, (T 1), copied from Manuscripts Class 1, (T 1) Treasury Board Papers 1557-1920, T. 1:512-519, in the Public Record Office, London.

——. War Office Papers, 1776-1783, Letters and enclosures, from officers in America to the secretary at war, Library and Archives Canada (MG 13), Great Britain War Office W.O. 1:10-13, photostatic copies of original documents presented to the Queen in 1957 Manuscripts (30/55), in the Public Record Office, London.

Haldimand, Sir Frederick. Official correspondence and papers. Library and Archives Canada (MG 21), copied courtesy of British Library (formerly British Museum), London, Gen. Sir Frederick Haldimand Manuscripts Collection, (MG 21) Manuscripts 21661-21892.

Wolcott, Oliver Jr. Papers, Mss, Volume 1, Folder 1.8, Hartford, Connecticut Historical Society.

Published Primary Source Materials

Adler, Jeanne Winston, ed. *Chainbreaker's War: A Seneca Chief Remembers the American Revolution*. Hansonville, N.Y.: Black Dome Press, 2002.

Butler, Zebulon. "Correspondence of Col. Zebulon Butler, Wyoming, June-December 1778." *Proceedings and Collections of the Wyoming Historical and Geological Society*, 7 (1902): 131-150.

Butler, Zebulon. "Orderly Book of Col. Zebulon Butler, at Wyoming, August-December 1778." *Proceedings and Collections of the Wyoming Historical and Geological Society*, 7 (1902): 106-130.

Calloway, Colin G., ed. *The World Turned Upside Down: Indian Voices from Early America*. Boston: Bedford/St. Martin's, 1994.

Clinton, George. *Public Papers of George Clinton*, First Governor of New York. Hugh Hastings, ed. 10 vols. Albany, N.Y.: State Historian, 1899-1914.

Commager, Henry Steele, and Richard B. Morris, eds. *The Spirit of Seventy Six: The Story of the American Revolution as Told by Participants*. New York: Harper-Collins, 1975; republished Da Capo Press, 1995.

Continental Congress. *Journals of the Continental Congress, 1774-1789*. Edited from the original records in the Library of Congress. Worthington C. Ford, ed. 34 vols. Washington, D.C.: Government Printing Office, 1904-1937.

Cook, Frederick, ed. *Journals of the Military Expedition of Major General John Sullivan against the Six Nations of Indians in 1779*. Auburn, N.Y.: Knapp, Peck & Thomson, 1887; reprint, Bowie, Md.: Heritage Books, 2000.

Documentary History of Dunmore's War 1774. Reuben G. Thwaites and Louise P. Kellogg, eds. Madison: Wisconsin Historical Society, 1905; reprint, Bowie, Md.: Heritage Books, 1989.

Drimmer, Frederick, ed. *Captured by the Indians: 15 Firsthand Accounts, 1750-1870*. New York: Dover, 1985, reprinted from *Scalps and Tomahawks: Narratives of Indian Captivity*, New York: Coward-McCann, 1961.

Gore, Obadiah, Jr. *The Revolutionary War Diary of Lieut. Obadiah Gore, Jr.* R. W. G. Vail, ed. New York: New York Public Library, 1929.

Greene, Nathanael. *The Papers of General Nathanael Greene*. Richard K. Showman, ed. 11 vols. Chapel Hill: University of North Carolina Press, 1983.

Johnson, William. *The Papers of Sir William Johnson.* J. J. Sullivan, ed. 14 vols. Albany: University of the State of New York, 1921-1965.

Journals of the House of Burgesses of Virginia, 1773-1776, Including the Records of the Committee of Correspondence. John Pendleton Kennedy, ed. Richmond, Va.: E. Waddey Company, 1905.

Letters of Delegates to Congress, 1774-1789. Paul H. Smith, ed. 26 vols. Washington, D.C.: Library of Congress and the Government Printing Office, 1976-2000.

The Manual Exercise as Ordered by His Majesty in 1764 Including the Fundamentals of Marching and Maneuvering. New York: H. Gaine Printing Office, 1775.

The Militia-Man: Containing Necessary Rules for Both Officer and Soldier, with an Explanation of the Manual Exercise of the Foot. London, circa 1740; reprint, Schenectady, N.Y.: United States Historical Research Service, 1995.

New York State. *Calendar of Historical Manuscripts Relating to the War of the Revolution.* 2 vols. Albany: Secretary of State of the State of New York, 1868.

Parker, Robert. "Journal of Lieutenant Robert Parker of the Second Continental Artillery, 1779." Thomas R. Bard, ed. *Pennsylvania Magazine of History and Biography,* 27 (1904): 12-25.

Pennsylvania Archives. Series 1. Samuel Hazard, ed. 12 vols. Philadelphia: Joseph Severns and Company, 1852-1856 (especially vols. 6 and 7).

Public Records of the Colony of Connecticut. 11 vols. Hartford, Conn.: Brown & Parsons, 1850-1890.

Public Records of the State of Connecticut. 39 vols. Hartford, Conn.: Press of the Case, Lockwood & Brainard, 1894-1931.

The Remembrancer: or Impartial repository of public events, 1775-1784. John Almon and Thomas Pownall. 17 vols. London: J. Almon, 1775-84.

Smith, James. *An Account of the Remarkable Occurrences in the Life of Col. James Smith, During His Captivity with the Indians, in the Years 1755, '56, '57, '58, & '59, Written by Himself.* Lexington, Ky.: John Bradford, 1799; reprint, Columbus: Ohio Historical Society, 1996.

St. Clair, Arthur. *The St. Clair Papers: The Life and Public Services of Arthur St. Clair.* William H. Smith, ed. 2 vols. Cincinnati, Ohio: Robert Clark & Company, 1882.

Stark, John. *Memoir and Official Correspondence of General John Stark, with notices of several other officers of the Revolution.* Caleb Stark, ed. Concord, N.H.: G. P. Lyon, 1860; reprint, Boston: Gregg Press, 1972.

Sullivan, John. *Letters and Papers of Major General John Sullivan, Continental Army.* Otis G. Hammond, ed. 3 vols. Concord: New Hampshire Historical Society, 1930-39.

Susquehanna Company Papers. Julian P. Boyd and Robert J. Taylor. 11 vols. Ithaca, N.Y.: Cornell University Press, 1930-1971.

Thatcher, James. *Military Journal of the American Revolution 1775-1783.* Hartford, Conn.: Hurlburt Williams & Company, 1862; reprint, Gansevoort, N.Y.: Corner House Historical Publications, 1998.

United States. American Archives: Consisting of a Collection of Authentic *Records, State Papers, Debates, and Letters and Other Notices of Publick Affairs, the Whole Forming a Documentary history of the Origin and Progress of the North American Colonies.* 9 vols. Peter Force, ed. Washington, D.C.: M. St. Clair Clarke and Peter Force, 1837-1853.

———. *Indian Affairs: Laws and Treaties.* Charles J. Kappler, ed. 2 vols. Washington, D.C.: Government Printing Office, 1904.

———. *The Public Statutes at Large of the United States of America by Authority of Congress.* Vol. 9, Section 1. Boston: Little, Brown, 1845-1866.

U.S. Army. Regulations for the Order and Discipline of the Troops of the United States. Compiled by Frederick William Baron von Steuben. Boston: I. Thomas and E. T. Andrews, 1794.

Warren, Benjamin. "Diary of Captain Benjamin Warren at Massacre of Cherry Valley." Transcribed by David E. Alexander. *Journal of American History,* 3, no. 1, New Haven, Conn.: Associated Publishers of American Records, 1909.

Washington, George. George *Washington Papers. The Varick Transcripts: The Continental Army Papers, 1776-1783.* Microfilm Collection, Library of Congress, Washington, D.C.

———. *The Writings of George Washington from the Original Manuscript Sources, 1745-1799.* John C. Fitzpatrick, ed. 39 vols. Washington, D.C.: Government Printing Office, 1931-1944.

———. *The Writings of George Washington.* Jared Sparks, ed. 12 vols. Boston: Ferdinand Andrews, 1833-1837.

———. *The Writings of George Washington.* Worthington C. Ford, ed. 14 vols. Washington, D.C.: Government Printing Office, 1889-1893.

Wasmus, Julius Friedrich. *An Eyewitness Account of the American Revolution and New England Life: The Journal of J. F. Wasmus, German Company Surgeon, 1776-1783.* Helga Doblin, trans., and Mary C. Lynn, ed. New York: Greenwood Press, 1990.

SECONDARY SOURCES

Abernathy, Thomas Perkins. *Western Lands and the American Revolution.* New York: Appleton-Century Company, 1937.

Allen, Robert S. *His Majesty's Indian Allies: British Indian Policy in the Defence of Canada, 1774-1815.* Toronto, Ontario: Dundurn Press, 1992.

Amory, Thomas C. *The Military Service and Public Life of Major General John Sullivan of the American Revolutionary Army.* Boston: Wiggin and Lunt, 1868.

Atkinson, George W. *History of Kanawha County, from Organization in 1789 until the Present Time.* Charleston: West Virginia Journal, 1876; reprint Waynesboro, N.C.: For the West Virginia Genealogical Society by Don Mills & Company, 1994.

Bell, Herbert C. *History of Northumberland County, Pennsylvania.* Chicago: Brown, Runk & Company, 1891.

Brady, William Young. "Brodhead's Trail up the Allegheny, 1779." *Western Pennsylvania Historical Magazine,* 37 (1954-1955): 19-31.

Busch, Clarence M., *Report of the Commission to Locate the Site of the Frontier Forts of Pennsylvania.* 2 vols. Harrisburg: State Printer of Pennsylvania, 1896.

Calloway, Colin G. *The American Revolution in Indian Country: Crisis and Diversity in Native American Communities.* New York: Cambridge University Press, 1995.

Cruikshank, Ernest, *The Story of Butler's Rangers and the Settlement of Niagara.* Welland, Ontario: Tribune Printing House, 1893; reprint, Niagara Falls, Ontario: Renown, 1982.

Curtis, Edward E. *The British Army in the American Revolution.* New Haven, Conn.: Corner House Publications, 1926; reprint, Gansevoort, N.Y.: Corner House Publications, 1998.

Dowd, Gregory Evans. *War Under Heaven: Pontiac, the Indian Nations, and the British Empire.* Baltimore: The Johns Hopkins University Press, 2002.

Downes, Randolph C. *Council Fires on the Upper Ohio.* Pittsburgh: University of Pittsburgh Press, 1940; reprint, 1969.

Eckert, Alan W. *That Dark and Bloody River: Chronicles of the Ohio River Valley.* New York: Bantam Books, 1995.

——. *The Wilderness War: A Narrative.* Boston: Little, Brown, 1978; reprint, Ashland, Ky.: Jesse Stuart Foundation, 2003.

Fischer, Joseph R. *A Well Executed Failure: The Sullivan Campaign Against the Iroquois, July-September 1779.* Columbia, South Carolina: University of South Carolina Press, 1997.

Fitzpatrick, John C. *Calendar of the Correspondence of George Washington, Commander in Chief of the Continental Army, with the Continental Congress (and) Calendar of the Correspondence with the Officers.* 4 vols. Washington, D.C.: Government Printing Office, 1906-1907.

Flick, Alexander C. *The American Revolution in New York: Its Political, Social and Economic Significance*. Albany: University of the State of New York, 1926.

Foote, Allan D., *Liberty March: The Battle of Oriskany*. Utica, N.Y.: North Country Books, 1998.

Graymont, Barbara. *The Iroquois in the American Revolution*. Syracuse, N.Y.: Syracuse University Press, 1972.

Hammon, Neal O., and Richard Taylor. *Virginia's Western War, 1775-1786*. Mechanicsburg, Pa.: Stackpole Books, 2002.

Harvey, Oscar Jewell. *A History of Wilkes-Barre, Luzerne County, Pennsylvania: from its first beginnings to the present time; including chapters of newly-discovered early Wyoming Valley history together with many biographical sketches and much Genealogical material*. 7 vols. Wilkes-Barre, Pa.: Oscar J. Harvey, 1909.

Hassler, Edgar W. *Old Westmoreland, A History of Western Pennsylvania During the Revolution*. Pittsburgh: J. R. Weldin & Company, 1900.

Jefferds, Joseph C. *Captain Matthew Arbuckle*. Charleston, W.Va.: Education Foundation, 1981.

Kercheval, Samuel. *A History of the Ohio Valley of West Virginia*. Woodstock, Va.: W. N. Grabill, 1902.

Ketchum, Richard M. *Saratoga: Turning Point of America's Revolutionary War*. New York: Henry Holt, 1997.

LaCrosse, Richard B. *Morgan's Riflemen and Their Role on the Northern Frontier, 1778-1783*. Bowie, Md.: Heritage Books, 2002.

Lewis, Virgil A. *History of the Battle of Point Pleasant*. Charleston: West Virginia Department of Archives and History, 1909; reprint, Westminster, Md.: Willow Bend Books, 1999.

Lobdell, Jared C., ed. *Indian Warfare in Western Pennsylvania and North West Virginia at the Time of the American Revolution*. Bowie, Md.: Heritage Books, 1992.

Lossing, Benson J. *The Pictorial Field-Book of the Revolution*. 2 vols. New York: Harper & Brothers, 1860.

Mayer, Holly. *Belonging to the Army: Camp Followers and Community During the American Revolution*. Columbia: University of South Carolina Press, 1996.

McKnight, Charles. *Our Western Border, Its Life, Forays, Scouts, Combats, Massacres, Red Chiefs, Adventures, Captivities, Pioneer Women, One Hundred Years Ago*. Philadelphia: J. C. McCurdy & Company, 1875.

Miner, Charles. *History of Wyoming, in a Series of letters from Charles Miner, to his son William Penn Miner, Esq*. Philadelphia: J. Crissy, 1845.

Mintz, Max M., *Seeds of Empire: The American Revolutionary Conquest of the Iroquois*, New York, New York University Press, 1999.

Nester, William R. *The Frontier War for Independence*. Mechanicsburg, Pa.: Stackpole Books, 2004.

Parker, Arthur. *The Constitution of the Five Nations*. Albany: University of the State of New York, 1916.

Pieper, Thomas I., and James B. Gidney. *Fort Laurens, 1778-1779: The Revolutionary War in Ohio*. Kent, Ohio: Kent State University Press, 1976.

Risch, Erna. *Supplying Washington's Army*. Washington, D.C.: U.S. Army Center of Military History, 1981.

Seaver, James E. *A Narrative of the Life of Mrs. Mary Jemison, the White Woman of Genesee*. Canandaigua, N.Y.: J. D. Bemis, 1824; reprint, Norman: University of Oklahoma Press, 1992.

Siebert, Wilbur H. *The Tories of the Upper Ohio*. Charleston: Department of Archives and History of the State of West Virginia, 1916.

Simms, Jeptha R. *Frontiersmen of New York: Showing Customs of the Indians, Vicissitudes of the Pioneer White Settlers, and Border Strife in Two Wars*. Albany, N.Y.: G. C. Riggs, 1882.

Stone, W. L. *The Life of Joseph Brant–Thayendanega: Including the Border Wars of the American Revolution*. 2 vols. New York: A. V. Blake, 1838.

Tanner, Helen Hornbeck, ed., Miklos Pinther, cartographer. *Atlas of Great Lakes Indian History*. Norman: University of Oklahoma Press, 1987.

Thwaites, Reuben G., and Louise P. Kellogg, eds. *Frontier Defense on the Upper Ohio, 1777-1778*. Madison: Wisconsin Historical Society, 1912.

———. *The Revolution on the Upper Ohio, 1775-1777*. Madison: Wisconsin Historical Society, 1912.

Williamson, James R., and Linda A. Fossler. *Zebulon Butler: Hero of the Revolutionary Frontier*. Westport, Conn.: Greenwood Press, 1995.

Wright, Albert Hazen. *The Sullivan Expedition of 1779: The Regimental Rosters of Men*. Finksburg, Md.: Pipe Creek Publications, 1993.

Wright, Robert K., Jr. *The Continental Army*. Washington, D.C.: U.S. Army Center of Military History, 1983.

Wright, Womack. *Some Notes on the Continental Army*. Cornwallville, N.Y.: Hope Farm Press, 1975.

Acknowledgements

I would like to extend my thanks and appreciation to a few people for their assistance, without which this project would not have been completed.

I developed my interest in the Iroquois Campaigns while working at National Park Service in the American Battlefield Protection Program, and was assigned to research and survey the sites of the 1777 attack on Fort Henry (Wheeling), 1778 battle of Wyoming, and the 1779 Upper Allegheny Expedition for the Revolutionary War Historic Preservation Study. Paul Hawke, Kristen Stevens, and Tanya Gossett, my friends and former colleagues at the American Battlefield Protection Program, and all those at the local, state, tribal, and national levels, tirelessly work to identify, research, interpret, and, most important, preserve America's historic battlefields.

Alan Shields of Olyphant, Pennsylvania, a local expert on the Wyoming Valley Massacre, took me to all the extant sites, as well as the locations of long-lost features associated with the July 1778 battle, in addition to allowing me access to his collection of authentic primary source documents and images from the Revolutionary War on the frontier. My cousin Kathleen Kaminski Towner and her husband Rick Towner of Honeoye, New York, took me to all the sites associated with the Sullivan-Clinton Campaign between Chemung and Fort Niagara, New York, including the sites of the Battle of Newtown and Groveland Ambuscade.

Barbara and Forrest Taylor of Cannons On Line were my primary source of information on eighteenth-century artillery. Maggie Parnall, of Ontario, Canada, assisted by locating Canadian documentary sources. I wish to give special thanks to all the archivists, librarians, curators, and historians in all the archives, libraries, museums, historical societies and other repositories of primary and secondary source information, who made my task of research markedly easier. Professors Joseph N. Tatarewicz, Ph.D., and Jon T. Sumida, Ph.D., mentored my scholarly development. My friend, colleague, and supervisor at the U.S. Army Center of Military History, Lieutenant Colonel Mark Reardon, allowed me to use the annual leave necessary to complete this project.

Finally, I have to credit my wife, Patricia, for encouraging me throughout, and putting up with the seemingly endless hours of research, pouring over notes, typing and retyping, and editing and re-editing the manuscript, and the myriad of tasks that interfered with other things she would rather have been doing with me. My brother Gregg E. Williams kept my temperamental computer running, performing such minor miracles as recovering files I thought were hopelessly lost after my machine decided to crash on me, probably in protest. My sons Michael, Edward, and Glenn Jr., and daughter-in-law Erin and grandson Austen, all lent valuable support and encouragement. .

Index